Unto this Last

AND OTHER WRITINGS BY

JOHN RUSKIN

Edited, with an introduction, commentary and notes, by

CLIVE WILMER

PENGUIN BOOKS

PENGUIN BOOKS

Published by the Penguin Group
27 Wrights Lane, London W8 5TZ, England
Viking Penguin Inc., 40 West 23rd Street, New York, New York 10010, USA
Penguin Books Australia Ltd, Ringwood, Victoria, Australia
Penguin Books Canada Ltd, 2801 John Street, Markham, Ontario, Canada L3R 1B4
Penguin Books (NZ) Ltd, 182–190 Wairau Road, Auckland 10, New Zealand

Penguin Books Ltd, Registered Offices: Harmondsworth, Middlesex, England

Published in Penguin Classics 1985
5 7 9 10 8 6 4

Printed and bound in Great Britain by
Cox & Wyman Ltd, Reading
Filmset in Aldus (Lintron 202) by
Rowland Phototypesetting Ltd,
Bury St Edmunds, Suffolk

PENGUIN CLASSICS

UNTO THIS LAST
and other writings by John Ruskin

John Ruskin was born in London in 1819, of Scottish descent. His father was a successful wine-merchant and art lover; his mother a strict Evangelical whose religious instruction affected him deeply. He entered Christ Church, Oxford, in 1836 and graduated in 1842. In 1843, the first of the five volumes of *Modern Painters* was published, a work written in defence of J. M. W. Turner. The other volumes survey the main traditions of European painting from Giotto to the nineteenth century. Ruskin was also passionately interested in Gothic architecture and published two works on the subject before the completion of *Modern Painters: The Seven Lamps of Architecture* (1849) and the three volumes of *The Stones of Venice* in 1851 and 1853. He married Effie Gray in 1848, but seven years later the marriage was annulled on grounds of non-consummation. In 1858 he met Rose la Touche, a girl of nine, with whom he fell in love and became increasingly obsessed, and in that year he finally lost his Evangelical faith. In 1860, disillusioned with a society in which poverty was rampant and the poor exploited, he began the first of four essays attacking the science of Political Economy. They were published in book form in 1862, under the title, *Unto this Last*. This was followed in 1863 by *Munera Pulveris*, which puts forward some positive proposals for economic change and reform. In 1869 he became the first Slade Professor of Fine Art at Oxford and in 1871 began writing *Fors Clavigera*, a series of open letters which draw connexions between diverse subjects. He also took part in many practical projects, many of which he directed by way of his Utopian pressure-group, the Guild of St George. When Rose la Touche died insane in 1875, however, he began to show signs of mental disturbance and suffered the first of seven mental breakdowns in 1878. In 1885 he began publishing his autobiography, *Praeterita*. This moving and lyrical book was brought to a premature conclusion by his last and most violent breakdown in 1889. He lived on, withdrawn and inactive, until 1900.

Clive Wilmer was born in 1945 and grew up in London. He graduated from King's College, Cambridge, and since then has spent most of his life living and teaching in Cambridge, apart from two years spent in Italy. A poet first and foremost, he has published two full-length collections of verse, *The Dwelling Place* (1977) and *Devotions* (1982), and has translated *Forced March* – selected poems of Miklós Radnóti – from the Hungarian in collaboration with George Gömöri. He has also edited a collection of essays by Thom Gunn, *The Occasions of Poetry*, and written critical essays, reviews, poems and verse translations from Italian, German, Polish and Hungarian for a wide variety of journals in England and America. His admiration of Ruskin, which he describes as almost a way of life, began when he was an undergraduate and developed during the time he spent in Florence and Venice.

CONTENTS

INTRODUCTION

1

In May 1860 John Ruskin delivered to his publishers the fifth and final volume of *Modern Painters*, his monumental study of landscape art. He was forty-one. The first volume had appeared in 1843 and established his reputation almost overnight as the most influential art critic in England, probably the most influential that English culture has ever known. It had been inspired by the greatest landscape artist of the early nineteenth century. The late paintings of J. M. W. Turner, with their unfocused washes of luminous colour, had moved conservative art critics to ridicule and contempt. Angered by what he judged prejudice and ignorance, Ruskin had risen to Turner's defence, never for a moment anticipating the scope of the finished work. As it grew, however, and as Ruskin's knowledge of art grew with it, the book began to encompass the whole field of European painting. But that was not the limit of Ruskin's interests and activities. The composition of *Modern Painters* was twice interrupted by studies of medieval architecture. He was much in demand as a public lecturer. He taught drawing free of charge at the new Working Men's College. He campaigned for sound principles of industrial design and interested himself in educational experiment. He helped to plan and build the Oxford Museum of Natural History. He spent a great deal of his time and money sorting, cleaning, framing and cataloguing the Turner bequest. Nor was he purely a theorist and critic. His ideas about art were based on a close study of nature, and his considerable powers of observation were reinforced by scientific knowledge of natural forms. His first great passion was geology – he had published essays on the subject at the age of fifteen – and he remained an original amateur of the subject for most of his life. He was a skilled and sensitive draughtsman and watercolourist, and illustrated most of his own books, making copies after great masters, architectural drawings, studies of natural forms. He was a considerable literary critic, and was widely regarded as the outstanding prose stylist of the age. Yet despite this reputation for various accomplishment, the subject of his next book took the public completely by surprise.

The completion of *Modern Painters* had exhausted him. Before the book appeared, he left for a holiday in the Swiss Alps, the landscape that from boyhood had inspired his love of nature. There, too, through Turner's impressions of it, he had learnt the role of the artist as interpreter of divine truth. Now, looking out on the scene he loved before all others, the 'cloudless peace of the snows of Chamouni', he turned his mind to the study of Political Economy. The first product of his meditations, the four essays later collected as *Unto this Last*, appeared that same year in the *Cornhill Magazine*, and with their publication Ruskin experienced what might have been judged the first setback of his career. The present selection has been designed to put *Unto this Last* in a context. Though the writings grouped around it illustrate the range of Ruskin's concerns, there is also a remarkable consistency of moral and social emphasis. It is the purpose of this Introduction to show that what then seemed at best a diversion, at worst an aberration, was in fact central to Ruskin's work and thought. It has become customary for critics and biographers to insist that the seeds of *Unto this Last* are to be found in his previous work and that no fundamental change of direction was involved. The arguments adduced to support this view are indisputable. Nevertheless, the book was, in subject and in manner, quite different from anything Ruskin had written before – disturbing to the complacency of his more genteel admirers. To feel something of its impact and originality, the modern reader needs to recognize this, and to learn by what paths Ruskin arrived at this unexpected point of departure.

2

Ruskin was an only child. He was born in 1819 in London but, like so many of those who have sought to explain the laws of economics, he was of Scottish descent. His father was a self-made man, a prosperous wine-merchant with a passion for Romantic literature and the visual arts. His mother was an inflexibly devout Evangelical; under her pious regime, Ruskin had to learn great tracts of the Bible by heart. As a child he was both spoilt and deprived: he had few companions and was denied many of the ordinary sensual delights of childhood, while his intellect and self-esteem were nourished and pampered. The denial of ordinary pleasures, as Ruskin suggests in his autobiography *Praeterita*, seems to have stimulated and refined his aesthetic sensibilities. In particular, it heightened his powers of sight, the faculty whose moral value his writings consistently stress. Modern biographers have tended to abominate his parents for their snobbery, their puritanism, and the suffocating excess of their devotion to their only son. But though Ruskin himself recognized these failings and the harm they had done him, he also praised his parents for the conduct of their lives and valued their commitment to honesty and hard work. Moreover, most of his attitudes and preoccupations can be traced to their teaching. To his mother he owed his religious awe, which set nature above all human endeavour, and his feeling for the rhythms of English prose, rooted as it is in the language of the Authorized Version. From his father he acquired his love of travel, landscape, painting, architecture, Byron and Scott and Turner; perhaps also something of his economic awareness.

Yet he despised their narrowness. Caricaturing their absurd ambitions for him in *Praeterita*, he wrote that they wanted him 'to write poetry as good as Byron's only pious; preach sermons as good as Bossuet's only Protestant; be made, at forty, Bishop of Winchester, and at fifty, Primate of England'. It is a beautifully neat sketch and only mildly exaggerated. It points quite clearly to the sources of Ruskin's thought in two movements of the late eighteenth century: Romanticism and Evangelical Protestantism. One wonders whether he ever realized how nearly fulfilled these parental ambitions were. If he never became a prince of the church, he certainly attained a comparable degree of public respect; and the literary manner he made his own might be seen as a marriage of poetry and the sermon.

His father did much to encourage the enthusiasm which led to *Modern Painters*. On his thirteenth birthday, Ruskin was given a copy of Samuel Rogers' *Italy*, a topographical poem illustrated with vignettes by Turner. He was ravished by these engravings. The following year the family went on holiday to Switzerland and there, for the first time, Ruskin glimpsed some of the mountain landscapes Turner had made his own. Soon, with his father's help, he was collecting Turner watercolours and the continental visit had become an annual event. In 1836, incensed by attacks in the quarterlies on Turner's late style, he launched himself into a spirited defence of those great paintings. The article was never published but its argument – that Turner shocked the critics because he was more 'truthful' than the conventional artists they praised – was the germ of the book Ruskin began in 1842, as soon as he had graduated from Oxford. 'Truth to Nature' is the theme of *Modern Painters*, and from the outset it has moral implications. If the criterion of greatness in art is truth, it follows that inferior art is bad because it is false. Good taste, therefore, is a moral quality. Ruskin did not shirk the awkwardness of this conclusion, and thereafter his development is marked by an inability to turn his back on disturbing questions.

It took Ruskin eighteen years to complete *Modern Painters*. He had originally conceived it as an essay, but the essay grew and, by the time the book was published, he was thinking in terms of three volumes. The second volume, which appeared in 1846, is hardly concerned with modern painting at all. It announces his discovery of Italian religious art – of Giotto, Fra Angelico, Bellini and, in a later period, Tintoretto. This discovery provoked a long but fruitful digression into the study of architecture, the outcome of which was four more books: *The Seven Lamps of Architecture* (1849) and the three volumes of *The Stones of Venice* (1851 and 1853). *Modern Painters* was shelved for nearly ten years; then, in 1856, Volumes III and IV appeared, only to be followed by more digressions – this time not only into writing but into projects of a practical and socially constructive nature. During this period he began addressing himself to religious and social questions and became, through his defence of the Pre-Raphaelite painters and his detailed annual reviews of the Royal Academy exhibition, a powerful influence on the course of contemporary art. By the time the last volume appeared, his mind was on other things and his views on most subjects had changed or developed. This is hardly surprising. He was twenty-four, precocious and opinionated, when the project began. He had studied a lot of pictures but his knowledge was far less wide-ranging than the autocratic tone of the first volume might suggest. As his knowledge increased, he noticed his errors and changed his mind. Moreover, the changes that took place in his personal development affected the book's focus and angle of vision. He had begun writing it as a pious Evangelical who saw nature as the visible language of God. By 1860 he had been 'unconverted' and the focus of his interest had moved from landscape to man.

This is as much as to say that *Modern Painters* is not one book, but five – as Ruskin himself realized. And yet, as he observed in his Preface to Volume V, there *is* a unifying theme: 'In the main aim and principle of the book, there is no variation from its first syllable to its last. It declares the perfectness and eternal beauty of the work of God; and tests all work of man by concurrence with, or subjection to that.' The development then, as he goes on to say, was organic: 'as the work changed like a tree, it was also rooted like a tree.' Ruskin's belief in the divinity of nature is Romantic. A quotation from Wordsworth appeared on the title-page of each volume of *Modern Painters*. This would seem to stress the modernity of Ruskin's thought, and not incorrectly. But his idea of creation, like Wordsworth's, is founded on the Natural Theology of the eighteenth century. Nature was, after the Bible, the second book of divine revelation. It could therefore be *read* by the pious observer. The function of art, Ruskin argued, was to interpret it and, thereby, the 'word' of God. And so the artist's main duty was to be truthful in his representation. Thus, when an artist was judged untruthful, as Turner had been, his only court of appeal was to nature herself. It was to her, therefore, that Ruskin turned in the painter's defence. The aspect of *Modern Painters* that is likely to seem most extraordinary to present-day readers is the detailed analysis and description of natural forms. Before we can judge the fidelity of a painting (these passages suggest) we must learn to perceive the subject correctly. Turner seems eccentric in his late work not because he distorts but because, on the contrary, his observation is so accurate. This is difficult to judge for two reasons: first, because the accuracy is not a matter of the single photographic image, but of overall impression (the painting has a context – in the larger landscape beyond the frame's confines and ultimately in the whole of the natural order); and, second, because people tend to judge pictures by the standards of other pictures. Turner's critics were hidebound by convention. They admired the kind of painting that emulated the Old Masters and observed the 'rules'. For Ruskin such pictures merely drew on the history of pictorial convention and, in so doing, perpetuated what might be falsehood, flattering human skill at the expense of truth. He condemned the neo-classical notion that nature should be idealized and that the artist should 'improve' it. On the contrary, he argued, the real world is the source of all our ideas of beauty: to idealize is to deform. The difficulty of Ruskin's criticism is that it also partakes of idealism. This is not a contradiction. He believed that the artist should render particulars with accuracy at the same time as giving the spectator an idea of the essence and meaning of created things. For this reason he also condemned what he saw as the debased and materialistic realism of Dutch genre painting. Beauty in nature was the signature of a loving God: it was the artist's duty to communicate that.

But beauty is not the only subject of art. From the outset, Ruskin realized that attention to truth involved knowledge of good and evil. The artists he praised as 'Naturalists' had the courage to look on evil as well as beauty. This is most clearly stated in the later volumes of *Modern Painters* (see, in the present selection, 'The Two Boyhoods'), but it is already apparent in the first. The early volumes were famed for their purple passages of descriptive prose. Here is one of the finest, the description in *Modern Painters I* of an oil by Turner that Ruskin owned, *Slavers throwing overboard the dead and dying* (1840):

> It is a sunset on the Atlantic, after prolonged storm; but the storm is partially lulled, and the torn and streaming rainclouds are moving in scarlet lines to lose themselves in the hollow of the night. The whole surface of sea included in the picture is divided into two ridges of

enormous swell, not high, nor local, but a low broad heaving of the whole ocean, like the lifting of its bosom by deep-drawn breath after the torture of the storm. Between these two ridges the fire of the sunset falls along the trough of the sea, dyeing it with an awful but glorious light, the intense and lurid splendour which burns like gold, and bathes like blood. Along this fiery path and valley, the tossing waves by which the swell of the sea is restlessly divided, lift themselves in dark, indefinite, fantastic forms, each casting a faint and ghastly shadow behind it along the illumined foam. They do not rise everywhere, but three or four together in wild groups, fitfully and furiously, as the under strength of the swell compels or permits them; leaving between them treacherous spaces of level and whirling water, now lighted with green and lamp-like fire, now flashing back the gold of the declining sun, now fearfully dyed from above with the undistinguishable images of the burning clouds, which fall upon them in flakes of crimson and scarlet, and give to the reckless waves the added motion of their own fiery flying. Purple and blue, the lurid shadows of the hollow breakers are cast upon the mist of night, which gathers cold and low, advancing like the shadow of death upon the guilty ship as it labours amidst the lightning of the sea, its thin masts written upon the sky in lines of blood, girded with condemnation in that fearful hue which signs the sky with horror, and mixes its flaming flood with the sunlight, and, cast far along the desolate heave of the sepulchral waves, incarnadines the multitudinous sea.

(*Library Edition* III, 571–2)

By the time he wrote *Unto this Last*, Ruskin had turned against 'fine writing' of this kind: it allowed the reader to admire the style without attending to the content. The passage is undeniably over-written. Yet the content could hardly have been expressed more powerfully or in any other way. The matter of the painting is described as if it were real: the very style has been influenced by Turner. By this means Ruskin's words unite with nature and the painter's hand in legible condemnation of the slavers' evil: '*written* upon the sky in lines of blood'. Even though the message is refracted through praise of a work of art, there is no mistaking Ruskin's generous outrage. The prophetic voice of Ruskin the social critic is heard here for the first time. In 1856 he wrote (in *Modern Painters III*): 'the greatest thing a human soul ever does in this world is to *see* something, and tell what he saw in a plain way . . . To see clearly is poetry, prophecy, and religion – all in one.' He was to be more and more tormented by the fact that sometimes he saw things only too well.

As *Modern Painters* develops, the broad theme of Truth to Nature increasingly takes on this darker colouring. As Ruskin grew older, the bold certainties of his Evangelical faith began to weaken. His travels and his knowledge of Christian art had removed his hatred of Catholicism, and he began to think of his parents' religion as sectarian, provincial and life-denying. More seriously, by 1858 (the year of his 'unconversion') the advances of modern science were troubling him. *The Origin of Species* appeared in 1859, but more disturbing to Ruskin – since his own knowledge confirmed it – was the evidence of geology. As early as 1851, he expressed his fear of the geologists' 'dreadful Hammers', the clink of which he heard 'at the end of every cadence of the Bible verses'. It seems unlikely that Ruskin ever became an atheist, but before he completed *Modern Painters* he had certainly lost his faith in the idea of the visible world as the language of a loving God. Accordingly, the author of Volumes IV and V finds that when he beholds the wonders of nature his eyes come to rest on pain, cruelty, corruption and death. Moreover, the digression that had led him from religious painting in *Modern Painters II* to religious architecture in *The Stones of Venice* also caused him to consider the response of human life to its natural context: for architecture, though it too may express delight in leaves and mountains, is above all a social art, 'born of man's necessities and expressive of his nature'. But when Ruskin looked at the social order around him, he found a way of life which did nothing to mitigate the hardness of the human lot and which, as far as the weaker members of society were concerned, did much to aggravate it. A society so dedicated to squalor and heartless brutality was, in Ruskin's view, indifferent to the beauty he had preached; and most of its professions of Christian charity were mere hypocrisy. Its real God was not the man of sorrows, but Mammon.

3

For Ruskin, the study of architecture had never been distinct from the study of landscape. Turner, like many of the watercolourists of his generation, had first made his mark as an architectural draughtsman, with cathedrals and ruined abbeys as his subjects. Among the lesser artists celebrated in *Modern Painters* are the engravers of popular architectural prints, Samuel Prout, David Roberts, Clarkson Stanfield and Ruskin's drawing master, J. D. Harding. These artists did much to popularize the revival of interest in medieval architecture that is part of Romanticism. But the tradition they belong to is connected with the movement of eighteenth-century taste known as the Picturesque. Picturesque landscape is not conventionally beautiful. The beauty lies in the handling; the scenes themselves are wild or disordered and associated with poverty. Often, antiquated buildings, usually falling into ruin, give focus and human meaning to the composition. The fashion for Gothic remains was closely connected with the Romantic nostalgia for the medieval. It was in origin sentimental and decorative, but by the early nineteenth century it had acquired dignity and antiquarian earnestness – mainly through the historical novels of Sir Walter Scott, which Ruskin devoured in his childhood.

Ruskin was, even in his teens, a superb architectural draughtsman – to begin with, very much of the Picturesque school. His first full-length prose work, *The Poetry of Architecture*, also belongs to the tradition: serialized in the *Architectural Magazine* in 1837, it deals with the relation of vernacular buildings to landscape. Ruskin's feeling for the Picturesque never quite diminished. The mouldering wall furred with lichen recurs throughout his writings. But he soon began trying to understand the emotion it generated, and wrote of the way the ageing of stone allows nature to blend with the man-made environment. And his work acquired a scholarly dimension. By the late 1840s, his knowledge of medieval iconography and the motifs of Gothic ornament in England, France and Italy was encyclopedic.

The first product of this knowledge was *The Seven Lamps of Architecture* (1849). Two preoccupations caused him to write it: his new estimation of early religious painting* and anxiety about the fate of the medieval heritage in modern times. In spite of – in some cases because of – the Gothic Revival, the great buildings of medieval Europe were under threat. Many of them were endangered by neglect; still more by the fashion for 'restoration' – at the hands of craftsmen and designers who were ignorant of medieval skills and unable to judge the value of the work they were so assiduously replacing. *The Seven Lamps* was written partly to make the case against the restorers and partly to record work that Ruskin believed was soon to be lost. As he both celebrated the art of the Middle Ages and lamented the failure of his own time to emulate or properly value it, he began to perceive the extent of the gulf that divided the two eras. He was forced to conclude that at some stage in its development, European culture had gone disastrously wrong.

This conclusion was new to Ruskin. *Modern Painters I* had championed modern artists and claimed to prove their 'Superiority in the Art of

---

* Much of the painting Ruskin called 'medieval' – Italian painting of the fifteenth century, for instance – now tends to be classed as 'early Renaissance'. He usually reserved the word 'Renaissance' for sixteenth-century painting and for architecture that used classical forms and conventions.

Landscape Painting to all the Ancient Masters'.* But during a long Italian tour in 1845, the religious masters from Giotto to Tintoretto took him by storm. He learnt that many of the claims he had made for the English landscapists could also be made for medieval painting. For instance, he praised fifteenth-century artists like Benozzo Gozzoli or Giovanni Bellini for what he called their 'naturalism': the way they paid homage to the hand of God in creation through the loving and accurate representation of natural forms. It was precisely this quality that he admired in Gothic architecture.

Anyone who has ever looked closely at a Gothic cathedral will have been struck by the proliferation of natural forms in its ornamentation. These forms are rarely abstract or idealized. They are usually particular, and identical motifs are rarely repeated. Pages of Ruskin are devoted to the study of all this richness. He sees it as one of the many ways in which the Gothic builders praised the glory of God's creation. The whole building honours the laws of the physical world. It respects the materials it is made of, being as much concerned to express the material's character as to convert it into wall or statue. In so doing, it harmonizes with the natural environment, seeming to grow out of the land. It further celebrates the beauty of natural forms by invoking them in its own formal dispositions – in rose-windows, in foliated tracery, in the analogies that may be drawn between forest and arcade, spire and mountain peak. And in the pursuit of organic beauty it discards formal perfection, thus in effect confessing the weakness of man and acknowledging that only God is perfect. It is because of this naturalism – as much as for dubiously historical reasons† – that Ruskin calls Gothic 'Christian architecture'.

With the coming of the Renaissance, however, naturalism gives way to conventions diametrically opposed to it. The decadent Catholicism of the late Middle Ages had given birth to a delusive self-confidence. The Gothic adoration of external things had opened perspectives into infinity; the art of the Renaissance confined itself to the study of man, beginning and ending in his physical being. For Ruskin, this was 'sensualism' – what is now called 'materialism' inflated with the sin of pride. This sensualism required a more worldly style to reflect its values. The result was Classicism: a revival of the architecture of pagan Rome. Where Gothic had confessed man's limitations, Classicism announced his perfections by means of symmetry, a mathematical concept of form, which centred on man and displayed the power of his intellect, but had no room for the wide world beyond him. The

---

* The sub-title of *Modern Painters I*.
† For an account of these reasons, see note 15 on p. 348.

change in style represented, in Ruskin's view, a covert rejection of Christianity, though Christian practice was to continue, as a mere form, into the nineteenth century.

Ruskin's fullest account of this cultural apostasy is to be found in *The Stones of Venice* (1851 and 1853). Venetian builders in the Middle Ages created their own eclectic variations on the Byzantine and Gothic styles. *
These were the styles the book was written to celebrate. When it appeared, Ruskin's architectural taste was still bafflingly unfashionable. To the amazement of his critics, he denounced the famed Palladio and the Renaissance, lavishing his praise on buildings that for two hundred years had been thought barbaric and grotesque. The modern tourist is amazed to learn that, before Ruskin, St Mark's and the Ducal Palace were not thought beautiful. Between 1849 and 1852, he spent long periods in Venice studying these ancient buildings, many of them obscure and disregarded. He studied them as exhaustively as he could: sketching, making daguerreotypes, writing voluminous notes, even climbing on the buildings to measure their proportions. At the same time he pursued their chronology in the city's archives and gradually unfolded his moralized tale of a culture's rise and fall.

Ruskin did not see buildings merely as works of art created by individuals for the use of other individuals. They were social artefacts and, as such, expressed the moral condition of the society in which and for which they were built. '. . . every noble form of architecture,' he wrote in Volume I, 'is in some sort the embodiment of the Polity, Life, History and Religious Faith of nations.' In the stones of Venice and their history, moreover, he believed it was possible to see the history of the European spirit neatly encapsulated. The period of the architecture he loved coincided exactly with the era of the city's greatness. Her adoption of the Renaissance style signalled her decline and anticipated her fall. That Ruskin idealized Venice and the Middle Ages in general, there can be no doubt. This is not greatly important. What the architectural works create is a myth, a Utopia projected back into the past. The relevance of the myth was to be felt in modern England, a greater maritime empire in a Europe fallen deeper into spiritual and cultural decay. As Byron, one of the heroes of Ruskin's youth, had put it:

> in the fall
> Of Venice think of thine.

* For an explanation of this, see note 1 on p. 318.

If *The Stones of Venice* were merely the lament of a conservative cultural pessimist, it would be of little account. But Ruskin's social critique has radical implications too. These are most plainly articulated in the central chapter of the work. 'The Nature of Gothic', an analysis of the style that is at once imaginative and scholarly, is one of Ruskin's masterpieces. However, the most innovative passage, though its implications for the future of art are profound, is scarcely about art at all. It is about work. In the last chapter of *The Seven Lamps*, Ruskin had already suggested that the quality of architectural ornament is affected by the conditions of labour in which it is produced. This argument has social implications, and in 'The Nature of Gothic' they combine with Ruskin's advocacy of 'naturalism'. Ornament may be classified not only in aesthetic terms but in terms of the *kind* of labour that goes into its production. In Renaissance architecture and the neo-classicism that grew from it, the ornament is *servile*. Because the variety of natural forms is reduced to certain fixed conventions – so that ornament may be made subservient to 'perfection' of design – the creative freedom of the workman is repressed and controlled. In the industrial age, this tendency has been hugely and grotesquely magnified by the conditions of mass production. Gothic ornament, by contrast, is *revolutionary*. Christianity recognizes 'the individual value of every soul' and sees the hand of God in the richness of creation. It thus gives freedom to the workman's imagination, encouraging him to respond as an individual to the various detail of the natural world. 'Work' and 'art' are thus virtually synonymous and remain so in Ruskin's vocabulary for the rest of his career. The society which fails to provide work that develops the workman's humanity in this way, he concludes, stands convicted of injustice.

Having once spoken out on these issues, Ruskin found it impossible to confine his work to questions of art. He began to dislike playing the part of what he was to call (in his lecture on 'Traffic') 'a respectable architectural man-milliner': a writer of purple prose and the darling of the increasingly wealthy middle class, of the people who collected modern pictures to enrich their drawing rooms and commissioned new town halls in the fashionable Gothic style. Partly because his family was wealthy, his conscience was deeply troubled by the sight of poverty or soulless drudgery. It made him angry to hear those who lived in comfort, their standard of living improving daily because of the labours of others, moralizing about the value of work – especially when the work was likely to be, literally, soul-destroying. Still more loathsome to him was the much-popularized science of Political Economy, which explained these inequities in terms of *natural* laws. Between 'The Nature of Gothic' in 1853 and the serialization of *Unto this*

Last in 1860, his social analyses surfaced in a variety of contexts: in the later volumes of *Modern Painters* (see 'The Two Boyhoods'), in his lectures (see 'The Work of Iron') and in a series of letters to the press on political questions which his cautious father persuaded him not to publish.

In the published writings, however, the social lessons were nearly always connected with art. The culmination of this phase of Ruskin's career came in 1857 when in Manchester he delivered the lectures he called *The Political Economy of Art*.* On this occasion he urged the state to involve itself in the promotion of art as an activity that gives fulfilment to society at large as well as to the individual. Fundamentally, the argument is for a practical application of the lessons he had preached in 'The Nature of Gothic', but it goes beyond that, implying the need for state intervention in the economy as a whole, and calling for a society based on co-operation rather than competition. The rhetoric is distinctly Tory and medievalist – he calls state intervention 'paternal government' – but he did not escape the charge of socialism.

With *The Political Economy of Art* the balance of Ruskin's work is turned on its head. He began as a critic of art who incidentally commented on the state of society. In the Manchester lectures he was transformed into a social critic who illustrates his arguments with observations about art. Great art was the product of a just social order, which was in turn the response of a nation to Christ's command that we love one another. Gothic art was great because it achieved an equable relationship between creativity and the given world; but it could not have been produced under modern conditions of labour. The architects of the modern Gothic Revival were therefore wasting their energy. For much the same reason it was fruitless for him to engage in the criticism of contemporary art. It was first necessary to change society. Only then would great art be attainable.

This is not to say that Ruskin criticized his age merely because its ugliness offended him. His condemnation of modern culture implied a condemnation of more deeply rooted social failures. What he sought to expose was a society statistically rich that could find no employment for its workers, lamented over-production as a cause of poverty, accepted the notion of planned obsolescence, encouraged an arms race as a source of economic growth, allowed extremes of poverty and starvation to co-exist with ostentatious luxury, professed Christianity but saw such poverty as a

---

* Later reprinted as *A Joy for ever; (and its Price in the Market)*. I refer to this book by its original title throughout.

law of nature not to be tampered with, and expected the majority of its people to rest content in conditions of squalor and brutal ugliness. The responsibility for these evils could not simply be laid at the door of wicked individuals who cared nothing for their fellow-humans. The causes were to be found in the great European apostasy he had begun tracing in the history of Venice. Victorian England was still, superficially, Christian, but its real philosophy was to be found elsewhere. It appeared under various names but its principles were constant: a mechanistic account of human nature, belief in liberty (though for many the reality of deprivation rendered such liberty worse than useless), the conviction that communal prosperity is only to be achieved by the individual's pursuit of his own interest. Ruskin had been stirred to social criticism by his sense of unjust conditions of labour. Labour conditions are shaped by the laws of the market. Not surprisingly, then, it was the new philosophy's account of those laws that Ruskin now chose to attack.

4

The modern science of Political Economy grew out of the empiricist tradition of English thought. It was a theoretical response to the vast expansion of manufacturing industry in the late eighteenth century and the consequent rise to power of middle-class entrepreneurs. For the first time ever, economic power was held by a class with no roots in the land. For this reason, the development of economic theory is connected with the beginnings of British democracy – in particular with the extension of the franchise to the urban middle class, eventually brought about by the Great Reform Bill of 1832.

The undisputed founder of 'classical' economics was Adam Smith (1723–90), whose book *The Wealth of Nations* (1776) was the first systematic study of the workings of modern economies. Smith's aim was to examine the causes of economic progress and its effects. Like the American revolutionaries, he takes it that men are born free. Prosperity, which he thinks of as the ever-increasing accumulation of material wealth, is most likely to be achieved in a society which declines to restrict freedom more than is necessary. This means that individuals, set free to pursue their own economic interests, benefit the community as a whole by adding to the sum of their nation's wealth. As Smith saw it, prosperity cannot be achieved by government. The state should play no role at all in the regulation of the economy, except to arbitrate – through the clear and firm administration of justice – when different self-interests come into conflict. Thus, in many respects, Smith's political views anticipate the nineteenth-century doctrine of *laissez-faire*.

The Wealth of Nations begins with the observation that 'the productive powers of labour' had been greatly improved in Smith's own time by what Ruskin was to call, with heavy irony, 'the great civilised invention of the division of labour'. This term refers to the method of production that is at the heart of industrial economies. When labour is divided, the individual worker ceases to be responsible for the manufacture of a whole product. On the contrary, he is obliged to work only on a part of it, so that his work becomes the specialized repetition of a single process. This system promotes greater speed and efficiency of production, but – as Ruskin, Marx and other moralists argued – alienates the worker from the products of his labour. Smith was aware of this problem, and disturbed by it. But, though he was by training and profession a moralist, he deliberately excluded moral considerations from his analysis of material problems. He was trying to initiate a science, a study of the laws that determine material prosperity.

These basic principles were developed and their detailed implications questioned and explored by David Ricardo (1772–1823) in his book *The Principles of Political Economy and Taxation* (1817). Ricardo systematized the laws of cause and effect in the theory, to give it a more scientific finish. His best-known contribution to the debate was the Labour Theory of Value, according to which, differences in the exchange value of commodities are determined by the relative quantities of labour that go into their production and distribution. (This argument had a clear effect on what Ruskin has to say about work and cost in *Unto this Last*.) Like Smith, Ricardo was a man of libertarian social attitudes, but he lacked something of the master's moral subtlety; and much of the inhumanity that appalled the critics of the classical economists had its origin in his work.

Still more disturbing to such critics were the theories of his contemporary, T. R. Malthus (1766–1834), author of *An Essay on the Principle of Population* (1798). He argued that, since population increases at a faster rate than the means of subsistence, the latter will control the growth of the former through the agency of starvation. Malthus's argument influenced Ricardo and resulted in the notorious 'Iron Law of Wages'. This law, first hinted at by Smith, states that there is a natural price for labour: one which enables the worker to subsist but, through the threat of starvation, prevents the working population from increasing or decreasing in number.

The theories of Smith, Ricardo and Malthus were championed by the Utilitarian school of philosophy, whose founder, Jeremy Bentham (1748–1832), had argued, in a famous sentence, that 'The greatest happiness of the greatest number is the foundation of morals and legislation'. In his view, the principles of human conduct were governed by pain and pleasure alone. Laws were good if they were useful – that is, if they promoted as much pleasure in the individual as was compatible with the pleasure of others, and protected him as far as possible from pain. Human actions were therefore motivated by self-interest. It was the function of law and institutions to ensure that the individual subordinated his own need for happiness to the happiness of the community.

Bentham and the classical economists had a great deal in common, and their ideas were brought together mainly through the efforts of James Mill (1773–1836) – who had first encouraged Ricardo to write – and his son John Stuart Mill (1806–73). The younger Mill's philosophical work goes far beyond the narrowly mechanistic materialism of those who inspired it. Nevertheless, it was he who became the main target of Ruskin's assault, largely because his *Principles of Political Economy* (1848), which sought to integrate and develop the theories I have outlined, was, in Ruskin's words, 'the most reputed essay on that subject which has appeared in modern times'.

The assumptions preserved by Mill and criticized by Ruskin may be briefly summarized. Economies are governed by natural laws which cannot be changed by human will, any more than the laws of physical nature can. Among the effects of these laws is the tragic but inescapable fact that some individuals are condemned to poverty. Any attempt by governments or other institutions to interfere with the operations of these laws is doomed to worse than failure: in seeking to improve the lot of individuals, it will damage the economy and thereby the welfare of the whole community. The task of governments, therefore, must be to create conditions in which enlightened self-interest and the laws of supply and demand can work more freely and effectively. The sufferings of the poor will to a large extent be reduced when they perceive their condition and regulate their population accordingly.

5

Ruskin's *Unto this Last* is first and foremost a cry of anger against injustice and inhumanity; the theories of the Political Economists had outraged his strongest moral convictions. But he was arguing against thinkers who claimed to have founded a science. To limit the book's message to questions of moral feeling would be to accept that he was what his critics called him, a sentimentalist who could not face reality. But the book is also a closely argued assault on the philosophical and scientific method the economists took for granted. Profoundly conservative Ruskin was resisting the whole tendency of modern civilization on intellectual as much as on moral grounds. He objected to a method, peculiar to modern times, which worked by specialization. He argued that this deformed reality by isolating the object of study and detaching moral from material considerations. Ruskin's argument may be connected with his objection to liberal democracy, which he thought of as the political expression of an outlook that sees each man as the sum of his own interests, detached from a social context. But of course Ruskin, quite as much as Mill, was a child of the nineteenth century. It is therefore necessary to trace the origins of the intellectual tradition he represents. This may be done under three headings: the scriptural tradition of Protestantism, high Tory paternalism, and the Romantic movement.

The first and most important key to Ruskin's politics is to be found in his mother's Biblical instruction. Evangelical Protestantism insists that the Bible is the word of God and must be taken literally. The Ruskin of the economic writings was no fundamentalist – when he wrote *Unto this Last* he was hardly a Christian at all – but, brought up in that tradition, he could not escape the implications of Biblical teaching on questions of money, labour, food and the status of the poor. It was no longer possible to regard the Genesis stories as historical, but there was no reason why the moral teaching of the New Testament should not be taken literally. Consider this passage on the Parable of the Talents*; all men are, he says,

> . . . stewards or ministers of whatever talents are entrusted to them.
> Only, is it not a strange thing, that while we more or less accept the meaning of that saying, so long as it is considered metaphorical, we never accept its meaning in its own terms? You know the lesson is given us under the form of a story about money. Money was given to the servants to make use of: the unprofitable servant dug in the earth, and hid his Lord's money. Well, we, in our poetical and spiritual application of this, say, that of course money doesn't mean money, it means wit, it means intellect, it means influence in high quarters, it means everything in the world except itself. And do not you see what a pretty and pleasant come-off there is for most of us in this spiritual application? Of course, if we had wit, we would use it for the good of our fellow-creatures. But we haven't wit. Of course if we had influence with the bishops, we would use it for the good of the Church; but we haven't any influence with the

* Matthew xxv. 14–30.

bishops. Of course, if we had political power, we would use it for the good of the nation; but we have no political power; we have no talents entrusted to *us* of any sort or kind. It is true we have a little money, but the parable can't possibly mean anything so vulgar as money; our money's our own.

I believe, if you think seriously of this matter, you will feel that the first and most literal application is just as necessary a one as any other – that the story does very specially mean what it says – plain money . . .

(from *The Political Economy of Art*, XVI, 98–9)

Literalism of this kind is uncommon and subversive. It blends, in Ruskin, with his peculiar honesty of temperament, an inability to turn away from what he had *seen*.

To the Biblical teaching of his mother was added the practical example of a high Tory father. John James Ruskin disapproved of his son's economic writings, and in later years their political differences put strains on their relationship. But the younger man consistently praised what he saw as his father's unfailing probity, and John James clearly provided him with a model of the honest tradesman. When the economic establishment reacted with alarm and contempt to the lessons of *Unto this Last*, it dismissed Ruskin as an amateur where practical business was concerned. There was small justification for this. Through his father, Ruskin had learnt as much about the operations of the market as Smith or Mill had; and though, detesting industry, he had little or no experience of its practice, his study of craftsmanship had taught him more about actual conditions of labour than was available to many 'professional' economists.

From his father he learned his political attitudes too. His autobiography begins with the words 'I am, and my father was before me, a violent Tory of the old school'.* This Toryism, comparable to that of Swift and Johnson and Coleridge, is based on a belief in hierarchy, established order and obedience to inherited authority. He detested both liberty and equality, blaming them, more than privilege, for the injustices he condemned. Only those who held power by right, as he saw it, could be moved by a sense of duty to serve and protect the weak. This is a side of Ruskin that is likely to confuse and even repel the modern reader, in particular the radical who finds his apparent socialism attractive. But in the nineteenth century political attitudes were not so neatly shared out between left and right as they are – or seem to be – today. Modern capitalist economics were then thought

---

* First used in *Fors Clavigera*, pp. 306–7 below.

progressive, being associated with the expansion of personal liberty. A radical liberal like John Stuart Mill, who championed democracy and the extension of personal rights and liberties, was also an advocate of doctrines which can be blamed for the degradations of the workhouse (Utilitarianism) and the extremes of Victorian poverty (*laissez-faire*). By contrast, Shaftesbury and Wilberforce, famous respectively for the Factory Acts and the abolition of slavery, were high Tories. State intervention in the economy and social welfare policies belonged to the right, for the right believed in the duty of government to govern – to secure social order and administer justice impartially.

No political label quite fits Ruskin's politics. Though he detested the Liberals, he was far from being a supporter of the Conservatives. His 'Toryism' was such that it could, in his own lifetime, inspire the socialism of William Morris and the founders of the Labour Party; and when he called himself a 'conservative', he usually meant a preserver of the environment – what we should call a 'conservationist'. The truth is that, despite an exceptional consistency of view, throughout his life, on most matters of principle, his specific opinions changed and developed as he grew older. His attitudes to war and imperialism and the rights of women, for instance, oscillate wildly between reaction and radicalism; and he in effect concedes the ambiguity of his position when, in *Fors Clavigera* (pp. 294 and 306–7 below), he calls himself, with conscious irony, both a Communist and a Tory. This complexity is partly due to the fact that Ruskin was never a political animal. One of his biggest failings as a social critic is his undiscriminating contempt for *all* political movements. At the same time, much of his strength derives from his indifference to partisan attitudes, which gives him the clear-sightedness of the boy who could not see the Emperor's new clothes.

This virtue is one of the qualities Ruskin shares with the only contemporary writer to have influenced his social views. It is thanks to Thomas Carlyle (1795–1881) that the Romantic nostalgia he inherited from his father took on a radical tinge. Carlyle called Political Economy 'the Dismal Science' and condemned it from a broadly Romantic viewpoint. But he also understood the industrial age and, in the 1830s and 40s, stood almost alone as the new philosophy's systematic opponent. Born in the same year as Keats, Carlyle was the only important English Romantic to survive into the Victorian era. Before the 1830s, when he began writing the apocalyptic history and social criticism for which he is now remembered, Carlyle had been mainly concerned with interpreting the literature and philosophy of modern Germany to the British public. Then, in early middle age, he turned his

Germanic transcendentalism to practical use. He had early lost his faith in Christianity but continued to believe in God. His philosophy retains the doctrines of predestination and divine justice, which he had learnt from his austerely Calvinist parents. He combines them with an unusually severe version of Romantic pantheism: not the Wordsworthian adoration of nature that Ruskin had imbibed, but belief in divinity as the indwelling principle of order in the universe. Man, in Carlyle's system, was a spiritual being who achieved his destined state of blessedness by following the moral imperative at the heart of his nature. To do so meant disregarding the prospect of material satisfaction. Thus, the idea of 'the greatest happiness of the greatest number' as the end of all social endeavour was morally abhorrent to Carlyle. Man's moral nature, as he saw it, was expressed through *work*. To deny him work – as *laissez-faire* governments, influenced by the economists, seemed to be doing – was not only injustice. It was a crime against nature.

Carlyle was probably the first thinker to insist that human beings have a right to work. He also thought they had a right to be governed. *Laissez-faire*, in his view, was the devil's philosophy. It was simply a way of saying that those with authority to govern need not do so. The distress of their subjects could simply be disregarded. But a nation's economy, as Carlyle understood it, was as much a social organism as its institutions. If parliaments could be reformed, why not economies? To counter the lethargy of modern government, he argued for government by great men and condemned the weakness of democracy. The hero as leader springs from Carlyle's metaphysics; he is a man who by his actions reveals his superiority to all other men, embodies in effect the will of God.

Ruskin's beliefs differed from Carlyle's in detail and in tone. Both men were authoritarian (if compassionate) and both were driven by the Protestant work ethic. But where Carlyle's obsession with men of power – which led him to the belief that 'might is right' – anticipates fascism, Ruskin believed in government by the wise. Carlyle was indiscriminate in his praise of work. Ruskin, equally convinced of its importance, looks at the quality of work and sees division of labour as a form of slavery. The terms of the discussion in *Unto this Last* are frequently Carlyle's, but it is conducted at a level that is profounder and less portentous. Carlyle had attacked the economists for the covert introduction – in an overtly scientific argument – of ideological values. But he had no head for the detail of their argument. It is the detail that Ruskin sets himself to demolish – the specifically economic issues. What moves us in *Unto this Last* is the way precise analysis unites with irony, passion and imagination. This has much to do with Ruskin's prose, which has also gained from the influence of Carlyle. There is an urgency that is new to Ruskin. The lyrical passages are there, but the prose is more functional than in *Modern Painters* and the tone more intimate. The combination of these contrasting elements gives the book an emotional and intellectual range beyond anything in Carlyle.

6

Unto this Last sets out to do two things: to define wealth and to demonstrate that certain moral conditions are essential to its attainment. It is not an attempt to outline a new economic theory or to propose specific policies, though inevitably the latter are touched upon. It is first and foremost a critique of current beliefs and ideas.

At the outset, Ruskin's objections to the classical theory are focused by a particular hypothesis. This is an abstract individual known as 'economic man', defined in an early essay of Mill's as a being who 'invariably does that by which he may obtain the greatest amount of necessaries, conveniences, and luxuries, with the smallest quantity of labour and physical self-denial with which they can be obtained in the existing state of knowledge'.* He was, in other words, motivated by nothing but the desire for material gain. Mill did not imagine that such an individual existed. He merely argued that it was necessary to isolate the object of one's investigation, 'because this is the mode in which science must necessarily proceed'. His aim was to discover how the laws of the market enabled interested persons to gain wealth, and economic man provided him with a model.

For Ruskin, this was precisely the way science ought not to proceed. If such an individual did not exist, how could he be used as a model for understanding real human actions?† Moreover, in cases of human nature, how was it possible to divide the understanding of an action from moral judgement of it? What Mill's theory *appeared* to propose – even if this was in no way his intention – was that society as a whole benefited from the greed and materialism of selfish individuals. It seemed to follow that Mill was *recommending* such behaviour. Many politicians and industrialists certainly understood him in this way and acted upon what they took to be

---

* 'On the Definition of Political Economy; and on the Method of Investigation Proper to it' (1836), reprinted in *Essays on Some Unsettled Questions of Political Economy*.

† One recalls Ruskin's objections to idealized landscape in his attacks on neo-classical art.

his advice, a fact which to Ruskin was sufficient proof of the method's irresponsibility.*

Man, as Ruskin depicts him, is fundamentally moral. To make such a statement is not to deny that man is capable of greed and lust and every species of heartlessness and immorality. It is simply to assert that we cannot understand humanity, cannot even understand the nature of wealth or greed, if we do not recognize that man is also capable of selflessness, honour, justice, love. What the abstracting scientific method appears to have discovered in him will not only be false (and therefore useless) but will go some way towards discouraging these virtues in the interest of, in this case, economic progress. And the individual, divided (as always) between higher and baser motives, will learn that the baser ones are beneficial to society and will therefore feel justified in the choice of selfishness.

The first essay of *Unto this Last*, 'The Roots of Honour', begins with Ruskin's attack on the notion of economic man. He argues that in most branches of human affairs – he cites the great professions – it is normal to regard personal gain as secondary to the disinterested service of one's fellows. The same should apply in industry and commerce: the job of the manufacturer and merchant should be to provide for the community. The second essay, 'The Veins of Wealth', anticipates the charge of sentimentality. With the help of some simple fables, Ruskin shows that honour in commercial affairs is not only desirable but essential to true prosperity. The Political Economists miss this point because they isolate the individual from society. Ruskin's model of the state is the family, in which survival and prosperity are grounded in interdependence. This leads naturally to a consideration of the fair reward for labour in 'Qui Judicatis Terram'. Here Ruskin argues that behind all human transactions is the concept of abstract justice. The concept is innate, and when it is violated the sufferer feels himself the victim of a crime. An unjust wage is therefore a form of theft. 'Ad Valorem', the last essay, begins with some redefinitions of key terms, misused – as Ruskin sees it – by Mill and Ricardo. The climax of the essay and of the book is a definition of 'value'. As in the case of 'justice', Ruskin finds it necessary to define this word in absolute terms. Adam Smith's distinction between value in use and value in exchange is relative and ultimately meaningless. The value of an object is its power to support life. It is thus intrinsic.

---

* This last point would presumably have been Ruskin's justification for his extreme unfairness to Mill, Smith and Ricardo in quoting them out of context. All three of them were aware that ideas had moral implications. Ruskin criticizes the *effect* of the ideas, and not necessarily the intention.

The argument, it now becomes clear, is an extension of Ruskin's view of art, for works of art, superficially useless, can only be justified by this conception of value. The book's final message, that 'There is no Wealth but Life', is the logical outcome, in social terms, of Ruskin's insistence on the morality of taste. The message of *Modern Painters* had been that 'All great art is the expression of man's delight in God's work, not in *his own*'. The target of Ruskin's attacks, aesthetic and economic, is the arrogance of the post-Renaissance intellect. Neo-classical theory had represented the artist as an improver of nature, and the result had been conventionalism – the artist imitating art, not humbly recording instances of nature. The economists saw wealth as the accumulation of money – not recognizing that money, too, is conventional, and that wealth is a quality anterior to the operation of markets. Just as neo-classical art missed reality by delighting in *man's* work, so economic theory flattered itself by contemplating its own hypotheses. As Ruskin's youthful fairy tale, *The King of the Golden River*, had suggested, the source of value is not gold – that is a token – but light and water, the sources of life itself.

7

The 'Four essays on the first principles of Political Economy' were written in the summer of 1860. Ruskin submitted them to the recently founded *Cornhill Magazine* in June of that year. The *Cornhill* was owned by his publisher, George Smith, and edited by the novelist Thackeray; both of them were, in a slight way, Ruskin's friends. The essays appeared as monthly instalments between August and November. As Ruskin tells us in his Preface, they were immediately 'reprobated in a violent manner': the critics savaged them and subscribers sent in letters of complaint. To give one example, the *Saturday Review* declared that the world would simply refuse to be 'preached to death by a mad governess' and denounced the essays as 'windy hysterics', 'absolute nonsense' and 'intolerable twaddle'. George Smith was seriously alarmed and instructed Thackeray to curtail publication: the essays were 'too deeply tainted with socialistic heresy to conciliate subscribers'. After the appearance of the third essay, Ruskin was informed 'that the magazine must only admit one Economical Essay more'. With Thackeray's permission, he 'made . . . the last one longer than the rest, and gave it blunt conclusion as well as I could – and so the book now stands'. This means that, in spite of the fourth essay's concentration, *Unto this Last* remains in some sense a fragment. It is nonetheless a well-constructed and powerfully written work. To the end of his life, Ruskin considered it the best and most valuable of all his books. So as neither to dilute this effect nor to tamper with the evidence, he published it in book form unrevised. This explains why a few undertakings he makes in the earlier essays are never carried out.

Unto this Last appeared in 1862. Ruskin wanted it to be on sale by the time his next book started appearing in serial form. This was *Munera Pulveris*, an attempt to complete the arguments begun in the four essays. Where the latter are essentially destructive of the classical position, *Munera Pulveris* attempts to replace it with positive proposals. Ruskin had 'resolved to make it the central work of my life to write an exhaustive treatise on Political Economy'. This ambition was never fulfilled, though some of Ruskin's devouter followers have claimed that these two books, read in conjunction with *Time and Tide* (1867) and *Fors Clavigera* (1871–84), constitute an exhaustively argued position. This is debatable. However, there can be no doubt that Ruskin was severely discouraged by the response his first essays provoked, even though the scale and hysteria of the opposition went a long way towards proving his arguments. *Munera Pulveris*, commissioned for *Fraser's Magazine* by a still more sympathetic friend – Carlyle's biographer, J. A. Froude – suffered the same fate as its predecessor, the series being cut short by the publisher. Most readers have conceded, too, that the proposals put forward in *Munera Pulveris* are disappointing when compared with the destructive force of *Unto this Last*, and that the conscientious sobriety of the style makes for uncharacteristically dull reading. The argument is clogged with dubious etymologies and references to Greek and Latin literature, both of which contribute to the suspicion that Ruskin no longer has his mind on nineteenth-century conditions. As for the later books, brilliant though in many ways they are, they are also eccentric and fragmentary and unpredictable, the work of a man on the verge of mental collapse. Moreover, by the time he wrote *Fors*, Ruskin had stopped attending to significant developments in economics, and much of his thought had hardened into reaction.

To begin with, *Unto this Last* sold badly. Ten years after its publication, the first edition of a thousand copies was still not exhausted. Yet when the book was reissued in the standard edition of Ruskin's works in 1877, it sold two thousand copies in the first year and continued to sell at that rate for the rest of the century. This must be seen partly as a measure of Ruskin's fame and status, which were at their height in the later Victorian age. But his fame as an art critic was already secure before 1860. It was the reputation of his economic writings that had advanced, and it had done so because professional economists had begun to recognize the flaws in the classical position. The belief in accumulation of wealth as the source of prosperity had receded; Ruskin's insistence on the importance of consumption – and the consequent danger of under-consumption – had been widely accepted. His influence on socialist thinkers like William Morris and the economist Henry George was by this time established, but it was not only socialists who recognized that the problems of the market were inseparable from social and, therefore, moral questions. By 1910, over a hundred thousand copies of *Unto this Last* had been sold and it had been translated into French, German, Italian and – by a certain M. K. Gandhi – into Gujarati. When the first twenty-nine Labour M Ps were elected to the House of Commons in 1906 a questionnaire was circulated among them which showed, according to Clement Attlee, that the book they considered had influenced them most deeply was *Unto this Last*. It is indeed possible to see Ruskin as an important influence on English social legislation for much of the twentieth century – notably on bills introduced by the government Attlee was eventually to lead. Writing of *Unto this Last* in 1964, Kenneth Clark said of Ruskin's social ideas that 'the greater part of them are now the truisms of the Welfare State'. Twenty years later, Clark's use of the word 'truism' sounds complacent, and the comment has an oddly period flavour; the interim has seen the rise of monetarism, a resurgence of *laissez-faire* without the insistence on non-economic liberties. Yet Clark's observation is in substance true. Ruskin's influence on our society has been incalculable.

8

Ruskin emerged as a critic of Political Economy in 1857. In 1869 he became a Professor of Fine Art. During those twelve years, he put most of his creative effort into public statements. The genre that dominates this phase of his career is the public lecture, the best examples of which are collected in *Sesame and Lilies* (1865) and *The Crown of Wild Olive* (1866). He also became a prolific contributor of letters to the press on issues of the day; as innumerable asides in the lectures 'Traffic' and 'Of Kings' Treasuries' indicate, he was now almost as concerned with the direction of foreign policy as with domestic questions. Though the period includes books on Greek mythology, for instance, and the formation of crystals, most of his writings are primarily concerned with topical problems. These can be strikingly diverse – war, commerce, work, education and public libraries, to name just a few at random. A by-product of this new emphasis is the juxtapository structure of his works, his many and various interests being brought together in a single lecture and made to reflect on one another.

In spite of Ruskin's habitually apocalyptic tone, the enterprise began with an assumption of optimism. He seemed not yet to have given up hope of persuading the middle classes to abandon the economics and social morality of the market. The nation was not in good health but the disease was curable. Hence the sermonizing manner, which presupposes confidence in his own powers of persuasion. As the period drew to a close, however, this hope was gradually darkened by despair and the public manner frequently yielded to subjectivity and inwardness. This had much to do with his personal life, which now turned towards tragedy. It was also because he had begun to feel the immensity of the task and to see the evils of the modern age as irreversible.

To understand these changes it will be necessary to look briefly at Ruskin's emotional life. In 1854, his seven-year-old marriage to Effie Gray was annulled on grounds of non-consummation. Effie alleged that this was due to her husband's impotence, a charge which Ruskin always denied. In any event, the marriage had been a terrible burden to both of them and Ruskin felt relieved that it was over. There can be no doubt that, even by Victorian standards, Ruskin's sexual repression was pathological. The whole emphasis on sight in his work, valuable as the depth of it is, must surely be connected with a neurotic distaste for physical intimacy. Much of the blame was presumably due to the overpowering possessiveness of his parents. In spite of growing disagreements, he continued to live with them and allowed much of his life to be ruled by them till their deaths. (His father died when he was forty-five; his mother when he was fifty-two.) The failure of his marriage was hardly tragic but it gives us a foretaste of the impending disaster. What made the repression wholly intolerable was his love for a girl thirty years his junior, which dominated his life for nearly seventeen years.

Ruskin met Rose La Touche in 1858 when she was nine and he was thirty-nine. This was the year in which he lost his religious faith: a dreadful irony, for Rose was soon to prove a religious fanatic. It seems probable that the sexuality of adult women terrified Ruskin and repelled him; in consequence, perhaps, he found it easier to direct his emotions to girls. In 1866, when Rose reached the age of sixteen, he asked her to marry him. Discouraged by her parents, she asked him to wait until she was older for an answer. He lived in hope for six years, aware all the while that her mind was increasingly threatened by religious mania. Gradually her neurosis began to express itself in symptoms of physical and mental illness. In 1872 she reached her decision and refused the offer of marriage. During the next few years, Ruskin staved off the emotional collapse that awaited him by increasing his already awesome load of work. In 1874, while studying the Giotto frescoes at Assisi, he even experienced a renewal of his religious faith, now purged of sectarian dogma. But in 1875 Rose died insane.

This tragic sequence of events ran through the busiest period of Ruskin's life. In 1869, just as he had begun to feel the hopelessness of the tasks he had set himself, he was given the opportunity to fulfil one of his greatest ambitions. He was asked to become the first Slade Professor of Fine Art at Oxford. This was a chance to provide the young with an art education on Ruskinian lines. It meant that he would be able, in one sphere of his interests, to influence the future of England substantially. He therefore accepted, but not without some searching of his conscience. The professorship, as Ruskin saw it, demanded a vast amount of work, for he was not prepared to give up his political endeavours. Inevitably, though he refused to exclude social comment from his lectures, most of his energy would have to go into his art work. This meant that social questions would have to be dealt with elsewhere. Part of the solution was provided by *Fors Clavigera*, which began appearing in 1871.

Fors is a series of open letters addressed 'to the Workmen and Labourers of Great Britain'. It was in effect a monthly periodical of which Ruskin was author, editor and publisher. It gave him the opportunity to speak on any subject and in any manner he chose. The epistolary form was a logical extension of his lecture-hall sermons. Characteristic of both is his use of the personal pronoun: the denunciatory 'you' with its Old Testament overtones modulating into the more ambiguous 'we' with its implications of shared guilt. By the late 1860s, the public lecture no longer met Ruskin's needs. Something more personal was required that could reach a less exclusively bourgeois audience and address a variety of topical themes, as they arose, without neglecting general principles. In *The Ethics of the Dust* (1866), a school textbook on geology, he experimented unsuccessfully with Platonic dialogue. He hit upon the genre he needed, however, as a result of his correspondence with Thomas Dixon, a cork-cutter from Sunderland and one of the many self-educated readers who drew sustenance from his writings. What began as a private correspondence developed into a series of open letters on 'the Laws of Work' published in 1867 as *Time and Tide*. A second series of these letters was promised but never written. The need for them was met instead by *Fors*.

Throughout the series of ninety-six letters, Ruskin manages to sustain the informal atmosphere of correspondence, including a large element of autobiography. This was necessitated by his growing pessimism and the inevitable inwardness that followed from it, exacerbated by the deepening disturbance of his mind. Pursuing his old technique of intermeshing disparate themes and expressing his judgements as much through juxta-position as through statement, he also achieves variety of tone. The urgency of what he has to say removes the last traces of 'fine writing' from his style. It is replaced by an unrivalled sense of rhythm, which modulates between anger, compassion, self-pity, satire, irony, tenderness, exasper-ation, confessional intimacy, lyrical description and a kind of controlled insanity. The variety is also hospitable to quotation – from the Bible, from classic literary texts, and from the daily papers.

The range of Ruskin's activities at this time is staggering. In 1875 alone, he was writing seven books at once, most of them for serial publication. These included guide-books to Italian cities and textbooks on natural history, both of which he judged necessary background to his Oxford lectures. He founded a museum in Sheffield and the Ruskin Art Collection in Oxford. He continued to draw and collect; he lectured; he published his own books. He also began to engage in what were intended as practical social projects for the renewal of England. In the first year of *Fors* he undertook to set a tithe of his income aside to contribute to 'a National Store instead of a National Debt' and asked his readers to do the same. This fund initiated what he was soon to christen the Guild of St George.

This Utopian body has been much misunderstood. Quixotic it un-doubtedly was, impractical and absurdly idiosyncratic. It was like a cross between the political structure of fourteenth-century Venice, an order of chivalry, a medieval craftsmen's guild and a modern, charitable pressure-group. Its purpose might be compared with the account of medieval labour in 'The Nature of Gothic'. That was to a large extent fantasy, whether Ruskin knew it or not. But the effect of the fantasy was to put modern conditions of labour in perspective, to provide an image of what work might be. In much the same way, the Guild should be understood as a living form of social criticism: one which reflected Ruskin's mental instability, no doubt, but also the madness of an unjust society. To cleanse a spring and cultivate a tiny plot of land around it, as Ruskin did in a village not far from London, or to build a strong country road through a neglected and potentially lovely village near Oxford, as he inspired a group of under-graduates to do, was to show in little what the whole of society might become. It is not impossible that Ruskin knew his enterprise was doomed to failure, yet any English reader who studies his work with care cannot fail to be impressed by how many of his endeavours, particularly those conducted through the Guild, have been absorbed into English life.

But Ruskin was going mad. His obsession with Rose La Touche began to penetrate every aspect of his work; it coloured his most public statements with subjective fantasy. With her death, the problem was exacerbated. He now began to suffer from hallucinations. His writing had always shown tendencies to instability, but the openly confessional form of *Fors* encouraged his extremity. In 1877 he launched a bitterly outspoken attack on the American painter, James Abbott McNeill Whistler, whom he considered guilty of shoddy craftsmanship. Whistler was an aesthete, and the real object of Ruskin's attack was the newly fashionable Aesthetic Movement with its rejection of the social value of art. Witty and iconoclastic, the painter saw his chance to unseat the art-dictator of mid-Victorian England. He sued Ruskin for libel, Ruskin was ordered to pay damages to the value of a farthing, and, in 1878, because the court had seemed to deny him the right to express critical judgements, he resigned his Oxford chair. But the resignation was already inevitable. Earlier in the year, Ruskin had suffered a savage mental breakdown. It was the first of seven. His last breakdown, in 1889, finished his creative life. Still more tragically, Ruskin survived in body, incapacitated and silent, for another ten years.

In the lucid intervals between his attacks of insanity, he continued to write and draw; and even, for a brief, erratic period, resumed his Oxford professorship. Notable among the works of this period are *The Bible of Amiens* (1880–85), another study of Gothic, which inspired Marcel Proust, and *Fiction, Fair and Foul* (1880–81), a book of essays which see death as the central theme of the Victorian novel. In 1884 he delivered a series of lectures called *The Storm-Cloud of the Nineteenth Century*. No other book of Ruskin's is so unmitigatedly pessimistic. In *Modern Painters III* he had said that nineteenth-century landscape might be characterized by its loving attention to cloud. The clouds of this late work are foul with pollution and driven across the land by plague winds. In six grim words he prophesies the future: 'Blanched sun, – blighted grass, – blinded man.' *The Storm-Cloud* is the most despairing, if also the most deranged, of Ruskin's attacks on the industrial age. It is followed by the most lyrical of his hymns to nature, an autobiography from which he deliberately excluded the remembrance of anything that caused him pain. *Praeterita* was the only book he wrote simply to give pleasure, yet its beauties are as remote as can be from those of *Modern Painters*. The theme of the book is memory, and its ecstasies occur not outside in the spacious world but within the author's mind. Ruskin's last and most violent breakdown brought this final attempt at wholeness to a premature close. Incapable of holding a pen, he dictated the final chapter to the woman who cared for him in his last years, his cousin Joan (or Joanna) Severn. He gave it the title 'Joanna's Care'. Nothing in his work better demonstrates the power and beauty of his prose. The character of the sentences is determined by his deployment of vividly particularized sensuous detail within a larger conceptual framework. There can be few writers in whose sentences time is so palpable a factor – both the time it takes us to read them and the larger time-scale of memory that our reading is meant to evoke. Ruskin is the master of the long sentence in English, the inclusiveness of the periods matching the range of his preoccupations. One is scarcely surprised to learn that Proust knew *Praeterita* by heart. Here is the last paragraph of Ruskin's published work. (He has just compared a rivulet in his English garden to the Fountain of Trevi in Rome and Fonte Branda in Siena.)

How things bind and blend themselves together! The last time I saw the Fountain of Trevi, it was from Arthur's father's room – Joseph Severn's, where we both took Joanie to see him in 1872, and the old man made a sweet drawing of his pretty daughter-in-law, now in her schoolroom; he himself then eager in finishing his last picture of the Marriage in Cana, which he had caused to take place under a vine trellis, and delighted himself by painting the crystal and ruby glittering of the changing rivulet of water out of the Greek vase, glowing into wine. Fonte Branda I last saw with Charles Norton, under the same arches where Dante saw it. We drank of it together, and walked together that evening on the hills above, where the fireflies among the scented thickets shone fitfully in the still undarkened air. *How* they shone! moving like fine-broken starlight through the purple leaves. How they shone! through the sunset that faded into thunderous night as I entered Siena three days before, the white edges of the mountainous clouds still lighted from the west, and the openly golden sky calm behind the Gate of Siena's heart, with its still golden words, 'Cor magis tibi Sena pandit,'* and the fireflies everywhere in sky and cloud rising and falling, mixed with the lightning, and more intense than the stars.

(XXXV, 561–62)

9

Ruskin was a writer who changed lives. *Unto this Last*, said Gandhi, 'captured me and made me transform my life'. For the young William Morris, 'The books of John Ruskin were . . . a sort of revelation . . .' In his

---

* 'More than her gates, Siena opens her heart to you': inscribed over the north gate of the city.

Introduction to *The Bible of Amiens*, Proust declared of Ruskin: 'He will teach me, for is not he, too, in some degree the Truth?' 'He was one of those rare men,' wrote Tolstoy, 'who think with their hearts, and so he thought and said not only what he himself had seen and felt, but what everyone will think and say in the future.' To these names may be added innumerable others, equally diverse. Nothing more effectively illustrates the range and depth of Ruskin's achievement than a roll-call of the people he influenced.

The present selection has been designed to demonstrate both his range and the unity underlying it. Nothing in his work seems more important than his refusal, in an age of growing specialization, to separate one discipline from another or to see questions of art and science as distinct from questions of morality. The refusal was, in many respects, an aspect of his conservatism. But the modern reader may feel it to be prophetic. In reacting against his time, he drew attention to values the industrial age was about to sweep away. Many of these – by no means all of them – our own age has begun to rediscover. He was, to use a term that was not then current, an ecological thinker. This is partly to say that he was the first important writer to recognize the dangers of industrial waste and pollution. For Ruskin, a profitable factory that pollutes the environment cannot be looked upon as a producer of wealth, for 'There is no Wealth but Life'. But I also intend 'ecological' in a broader sense. Ecology studies the forms of life in the context of their environment. Ruskin applied this principle to everything that concerned him. However detailed his scrutiny of particulars, he shows himself incapable, from first to last, of abstracting anything from its context.

In order to focus on *Unto this Last*, however, I have chosen pieces that easily connect with it. They cover a variety of topics, but each of them at some point touches on the themes of wealth, labour, justice and social order. I have also drawn mainly on the writings of Ruskin's middle period, the phase of his life to which *Unto this Last* belongs. I have therefore denied the reader some of the pleasures of reading him. The selection contains few of the ecstatic descriptions of nature or architecture that make the early books so memorable; and, apart from two letters from *Fors Clavigera*, I have included nothing from the more personal and fragmentary books of his last period. In particular, with great regret, I have excluded *Praeterita*, though one of the passages from *Fors* recurs in the first chapter of that great book. This decision was made partly because it is difficult to make extracts from *Praeterita*, partly because the book is one of the few that are still in print, and partly because I could find no extended passage that would throw light on the themes of this selection. I wanted at all costs to avoid something which Ruskin himself detested and which has bedevilled his reputation from the start: the anthologizing of short purple passages, removed from their intended contexts. All the essays and lectures, with the exception of 'The Nature of Gothic', are virtually complete, though I have cut a few footnotes and sentences that were too ephemerally topical to be anything but distracting to a modern reader. The missing footnotes I have left unacknowledged, but cuts in the main text are indicated thus: [. . .]. Asterisks and daggers left in the text are Ruskin's and refer to those of his footnotes that remain; numbers refer to my notes, which I have placed at the end of the book, so that readers may disregard them if they choose. I have ignored Ruskin's practice of numbering paragraphs.

The text I have used is *The Library Edition of the Works of John Ruskin*, edited by E. T. Cook and Alexander Wedderburn, which I describe more fully in the Select Bibliography, p. 43. All references in this introduction and in the notes are to that edition.

CLIVE WILMER
Cambridge
November 1984

CHRONOLOGY

1819 8 February, Ruskin born in London, the son of John James Ruskin and Margaret Ruskin (née Cox)

1823 The family moves to Herne Hill, south of London

1825 First continental tour (Paris, Brussels, Waterloo)

1826 Begins writing poetry

1832 Receives Samuel Rogers' *Italy* as a birthday present. Illustrated with vignettes by Turner, the book begins the central enthusiasm of Ruskin's life

1833 Continental tour includes first visit to Switzerland, notably to the Vale of Chamonix, one of 'my two bournes of earth'

1834 Begins life-long study of Alpine geology. Two essays on geology – his first published works – appear in the *Magazine of Natural History*

1835 Continental tour includes first visit to his other bourne of earth, Italy, and, more specifically, Venice

1836 Falls sentimentally in love with Adèle Domecq, daughter of his father's French partner. Writes essay defending Turner against his critics in the reviews but does not publish it. Goes up to Christ Church, Oxford

1837 Publishes *The Poetry of Architecture* (1837–8) in the *Architectural Magazine*

1839 Meets Turner. Suffers from depression and suspected consumption and goes on long tour with parents to recover health. First visit to Rome

1841 Returns to England and meets distant cousin, Euphemia ('Effie') Gray. Writes *The King of the Golden River* for her

1842 Returns to Oxford and takes B.A. Family moves to Denmark Hill, London. Ruskin begins *Modern Painters*

1843 *Modern Painters I* published anonymously ('by a Graduate of Oxford')

1845 First continental tour without parents. Realizes the greatness of early Italian painting and discovers Tintoretto

1846 Publishes *Modern Painters II*

1848 Marries Effie Gray. They tour Normandy together, Ruskin studying Gothic architecture. He begins *The Seven Lamps of Architecture*

1849   Long stay in Venice (1849–50); begins systematic study of Venetian architecture. Publishes *The Seven Lamps*. Embarks on *The Stones of Venice*

1851   Meets Carlyle. Publishes *The Stones of Venice I*. Sees first Pre-Raphaelite pictures at the Royal Academy and writes letter to *The Times* defending them against their critics. Returns to Venice for second long stay (1851–2). Turner dies; Ruskin is named executor in his will

1852   Social criticism begins with three letters on social and economic problems intended for publication in *The Times*, but John James suppresses them

1853   *The Stones of Venice II* and *III* published. Spends summer with Effie and J. E. Millais at Glenfinlas. Effie and Millais fall in love. Ruskin delivers his first lectures in Edinburgh (*Lectures on Architecture and Painting*, published 1854)

1854   Marriage annulled on grounds of non-consummation. Ruskin begins lecturing at the Working Men's College. Friendship with Rossetti begins

1855   Begins working with Benjamin Woodward on designs for the new Museum of Natural History in Oxford; Ruskin takes charge of the sculptural schemes. Effie marries Millais. Ruskin begins the series of *Academy Notes*, an annual commentary on the Royal Academy exhibitions

1856   Publishes *Modern Painters III* and *IV* and *The Harbours of England*

1857   Publishes *The Elements of Drawing*. Lectures on *The Political Economy of Art* in Manchester. Begins sorting and cataloguing the drawings in the Turner bequest (1857–8)

1858   Lectures on 'The Work of Iron'. Meets the nine-year-old Rose La Touche, with whom he is soon to fall in love. In Turin experiences an 'unconversion' which turns him against his rigid Protestantism and undermines his belief in Christianity

1859   Publishes *The Two Paths* and *The Elements of Perspective*. Meets Margaret Bell, the headmistress of a progressive girls' school in Cheshire, Winnington Hall; is affected by her ideas and becomes a regular visitor to the school (until 1868)

1860   Publishes *Modern Painters V* and, at Chamonix, begins *Unto this Last*. The latter serialized in the *Cornhill Magazine*, but hostile public reaction halts publication prematurely

1862   *Unto this Last* appears in book form

1863   *Munera Pulveris* serialized in *Fraser's Magazine*

1864 Death of John James Ruskin. Ruskin's cousin Joan Agnew (later Mrs Arthur Severn) comes to live at Denmark Hill and takes care of Ruskin and his mother for the rest of their lives. The lectures 'Traffic' and 'Of Kings' Treasuries' delivered

1865 *Sesame and Lilies* published. Joins Carlyle in forming a Defence and Aid Fund in support of Governor Eyre, who has ruthlessly suppressed an insurrection in Jamaica and is now in danger of impeachment

1866 Proposes marriage to Rose La Touche, but she postpones her decision. Publishes *The Ethics of the Dust*, a dialogue on crystallography written for the girls at Winnington, and *The Crown of Wild Olive*

1867 Publishes *Time and Tide*, a book of letters on 'the Laws of Work' addressed to Thomas Dixon, a cork-cutter of Sunderland

1869 Publishes *The Queen of the Air*, lectures on classical mythology. Elected first Slade Professor of Fine Art at Oxford

1870 First series of Slade *Lectures on Art*

1871 Begins publishing *Fors Clavigera* in monthly instalments. Founds the St George's Fund (later the Guild of St George) for the renewal of England and undertakes to pay a tithe of his income to it. Endows drawing mastership at Oxford and begins the Ruskin Art Collection there. Purchases Brantwood on Coniston Water, which now becomes his main residence. Begins series of social experiments, notably a housing scheme in Marylebone run by Octavia Hill. Margaret Ruskin dies, ninety years old

1872 Publishes *Aratra Pentelici* (on sculpture) and *The Eagle's Nest* (on science and art). Rose La Touche seriously ill both physically and mentally; she finally rejects Ruskin's proposal

1873 Publishes *Love's Meinie* (1873–81) and *Ariadne Florentina*. The former, a study of birds, is the first of three books on natural history

1874 Publishes *Val d'Arno*, lectures on Tuscan sculpture. In Assisi to study the Giotto frescoes, Ruskin recovers his Christian faith while living in a sacristan's cell

1875 Publishes first instalments of *Mornings in Florence* (1875–7) and the other two books on natural history, *Proserpina* (on botany; 1875–86) and *Deucalion* (on geology; 1875–83). Founds the Sheffield Museum, Walkley. Rose La Touche dies insane. Ruskin gives only one series of lectures at Oxford and is excused his duties till 1877

1876 Begins editing his *Bibliotheca Pastorum* (1876–85): the first volume is the *Economist* of Xenophon. In Venice, meets Count Alvise Zorzi; together they campaign to save St Mark's from proposed 'restorations'. A series of hallucinations in Venice at Christmas-time anticipates mental collapse

1877   Begins publishing *St Mark's Rest* (1877–84), on Venice. In *Fors* accuses Whistler of asking 'two hundred guineas for flinging a pot of paint in the public's face'; Whistler sues him for libel

1878   First mental breakdown. Suspends publication of *Fors*. Fined a farthing damages for libelling Whistler and, in protest, resigns professorship

1880   Resumes publication of *Fors*, which continues intermittently until 1884. Begins publishing *The Bible of Amiens* (1880–85) and *Fiction, Fair and Foul* (1880–81)

1881   Carlyle dies

1882   Rossetti dies

1883   Resumes Slade professorship after a year without mental attacks

1884   Publishes *The Storm-Cloud of the Nineteenth Century*, a visionary account of the disturbance of natural order in modern times

1885   Resigns professorship in protest against vivisection in the University of Oxford. Begins publishing his autobiography, *Praeterita* (1885–9)

1888   Last continental tour

1889   *Praeterita* concluded prematurely after his last and most severe attack of madness. He survives another ten years, incapacitated, living in seclusion and virtual silence

1900   Dies at Brantwood of influenza, 20 January. Buried in Coniston churchyard

SELECT BIBLIOGRAPHY

Most of Ruskin's books are out of print. Anyone who takes more than a passing interest in his work should look for the standard edition in a library. This is *The Library Edition of the Works of John Ruskin*, edited by E. T. Cook and Alexander Wedderburn, London, 1903–12. It was published in thirty-nine large volumes, and the index alone fills one of them. It is a masterpiece of editorial scholarship and very easy to use. The introductions to each volume are unusually long, well-written and informative; it is beautifully illustrated, mainly with Ruskin's drawings; the notes are incomparable.

Of complete books in print, the only ones easily available that include material not in this selection are *The Elements of Drawing* (Dover) and *Praeterita* (OUP). There is also a handsome edition of *The Stones of Venice* (Faber and Faber), which includes some splendid colour reproductions; but it is heavily abridged and the cuts are nowhere indicated. There are also a number of selections in print. Of these, by far the best is *The Genius of John Ruskin*, edited by J. D. Rosenberg, London (Allen and Unwin), 1964. This includes much longer extracts than is customary and attempts to cover every phase and manner of Ruskin's career. Many collections of diaries and letters have been published. Much the most important of these, *The Diaries of John Ruskin*, selected and edited by Joan Evans and J. H. Waterhouse, three volumes, Oxford, 1956–9, is out of print. Fortunately, certain of Ruskin's books are still easy to find in second-hand bookshops, though they are neither as cheap nor as common as they were until quite recently, and many specific works are rare.

The quantity of secondary literature is staggering. Of the innumerable biographies, three merit particular attention. E. T. Cook's *The Life of John Ruskin*, two volumes, London, 1893, is the standard work. It is reverential but neither pompous nor fussy; most of the material appears in the Introductions to the *Library Edition*. Derrick Leon's *Ruskin: The Great Victorian*, London, 1949, is probably the fullest and most sympathetic biography. Unlike most modern critics, Leon was very much a Ruskinian. John Dixon Hunt's *The Wider Sea*, London (Dent), 1982, is the most up-to-date account. Tim Hilton's *John Ruskin: The Early Years*, New Haven (Yale), 1985, published in the month this book goes to press, sounds as if it is likely soon to become the standard biography. It deals with Ruskin's life up until 1860; a second volume dealing with the later years is promised. The most interesting critical studies of recent years are, in my view, J. D. Rosenberg's *The Darkening Glass*, London (Routledge), 1963, and Robert Hewison's *John Ruskin: The Argument of the Eye*, London (Thames and Hudson), 1976. Both make original observations and both use biographical material.

Ruskin was a superb draughtsman and watercolourist. Evidence of this is to be found in the *Library Edition*, in Paul H. Walton's *The Drawings of John Ruskin*, Oxford (Clarendon Press), 1972, in Robert Hewison's *Ruskin and Venice*, London (Thames and Hudson), 1978, and in *John Ruskin*, the catalogue to the Arts Council travelling exhibition of 1983.

The King of the Golden River

or

THE BLACK BROTHERS

A Legend of Stiria

Written 1841
Published 1850

COMMENTARY

The King of the Golden River was written in 1841 as a gift for the thirteen-year-old Effie Gray (who was later to become Ruskin's wife). Ruskin's first biographer, W. G. Collingwood, relates the circumstances as follows: 'The story goes that she challenged the melancholy John, engrossed in his drawing and geology, to write a fairy tale – as the least likely task for him to fulfil. Upon which he produced at a couple of sittings *The King of the Golden River*, a pretty medley of Grimm's grotesque and Dickens' kindliness and the true Ruskinian ecstasy of the Alps.' The story was never intended for the general public and remained unpublished till 1850, when Ruskin gave his 'passive assent' to its publication. Charmingly illustrated by Richard Doyle, it was quickly successful and remained so throughout the nineteenth century.

The influences named by Collingwood were noted by Ruskin himself in *Praeterita*. He was an enthusiastic follower of Dickens and read all his stories and novels as they appeared. He first read Grimm's fairy tales as a small boy. Edgar Taylor's *German Popular Stories* of 1826, splendidly illustrated with etchings by George Cruikshank, grafted itself upon his imagination, and in 1868 he wrote the introduction to a new edition of it, emphasizing the importance for developing imaginations of the traditional tale and its power to animate 'the material world with inextinguishable life'.

Neither Ruskin nor Collingwood mentions the influence of Turner's Alpine paintings. It is clear, even from a single reading of the story, that Ruskin was already searching for a way of expressing in words the same feeling for landscape that he found in Turner. Without the discovery that the fairy tale represents, *Modern Painters* might not have been possible. Moreover, what Ruskin most admired in Turner was his ability to combine the truthful depiction of natural wonders with an awareness of the moral order underpinning them. Thus, when the wicked brothers in this tale are judged by the 'red glory of the sunset', the conception is Turnerian and something more than a pleasant fancy.

When Northrop Frye in his *Anatomy of Criticism* argues that 'Ruskin's treatment of wealth in his economic works' is 'essentially a commentary on this fairy tale', he exaggerates. It is nonetheless surprising to find how much of *Unto this Last* is there in embryo. If one wished to extract a moral from the allegory, one could hardly do better than the dictum from *Unto this Last*: 'There is no Wealth but Life'.

THE KING
OF THE GOLDEN RIVER
or
THE BLACK BROTHERS

CHAPTER I

HOW THE AGRICULTURAL SYSTEM OF THE BLACK BROTHERS
WAS INTERFERED WITH BY SOUTH-WEST WIND,
ESQUIRE

In a secluded and mountainous part of Stiria there was, in old time, a valley of the most surprising and luxuriant fertility. It was surrounded, on all sides, by steep and rocky mountains, rising into peaks, which were always covered with snow, and from which a number of torrents descended in constant cataracts. One of these fell westward, over the face of a crag so high, that, when the sun had set to everything else, and all below was darkness, his beams still shone full upon this waterfall, so that it looked like a shower of gold. It was, therefore, called by the people of the neighbour-hood, the Golden River. It was strange that none of these streams fell into the valley itself. They all descended on the other side of the mountains, and wound away through broad plains and by populous cities. But the clouds were drawn so constantly to the snowy hills, and rested so softly in the circular hollow, that in time of drought and heat, when all the country round was burnt up, there was still rain in the little valley; and its crops were so heavy, and its hay so high, and its apples so red, and its grapes so blue, and its wine so rich, and its honey so sweet, that it was a marvel to every one who beheld it, and was commonly called the Treasure Valley.

The whole of this little valley belonged to three brothers, called Schwartz, Hans, and Gluck. Schwartz and Hans, the two elder brothers, were very ugly men, with over-hanging eyebrows and small dull eyes, which were always half shut, so that you couldn't see into *them*, and always fancied they saw very far into *you*. They lived by farming the Treasure Valley, and very good farmers they were. They killed everything that did not pay for its eating. They shot the blackbirds, because they pecked the fruit; and killed the hedgehogs, lest they should suck the cows; they poisoned the crickets for eating the crumbs in the kitchen; and smothered the cicadas, which used to sing all summer in the lime trees. They worked their servants without any wages, till they would not work any more, and then quarrelled with them, and turned them out of doors without paying them. It would have been very odd, if with such a farm, and such a system of farming, they hadn't got very rich; and very rich they *did* get. They generally contrived to keep their corn by them till it was very dear, and then sell it for twice its value; they had heaps of gold lying about on their floors, yet it was never known that they had given so much as a penny or a crust in charity; they never went to mass; grumbled perpetually at paying tithes; and were, in a word, of so cruel and grinding a temper, as to receive from all those with whom they had any dealings, the nick-name of the 'Black Brothers.'

The youngest brother, Gluck, was as completely opposed, in both appearance and character, to his seniors as could possibly be imagined or desired. He was not above twelve years old, fair, blue-eyed, and kind in temper to every living thing. He did not, of course, agree particularly well with his brothers, or rather, they did not agree with *him*. He was usually appointed to the honourable office of turnspit, when there was anything to roast, which was not often; for, to do the brothers justice, they were hardly less sparing upon themselves than upon other people. At other times he used to clean the shoes, floors, and sometimes the plates, occasionally getting what was left on them, by way of encouragement, and a wholesome quantity of dry blows, by way of education.

Things went on in this manner for a long time. At last came a very wet summer, and everything went wrong in the country around. The hay had hardly been got in, when the haystacks were floated bodily down to the sea by an inundation; the vines were cut to pieces with the hail; the corn was all killed by a black blight; only in the Treasure Valley, as usual, all was safe. As it had rain when there was rain nowhere else, so it had sun when there was sun nowhere else. Everybody came to buy corn at the farm, and went away pouring maledictions on the Black Brothers. They asked what they liked, and got it, except from the poor people, who could only beg, and several of whom were starved at their very door, without the slightest regard or notice.

It was drawing towards winter, and very cold weather, when one day the two elder brothers had gone out, with their usual warning to little Gluck, who was left to mind the roast, that he was to let nobody in, and give nothing out. Gluck sat down quite close to the fire, for it was raining very hard, and the kitchen walls were by no means dry or comfortable looking. He turned and turned, and the roast got nice and brown. 'What a pity,' thought Gluck, 'my brothers never ask anybody to dinner. I'm sure, when they've got such a nice piece of mutton as this, and nobody else has got so much as a piece of dry bread, it would do their hearts good to have somebody to eat it with them.'

Just as he spoke, there came a double knock at the house door, yet heavy and dull, as though the knocker had been tied up – more like a puff than a knock.

'It must be the wind,' said Gluck; 'nobody else would venture to knock double knocks at our door.'

No; it wasn't the wind: there it came again very hard, and what was particularly astounding, the knocker seemed to be in a hurry, and not to be in the least afraid of the consequences. Gluck went to the window, opened it, and put his head out to see who it was.

It was the most extraordinary looking little gentleman he had ever seen in his life. He had a very large nose, slightly brass-coloured; his cheeks were very round, and very red, and might have warranted a supposition that he had been blowing a refractory fire for the last eight-and-forty hours; his eyes twinkled merrily through long silky eyelashes, his moustaches curled twice round like a corkscrew on each side of his mouth, and his hair, of a curious mixed pepper-and-salt colour, descended far over his shoulders. He was about four-feet-six in height, and wore a conical pointed cap of nearly the same altitude, decorated with a black feather some three feet long. His doublet was prolonged behind into something resembling a violent exaggeration of what is now termed a 'swallow tail,' but was much obscured by the swelling folds of an enormous black, glossy-looking cloak, which must have been very much too long in calm weather, as the wind, whistling round the old house, carried it clear out from the wearer's shoulders to about four times his own length.

Gluck was so perfectly paralyzed by the singular appearance of his visitor, that he remained fixed without uttering a word, until the old gentleman, having performed another, and a more energetic concerto on the knocker, turned round to look after his fly-away cloak. In so doing he caught sight of Gluck's little yellow head jammed in the window, with its mouth and eyes very wide open indeed.

'Hollo!' said the little gentleman, 'that's not the way to answer the door: I'm wet, let me in.'

To do the little gentleman justice, he *was* wet. His feather hung down between his legs like a beaten puppy's tail, dripping like an umbrella; and from the ends of his moustaches the water was running into his waistcoat pockets, and out again like a mill stream.

'I beg pardon, sir,' said Gluck, 'I'm very sorry, but I really can't.'

'Can't what?' said the old gentleman.

'I can't let you in, sir, – I can't indeed; my brothers would beat me to death, sir, if I thought of such a thing. What do you want, sir?'

'Want?' said the old gentleman, petulantly. 'I want fire, and shelter; and there's your great fire there blazing, crackling, and dancing on the walls, with nobody to feel it. Let me in, I say; I only want to warm myself.'

Gluck had had his head, by this time, so long out of the window, that he began to feel it was really unpleasantly cold, and when he turned, and saw the beautiful fire rustling and roaring, and throwing long bright tongues up the chimney, as if it were licking its chops at the savoury smell of the leg of mutton, his heart melted within him that it should be burning away for nothing. 'He does look *very* wet,' said little Gluck; 'I'll just let him in for a quarter of an hour.' Round he went to the door, and opened it; and as the little gentleman walked in, there came a gust of wind through the house, that made the old chimneys totter.

'That's a good boy,' said the little gentleman. 'Never mind your brothers. I'll talk to them.'

'Pray, sir, don't do any such thing,' said Gluck. 'I can't let you stay till they come; they'd be the death of me.'

'Dear me,' said the old gentleman, 'I'm very sorry to hear that. How long may I stay?'

'Only till the mutton's done, sir,' replied Gluck, 'and it's very brown.'

Then the old gentleman walked into the kitchen, and sat himself down on the hob, with the top of his cap accommodated up the chimney, for it was a great deal too high for the roof.

'You'll soon dry there, sir,' said Gluck, and sat down again to turn the mutton. But the old gentleman did *not* dry there, but went on drip, drip, dripping among the cinders, and the fire fizzed, and sputtered, and began to look very black, and uncomfortable: never was such a cloak; every fold in it ran like a gutter.

'I beg pardon, sir,' said Gluck at length, after watching the water spreading in long, quicksilver-like streams over the floor for a quarter of an hour; 'mayn't I take your cloak?'

'No, thank you,' said the old gentleman.

'Your cap, sir?'

'I am all right, thank you,' said the old gentleman, rather gruffly.

'But, – sir, – I'm very sorry,' said Gluck, hesitatingly; 'but – really, sir, – you're – putting the fire out.'

'It'll take longer to do the mutton, then,' replied his visitor, drily.

Gluck was very much puzzled by the behaviour of his guest; it was such a strange mixture of coolness and humility. He turned away at the string meditatively for another five minutes.

'That mutton looks very nice,' said the old gentleman at length. 'Can't you give me a little bit?'

'Impossible, sir,' said Gluck.

'I'm very hungry,' continued the old gentleman: 'I've had nothing to eat yesterday, nor to-day. They surely couldn't miss a bit from the knuckle!'

He spoke in so very melancholy a tone, that it quite melted Gluck's heart. 'They promised me one slice to-day, sir,' said he; 'I can give you that, but not a bit more.'

'That's a good boy,' said the old gentleman again.

Then Gluck warmed a plate, and sharpened a knife. 'I don't care if I do get beaten for it,' thought he. Just as he had cut a large slice out of the mutton, there came a tremendous rap at the door. The old gentleman jumped off the hob, as if it had suddenly become inconveniently warm. Gluck fitted the slice into the mutton again, with desperate efforts at exactitude, and ran to open the door.

'What did you keep us waiting in the rain for?' said Schwartz, as he walked in, throwing his umbrella in Gluck's face. 'Ay! what for, indeed, you little vagabond?' said Hans, administering an educational box on the ear, as he followed his brother into the kitchen.

'Bless my soul!' said Schwartz when he opened the door.

'Amen,' said the little gentleman, who had taken his cap off, and was standing in the middle of the kitchen, bowing with the utmost possible velocity.

'Who's that?' said Schwartz, catching up a rolling-pin, and turning to Gluck with a fierce frown.

'I don't know, indeed, brother,' said Gluck in great terror.

'How did he get in?' roared Schwartz.

'My dear brother,' said Gluck, deprecatingly, 'he was so *very* wet!'

The rolling-pin was descending on Gluck's head; but, at the instant, the old gentleman interposed his conical cap, on which it crashed with a shock that shook the water out of it all over the room. What was very odd, the rolling-pin no sooner touched the cap, than it flew out of Schwartz's hand, spinning like a straw in a high wind, and fell into the corner at the further end of the room.

'Who are you, sir?' demanded Schwartz, turning upon him.

'What's your business?' snarled Hans.

'I'm a poor old man, sir,' the little gentleman began very modestly, 'and I saw your fire through the window, and begged shelter for a quarter of an hour.'

'Have the goodness to walk out again, then,' said Schwartz. 'We've quite enough water in our kitchen, without making it a drying-house.'

'It is a cold day to turn an old man out in, sir; look at my grey hairs.' They hung down to his shoulders, as I told you before.

'Ay!' said Hans, 'there are enough of them to keep you warm. Walk!'

'I'm very, very hungry, sir; couldn't you spare me a bit of bread before I go?'

'Bread, indeed!' said Schwartz; 'do you suppose we've nothing to do with our bread but to give it to such red-nosed fellows as you?'

'Why don't you sell your feather?' said Hans, sneeringly. 'Out with you!'

'A little bit,' said the old gentleman.

'Be off!' said Schwartz.

'Pray, gentlemen —'

'Off, and be hanged!' cried Hans, seizing him by the collar. But he had no sooner touched the old gentleman's collar, than away he went after the rolling-pin, spinning round and round, till he fell into the corner on the top of it. Then Schwartz was very angry, and ran at the old gentleman to turn him out; but he also had hardly touched him, when away he went after Hans and the rolling-pin, and hit his head against the wall as he tumbled into the corner. And so there they lay, all three.

Then the old gentleman spun himself round with velocity in the opposite direction; continued to spin until his long cloak was all wound neatly about him; clapped his cap on his head, very much on one side (for it could not stand upright without going through the ceiling), gave an additional twist to his corkscrew moustaches, and replied with perfect coolness: 'Gentlemen, I wish you a very good morning. At twelve o'clock to-night I'll call again; after such a refusal of hospitality as I have just experienced, you will not be surprised if that visit is the last I ever pay you.'

'If ever I catch you here again,' muttered Schwartz, coming, half frightened, out of the corner – but, before he could finish his sentence, the old gentleman had shut the house door behind him with a great bang: and there drove past the window, at the same instant, a wreath of ragged cloud, that whirled and rolled away down the valley in all manner of shapes; turning over and over in the air, and melting away at last in a gush of rain.

'A very pretty business, indeed, Mr Gluck!' said Schwartz. 'Dish the mutton, sir. If ever I catch you at such a trick again – bless me, why, the mutton's been cut!'

'You promised me one slice, brother, you know,' said Gluck.

'Oh! and you were cutting it hot, I suppose, and going to catch all the gravy. It'll be long before I promise you such a thing again. Leave the room, sir; and have the kindness to wait in the coal-cellar till I call you.'

Gluck left the room melancholy enough. The brothers ate as much mutton as they could, locked the rest in the cupboard, and proceeded to get very drunk after dinner.

Such a night as it was! Howling wind, and rushing rain, without intermission. The brothers had just sense enough left to put up all the shutters, and double bar the door, before they went to bed. They usually slept in the same room. As the clock struck twelve, they were both awakened by a tremendous crash. Their door burst open with a violence that shook the house from top to bottom.

'What's that?' cried Schwartz, starting up in his bed.

'Only I,' said the little gentleman.

The two brothers sat up on their bolster, and stared into the darkness. The room was full of water, and by a misty moonbeam, which found its way through a hole in the shutter, they could see in the midst of it an enormous foam globe, spinning round, and bobbing up and down like a cork, on which, as on a most luxurious cushion, reclined the little old gentleman, cap and all. There was plenty of room for it now, for the roof was off.

'Sorry to incommode you,' said their visitor, ironically. 'I'm afraid your beds are dampish; perhaps you had better go to your brother's room: I've left the ceiling on, there.'

They required no second admonition, but rushed into Gluck's room, wet through, and in an agony of terror.

'You'll find my card on the kitchen table,' the old gentleman called after them. 'Remember, the *last* visit.'

'Pray Heaven it may!' said Schwartz, shuddering. And the foam globe disappeared.

Dawn came at last, and the two brothers looked out of Gluck's little window in the morning. The Treasure Valley was one mass of ruin and desolation. The inundation had swept away trees, crops, and cattle, and left in their stead a waste of red sand and grey mud. The two brothers crept shivering and horror-struck into the kitchen. The water had gutted the whole first floor; corn, money, almost every movable thing had been swept away, and there was left only a small white card on the kitchen table. On it, in large, breezy, long-legged letters, were engraved the words:

SOUTH-WEST WIND, ESQUIRE.

CHAPTER II

OF THE PROCEEDINGS OF THE THREE BROTHERS
AFTER THE VISIT OF SOUTH-WEST WIND, ESQUIRE;
AND HOW LITTLE GLUCK HAD AN INTERVIEW WITH
THE KING OF THE GOLDEN RIVER

SOUTH-WEST WIND, Esquire, was as good as his word. After the momentous visit above related, he entered the Treasure Valley no more; and, what was worse, he had so much influence with his relations, the Wet Winds in general, and used it so effectually, that they all adopted a similar line of conduct. So no rain fell in the valley from one year's end to another. Though everything remained green and flourishing in the plains below, the inheritance of the Three Brothers was a desert. What had once been the richest soil in the kingdom, became a shifting heap of red sand; and the brothers, unable longer to contend with the adverse skies, abandoned their valueless patrimony in despair, to seek some means of gaining a livelihood among the cities and people of the plains. All their money was gone, and they had nothing left but some curious old-fashioned pieces of gold plate, the last remnants of their ill-gotten wealth.

'Suppose we turn goldsmiths?' said Schwartz to Hans, as they entered the large city. 'It is a good knave's trade; we can put a great deal of copper into the gold, without any one's finding it out.'[1]

The thought was agreed to be a very good one; they hired a furnace, and turned goldsmiths. But two slight circumstances affected their trade: the first, that people did not approve of the coppered gold; the second, that the two elder brothers, whenever they had sold anything, used to leave little Gluck to mind the furnace, and go and drink out the money in the ale-house next door. So they melted all their gold, without making money enough to buy more, and were at last reduced to one large drinking mug, which an uncle of his had given to little Gluck, and which he was very fond of, and would not have parted with for the world; though he never drank anything out of it but milk and water. The mug was a very odd mug to look at. The handle was formed of two wreaths of flowing golden hair, so finely spun that it looked more like silk than metal, and these wreaths descended into, and mixed with, a beard and whiskers of the same exquisite workmanship, which surrounded and decorated a very fierce little face, of the reddest gold imaginable, right in the front of the mug, with a pair of eyes in it which seemed to command its whole circumference. It was impossible to drink out of the mug without being subjected to an intense gaze out of the side of these eyes; and Schwartz positively averred, that once, after emptying it, full of Rhenish, seventeen times, he had seen them wink! When it came to the mug's turn to be made into spoons, it half broke poor little Gluck's heart; but the brothers only laughed at him, tossed the mug into the melting-pot, and staggered out to the ale-house: leaving him, as usual, to pour the gold into bars, when it was all ready.

When they were gone, Gluck took a farewell look at his old friend in the melting-pot. The flowing hair was all gone; nothing remained but the red nose, and the sparkling eyes, which looked more malicious than ever. 'And no wonder,' thought Gluck, 'after being treated in that way.' He sauntered disconsolately to the window, and sat himself down to catch the fresh evening air, and escape the hot breath of the furnace. Now this window commanded a direct view of the range of mountains, which, as I told you before, overhung the Treasure Valley, and more especially of the peak from which fell the Golden River. It was just at the close of the day, and when Gluck sat down at the window, he saw the rocks of the mountain tops, all crimson, and purple with the sunset; and there were bright tongues of fiery cloud burning and quivering about them; and the river, brighter than all, fell, in a waving column of pure gold, from precipice to precipice, with the double arch of a broad purple rainbow stretched across it, flushing and fading alternately in the wreaths of spray.

'Ah!' said Gluck aloud, after he had looked at it for a little while, 'if that river were really all gold, what a nice thing it would be.'

'No it wouldn't, Gluck,' said a clear metallic voice, close at his ear.

'Bless me! what's that?' exclaimed Gluck, jumping up. There was nobody there. He looked round the room, and under the table, and a great many times behind him, but there was certainly nobody there, and he sat down again at the window. This time he didn't speak, but he couldn't help thinking again that it would be very convenient if the river were really all gold.

'Not at all, my boy,' said the same voice, louder than before.

'Bless me!' said Gluck again, 'what *is* that?' He looked again into all the corners and cupboards, and then began turning round, and round, as fast as he could in the middle of the room, thinking there was somebody behind him, when the same voice struck again on his ear. It was singing now very merrily, 'Lala-lira-la;' no words, only a soft running effervescent melody, something like that of a kettle on the boil. Gluck looked out of the window. No, it was certainly in the house. Upstairs, and downstairs. No, it was certainly in that very room, coming in quicker time, and clearer notes, every moment. 'Lala-lira-la.' All at once it struck Gluck that it sounded louder near the furnace. He ran to the opening, and looked in: yes, he saw right, it seemed to be coming, not only out of the furnace, but out of the pot. He uncovered it, and ran back in a great fright, for the pot was certainly singing! He stood in the farthest corner of the room, with his hands up, and his mouth open, for a minute or two, when the singing stopped, and the voice became clear, and pronunciative.

'Hollo!' said the voice.

Gluck made no answer.

'Hollo! Gluck, my boy,' said the pot again.

Gluck summoned all his energies, walked straight up to the crucible, drew it out of the furnace, and looked in. The gold was all melted, and its surface as smooth and polished as a river; but instead of reflecting little Gluck's head, as he looked in, he saw meeting his glance from beneath the gold the red nose and sharp eyes of his old friend of the mug, a thousand times redder and sharper than ever he had seen them in his life.

'Come, Gluck, my boy,' said the voice out of the pot again, 'I'm all right; pour me out.'

But Gluck was too much astonished to do anything of the kind.

'Pour me out, I say,' said the voice, rather gruffly.

Still Gluck couldn't move.

'*Will* you pour me out?' said the voice, passionately, 'I'm too hot.'

By a violent effort, Gluck recovered the use of his limbs, took hold of the crucible, and sloped it so as to pour out the gold. But instead of a liquid stream, there came out, first, a pair of pretty little yellow legs, then some coat tails, then a pair of arms stuck a-kimbo, and, finally, the well-known head of his friend the mug; all which articles, uniting as they rolled out, stood up energetically on the floor, in the shape of a little golden dwarf, about a foot and a half high.

'That's right!' said the dwarf, stretching out first his legs, and then his arms, and then shaking his head up and down, and as far round as it would go, for five minutes, without stopping; apparently with the view of ascertaining if he were quite correctly put together, while Gluck stood contemplating him in speechless amazement. He was dressed in a slashed doublet of spun gold, so fine in its texture, that the prismatic colours gleamed over it, as if on a surface of mother of pearl; and, over this brilliant doublet, his hair and beard fell full halfway to the ground, in waving curls, so exquisitely delicate, that Gluck could hardly tell where they ended; they seemed to melt into air. The features of the face, however, were by no means finished with the same delicacy; they were rather coarse, slightly inclining to coppery in complexion, and indicative, in expression, of a very pertinacious and intractable disposition in their small proprietor. When the dwarf had finished his self-examination, he turned his small sharp eyes full on Gluck, and stared at him deliberately for a minute or two. 'No, it wouldn't, Gluck, my boy,' said the little man.

This was certainly rather an abrupt and unconnected mode of commencing conversation. It might indeed be supposed to refer to the course of Gluck's thoughts, which had first produced the dwarf's observations out of the pot; but whatever it referred to, Gluck had no inclination to dispute the dictum.

'Wouldn't it, sir?' said Gluck, very mildly and submissively indeed.

'No,' said the dwarf, conclusively. 'No, it wouldn't.' And with that, the dwarf pulled his cap hard over his brows, and took two turns, of three feet long, up and down the room, lifting his legs up very high, and setting them down very hard. This pause gave time for Gluck to collect his thoughts a little, and, seeing no great reason to view his diminutive visitor with dread, and feeling his curiosity overcome his amazement, he ventured on a question of peculiar delicacy.

'Pray, sir,' said Gluck, rather hesitatingly, 'were you my mug?'

On which the little man turned sharp round, walked straight up to Gluck, and drew himself up to his full height. 'I,' said the little man, 'am the King of the Golden River.' Whereupon he turned about again, and took two more turns, some six feet long, in order to allow time for the consternation which this announcement produced in his auditor to evaporate. After which, he again walked up to Gluck and stood still, as if expecting some comment on his communication.

Gluck determined to say something at all events. 'I hope your Majesty is very well,' said Gluck.

'Listen!' said the little man, deigning no reply to this polite inquiry. 'I am the King of what you mortals call the Golden River. The shape you saw me in was owing to the malice of a stronger king, from whose enchantments you have this instant freed me. What I have seen of you, and your conduct to your wicked brothers, renders me willing to serve you; therefore, attend to what I tell you. Whoever shall climb to the top of that mountain from which you see the Golden River issue, and shall cast into the stream at its source three drops of holy water, for him, and for him only, the river shall turn to gold. But no one failing in his first, can succeed in a second attempt;

and if any one shall cast unholy water into the river, it will overwhelm him, and he will become a black stone.' So saying, the King of the Golden River turned away and deliberately walked into the centre of the hottest flame of the furnace. His figure became red, white, transparent, dazzling, – a blaze of intense light – rose, trembled, and disappeared. The King of the Golden River had evaporated.

'Oh!' cried poor Gluck, running to look up the chimney after him; 'oh dear, dear, dear me! My mug! my mug! my mug!'

CHAPTER III

THE King of the Golden River had hardly made the extraordinary exit related in the last chapter, before Hans and Schwartz came roaring into the house, very savagely drunk. The discovery of the total loss of their last piece of plate had the effect of sobering them just enough to enable them to stand over Gluck, beating him very steadily for a quarter of an hour; at the expiration of which period they dropped into a couple of chairs, and requested to know what he had got to say for himself. Gluck told them his story, of which, of course, they did not believe a word. They beat him again, till their arms were tired, and staggered to bed. In the morning, however, the steadiness with which he adhered to his story obtained him some degree of credence; the immediate consequence of which was, that the two brothers, after wrangling a long time on the knotty question, which of them should try his fortune first, drew their swords and began fighting. The noise of the fray alarmed the neighbours, who, finding they could not pacify the combatants, sent for the constable.

Hans, on hearing this, contrived to escape, and hid himself; but Schwartz was taken before the magistrate, fined for breaking the peace, and, having drunk out his last penny the evening before, was thrown into prison till he should pay.

When Hans heard this, he was much delighted, and determined to set out immediately for the Golden River. How to get the holy water was the question. He went to the priest, but the priest could not give any holy water to so abandoned a character. So Hans went to vespers in the evening for the first time in his life, and, under pretence of crossing himself, stole a cupful, and returned home in triumph.

Next morning he got up before the sun rose, put the holy water into a strong flask, and two bottles of wine and some meat in a basket, slung them over his back, took his alpine staff in his hand, and set off for the mountains.

On his way out of the town he had to pass the prison, and as he looked in at the windows, whom should he see but Schwartz himself peeping out of the bars, and looking very disconsolate.

'Good morning, brother,' said Hans; 'have you any message for the King of the Golden River?'

Schwartz gnashed his teeth with rage, and shook the bars with all his strength; but Hans only laughed at him, and advising him to make himself comfortable till he came back again, shouldered his basket, shook the bottle of holy water in Schwartz's face till it frothed again, and marched off in the highest spirits in the world.

It was, indeed, a morning that might have made any one happy, even with no Golden River to seek for. Level lines of dewy mist lay stretched along the valley, out of which rose the massy mountains – their lower cliffs in pale grey shadow, hardly distinguishable from the floating vapour, but gradually ascending till they caught the sunlight, which ran in sharp touches of ruddy colour along the angular crags, and pierced, in long level rays, through their fringes of spear-like pine. Far above, shot up red splintered masses of castellated rock, jagged and shivered into myriads of fantastic forms, with here and there a streak of sunlit snow, traced down their chasms like a line of forked lightning; and, far beyond, and far above all these, fainter than the morning cloud, but purer and changeless, slept, in the blue sky, the utmost peaks of the eternal snow.[2]

The Golden River, which sprang from one of the lower and snowless elevations, was now nearly in shadow; all but the uppermost jets of spray, which rose like slow smoke above the undulating line of the cataract, and floated away in feeble wreaths upon the morning wind.

On this object, and on this alone, Hans' eyes and thoughts were fixed; forgetting the distance he had to traverse, he set off at an imprudent rate of walking, which greatly exhausted him before he had scaled the first range of the green and low hills. He was, moreover, surprised, on surmounting them, to find that a large glacier, of whose existence, notwithstanding his previous knowledge of the mountains, he had been absolutely ignorant, lay between him and the source of the Golden River. He entered on it with the boldness of a practised mountaineer; yet he thought he had never traversed so strange or so dangerous a glacier in his life. The ice was excessively slippery, and out of all its chasms came wild sounds of gushing water; not monotonous or low, but changeful and loud, rising occasionally into drifting passages of wild melody, then breaking off into short melancholy tones, or sudden shrieks, resembling those of human voices in distress or pain. The ice was broken into thousands of confused shapes, but none, Hans thought, like the ordinary forms of splintered ice. There seemed a curious *expression* about all their outlines – a perpetual resemblance to living features, distorted and scornful. Myriads of deceitful shadows, and lurid lights, played and floated about and through the pale blue pinnacles, dazzling and confusing the sight of the traveller; while his ears grew dull and his head giddy with the constant gush and roar of the concealed waters. These painful circumstances increased upon him as he advanced; the ice crashed and yawned into fresh chasms at his feet, tottering spires nodded around him, and fell thundering across his path; and though he had repeatedly faced these dangers on the most terrific glaciers, and in the wildest weather, it was with a new and oppressive feeling of panic terror that he leaped the last chasm, and flung himself, exhausted and shuddering, on the firm turf of the mountain.

He had been compelled to abandon his basket of food, which became a perilous incumbrance on the glacier, and had now no means of refreshing himself but by breaking off and eating some of the pieces of ice. This, however, relieved his thirst; an hour's repose recruited his hardy frame, and with the indomitable spirit of avarice, he resumed his laborious journey.

His way now lay straight up a ridge of bare red rocks, without a blade of grass to ease the foot, or a projecting angle to afford an inch of shade from the south sun. It was past noon, and the rays beat intensely upon the steep path, while the whole atmosphere was motionless, and penetrated with heat. Intense thirst was soon added to the bodily fatigue with which Hans was now afflicted; glance after glance he cast on the flask of water which hung at his belt. 'Three drops are enough,' at last thought he; 'I may, at least, cool my lips with it.'

He opened the flask, and was raising it to his lips, when his eye fell on an object lying on the rock beside him; he thought it moved. It was a small dog, apparently in the last agony of death from thirst. Its tongue was out, its jaws dry, its limbs extended lifelessly, and a swarm of black ants were crawling about its lips and throat. Its eye moved to the bottle which Hans held in his hand. He raised it, drank, spurned the animal with his foot, and passed on. And he did not know how it was, but he thought that a strange shadow had suddenly come across the blue sky.

The path became steeper and more rugged every moment; and the high hill air, instead of refreshing him, seemed to throw his blood into a fever. The noise of the hill cataracts sounded like mockery in his ears; they were all distant, and his thirst increased every moment. Another hour passed, and he again looked down to the flask at his side; it was half empty; but there was much more than three drops in it. He stopped to open it, and again, as he did so, something moved in the path above him. It was a fair child, stretched nearly lifeless on the rock, its breast heaving with thirst, its eyes closed, and its lips parched and burning. Hans eyed it deliberately, drank, and passed on. And a dark grey cloud came over the sun, and long, snake-like shadows crept up along the mountain sides. Hans struggled on. The sun was sinking, but its descent seemed to bring no coolness; the leaden weight of the dead air pressed upon his brow and heart, but the goal was near. He saw the cataract of the Golden River springing from the hill-side, scarcely five hundred feet above him. He paused for a moment to breathe, and sprang on to complete his task.

At this instant a faint cry fell on his ear. He turned, and saw a grey-haired old man extended on the rocks. His eyes were sunk, his features deadly pale, and gathered into an expression of despair. 'Water!' he stretched his arms to Hans, and cried feebly, 'Water! I am dying.'

'I have none,' replied Hans; 'thou hast had thy share of life.' He strode over the prostrate body, and darted on. And a flash of blue lightning rose out of the East, shaped like a sword; it shook thrice over the whole heaven, and left it dark with one heavy, impenetrable shade. The sun was setting; it plunged towards the horizon like a red-hot ball.

The roar of the Golden River rose on Hans' ear. He stood at the brink of the chasm through which it ran. Its waves were filled with the red glory of the sunset: they shook their crests like tongues of fire, and flashes of bloody light gleamed along their foam. Their sound came mightier and mightier on his senses; his brain grew giddy with the prolonged thunder. Shuddering he drew the flask from his girdle, and hurled it into the centre of the torrent. As he did so, an icy chill shot through his limbs: he staggered, shrieked, and fell. The waters closed over his cry. And the moaning of the river rose wildly into the night, as it gushed over

THE BLACK STONE.

CHAPTER IV

POOR little Gluck waited very anxiously alone in the house for Hans' return. Finding he did not come back, he was terribly frightened, and went and told Schwartz in the prison all that had happened. Then Schwartz was very much pleased, and said that Hans must certainly have been turned into a black stone, and he should have all the gold to himself. But Gluck was very sorry, and cried all night. When he got up in the morning there was no bread in the house, nor any money; so Gluck went and hired himself to another goldsmith, and he worked so hard, and so neatly, and so long every day, that he soon got money enough together to pay his brother's fine, and he went and gave it all to Schwartz, and Schwartz got out of prison. Then Schwartz was quite pleased, and said he should have some of the gold of the river. But Gluck only begged he would go and see what had become of Hans.

Now when Schwartz had heard that Hans had stolen the holy water, he thought to himself that such a proceeding might not be considered altogether correct by the King of the Golden River, and determined to manage matters better. So he took some more of Gluck's money, and went to a bad priest, who gave him some holy water very readily for it. Then Schwartz was sure it was all quite right. So Schwartz got up early in the morning before the sun rose, and took some bread and wine in a basket, and put his holy water in a flask, and set off for the mountains. Like his brother, he was much surprised at the sight of the glacier, and had great difficulty in crossing it, even after leaving his basket behind him. The day was cloudless, but not bright: there was a heavy purple haze hanging over the sky, and the hills looked lowering and gloomy. And as Schwartz climbed the steep rock path, the thirst came upon him, as it had upon his brother, until he lifted his flask to his lips to drink. Then he saw the fair child lying near him on the rocks, and it cried to him, and moaned for water.

'Water, indeed,' said Schwartz; 'I haven't half enough for myself,' and passed on. And as he went he thought the sunbeams grew more dim, and he saw a low bank of black cloud rising out of the West; and, when he had climbed for another hour the thirst overcame him again, and he would have drunk. Then he saw the old man lying before him on the path, and heard him cry out for water. 'Water, indeed,' said Schwartz; 'I haven't half enough for myself,' and on he went.

Then again the light seemed to fade from before his eyes, and he looked up, and, behold, a mist, of the colour of blood, had come over the sun; and the bank of black cloud had risen very high, and its edges were tossing and tumbling like the waves of the angry sea. And they cast long shadows, which flickered over Schwartz's path.

Then Schwartz climbed for another hour, and again his thirst returned; and as he lifted his flask to his lips, he thought he saw his brother Hans lying exhausted on the path before him, and, as he gazed, the figure stretched its arms to him, and cried for water. 'Ha, ha,' laughed Schwartz, 'are you there? remember the prison bars, my boy. Water, indeed! do you suppose I carried it all the way up here for *you!*' And he strode over the figure; yet, as he passed, he thought he saw a strange expression of mockery about its lips. And, when he had gone a few yards farther, he looked back; but the figure was not there.

And a sudden horror came over Schwartz, he knew not why; but the thirst for gold prevailed over his fear, and he rushed on. And the bank of black cloud rose to the zenith, and out of it came bursts of spiry lightning, and waves of darkness seemed to heave and float between their flashes over the whole heavens. And the sky where the sun was setting was all level, and like a lake of blood; and a strong wind came out of that sky, tearing its crimson clouds into fragments, and scattering them far into the darkness.[3] And when Schwartz stood by the brink of the Golden River, its waves were black, like thunder clouds, but their foam was like fire; and the roar of the waters below, and the thunder above, met, as he cast the flask into the stream. And, as he did so, the lightning glared into his eyes, and the earth gave way beneath him, and the waters closed over his cry. And the moaning of the river rose wildly into the night, as it gushed over the

TWO BLACK STONES.

CHAPTER V

HOW LITTLE GLUCK SET OFF ON AN EXPEDITION
TO THE GOLDEN RIVER, AND HOW HE PROSPERED THEREIN;
WITH OTHER MATTERS OF INTEREST

WHEN Gluck found that Schwartz did not come back he was very sorry, and did not know what to do. He had no money, and was obliged to go and hire himself again to the goldsmith, who worked him very hard, and gave him very little money. So, after a month or two, Gluck grew tired, and made up his mind to go and try his fortune with the Golden River. 'The little king looked very kind,' thought he. 'I don't think he will turn me into a black stone.' So he went to the priest, and the priest gave him some holy water as soon as he asked for it. Then Gluck took some bread in his basket, and the bottle of water, and set off very early for the mountains.

If the glacier had occasioned a great deal of fatigue to his brothers, it was twenty times worse for him, who was neither so strong nor so practised on the mountains. He had several very bad falls, lost his basket and bread, and was very much frightened at the strange noises under the ice. He lay a long time to rest on the grass, after he had got over, and began to climb the hill just in the hottest part of the day. When he had climbed for an hour, he got dreadfully thirsty, and was going to drink like his brothers, when he saw an old man coming down the path above him, looking very feeble, and leaning on a staff. 'My son,' said the old man, 'I am faint with thirst, give me some of that water.' Then Gluck looked at him, and when he saw that he was pale and weary, he gave him the water; 'Only pray don't drink it all,' said Gluck. But the old man drank a great deal, and gave him back the bottle two-thirds empty. Then he bade him good speed, and Gluck went on again merrily. And the path became easier to his feet, and two or three blades of grass appeared upon it, and some grasshoppers began singing on the bank beside it; and Gluck thought he had never heard such merry singing.

Then he went on for another hour, and the thirst increased on him so that he thought he should be forced to drink. But, as he raised the flask, he saw a little child lying panting by the roadside, and it cried out piteously for water. Then Gluck struggled with himself, and determined to bear the thirst a little longer; and he put the bottle to the child's lips, and it drank it all but a few drops. Then it smiled on him, and got up, and ran down the hill; and Gluck looked after it, till it became as small as a little star, and then turned and began climbing again. And then there were all kinds of sweet flowers growing on the rocks, bright green moss, with pale pink starry flowers, and soft belled gentians, more blue than the sky at its deepest, and pure white transparent lilies. And crimson and purple butterflies darted hither and thither, and the sky sent down such pure light, that Gluck had never felt so happy in his life.

Yet, when he had climbed for another hour, his thirst became intolerable again; and, when he looked at his bottle, he saw that there were only five or six drops left in it, and he could not venture to drink. And, as he was hanging the flask to his belt again, he saw a little dog lying on the rocks, gasping for breath – just as Hans had seen it on the day of his ascent. And Gluck stopped and looked at it, and then at the Golden River, not five hundred yards above him; and he thought of the dwarf's words, 'that no one could succeed, except in his first attempt'; and he tried to pass the dog, but it whined piteously, and Gluck stopped again. 'Poor beastie,' said Gluck, 'it'll be dead when I come down again, if I don't help it.' Then he looked closer and closer at it, and its eye turned on him so mournfully, that he could not stand it. 'Confound the King and his gold too,' said Gluck; and he opened the flask, and poured all the water into the dog's mouth.

The dog sprang up and stood on its hind legs. Its tail disappeared, its ears became long, longer, silky, golden; its nose became very red, its eyes became very twinkling; in three seconds the dog was gone, and before Gluck stood his old acquaintance, the King of the Golden River.

'Thank you,' said the monarch; 'but don't be frightened, it's all right;' for Gluck showed manifest symptoms of consternation at this unlooked-for reply to his last observation. 'Why didn't you come before,' continued the dwarf, 'instead of sending me those rascally brothers of yours, for me to have the trouble of turning into stones? Very hard stones they make too.'

'Oh dear me!' said Gluck, 'have you really been so cruel?'

'Cruel!' said the dwarf, 'they poured unholy water into my stream: do you suppose I'm going to allow that?'

'Why,' said Gluck, 'I am sure, sir – your majesty, I mean – they got the water out of the church font.'

'Very probably,' replied the dwarf; 'but,' and his countenance grew stern as he spoke, 'the water which has been refused to the cry of the weary and dying, is unholy, though it had been blessed by every saint in heaven; and the water which is found in the vessel of mercy is holy, though it had been defiled with corpses.'

So saying, the dwarf stooped and plucked a lily that grew at his feet. On its white leaves there hung three drops of clear dew. And the dwarf shook them into the flask which Gluck held in his hand. 'Cast these into the river,' he said, 'and descend on the other side of the mountains into the Treasure Valley. And so good speed.'

As he spoke, the figure of the dwarf became indistinct. The playing colours of his robe formed themselves into a prismatic mist of dewy light; he stood for an instant veiled with them as with the belt of a broad rainbow. The colours grew faint, the mist rose into the air; the monarch had evaporated.

And Gluck climbed to the brink of the Golden River, and its waves were as clear as crystal, and as brilliant as the sun. And, when he cast the three drops of dew into the stream, there opened where they fell a small circular whirlpool, into which the waters descended with a musical noise.

Gluck stood watching it for some time, very much disappointed, because not only the river was not turned into gold, but its waters seemed much diminished in quantity. Yet he obeyed his friend the dwarf, and descended the other side of the mountains towards the Treasure Valley; and, as he went, he thought he heard the noise of water working its way under the ground. And, when he came in sight of the Treasure Valley, behold, a river, like the Golden River, was springing from a new cleft of the rocks above it, and was flowing in innumerable streams among the dry heaps of red sand.

And as Gluck gazed, fresh grass sprang beside the new streams, and creeping plants grew, and climbed among the moistening soil. Young flowers opened suddenly along the river sides, as stars leap out when twilight is deepening, and thickets of myrtle, and tendrils of vine, cast lengthening shadows over the valley as they grew. And thus the Treasure Valley became a garden again, and the inheritance, which had been lost by cruelty, was regained by love.[4]

And Gluck went, and dwelt in the valley, and the poor were never driven from his door: so that his barns became full of corn, and his house of treasure. And, for him, the river had, according to the dwarf's promise, become a River of Gold.

And, to this day, the inhabitants of the valley point out the place where the three drops of holy dew were cast into the stream, and trace the course of the Golden River under the ground, until it emerges in the Treasure Valley. And at the top of the cataract of the Golden River, are still to be seen two BLACK STONES, round which the waters howl mournfully every day at sunset; and these stones are still called by the people of the valley

THE BLACK BROTHERS.

from

The Stones of Venice

VOLUME II

The Sea-Stories

Published 1853

COMMENTARY

The structure of *The Stones of Venice* has been compared to that of a Gothic cathedral, complex, allegorical and organic. It is not impossible that Ruskin had this analogy in mind, for the work is a celebration of the Gothic style. There are three volumes, and 'The Nature of Gothic' is the central chapter of the middle volume. The sub-titles of the separate volumes – 'The Foundations', 'The Sea-Stories' ('storeys' *and* 'stories') and 'The Fall' – sustain the architectural analogy, though they also bear moral and poetic significances. The overall title is similarly resonant. It suggests Ruskin's concern with the physical fact of stone as the medium of architecture, and hints at his sense of Venice as a great civilization fallen into ruin. Morally speaking, the stones of Venice are also touchstones – of social health and disease, moral grandeur and decay. Carlyle called the book a '*Sermon in Stones*'; and it is that quite as much as a study of architectural styles.

'The Nature of Gothic' was profoundly influential. In 1854, the year after it appeared, the Working Men's College opened in London. One of its philanthropic founders, F. J. Furnivall, asked Ruskin if the chapter might be reprinted as a pamphlet to be given free of charge to all working men attending the courses. Ruskin agreed and, into the bargain, offered the college the profits he made on sales. Around the same time, *The Stones of Venice* changed the lives of two young Oxford students, Edward Burne-Jones and William Morris. Thirty-eight years later, Morris's Kelmscott Press reissued 'The Nature of Gothic' as a single book. In the introduction he wrote for it Morris says: 'the lesson Ruskin . . . teaches us, is that art is the expression of man's pleasure in his labour'. He describes the essay as 'one of the very few necessary and inevitable utterances of the century. To some of us when we first read it, now many years ago, it seemed to point out a new road on which the world should travel.' Though Ruskin himself avoided the word, the name of that road was Socialism.

The Stones of Venice had an incalculable effect on English architecture and on the preservation of historic buildings. The book had been written in response to what Ruskin feared would be the destruction of medieval Venice through 'restoration' or neglect. In this respect it met with some limited success. In England it was eventually to inspire Morris's Society for the Preservation of Ancient Buildings. Its effect on new architecture, however, may be judged a mixed blessing. It gave enormous impetus and critical weight to the Gothic Revival, inspiring many of its best architects (notably Butterfield, Street and Waterhouse). But it was also responsible for the introduction of the polychromatic elaboration of Venetian Gothic into the cold, rainy, polluted cities of industrial England. Ruskin detested these buildings and, as the lecture on 'Traffic' shows, he deplored the fashion for the stylistic details of Gothic, because it took no account of the social and spiritual conditions from which – so he argued – the style first sprang.

THE NATURE OF GOTHIC

I F the reader will look back to the division of our subject which was made in the first chapter of the first volume,[1] he will find that we are now about to enter upon the examination of that school of Venetian architecture which forms an intermediate step between the Byzantine and Gothic forms; but which I find may be conveniently considered in its connexion with the latter style. In order that we may discern the tendency of each step of this change, it will be wise in the outset to endeavour to form some general idea of its final result. We know already what the Byzantine architecture is from which the transition was made, but we ought to know something of the Gothic architecture into which it led. I shall endeavour therefore to give the reader in this chapter an idea, at once broad and definite, of the true nature of *Gothic* architecture, properly so called; not of that of Venice only, but of universal Gothic: for it will be one of the most interesting parts of our subsequent inquiry to find out how far Venetian architecture reached the universal or perfect type of Gothic, and how far it either fell short of it, or assumed foreign and independent forms.

The principal difficulty in doing this arises from the fact that every building of the Gothic period differs in some important respect from every other; and many include features which, if they occurred in other buildings, would not be considered Gothic at all; so that all we have to reason upon is merely, if I may be allowed so to express it, a greater or less degree of *Gothicness* in each building we examine. And it is this Gothicness, – the character which, according as it is found more or less in a building, makes it more or less Gothic, – of which I want to define the nature; and I feel the same kind of difficulty in doing so which would be encountered by any one who undertook to explain, for instance, the nature of Redness, without any actually red thing to point to, but only orange and purple things. Suppose he had only a piece of heather and a dead oak-leaf to do it with. He might say, the colour which is mixed with the yellow in this oak-leaf, and with the blue in this heather, would be red, if you had it separate; but it would be difficult, nevertheless, to make the abstraction perfectly intelligible: and it is so in a far greater degree to make the abstraction of the Gothic character intelligible, because that character itself is made up of many mingled ideas, and can consist only in their union. That is to say, pointed arches do not constitute Gothic, nor vaulted roofs, nor flying buttresses, nor grotesque sculptures; but all or some of these things, and many other things with them, when they come together so as to have life.

Observe also, that, in the definition proposed, I shall only endeavour to analyze the idea which I suppose already to exist in the reader's mind. We all have some notion, most of us a very determined one, of the meaning of the term Gothic, but I know that many persons have this idea in their minds without being able to define it: that is to say, understanding generally that Westminster Abbey is Gothic, and St Paul's is not, that Strasburg Cathedral is Gothic, and St Peter's is not, they have, nevertheless, no clear notion of what it is that they recognize in the one or miss in the other, such as would enable them to say how far the work at Westminster or Strasburg is good and pure of its kind; still less to say of any nondescript building, like St James's Palace or Windsor Castle, how much right Gothic element there is in it, and how much wanting. And I believe this inquiry to be a pleasant and profitable one; and that there will be found something more than usually interesting in tracing out this grey, shadowy, many-pinnacled image of the Gothic spirit within us; and discerning what fellowship there is between it and our Northern hearts. And if, at any point of the inquiry, I should interfere with any of the reader's previously formed conceptions, and use the term Gothic in any sense which he would not willingly attach to it, I do not ask him to accept, but only to examine and understand, my interpretation, as necessary to the intelligibility of what follows in the rest of the work.

We have, then, the Gothic character submitted to our analysis, just as the rough mineral is submitted to that of the chemist, entangled with many other foreign substances, itself perhaps in no place pure, or ever to be obtained or seen in purity for more than an instant; but nevertheless a thing of definite and separate nature, however inextricable or confused in appearance. Now observe: the chemist defines his mineral by two separate kinds of character; one external, its crystalline form, hardness, lustre, etc.; the other internal, the proportions and nature of its constituent atoms. Exactly in the same manner, we shall find that Gothic architecture has external forms and internal elements. Its elements are certain mental tendencies of the builders, legibly expressed in it; as fancifulness, love of variety, love of richness, and such others. Its external forms are pointed arches, vaulted roofs, etc. And unless both the elements and the forms are there, we have no right to call the style Gothic. It is not enough that it has the Form, if it have not also the power and life. It is not enough that it has the Power, if it have not the form. We must therefore inquire into each of these characters successively; and determine first, what is the Mental Expression, and secondly, what the Material Form of Gothic architecture, properly so called.

1st Mental Power or Expression. What characters, we have to discover, did the Gothic builders love, or instinctively express in their work, as distinguished from all other builders?

Let us go back for a moment to our chemistry, and note that, in defining a mineral by its constituent parts, it is not one nor another of them, that can make up the mineral, but the union of all: for instance, it is neither in charcoal, nor in oxygen, nor in lime, that there is the making of chalk, but in the combination of all three in certain measures; they are all found in very different things from chalk, and there is nothing like chalk either in charcoal or in oxygen, but they are nevertheless necessary to its existence.

So in the various mental characters which make up the soul of Gothic. It is not one nor another that produces it; but their union in certain measures. Each one of them is found in many other architectures beside Gothic; but Gothic cannot exist where they are not found, or, at least, where their place is not in some way supplied. Only there is this great difference between the composition of the mineral and of the architectural style, that if we withdraw one of its elements from the stone, its form is utterly changed, and its existence as such and such a mineral is destroyed; but if we withdraw one of its mental elements from the Gothic style, it is only a little less Gothic than it was before, and the union of two or three of its elements is enough already to bestow a certain Gothicness of character, which gains in intensity as we add the others, and loses as we again withdraw them.

I believe, then, that the characteristic or moral elements of Gothic are the following, placed in the order of their importance:

1. Savageness.
2. Changefulness.
3. Naturalism.
4. Grotesqueness.
5. Rigidity.
6. Redundance.

These characters are here expressed as belonging to the building; as belonging to the builder, they would be expressed thus: – 1. Savageness or Rudeness. 2. Love of Change. 3. Love of Nature. 4. Disturbed Imagination. 5. Obstinacy. 6. Generosity. And I repeat, that the withdrawal of any one, or any two, will not at once destroy the Gothic character of a building, but the removal of a majority of them will. I shall proceed to examine them in their order.

SAVAGENESS. I am not sure when the word 'Gothic' was first generically applied to the architecture of the North; but I presume that, whatever the date of its original usage, it was intended to imply reproach, and express the barbaric character of the nations among whom that architecture arose.[2] It never implied that they were literally of Gothic lineage, far less that their architecture had been originally invented by the Goths themselves; but it did imply that they and their buildings together exhibited a degree of sternness and rudeness, which, in contradistinction to the character of Southern and Eastern nations, appeared like a perpetual reflection of the contrast between the Goth and the Roman in their first encounter. And when that fallen Roman, in the utmost impotence of his luxury, and insolence of his guilt, became the model for the imitation of civilized Europe, at the close of the so-called Dark ages, the word Gothic became a term of unmitigated contempt, not unmixed with aversion. From that contempt, by the exertion of the antiquaries and architects of this century, Gothic architecture has been sufficiently vindicated; and perhaps some among us, in our admiration of the magnificent science of its structure, and sacredness of its expression, might desire that the term of ancient reproach should be withdrawn, and some other, of more apparent honourableness, adopted in its place. There is no chance, as there is no need, of such a substitution. As far as the epithet was used scornfully, it was used falsely; but there is no reproach in the word, rightly understood; on the contrary, there is a profound truth, which the instinct of mankind almost unconsciously recognizes. It is true, greatly and deeply true, that the architecture of the North is rude and wild; but it is not true, that, for this reason, we are to condemn it, or despise. Far otherwise: I believe it is in this very character that it deserves our profoundest reverence.

The charts of the world which have been drawn up by modern science have thrown into a narrow space the expression of a vast amount of knowledge, but I have never yet seen any one pictorial enough to enable the spectator to imagine the kind of contrast in physical character which exists between Northern and Southern countries. We know the differences in detail, but we have not that broad glance and grasp which would enable us to feel them in their fulness. We know that gentians grow on the Alps, and olives on the Apennines; but we do not enough conceive for ourselves that variegated mosaic of the world's surface which a bird sees in its migration, that difference between the district of the gentian and of the olive which the stork and the swallow see far off, as they lean upon the sirocco wind. Let us, for a moment, try to raise ourselves even above the level of their flight, and imagine the Mediterranean lying beneath us like an irregular lake, and all its ancient promontories sleeping in the sun: here and there an angry spot of thunder, a grey stain of storm, moving upon the burning field; and here and there a fixed wreath of white volcano smoke, surrounded by its circle of ashes; but for the most part a great peacefulness of light, Syria and Greece, Italy and Spain, laid like pieces of a golden pavement into the sea-blue, chased, as we stoop nearer to them, with bossy beaten work of mountain chains, and glowing softly with terraced gardens, and flowers heavy with frankincense, mixed among masses of laurel, and orange, and plumy palm, that abate with their grey-green shadows the burning of the marble rocks, and of the ledges of porphyry sloping under lucent sand. Then let us pass farther towards the north, until we see the orient colours change gradually into a vast belt of rainy green, where the pastures of Switzerland, and poplar valleys of France, and dark forests of the Danube and Carpathians stretch from the mouths of the Loire to those of the Volga, seen through clefts in grey swirls of rain-cloud and flaky veils of the mist of the brooks, spreading low along the pasture lands: and then, farther north still, to see the earth heave into mighty masses of leaden rock and heathy moor, bordering with a broad waste of gloomy purple that belt of field and wood, and splintering into irregular and grisly islands amidst the northern seas, beaten by storm, and chilled by ice-drift, and tormented by furious pulses of contending tide, until the roots of the last forests fail from among the hill ravines, and the hunger of the north wind bites their peaks into barrenness; and, at last, the wall of ice, durable like iron, sets, deathlike, its white teeth against us out of the polar twilight. And, having once traversed in thought this gradation of the zoned iris of the earth in all its material vastness, let us go down nearer to it, and watch the parallel change in the belt of animal life; the multitudes of swift and brilliant creatures that glance in the air and sea, or tread the sands of the southern zone; striped zebras and spotted leopards, glistening serpents, and birds arrayed in purple and scarlet. Let us contrast their delicacy and brilliancy of colour, and swiftness of motion, with the frost-cramped strength, and shaggy covering, and dusky plumage of the northern tribes; contrast the Arabian horse with the Shetland, the tiger and leopard with the wolf and bear, the antelope with the elk, the bird of paradise with the osprey; and then, submissively acknowledging the great laws by which the earth and all that it bears are ruled throughout their being, let us not condemn, but rejoice in the expression by man of his own rest in the statutes of the lands that gave him birth. Let us watch him with reverence as he sets side by side the burning gems, and smooths with soft sculpture the jasper pillars, that are to reflect a ceaseless sunshine, and rise into a cloudless sky: but not with less reverence let us stand by him, when, with rough strength and hurried stroke, he smites an uncouth animation out of the rocks which he has torn from among the moss of the moorland, and heaves into the darkened air the pile of iron buttress and rugged wall, instinct with work of an imagination as wild and wayward as the northern sea; creatures of ungainly shape and rigid limb, but full of wolfish life; fierce as the winds that beat, and changeful as the clouds that shade them.

There is, I repeat, no degradation, no reproach in this, but all dignity and honourableness: and we should err grievously in refusing either to recognize as an essential character of the existing architecture of the North, or to admit as a desirable character in that which it yet may be, this wildness of thought, and roughness of work; this look of mountain brotherhood between the cathedral and the Alp; this magnificence of sturdy power, put forth only the more energetically because the fine finger-touch was chilled away by the frosty wind, and the eye dimmed by the moor-mist, or blinded by the hail; this out-speaking of the strong spirit of men who may not gather redundant fruitage from the earth, nor bask in dreamy benignity of sunshine, but must break the rock for bread, and cleave the forest for fire, and show, even in what they did for their delight, some of the hard habits of the arm and heart that grew on them as they swung the axe or pressed the plough.

If, however, the savageness of Gothic architecture, merely as an expression of its origin among Northern nations, may be considered, in some sort, a noble character, it possesses a higher nobility still, when considered as an index, not of climate, but of religious principle.

In the 13th and 14th paragraphs of Chapter XXI of the first volume of this work,[3] it was noticed that the systems of architectural ornament, properly so called, might be divided into three: – 1. Servile ornament, in which the execution or power of the inferior workman is entirely subjected to the intellect of the higher; – 2. Constitutional ornament, in which the executive inferior power is, to a certain point, emancipated and independent, having a will of its own, yet confessing its inferiority and rendering obedience to higher powers; – and 3. Revolutionary ornament, in which no executive inferiority is admitted at all. I must here explain the nature of these divisions at somewhat greater length.

Of Servile ornament, the principal schools are the Greek, Ninevite, and Egyptian[4]; but their servility is of different kinds. The Greek master-workman was far advanced in knowledge and power above the Assyrian or Egyptian. Neither he nor those for whom he worked could endure the appearance of imperfection in anything; and, therefore, what ornament he appointed to be done by those beneath him was composed of mere geometrical forms, – balls, ridges, and perfectly symmetrical foliage, –

which could be executed with absolute precision by line and rule, and were as perfect in their way, when completed, as his own figure sculpture. The Assyrian and Egyptian, on the contrary, less cognisant of accurate form in anything, were content to allow their figure sculpture to be executed by inferior workmen, but lowered the method of its treatment to a standard which every workman could reach, and then trained him by discipline so rigid, that there was no chance of his falling beneath the standard appointed. The Greek gave to the lower workman no subject which he could not perfectly execute. The Assyrian gave him subjects which he could only execute imperfectly, but fixed a legal standard for his imperfection. The workman was, in both systems, a slave.

But in the mediæval, or especially Christian, system of ornament,[5] this slavery is done away with altogether; Christianity having recognized, in small things as well as great, the individual value of every soul. But it not only recognizes its value; it confesses its imperfection, in only bestowing dignity upon the acknowledgment of unworthiness. That admission of lost power and fallen nature, which the Greek or Ninevite felt to be intensely painful, and, as far as might be, altogether refused, the Christian makes daily and hourly, contemplating the fact of it without fear, as tending, in the end, to God's greater glory. Therefore, to every spirit which Christianity summons to her service, her exhortation is: Do what you can, and confess frankly what you are unable to do; neither let your effort be shortened for fear of failure, nor your confession silenced for fear of shame. And it is, perhaps, the principal admirableness of the Gothic schools of architecture, that they thus receive the results of the labour of inferior minds; and out of fragments full of imperfection, and betraying that imperfection in every touch, indulgently raise up a stately and unaccusable whole.

But the modern English mind has this much in common with that of the Greek, that it intensely desires, in all things, the utmost completion or perfection compatible with their nature. This is a noble character in the abstract, but becomes ignoble when it causes us to forget the relative dignities of that nature itself, and to prefer the perfectness of the lower nature to the imperfection of the higher; not considering that as, judged by such a rule, all the brute animals would be preferable to man, because more perfect in their functions and kind, and yet are always held inferior to him, so also in the works of man, those which are more perfect in their kind are always inferior to those which are, in their nature, liable to more faults and shortcomings. For the finer the nature, the more flaws it will show through the clearness of it; and it is a law of this universe, that the best things shall be seldomest seen in their best form. The wild grass grows well and strongly, one year with another; but the wheat is, according to the greater nobleness of its nature, liable to the bitterer blight. And therefore, while in all things that we see or do, we are to desire perfection, and strive for it, we are nevertheless not to set the meaner thing, in its narrow accomplishment, above the nobler thing, in its mighty progress; not to esteem smooth minuteness above shattered majesty; not to prefer mean victory to honourable defeat; not to lower the level of our aim, that we may the more surely enjoy the complacency of success. But, above all, in our dealings with the souls of other men, we are to take care how we check, by severe requirement or narrow caution, efforts which might otherwise lead to a noble issue; and, still more, how we withhold our admiration from great excellencies, because they are mingled with rough faults. Now, in the make and nature of every man, however rude or simple, whom we employ in manual labour, there are some powers for better things; some tardy imagination, torpid capacity of emotion, tottering steps of thought, there are, even at the worst; and in most cases it is all our own fault that they *are* tardy or torpid. But they cannot be strengthened, unless we are content to take them in their feebleness, and unless we prize and honour them in their imperfection above the best and most perfect manual skill. And this is what we have to do with all our labourers; to look for the *thoughtful* part of them, and get that out of them, whatever we lose for it, whatever faults and errors we are obliged to take with it. For the best that is in them cannot manifest itself, but in company with much error. Understand this clearly: You can teach a man to draw a straight line, and to cut one; to strike a curved line, and to carve it; and to copy and carve any number of given lines or forms, with admirable speed and perfect precision; and you find his work perfect of its kind: but if you ask him to think about any of those forms, to consider if he cannot find any better in his own head, he stops; his execution becomes hesitating; he thinks, and ten to one he thinks wrong; ten to one he makes a mistake in the first touch he gives to his work as a thinking being. But you have made a man of him for all that. He was only a machine before, an animated tool.

And observe, you are put to stern choice in this matter. You must either make a tool of the creature, or a man of him. You cannot make both. Men were not intended to work with the accuracy of tools, to be precise and perfect in all their actions. If you will have that precision out of them, and make their fingers measure degrees like cog-wheels, and their arms strike curves like compasses, you must unhumanize them. All the energy of their spirits must be given to make cogs and compasses of themselves. All their attention and strength must go to the accomplishment of the mean act. The eye of the soul must be bent upon the finger-point, and the soul's force must fill all the invisible nerves that guide it, ten hours a day, that it may not err from its steely precision, and so soul and sight be worn away, and the whole human being be lost at last – a heap of sawdust, so far as its intellectual work in this world is concerned: saved only by its Heart, which cannot go into the form of cogs and compasses, but expands, after the ten hours are over, into fireside humanity. On the other hand, if you will make a man of the working creature, you cannot make a tool. Let him but begin to imagine, to think, to try to do anything worth doing; and the engine-turned precision is lost at once. Out come all his roughness, all his dulness, all his incapability; shame upon shame, failure upon failure, pause after pause: but out comes the whole majesty of him also; and we know the height of it only when we see the clouds settling upon him. And, whether the clouds be bright or dark, there will be transfiguration behind and within them.

And now, reader, look round this English room of yours, about which you have been proud so often, because the work of it was so good and strong, and the ornaments of it so finished. Examine again all those accurate mouldings, and perfect polishings, and unerring adjustments of the seasoned wood and tempered steel. Many a time you have exulted over them, and thought how great England was, because her slightest work was done so thoroughly. Alas! if read rightly, these perfectnesses are signs of a slavery in our England a thousand times more bitter and more degrading than that of the scourged African, or helot Greek. Men may be beaten, chained, tormented, yoked like cattle, slaughtered like summer flies, and yet remain in one sense, and the best sense, free. But to smother their souls with them, to blight and hew into rotting pollards the suckling branches of their human intelligence, to make the flesh and skin which, after the worm's work on it, is to see God,[6] into leathern thongs to yoke machinery with, – this is to be slave-masters indeed; and there might be more freedom in England, though her feudal lords' lightest words were worth men's lives, and though the blood of the vexed husbandman dropped in the furrows of her fields, than there is while the animation of her multitudes is sent like fuel to feed the factory smoke, and the strength of them is given daily to be wasted into the fineness of a web, or racked into the exactness of a line.

And, on the other hand, go forth again to gaze upon the old cathedral front, where you have smiled so often at the fantastic ignorance of the old sculptors: examine once more those ugly goblins, and formless monsters, and stern statues, anatomiless and rigid; but do not mock at them, for they are signs of the life and liberty of every workman who struck the stone; a freedom of thought, and rank in scale of being, such as no laws, no charters, no charities can secure; but which it must be the first aim of all Europe at this day to regain for her children.

Let me not be thought to speak wildly or extravagantly. It is verily this degradation of the operative into a machine, which, more than any other evil of the times, is leading the mass of the nations everywhere into vain, incoherent, destructive struggling for a freedom of which they cannot explain the nature to themselves. Their universal outcry against wealth, and against nobility, is not forced from them either by the pressure of famine, or the sting of mortified pride. These do much, and have done much in all ages; but the foundations of society were never yet shaken as they are at this day. It is not that men are ill fed, but that they have no pleasure in the work by which they make their bread, and therefore look to wealth as the only means of pleasure. It is not that men are pained by the scorn of the upper classes, but they cannot endure their own; for they feel that the kind of labour to which they are condemned is verily a degrading one, and makes them less than men. Never had the upper classes so much sympathy with the lower, or charity for them, as they have at this day, and yet never were they so much hated by them: for, of old, the separation between the noble and the poor was merely a wall built by law; now it is a veritable difference in level of standing, a precipice between upper and lower grounds in the field of humanity, and there is pestilential air at the bottom of it. I know not if a day is ever to come when the nature of right freedom will be understood, and when men will see that to obey another man, to labour for him, yield reverence to him or to his place, is not slavery. It is often the best kind of liberty, – liberty from care. The man who says to one, Go, and he goeth, and to another, Come, and he cometh,[7] has, in most cases, more sense of restraint and difficulty than the man who obeys him. The movements of the one are hindered by the burden on his shoulder; of the other by the bridle on his lips: there is no way by which the burden may be lightened; but we need not suffer from the bridle if we do not champ at it. To yield reverence to another, to hold ourselves and our likes at his disposal, is not slavery; often it is the noblest state in which a man can live in this world. There is, indeed, a reverence which is servile, that is to say, irrational or selfish: but there is also noble reverence, that is to say, reasonable and loving; and a man is never so noble as when he is reverent in this kind; nay, even if the feeling pass the bounds of mere reason, so that it be loving, a man is raised by it. Which had, in reality, most of the serf nature in him, – the Irish peasant who was lying in wait yesterday for his landlord, with his musket muzzle thrust through the ragged hedge[8]; or that old mountain servant, who 200 years ago, at Inverkeithing, gave up his own life and the lives of his seven sons for his chief? – as each fell, calling forth his brother to the death, 'Another for Hector!'[9] And therefore, in all ages and all countries, reverence has been paid and sacrifice made by men to each other, not only without complaint, but rejoicingly; and famine, and peril, and sword, and all evil, and all shame, have been borne willingly in the causes of masters and kings; for all these gifts of the heart ennobled the men who gave, not less than the men who received them, and nature prompted, and God rewarded the sacrifice. But to feel their souls withering within them, unthanked, to find their whole being sunk into an unrecognized abyss, to be counted off into a heap of mechanism numbered with its wheels, and weighed with its hammer strokes – this, nature bade not, – this, God blesses not, – this, humanity for no long time is able to endure.

We have much studied and much perfected, of late, the great civilized invention of the division of labour[10]; only we give it a false name. It is not, truly speaking, the labour that is divided; but the men: – Divided into mere segments of men – broken into small fragments and crumbs of life; so that all the little piece of intelligence that is left in a man is not enough to make a pin, or a nail, but exhausts itself in making the point of a pin or the head of a nail. Now it is a good and desirable thing, truly, to make many pins in a day; but if we could only see with what crystal sand their points were polished, – sand of human soul, much to be magnified before it can be discerned for what it is – we should think there might be some loss in it also. And the great cry that rises from all our manufacturing cities, louder than their furnace blast, is all in very deed for this, – that we manufacture everything there except men; we blanch cotton, and strengthen steel, and refine sugar, and shape pottery; but to brighten, to strengthen, to refine, or to form a single living spirit, never enters into our estimate of advantages. And all the evil to which that cry is urging our myriads can be met only in one way: not by teaching nor preaching, for to teach them is but to show them their misery, and to preach to them, if we do nothing more than preach, is to mock at it. It can be met only by a right understanding, on the part of all classes, of what kinds of labour are good for men, raising them, and making them happy; by a determined sacrifice of such convenience, or beauty, or cheapness as is to be got only by the degradation of the workman; and by equally determined demand for the products and results of healthy and ennobling labour.

And how, it will be asked, are these products to be recognized, and this demand to be regulated? Easily: by the observance of three broad and simple rules:

1. Never encourage the manufacture of any article not absolutely necessary, in the production of which *Invention* has no share.

2. Never demand an exact finish for its own sake, but only for some practical or noble end.

3. Never encourage imitation or copying of any kind, except for the sake of preserving records of great works.

The second of these principles is the only one which directly rises out of the consideration of our immediate subject; but I shall briefly explain the meaning and extent of the first also, reserving the enforcement of the third for another place.

1. Never encourage the manufacture of anything not necessary, in the production of which invention has no share.

For instance. Glass beads are utterly unnecessary, and there is no design or thought employed in their manufacture. They are formed by first drawing out the glass into rods; these rods are chopped up into fragments of the size of beads by the human hand, and the fragments are then rounded in the furnace. The men who chop up the rods sit at their work all day, their hands vibrating with a perpetual and exquisitely timed palsy, and the beads dropping beneath their vibration like hail.[11] Neither they, nor the men who draw out the rods or fuse the fragments, have the smallest occasion for the use of any single human faculty; and every young lady, therefore, who buys glass beads is engaged in the slave-trade, and in a much more cruel one than that which we have so long been endeavouring to put down.[12]

But glass cups and vessels may become the subjects of exquisite invention; and if in buying these we pay for the invention, that is to say, for the beautiful form, or colour, or engraving, and not for mere finish of execution, we are doing good to humanity.

So, again, the cutting of precious stones, in all ordinary cases, requires little exertion of any mental faculty; some tact and judgment in avoiding flaws, and so on, but nothing to bring out the whole mind. Every person who wears cut jewels merely for the sake of their value is, therefore, a slave-driver.

But the working of the goldsmith, and the various designing of grouped jewellery and enamel-work, may become the subject of the most noble human intelligence. Therefore, money spent in the purchase of well-designed plate, of precious engraved vases, cameos, or enamels, does good to humanity; and, in work of this kind, jewels may be employed to heighten its splendour; and their cutting is then a price paid for the attainment of a noble end, and thus perfectly allowable.

I shall perhaps press this law farther elsewhere, but our immediate concern is chiefly with the second, namely, never to demand an exact finish, when it does not lead to a noble end. For observe, I have only dwelt upon the rudeness of Gothic, or any other kind of imperfectness, as admirable, where it was impossible to get design or thought without it. If you are to have the thought of a rough and untaught man, you must have it in a rough and untaught way; but from an educated man, who can without effort express his thoughts in an educated way, take the graceful expression, and be thankful. Only *get* the thought, and do not silence the peasant because he cannot speak good grammar, or until you have taught him his grammar. Grammar and refinement are good things, both, only be sure of the better thing first. And thus in art, delicate finish is desirable from the greatest masters, and is always given by them. In some places Michael Angelo, Leonardo, Phidias, Perugino, Turner, all finished with the most exquisite care; and the finish they give always leads to the fuller accomplishment of their noble purposes. But lower men than these cannot finish, for it requires consummate knowledge to finish consummately, and then we must take their thoughts as they are able to give them. So the rule is simple: Always look for invention first, and after that, for such execution as will help the invention, and as the inventor is capable of without painful effort, and *no more*. Above all, demand no refinement of execution where there is no thought, for that is slaves' work, unredeemed. Rather choose rough work than smooth work, so only that the practical purpose be answered, and never imagine there is reason to be proud of anything that may be accomplished by patience and sand-paper.

I shall only give one example, which however will show the reader what I mean, from the manufacture already alluded to, that of glass. Our modern glass is exquisitely clear in its substance, true in its form, accurate in its cutting. We are proud of this. We ought to be ashamed of it. The old Venice glass was muddy, inaccurate in all its forms, and clumsily cut, if at all. And the old Venetian was justly proud of it. For there is this difference between the English and Venetian workman, that the former thinks only of accurately matching his patterns, and getting his curves perfectly true and his edges perfectly sharp, and becomes a mere machine for rounding curves and sharpening edges; while the old Venetian cared not a whit whether his edges were sharp or not, but he invented a new design for every glass that he made, and never moulded a handle or a lip without a new fancy in it. And therefore, though some Venetian glass is ugly and clumsy enough when made by clumsy and uninventive workmen, other Venetian glass is so lovely in its forms that no price is too great for it; and we never see the same form in it twice. Now you cannot have the finish and the varied form too. If the workman is thinking about his edges, he cannot be thinking of his design; if of his design, he cannot think of his edges. Choose whether you will pay for the lovely form or the perfect finish, and choose at the same moment whether you will make the worker a man or a grindstone.

Nay, but the reader interrupts me, – 'If the workman can design beautifully, I would not have him kept at the furnace. Let him be taken away and made a gentleman, and have a studio, and design his glass there, and I will have it blown and cut for him by common workmen, and so I will have my design and my finish too.'

All ideas of this kind are founded upon two mistaken suppositions: the first, that one man's thoughts can be, or ought to be, executed by another man's hands; the second, that manual labour is a degradation, when it is governed by intellect.

On a large scale, and in work determinable by line and rule, it is indeed both possible and necessary that the thoughts of one man should be carried out by the labour of others; in this sense I have already defined the best architecture to be the expression of the mind of manhood by the hands of childhood.[13] But on a smaller scale, and in a design which cannot be mathematically defined, one man's thoughts can never be expressed by another: and the difference between the spirit of touch of the man who is inventing, and of the man who is obeying directions, is often all the difference between a great and a common work of art. How wide the separation is between original and second-hand execution, I shall endeavour to show elsewhere[14]; it is not so much to our purpose here as to mark the other and more fatal error of despising manual labour when governed by intellect; for it is no less fatal an error to despise it when thus regulated by intellect, than to value it for its own sake. We are always in these days endeavouring to separate the two; we want one man to be always thinking, and another to be always working, and we call one a gentleman, and the other an operative; whereas the workman ought often to be thinking, and the thinker often to be working, and both should be gentlemen, in the best sense. As it is, we make both ungentle, the one envying, the other despising, his brother; and the mass of society is made up of morbid thinkers, and miserable workers. Now it is only by labour that thought can be made healthy, and only by thought that labour can be made happy, and the two cannot be separated with impunity. It would be well if all of us were good handicraftsmen in some kind, and the dishonour of manual labour done away with altogether; so that though there should still be a trenchant distinction of race between nobles and commoners, there should not, among the latter, be a trenchant distinction of employment, as between idle and working men, or between men of liberal and illiberal professions. All professions should be liberal, and there should be less pride felt in peculiarity of employment, and more in excellence of achievement. And yet more, in each several profession, no master should be too proud to do its hardest work. The painter should grind his own colours; the architect work in the mason's yard with his men; the master-manufacturer be himself a more skilful operative than any man in his mills; and the distinction between one man and another be only in experience and skill, and the authority and wealth which these must naturally and justly obtain.

I should be led far from the matter in hand, if I were to pursue this interesting subject. Enough, I trust, has been said to show the reader that the rudeness or imperfection which at first rendered the term 'Gothic' one of reproach is indeed, when rightly understood, one of the most noble characters of Christian architecture, and not only a noble but an *essential* one. It seems a fantastic paradox, but it is nevertheless a most important truth, that no architecture can be truly noble which is *not* imperfect. And this is easily demonstrable. For since the architect, whom we will suppose capable of doing all in perfection, cannot execute the whole with his own hands, he must either make slaves of his workmen in the old Greek, and present English fashion, and level his work to a slave's capacities, which is to degrade it; or else he must take his workmen as he finds them, and let them show their weaknesses together with their strength, which will involve the Gothic imperfection, but render the whole work as noble as the intellect of the age can make it.

But the principle may be stated more broadly still. I have confined the illustration of it to architecture, but I must not leave it as if true of architecture only. Hitherto I have used the words imperfect and perfect merely to distinguish between work grossly unskilful, and work executed with average precision and science; and I have been pleading that any degree of unskilfulness should be admitted, so only that the labourer's mind had room for expression. But, accurately speaking, no good work whatever can be perfect, and *the demand for perfection is always a sign of a misunderstanding of the ends of art.*

This is for two reasons, both based on everlasting laws. The first, that no great man ever stops working till he has reached his point of failure: that is to say, his mind is always far in advance of his powers of execution, and the latter will now and then give way in trying to follow it; besides that he will always give to the inferior portions of his work only such inferior attention as they require; and according to his greatness he becomes so accustomed to the feeling of dissatisfaction with the best he can do, that in moments of lassitude or anger with himself he will not care though the beholder be dissatisfied also. I believe there has only been one man who would not acknowledge this necessity, and strove always to reach perfection, Leonardo; the end of his vain effort being merely that he would take ten years to a picture and leave it unfinished. And therefore, if we are to have great men working at all, or less men doing their best, the work will be imperfect, however beautiful. Of human work none but what is bad can be perfect, in its own bad way.*

The second reason is, that imperfection is in some sort essential to all that we know of life. It is the sign of life in a mortal body, that is to say, of a state of progress and change. Nothing that lives is, or can be, rigidly perfect; part of it is decaying, part nascent. The foxglove blossom, – a third part bud, a third part past, a third part in full bloom, – is a type of the life of this world. And in all things that live there are certain irregularities and deficiencies which are not only signs of life, but sources of beauty. No human face is exactly the same in its lines on each side, no leaf perfect in its lobes, no branch in its symmetry. All admit irregularity as they imply change; and to banish imperfection is to destroy expression, to check exertion, to paralyze vitality. All things are literally better, lovelier, and more beloved for the imperfections which have been divinely appointed, that the law of human life may be Effort, and the law of human judgment, Mercy.

Accept this then for a universal law, that neither architecture nor any other noble work of man can be good unless it be imperfect ; and let us be prepared for the otherwise strange fact, which we shall discern clearly as we approach the period of the Renaissance, that the first cause of the fall of the arts of Europe was a relentless requirement of perfection, incapable alike either of being silenced by veneration for greatness, or softened into forgiveness of simplicity.

Thus far then of the Rudeness or Savageness, which is the first mental element of Gothic architecture. It is an element in many other healthy architectures also, as the Byzantine and Romanesque; but true Gothic cannot exist without it.

The second mental element above named was CHANGEFULNESS, or Variety.

I have already enforced the allowing independent operation to the inferior workman, simply as a duty *to him*, and as ennobling the architecture by

* The Elgin marbles are supposed by many persons to be 'perfect.' In the most important portions they indeed approach perfection, but only there. The draperies are unfinished, the hair and wool of the animals are unfinished, and the entire bas-reliefs of the frieze are roughly cut.

rendering it more Christian. We have now to consider what reward we obtain for the performance of this duty, namely, the perpetual variety of every feature of the building.

Wherever the workman is utterly enslaved, the parts of the building must of course be absolutely like each other; for the perfection of his execution can only be reached by exercising him in doing one thing, and giving him nothing else to do. The degree in which the workman is degraded may be thus known at a glance, by observing whether the several parts of the building are similar or not; and if, as in Greek work, all the capitals are alike, and all the mouldings unvaried, then the degradation is complete; if, as in Egyptian or Ninevite work, though the manner of executing certain figures is always the same, the order of design is perpetually varied, the degradation is less total; if, as in Gothic work, there is perpetual change both in design and execution, the workman must have been altogether set free.

How much the beholder gains from the liberty of the labourer may perhaps be questioned in England, where one of the strongest instincts in nearly every mind is that Love of Order which makes us desire that our house windows should pair like our carriage horses, and allows us to yield our faith unhesitatingly to architectural theories which fix a form for everything, and forbid variation from it. I would not impeach love of order: it is one of the most useful elements of the English mind; it helps us in our commerce and in all purely practical matters; and it is in many cases one of the foundation stones of morality. Only do not let us suppose that love of order is love of art. It is true that order, in its highest sense, is one of the necessities of art, just as time is a necessity of music; but love of order has no more to do with our right enjoyment of architecture or painting, than love of punctuality with the appreciation of an opera. Experience, I fear, teaches us that accurate and methodical habits in daily life are seldom characteristic of those who either quickly perceive, or richly possess, the creative powers of art; there is, however, nothing inconsistent between the two instincts, and nothing to hinder us from retaining our business habits, and yet fully allowing and enjoying the noblest gifts of Invention. We already do so, in every other branch of art except architecture, and we only do *not* so there because we have been taught that it would be wrong. Our architects gravely inform us that, as there are four rules of arithmetic, there are five orders of architecture; we, in our simplicity, think that this sounds consistent, and believe them. They inform us also that there is one proper form for Corinthian capitals, another for Doric, and another for Ionic. We, considering that there is also a proper form for the letters A, B, and C, think that this also sounds consistent, and accept the proposition. Understanding, therefore, that one form of the said capitals is proper, and no other, and having a conscientious horror of all impropriety, we allow the architect to provide us with the said capitals, of the proper form, in such and such a quantity, and in all other points to take care that the legal forms are observed; which having done, we rest in forced confidence that we are well housed.

But our higher instincts are not deceived. We take no pleasure in the building provided for us, resembling that which we take in a new book or a new picture. We may be proud of its size, complacent in its correctness, and happy in its convenience. We may take the same pleasure in its symmetry and workmanship as in a well-ordered room, or a skilful piece of manufacture. And this we suppose to be all the pleasure that architecture was ever intended to give us. The idea of reading a building as we would read Milton or Dante, and getting the same kind of delight out of the stones as out of the stanzas, never enters our mind for a moment. And for good reason; – There is indeed rhythm in the verses, quite as strict as the symmetries or rhythm of the architecture, and a thousand times more beautiful, but there is something else than rhythm. The verses were neither made to order, nor to match, as the capitals were; and we have therefore a kind of pleasure in them other than a sense of propriety. But it requires a strong effort of common sense to shake ourselves quit of all that we have been taught for the last two centuries, and wake to the perception of a truth just as simple and certain as it is new: that great art, whether expressing itself in words, colours, or stones, does *not* say the same thing over and over again; that the merit of architectural, as of every other art, consists in its saying new and different things; that to repeat itself is no more a characteristic of genius in marble than it is of genius in print; and that we may, without offending any laws of good taste, require of an architect, as we do of a novelist, that he should be not only correct, but entertaining.

Yet all this is true, and self-evident; only hidden from us, as many other self-evident things are, by false teaching. Nothing is a great work of art, for the production of which either rules or models can be given. Exactly so far as architecture works on known rules, and from given models, it is not an art, but a manufacture; and it is, of the two procedures, rather less rational (because more easy) to copy capitals or mouldings from Phidias, and call ourselves architects, than to copy heads and hands from Titian, and call ourselves painters.

Let us then understand at once that change or variety is as much a necessity to the human heart and brain in buildings as in books; that there is no merit, though there is some occasional use, in monotony; and that we must no more expect to derive either pleasure or profit from an architecture whose ornaments are of one pattern, and whose pillars are of one proportion, than we should out of a universe in which the clouds were all of one shape, and the trees all of one size.

And this we confess in deeds, though not in words. All the pleasure which the people of the nineteenth century take in art, is in pictures, sculpture, minor objects of virtù, or mediæval architecture, which we enjoy under the term picturesque: no pleasure is taken anywhere in modern buildings, and we find all men of true feeling delighting to escape out of modern cities into natural scenery: hence, as I shall hereafter show, that peculiar love of landscape, which is characteristic of the age.[15] It would be well, if in all other matters, we were as ready to put up with what we dislike, for the sake of compliance with established law, as we are in architecture.

How so debased a law ever came to be established, we shall see when we come to describe the Renaissance schools; here we have only to note, as a second most essential element of the Gothic spirit, that it broke through that law wherever it found it in existence; it not only dared, but delighted in, the infringement of every servile principle; and invented a series of forms of which the merit was, not merely that they were new, but that they were *capable of perpetual novelty*. The pointed arch was not merely a bold variation from the round, but it admitted of millions of variations in itself; for the proportions of a pointed arch are changeable to infinity, while a circular arch is always the same. The grouped shaft[16] was not merely a bold variation from the single one, but it admitted of millions of variations in its grouping, and in the proportions resultant from its grouping. The introduction of tracery was not only a startling change in the treatment of window lights,[17] but admitted endless changes in the interlacement of the tracery bars themselves. So that, while in all living Christian architecture the love of variety exists, the Gothic schools exhibited that love in culminating energy; and their influence, wherever it extended itself, may be sooner and farther traced by this character than by any other; the tendency to the adoption of Gothic types being always first shown by greater irregularity, and richer variation in the forms of architecture it is about to supersede, long before the appearance of the pointed arch or of any other recognizable *outward* sign of the Gothic mind.

We must, however, herein note carefully what distinction there is between a healthy and a diseased love of change; for as it was in healthy love of change that the Gothic architecture rose, it was partly in consequence of diseased love of change that it was destroyed. In order to understand this clearly, it will be necessary to consider the different ways in which change and monotony are presented to us in nature; both having their use, like darkness and light, and the one incapable of being enjoyed without the other: change being most delightful after some prolongation of monotony, as light appears most brilliant after the eyes have been for some time closed.

I believe that the true relations of monotony and change may be most simply understood by observing them in music. We may therein notice first, that there is a sublimity and majesty in monotony, which there is not in rapid or frequent variation. This is true throughout all nature. The greater part of the sublimity of the sea depends on its monotony; so also that of desolate moor and mountain scenery; and especially the sublimity of motion, as in the quiet, unchanged fall and rise of an engine beam. So also there is sublimity in darkness which there is not in light.

Again, monotony after a certain time, or beyond a certain degree, becomes either uninteresting or intolerable, and the musician is obliged to break it in one of two ways: either while the air or passage is perpetually repeated, its notes are variously enriched and harmonized; or else, after a certain number of repeated passages, an entirely new passage is introduced, which is more or less delightful according to the length of the previous monotony. Nature, of course, uses both these kinds of variation perpetually.[18] The sea-waves, resembling each other in general mass, but none like its brother in minor divisions and curves, are a monotony of the first kind; the great plain, broken by an emergent rock or clump of trees, is a monotony of the second.

Farther: in order to the enjoyment of the change in either case, a certain degree of patience is required from the hearer or observer. In the first case, he must be satisfied to endure with patience the recurrence of the great masses of sound or form, and to seek for entertainment in a careful watchfulness of the minor details. In the second case, he must bear patiently the infliction of the monotony for some moments, in order to feel the full refreshment of the change. This is true even of the shortest musical passage in which the element of monotony is employed. In cases of more majestic monotony, the patience required is so considerable that it becomes a kind of pain, – a price paid for the future pleasure.

Again: the talent of the composer is not in the monotony, but in the changes: he may show feeling and taste by his use of monotony in certain places or degrees; that is to say, by his *various* employment of it; but it is always in the new arrangement or invention that his intellect is shown, and not in the monotony which relieves it.

Lastly: if the pleasure of change be too often repeated, it ceases to be delightful, for then change itself becomes monotonous, and we are driven to seek delight in extreme and fantastic degrees of it. This is the diseased love of change of which we have above spoken.

From these facts we may gather generally that monotony is, and ought to be, in itself painful to us, just as darkness is; that an architecture which is altogether monotonous is a dark or dead architecture; and of those who love it, it may be truly said, 'they love darkness rather than light.'[19] But monotony in certain measure, used in order to give value to change, and above all, that *transparent* monotony, which, like the shadows of a great painter, suffers all manner of dimly suggested form to be seen through the body of it, is an essential in architectural as in all other composition; and the endurance of monotony has about the same place in a healthy mind that the endurance of darkness has: that is to say, as a strong intellect will have pleasure in the solemnities of storm and twilight, and in the broken and mysterious lights that gleam among them, rather than in mere brilliancy and glare, while a frivolous mind will dread the shadow and the storm; and as a great man will be ready to endure much darkness of fortune in order to reach greater eminence of power or felicity, while an inferior man will not pay the price; exactly in like manner a great mind will accept, or even delight in, monotony which would be wearisome to an inferior intellect, because it has more patience and power of expectation, and is ready to pay the full price for the great future pleasure of change. But in all cases it is not that the noble nature loves monotony, any more than it loves darkness or pain. But it can bear with it, and receive a high pleasure in the endurance or patience, a pleasure necessary to the well-being of this world; while those who will not submit to the temporary sameness, but rush from one change to another, gradually dull the edge of change itself, and bring a shadow and weariness over the whole world from which there is no more escape.

From these general uses of variety in the economy of the world, we may at once understand its use and abuse in architecture. The variety of the Gothic schools is the more healthy and beautiful, because in many cases it is entirely unstudied, and results, not from mere love of change, but from practical necessities. For in one point of view Gothic is not only the best, but the *only rational* architecture, as being that which can fit itself most easily to all services, vulgar or noble. Undefined in its slope of roof, height of shaft, breadth of arch, or disposition of ground plan, it can shrink into a turret, expand into a hall, coil into a staircase, or spring into a spire, with undegraded grace and unexhausted energy; and whenever it finds occasion for change in its form or purpose, it submits to it without the slightest sense of loss either to its unity or majesty, – subtle and flexible like a fiery serpent, but ever attentive to the voice of the charmer. And it is one of the chief virtues of the Gothic builders, that they never suffered ideas of outside symmetries and consistencies to interfere with the real use and value of what they did. If they wanted a window, they opened one; a room, they added one; a buttress, they built one; utterly regardless of any established conventionalities of external appearance, knowing (as indeed it always happened) that such daring interruptions of the formal plan would rather give additional interest to its symmetry than injure it. So that, in the best times of Gothic, a useless window would rather have been opened in an unexpected place for the sake of the surprise, than a useful one forbidden for the sake of symmetry. Every successive architect, employed upon a great work, built the pieces he added in his own way, utterly regardless of the style adopted by his predecessors; and if two towers were raised in nominal correspondence at the sides of a cathedral front, one was nearly sure to be different from the other, and in each the style at the top to be different from the style at the bottom.

These marked variations were, however, only permitted as part of the great system of perpetual change which ran through every member of Gothic design, and rendered it as endless a field for the beholder's inquiry as for the builder's imagination: change, which in the best schools is subtle and delicate, and rendered more delightful by intermingling of a noble monotony; in the more barbaric schools is somewhat fantastic and redundant; but, in all, a necessary and constant condition of the life of the school. Sometimes the variety is in one feature, sometimes in another; it may be in the capitals or crockets, in the niches or the traceries, or in all together, but in some one or other of the features it will be found always. If the mouldings are constant, the surface sculpture will change; if the capitals are of a fixed design, the traceries will change; if the traceries are monotonous, the capitals will change; and if even, as in some fine schools, the early English[20] for example, there is the slightest approximation to an unvarying type of mouldings, capitals, and floral decoration, the variety is found in the disposition of the masses, and in the figure sculpture.

I must now refer for a moment, before we quit the consideration of this, the second mental element of Gothic, to the opening of the third chapter of the *Seven Lamps of Architecture*,[21] in which the distinction was drawn between man gathering and man governing; between his acceptance of the sources of delight from nature, and his development of authoritative or imaginative power in their arrangement: for the two mental elements, not only of Gothic, but of all good architecture, which we have just been examining, belong to it, and are admirable in it, chiefly as it is, more than any other subject of art, the work of man, and the expression of the average power of man. A picture or poem is often little more than a feeble utterance of man's admiration of something out of himself; but architecture approaches more to a creation of his own, born of his necessities, and expressive of his nature. It is also, in some sort, the work of the whole race, while the picture or statue is the work of one only, in most cases more highly gifted than his fellows. And therefore we may expect that the first two elements of good architecture should be expressive of some great truths commonly belonging to the whole race, and necessary to be understood or felt by them in all their work that they do under the sun. And observe what they are: the confession of Imperfection, and the confession of Desire of Change. The building of the bird and the bee needs not express anything like this. It is perfect and unchanging. But just because we are something better than birds or bees, our building must confess that we have not reached the perfection we can imagine, and cannot rest in the condition we have attained. If we pretend to have reached either perfection or satisfaction, we have degraded ourselves and our work. God's work only may express that; but ours may never have that sentence written upon it, – 'And behold, it was very good.'[22] And, observe again, it is not merely as it renders the edifice a book of various knowledge, or a mine of precious thought, that variety is essential to its nobleness. The vital principle is not the love of *Knowledge*, but the love of *Change*. It is that strange *disquietude* of the Gothic spirit that is its greatness; that restlessness of the dreaming mind, that wanders hither and thither among the niches, and flickers feverishly around the pinnacles, and frets and fades in labyrinthine knots and shadows along wall and roof, and yet is not satisfied, nor shall be satisfied. The Greek could stay in his triglyph[23] furrow, and be at peace; but the work of the Gothic heart is fretwork still, and it can neither rest in, nor from, its labour, but must pass on, sleeplessly, until its love of change shall be pacified for ever in the change that must come alike on them that wake and them that sleep.[24]

The third constituent element of the Gothic mind was stated to be NATURALISM; that is to say, the love of natural objects for their own sake, and the effort to represent them frankly, unconstrained by artistical laws.

This characteristic of the style partly follows in necessary connection with those named above. For, so soon as the workman is left free to represent what subjects he chooses, he must look to the nature that is round him for material, and will endeavour to represent it as he sees it, with more or less accuracy according to the skill he possesses, and with much play of fancy, but with small respect for law. There is, however, a marked distinction between the imaginations of the Western and Eastern races, even when both are left free; the Western, or Gothic, delighting most in the representation of facts, and the Eastern (Arabian, Persian, and Chinese) in the harmony of colours and forms. Each of these intellectual dispositions has its particular forms of error and abuse [. . .][25]

Of the various forms of resultant mischief it is not here the place to speak; the reader may already be somewhat wearied with a statement which has led us apparently so far from our immediate subject. But the digression was necessary, in order that I might clearly define the sense in which I use the word Naturalism when I state it to be the third most essential characteristic of Gothic architecture. I mean that the Gothic builders belong to the central or greatest rank in *both* the classifications of artists which we have just made; that considering all artists as either men of design, men of facts, or men of both, the Gothic builders were men of both; and that again, considering all artists as either Purists, Naturalists, or Sensualists, the Gothic builders were Naturalists.

I say first, that the Gothic builders were of that central class which unites fact with design; but that the part of the work which was more especially their own was the truthfulness. Their power of artistical invention or arrangement was not greater than that of Romanesque and Byzantine workmen: by those workmen they were taught the principles, and from them received their models, of design; but to the ornamental feeling and rich fancy of the Byzantine the Gothic builder added a love of *fact* which is never found in the South. Both Greek and Roman used conventional foliage in their ornament, passing into something that was not foliage at all, knotting itself into strange cup-like buds or clusters, and growing out of lifeless rods instead of stems; the Gothic sculptor received these types, at first, as things that ought to be, just as we have a second time received them; but he could not rest in them. He saw there was no veracity in them, no knowledge, no vitality. Do what he would, he could not help liking the true leaves better; and cautiously, a little at a time, he put more of nature into his work, until at last it was all true, retaining, nevertheless, every valuable character of the original well-disciplined and designed arrangement.

Nor is it only in external and visible subject that the Gothic workman wrought for truth: he is as firm in his rendering of imaginative as of actual truth; that is to say, when an idea would have been by a Roman, or Byzantine, symbolically represented, the Gothic mind realizes it to the utmost. For instance, the purgatorial fire is represented in the mosaic of Torcello (Romanesque)[26] as a red stream, longitudinally striped like a riband, descending out of the throne of Christ, and gradually extending itself to envelop the wicked. When we are once informed what this means, it is enough for its purpose; but the Gothic inventor does not leave the sign in need of interpretation. He makes the fire as like real fire as he can; and in the porch of St Maclou at Rouen[27] the sculptured flames burst out of the Hades gate, and flicker up, in writhing tongues of stone, through the interstices of the niches, as if the church itself were on fire. This is an extreme instance, but it is all the more illustrative of the entire difference in temper and thought between the two schools of art, and of the intense love of veracity which influenced the Gothic design.

I do not say that this love of veracity is always healthy in its operation. I have above noticed the errors into which it falls from despising design; and there is another kind of error noticeable in the instance just given, in which the love of truth is too hasty, and seizes on a surface truth instead of an inner one. For in representing the Hades fire, it is not the mere *form* of the flame which needs most to be told, but its unquenchableness, its Divine ordainment and limitation, and its inner fierceness, not physical and material, but in being the expression of the wrath of God. And these things are not to be told by imitating the fire that flashes out of a bundle of sticks. If we think over his symbol a little, we shall perhaps find that the Romanesque builder told more truth in that likeness of a blood-red stream, flowing between definite shores, and out of God's throne, and expanding, as if fed by a perpetual current, into the lake wherein the wicked are cast, than the Gothic builder in those torch-flickerings about his niches. But this is not to our immediate purpose; I am not at present to insist upon the faults into which the love of truth was led in the later Gothic times, but on the feeling itself, as a glorious and peculiar characteristic of the Northern builders. For, observe, it is not, even in the above instance, love of truth, but want of thought, which *causes* the fault. The love of truth, as such, is good, but when it is misdirected by thoughtlessness or over-excited by vanity, and either seizes on facts of small value, or gathers them chiefly that it may boast of its grasp and apprehension, its work may well become dull or offensive. Yet let us not, therefore, blame the inherent love of facts, but the incautiousness of their selection, and impertinence of their statement.

I said, in the second place, that Gothic work, when referred to the arrangement of all art, as purist, naturalist, or sensualist, was naturalist. This character follows necessarily on its extreme love of truth, prevailing over the sense of beauty, and causing it to take delight in portraiture of every kind, and to express the various characters of the human countenance and form, as it did the varieties of leaves and the ruggedness of branches. And this tendency is both increased and ennobled by the same Christian humility which we saw expressed in the first character of Gothic work, its rudeness. For as that resulted from a humility which confessed the imperfection of the *workman*, so this naturalist portraiture is rendered more faithful by the humility which confesses the imperfection of the *subject*. The Greek sculptor could neither bear to confess his own feebleness, nor to tell the faults of the forms that he portrayed. But the Christian workman, believing that all is finally to work together for good,[28] freely confesses both, and neither seeks to disguise his own roughness of work, nor his subject's roughness of make. Yet this frankness being joined, for the most part, with depth of religious feeling in other directions, and especially with charity, there is sometimes a tendency to Purism in the best Gothic sculpture; so that it frequently reaches great dignity of form and tenderness of expression, yet never so as to lose the veracity of portraiture wherever portraiture is possible: not exalting its kings into demi-gods, nor its saints into archangels, but giving what kingliness and sanctity was in them, to the full, mixed with due record of their faults; and this in the most part with a great indifference like that of Scripture history, which sets down, with unmoved and unexcusing resoluteness, the virtues and errors of all men of whom it speaks, often leaving the reader to form his own estimate of them, without an indication of the judgment of the historian. And this veracity is carried out by the Gothic sculptors in the minuteness and generality, as well as the equity, of their delineation: for they do not limit their art to the portraiture of saints and kings, but introduce the most familiar scenes and most simple subjects: filling up the backgrounds of Scripture histories with vivid and curious representations of the commonest incidents of daily life, and availing themselves of every occasion in which, either as a symbol, or an explanation of a scene or time, the things familiar to the eye of the workman could be introduced and made of account. Hence Gothic sculpture and painting are not only full of valuable portraiture of the greatest men, but copious records of all the domestic customs and inferior arts of the ages in which it flourished. *

There is, however, one direction in which the Naturalism of the Gothic workmen is peculiarly manifested; and this direction is even more characteristic of the school than the Naturalism itself; I mean their peculiar

---

* The best art either represents the facts of its own day, or, if facts of the past, expresses them with accessaries of the time in which the work was done. All good art, representing past events, is therefore full of the most frank anachronism, and always *ought* to be. No painter has any business to be an antiquarian. We do not want his impressions or suppositions respecting things that are past. We want his clear assertions respecting things present.

fondness for the forms of Vegetation. In rendering the various circumstances of daily life, Egyptian and Ninevite sculpture is as frank and as diffuse as the Gothic. From the highest pomps of state or triumphs of battle, to the most trivial domestic arts and amusements, all is taken advantage of to fill the field of granite with the perpetual interest of a crowded drama; and the early Lombardic and Romanesque sculpture[29] is equally copious in its description of the familiar circumstances of war and the chase. But in all the scenes portrayed by the workmen of these nations, vegetation occurs only as an explanatory accessary; the reed is introduced to mark the course of the river, or the tree to mark the covert of the wild beast, or the ambush of the enemy, but there is no especial interest in the forms of the vegetation strong enough to induce them to make it a subject of separate and accurate study. Again, among the nations who followed the arts of design exclusively, the forms of foliage introduced were meagre and general, and their real intricacy and life were neither admired nor expressed. But to the Gothic workman the living foliage became a subject of intense affection, and he struggled to render all its characters with as much accuracy as was compatible with the laws of his design and the nature of his material,[30] not unfrequently tempted in his enthusiasm to transgress the one and disguise the other.

There is a peculiar significance in this, indicative both of higher civilization and gentler temperament, than had before been manifested in architecture. Rudeness, and the love of change, which we have insisted upon as the first elements of Gothic, are also elements common to all healthy schools. But here is a softer element mingled with them, peculiar to the Gothic itself. The rudeness or ignorance which would have been painfully exposed in the treatment of the human form, are still not so great as to prevent the successful rendering of the wayside herbage; and the love of change, which becomes morbid and feverish in following the haste of the hunter and the rage of the combatant, is at once soothed and satisfied as it watches the wandering of the tendril, and the budding of the flower. Nor is this all: the new direction of mental interest marks an infinite change in the means and the habits of life. The nations whose chief support was in the chase, whose chief interest was in the battle, whose chief pleasure was in the banquet, would take small care respecting the shapes of leaves and flowers; and notice little in the forms of the forest trees which sheltered them, except the signs indicative of the wood which would make the toughest lance, the closest roof, or the clearest fire. The affectionate observation of the grace and outward character of vegetation is the sure sign of a more tranquil and gentle existence, sustained by the gifts, and gladdened by the splendour, of the earth. In that careful distinction of species, and richness of delicate and undisturbed organization, which characterize the Gothic design, there is the history of rural and thoughtful life, influenced by habitual tenderness, and devoted to subtle inquiry; and every discriminating and delicate touch of the chisel, as it rounds the petal or guides the branch, is a prophecy of the development of the entire body of the natural sciences, beginning with that of medicine, of the recovery of literature,[31] and the establishment of the most necessary principles of domestic wisdom and national peace.

I have before alluded to the strange and vain supposition, that the original conception of Gothic architecture had been derived from vegetation, – from the symmetry of avenues, and the interlacing of branches.[32] It is a supposition which never could have existed for a moment in the mind of any person acquainted with early Gothic; but, however idle as a theory, it is most valuable as a testimony to the character of the perfected style. It is precisely because the reverse of this theory is the fact, because the Gothic did not arise out of, but developed itself into a resemblance to vegetation, that this resemblance is so instructive as an indication of the temper of the builders. It was no chance suggestion of the form of an arch from the bending of a bough, but a gradual and continual discovery of a beauty in natural forms which could be more and more perfectly transferred into those of stone, that influenced at once the heart of the people, and the form of the edifice. The Gothic architecture arose in massy and mountainous strength, axe-hewn, and iron-bound, block heaved upon block by the monk's enthusiasm and the soldier's force; and cramped and stanchioned into such weight of grisly wall, as might bury the anchoret[33] in darkness, and beat back the utmost storm of battle, suffering but by the same narrow crosslet[34] the passing of the sunbeam, or of the arrow. Gradually, as that monkish enthusiasm became more thoughtful, and as the sound of war became more and more intermittent beyond the gates of the convent or the keep, the stony pillar grew slender and the vaulted roof grew light, till they had wreathed themselves into the semblance of the summer woods at their fairest, and of the dead field-flowers, long trodden down in blood, sweet monumental statues were set to bloom for ever, beneath the porch of the temple, or the canopy of the tomb.

Nor is it only as a sign of greater gentleness or refinement of mind, but as a proof of the best possible direction of this refinement, that the tendency of the Gothic to the expression of vegetative life is to be admired. That sentence of Genesis,[35] 'I have given thee every green herb for meat,' like all the rest of the book, has a profound symbolical as well as a literal meaning. It is not merely the nourishment of the body, but the food of the soul, that is intended. The green herb is, of all nature, that which is most essential to the healthy spiritual life of man. Most of us do not need fine scenery; the precipice and the mountain peak are not intended to be seen by all men, – perhaps their power is greatest over those who are unaccustomed to them. But trees and fields and flowers were made for all, and are necessary for all. God has connected the labour which is essential to the bodily sustenance with the pleasures which are healthiest for the heart; and while He made the ground stubborn, He made its herbage fragrant, and its blossoms fair. The proudest architecture that man can build has no higher honour than to bear the image and recall the memory of that grass of the field which is, at once, the type and the support of his existence; the goodly building is then most glorious when it is sculptured into the likeness of the leaves of Paradise; and the great Gothic spirit, as we showed it to be noble in its disquietude, is also noble in its hold of nature; it is, indeed, like the dove of Noah, in that she found no rest upon the face of the waters, – but like her in this also, 'LO, IN HER MOUTH WAS AN OLIVE BRANCH, PLUCKED OFF.'[36]

The fourth essential element of the Gothic mind was above stated to be the sense of the GROTESQUE; but I shall defer the endeavour to define this most curious and subtle character until we have occasion to examine one of the divisions of the Renaissance schools, which was morbidly influenced by it.[37] It is the less necessary to insist upon it here, because every reader familiar with Gothic architecture must understand what I mean, and will, I believe, have no hesitation in admitting, that the tendency to delight in fantastic and ludicrous, as well as in sublime, images, is a universal instinct of the Gothic imagination.

The fifth element above named was RIGIDITY; and this character I must endeavour carefully to define, for neither the word I have used, nor any other that I can think of, will express it accurately. For I mean, not merely stable, but *active* rigidity; the peculiar energy which gives tension to movement, and stiffness to resistance, which makes the fiercest lightning forked rather than curved, and the stoutest oak-branch angular rather than bending, and is as much seen in the quivering of the lance as in the glittering of the icicle.

I have before had occasion[38] to note some manifestations of this energy or fixedness; but it must be still more attentively considered here, as it shows itself throughout the whole structure and decoration of Gothic work. Egyptian and Greek buildings stand, for the most part, by their own weight and mass, one stone passively incumbent on another; but in the Gothic vaults and traceries there is a stiffness analogous to that of the bones of a limb, or fibres of a tree; an elastic tension and communication of force from part to part, and also a studious expression of this throughout every visible line of the building. And, in like manner, the Greek and Egyptian ornament is either mere surface engraving, as if the face of the wall had been stamped with a seal, or its lines are flowing, lithe, and luxuriant; in either case, there is no expression of energy in the framework of the ornament itself. But the Gothic ornament stands out in prickly independence, and frosty fortitude, jutting into crockets, and freezing into pinnacles; here starting up into a monster, there germinating into a blossom, anon knitting itself into a branch, alternately thorny, bossy, and bristly, or writhed into every form of nervous entanglement; but, even when most graceful, never for an instant languid, always quickset: erring, if at all, ever on the side of brusquerie.

The feelings or habits in the workman which give rise to this character in the work, are more complicated and various than those indicated by any other sculptural expression hitherto named. There is, first, the habit of hard and rapid working; the industry of the tribes of the North, quickened by the coldness of the climate, and giving an expression of sharp energy to all they do, as opposed to the languor of the Southern tribes, however much of fire there may be in the heart of that languor, for lava itself may flow languidly. There is also the habit of finding enjoyment in the signs of cold, which is never found, I believe, in the inhabitants of countries south of the Alps. Cold is to them an unredeemed evil, to be suffered and forgotten as soon as may be; but the long winter of the North forces the Goth (I mean the Englishman, Frenchman, Dane, or German), if he would lead a happy life at all, to find resources of happiness in foul weather as well as fair, and to rejoice in the leafless as well as in the shady forest. And this we do with all our hearts; finding perhaps nearly as much contentment by the Christmas fire as in the summer sunshine, and gaining health and strength on the ice-fields of winter, as well as among the meadows of spring. So that there is nothing adverse or painful to our feelings in the cramped and stiffened structure of vegetation checked by cold; and instead of seeking, like the Southern sculpture, to express only the softness of leafage nourished in all tenderness, and tempted into all luxuriance by warm winds and glowing rays, we find pleasure in dwelling upon the crabbed, perverse, and morose animation of plants that have known little kindness from earth or heaven, but, season after season, have had their best efforts palsied by frost, their brightest buds buried under snow, and their goodliest limbs lopped by tempest.

There are many subtle sympathies and affections which join to confirm the Gothic mind in this peculiar choice of subject; and when we add to the influence of these, the necessities consequent upon the employment of a rougher material, compelling the workman to seek for vigour of effect, rather than refinement of texture or accuracy of form, we have direct and manifest causes for much of the difference between the Northern and Southern cast of conception: but there are indirect causes holding a far more important place in the Gothic heart, though less immediate in their influence on design. Strength of will, independence of character, resolute-ness of purpose, impatience of undue control, and that general tendency to set the individual reason against authority, and the individual deed against destiny, which, in the Northern tribes, has opposed itself throughout all ages, to the languid submission, in the Southern, of thought to tradition, and purpose to fatality, are all more or less traceable in the rigid lines, vigorous and various masses, and daringly projecting and independent structure of the Northern Gothic ornament: while the opposite feelings are in like manner legible in the graceful and softly guided waves and wreathed bands, in which Southern decoration is constantly disposed; in its tendency to lose its independence, and fuse itself into the surface of the masses upon which it is traced; and in the expression seen so often, in the arrangement of those masses themselves, of an abandonment of their strength to an inevitable necessity, or a listless repose.

There is virtue in the measure, and error in the excess, of both these characters of mind, and in both of the styles which they have created; the best architecture, and the best temper, are those which unite them both; and this fifth impulse of the Gothic heart is therefore that which needs most caution in its indulgence. It is more definitely Gothic than any other, but the best Gothic building is not that which is *most* Gothic: it can hardly be too frank in its confession of rudeness, hardly too rich in its changefulness, hardly too faithful in its naturalism; but it may go too far in its rigidity, and, like the great Puritan spirit in its extreme, lose itself either in frivolity of division, or perversity of purpose. It actually did so in its later times; but it is gladdening to remember that in its utmost nobleness, the very temper which has been thought most adverse to it, the Protestant spirit of self-dependence and inquiry, was expressed in its every line.[39] Faith and aspiration there were, in every Christian ecclesiastical building, from the first century to the fifteenth; but the moral habits to which England in this age owes the kind of greatness that she has, – the habits of philosophical investigation, of accurate thought, of domestic seclusion and independence, of stern self-reliance and sincere upright searching into religious truth, – were only traceable in the features which were the distinctive creation of the

Gothic schools, in the veined foliage, and thorny fretwork, and shadowy niche, and buttressed pier, and fearless height of subtle pinnacle and crested tower, sent like an 'unperplexed question up to Heaven.'[40]

Last, because the least essential, of the constituent elements of this noble school, was placed that of REDUNDANCE, – the uncalculating bestowal of the wealth of its labour. There is, indeed, much Gothic, and that of the best period, in which this element is hardly traceable, and which depends for its effect almost exclusively on loveliness of simple design and grace of uninvolved proportion; still, in the most characteristic buildings, a certain portion of their effect depends upon accumulation of ornament; and many of those which have most influence on the minds of men, have attained it by means of this attribute alone. And although, by careful study of the school, it is possible to arrive at a condition of taste which shall be better contented by a few perfect lines than by a whole façade covered with fretwork, the building which only satisfies such a taste is not to be considered the best. For the very first requirement of Gothic architecture being, as we saw above, that it shall both admit the aid, and appeal to the admiration, of the rudest as well as the most refined minds, the richness of the work is, paradoxical as the statement may appear, a part of its humility. No architecture is so haughty as that which is simple; which refuses to address the eye, except in a few clear and forceful lines; which implies, in offering so little to our regards, that all it has offered is perfect; and disdains, either by the complexity or the attractiveness of its features, to embarrass our investigation, or betray us into delight. That humility, which is the very life of the Gothic school, is shown not only in the imperfection, but in the accumulation, of ornament. The inferior rank of the workman is often shown as much in the richness, as the roughness, of his work; and if the co-operation of every hand, and the sympathy of every heart, are to be received, we must be content to allow the redundance which disguises the failure of the feeble, and wins the regard of the inattentive. There are, however, far nobler interests mingling, in the Gothic heart, with the rude love of decorative accumulation: a magnificent enthusiasm, which feels as if it never could do enough to reach the fulness of its ideal; an unselfishness of sacrifice, which would rather cast fruitless labour before the altar than stand idle in the market[41]; and, finally, a profound sympathy with the fulness and wealth of the material universe, rising out of that Naturalism whose operation we have already endeavoured to define. The sculptor who sought for his models among the forest leaves, could not but quickly and deeply feel that complexity need not involve the loss of grace, nor richness that of repose; and every hour which he spent in the study of the minute and various work of Nature, made him feel more forcibly the barrenness of what was best in that of man: nor is it to be wondered at, that, seeing her perfect and exquisite creations poured forth in a profusion which conception could not grasp nor calculation sum, he should think that it ill became him to be niggardly of his own rude craftsmanship; and where he saw throughout the universe a faultless beauty lavished on measureless spaces of broidered field and blooming mountain, to grudge his poor and imperfect labour to the few stones that he had raised one upon another, for habitation or memorial. The years of his life passed away before his task was accomplished; but generation succeeded generation with unwearied enthusiasm, and the cathedral front was at last lost in the tapestry of its traceries, like a rock among the thickets and herbage of spring.

We have now, I believe, obtained a view approaching to completeness of the various moral or imaginative elements which composed the inner spirit of Gothic architecture [. . .][42]

from

The Two Paths

LECTURES ON ART

and its application to
Decoration and Manufacture

Published 1859

COMMENTARY

The Two Paths was published in 1859. It brings together five of Ruskin's lectures on applied art, all of which were composed in response to government policy on manufacture and design. In 1835, a House of Commons Select Committee had recognized that the expansion of manufacturing industry was creating problems of taste which modern artisans were ill-equipped to meet. The committee recommended the creation of a Government School of Design, but the brief given the first such school proved too limited. After a number of false starts, a Department of Science and Art was set up (in 1853) and made responsible for what are now called Colleges of Art and Technology. These were established in industrial centres all over the country. Ruskin approved in principle of governmental involvement in art education but was critical of the specific policies adopted. He argued that design could not be taught by rule and for strictly limited purposes. He also considered it wrong that the schools were to be confined to artisans and that the design taught was to be seen only in relation to manufacturing industry. What was needed was a programme to educate public taste; the role of the consumer in improving design was quite as important as that of the craftsman. If design was taught only in relation to manufacture, the result would be what Ruskin most despised, the conventionalization of natural forms. He advocated instead the teaching of *drawing*, since drawing compels the student to study nature, and it is in nature that our sense of form and beauty has its origin. These concerns inform every lecture in *The Two Paths*, the title of which refers to the two approaches to design that Ruskin contrasts – conventionalism and truth to nature.

'The Work of Iron, in Nature, Art, and Policy' is less concerned than the other lectures in *The Two Paths* with the specific issue of design. Its main interest lies in the way Ruskin's concern with naturalism brings him to the threshold of *Unto this Last*. The critic Nick Shrimpton has argued that this lecture, more than any other work of Ruskin's, marks the transition from art criticism to social criticism in his writing. It was delivered in Tunbridge Wells in 1858. It begins as a meditation on the health-giving mineral springs for which the town is famous and focuses at the outset on two of Ruskin's earliest preoccupations – colour and geology: in this case, the 'saffron stain' on the well-rims – rust – which is caused by the interaction of iron in the soil and oxygen in water. Throughout nature, he argues, iron is a source of colour. Without it, the world would be like a desert – which he then evokes, in terms which obliquely call to mind the desolating encroachments on nature of modern manufacturing industry. Shrimpton is surely right to suggest that for the symbolic force of these apocalyptic landscapes Ruskin is indebted to the later novels of Dickens, in particular to the descriptive passages in *Dombey and Son* and *Bleak House*. This Dickensian suggestiveness finds in Ruskin a habit of mind schooled in medieval typology. Along the lines of his medieval discipline, he takes the union of iron and air as a type of the union of body and soul. This leads him on to such apparently diverse themes as truth to material in art, the Victorian fashion for railings, the Crimean War and his first major attack on the selfishness of the capitalist system. In this way it anticipates the works of Ruskin's later life – books like *Fors Clavigera* – which become compendia of all his preoccupations.

THE WORK OF IRON,
IN NATURE, ART, AND POLICY

A Lecture delivered at Tunbridge Wells,
February 16th, 1858

WHEN first I heard that you wished me to address you this evening, it was a matter of some doubt with me whether I could find any subject that would possess any sufficient interest for you to justify my bringing you out of your comfortable houses on a winter's night. When I venture to speak about my own special business of art, it is almost always before students of art, among whom I may sometimes permit myself to be dull, if I can feel that I am useful: but a mere talk about art, especially without examples to refer to (and I have been unable to prepare any careful illustrations for this lecture), is seldom of much interest to a general audience. As I was considering what you might best bear with me in speaking about, there came naturally into my mind a subject connected with the origin and present prosperity of the town you live in; and, it seemed to me, in the outbranchings of it, capable of a very general interest. When, long ago (I am afraid to think how long), Tunbridge Wells was my Switzerland, and I used to be brought down here in the summer, a sufficiently active child, rejoicing in the hope of clambering sandstone cliffs of stupendous height above the common, there used sometimes, as, I suppose, there are in the lives of all children at the Wells, to be dark days in my life – days of condemnation to the pantiles and band – under which calamities my only consolation used to be in watching, at every turn in my walk, the welling forth of the spring over the orange rim of its marble basin. The memory of the clear water, sparkling over its saffron stain, came back to me as the strongest image connected with the place; and it struck me that you might not be unwilling, to-night, to think a little over the full significance of that saffron stain, and of the power, in other ways and other functions, of the steely element to which so many here owe returning strength and life; – chief as it has been always, and is yet more and more markedly so day by day, among the precious gifts of the earth.

The subject is, of course, too wide to be more than suggestively treated; and even my suggestions must be few, and drawn chiefly from my own fields of work; nevertheless, I think I shall have time to indicate some courses of thought which you may afterwards follow out for yourselves if they interest you; and so I will not shrink from the full scope of the subject which I have announced to you – the functions of Iron, in Nature, Art, and Policy.

Without more preface, I will take up the first head.

I. IRON IN NATURE. – You all probably know that the ochreous stain, which, perhaps, is often thought to spoil the basin of your spring, is iron in a state of rust: and when you see rusty iron in other places you generally think, not only that it spoils the places it stains, but that it is spoiled itself – that rusty iron is spoiled iron.

For most of our uses it generally is so; and because we cannot use a rusty knife or razor so well as a polished one, we suppose it to be a great defect in iron that it is subject to rust. But not at all. On the contrary, the most perfect and useful state of it is that ochreous stain; and therefore it is endowed with so ready a disposition to get itself into that state. It is not a fault in the iron, but a virtue, to be so fond of getting rusted, for in that condition it fulfils its most important functions in the universe, and most kindly duties to mankind. Nay, in a certain sense, and almost a literal one, we may say that iron rusted is Living; but when pure or polished, Dead. You all probably know that in the mixed air we breathe, the part of it essentially needful to us is called oxygen; and that this substance is to all animals, in the most accurate sense of the word, 'breath of life.'[1] The nervous power of life is a different thing; but the supporting element of the breath, without which the blood, and therefore the life, cannot be nourished, is this oxygen. Now it is this very same air which the iron breathes when it gets rusty. It takes the oxygen from the atmosphere as eagerly as we do, though it uses it differently. The iron keeps all that it gets; we, and other animals, part with it again; but the metal absolutely keeps what it has once received of this aërial gift; and the ochreous dust which we so much despise is, in fact, just so much nobler than pure iron, in so far as it is *iron and the air*. Nobler, and more useful – for, indeed, as I shall be able to show you presently – the main service of this metal, and of all other metals, to us, is not in making knives, and scissors, and pokers, and pans, but in making the ground we feed from, and nearly all the substances first needful to our existence. For these are all nothing but metals and oxygen – metals with breath put into them. Sand, lime, clay, and the rest of the earths – potash and soda, and the rest of the alkalies – are all of them metals which have undergone this, so to speak, vital change, and have been rendered fit for the service of man by permanent unity with the purest air which he himself breathes. There is only one metal which does not rust readily; and that in its influence on Man hitherto, has caused Death rather than Life; it will not be put to its right use till it is made a pavement of, and so trodden under foot.[2]

Is there not something striking in this fact, considered largely as one of the types, or lessons, furnished by the inanimate creation? Here you have your hard, bright, cold, lifeless metal – good enough for swords and scissors – but not for food. You think, perhaps, that your iron is wonderfully useful in a pure form, but how would you like the world, if all your meadows, instead of grass, grew nothing but iron wire – if all your arable ground, instead of being made of sand and clay, were suddenly turned into flat surfaces of steel – if the whole earth, instead of its green and glowing sphere, rich with forest and flower, showed nothing but the image of the vast furnace of a ghastly engine – a globe of black, lifeless, excoriated metal?[3] It would be that, – probably it was once that; but assuredly it would be, were it not that all the substance of which it is made sucks and breathes the brilliancy of the atmosphere; and, as it breathes, softening from its merciless hardness, it falls into fruitful and beneficent dust; gathering itself again into the earths from which we feed, and the stones with which we build; – into the rocks that frame the mountains, and the sands that bind the sea.

Hence, it is impossible for you to take up the most insignificant pebble at your feet, without being able to read, if you like, this curious lesson in it. You look upon it at first as if it were earth only. Nay, it answers, 'I am not earth – I am earth and air in one; part of that blue heaven which you love, and long for, is already in me; it is all my life – without it I should be nothing, and able for nothing; I could not minister to you, nor nourish you – I should be a cruel and helpless thing; but, because there is, according to my need and place in creation, a kind of soul in me, I have become capable of good, and helpful in the circles of vitality.'[4]

Thus far the same interest attaches to all the earths, and all the metals of which they are made; but a deeper interest and larger beneficence belong to that ochreous earth of iron which stains the marble of your springs. It stains much besides that marble. It stains the great earth wheresoever you can see it, far and wide – it is the colouring substance appointed to colour the globe for the sight, as well as subdue it to the service of man. You have just seen your hills covered with snow, and, perhaps, have enjoyed, at first, the contrast of their fair white with the dark blocks of pine woods; but have you ever considered how you would like them always white – not pure white, but dirty white – the white of thaw, with all the chill of snow in it, but none of its brightness? That is what the colour of the earth would be without its iron; that would be its colour, not here or there only, but in all places, and at all times. Follow out that idea till you get it in some detail. Think first of your pretty gravel walks in your gardens, and fine, like plots of sunshine between the yellow flower-beds; fancy them all suddenly turned to the colour of ashes. That is what they would be without iron ochre. Think of your winding walks over the common, as warm to the eye as they are dry to the foot, and imagine them all laid down suddenly with gray cinders. Then pass beyond the common into the country, and pause at the first ploughed field that you see sweeping up the hill sides in the sun, with its deep brown furrows, and wealth of ridges all a-glow, heaved aside by the ploughshare, like deep folds of a mantle of russet velvet – fancy it all changed suddenly into grisly furrows in a field of mud. That is what it would be without iron. Pass on, in fancy, over hill and dale, till you reach the bending line of the sea shore; go down upon its breezy beach – watch the white foam flashing among the amber of it, and all the blue sea embayed in belts of gold: then fancy those circlets of far sweeping shore suddenly put into mounds of mourning – all those golden sands turned into gray slime; the fairies no more able to call to each other, 'Come unto these yellow sands;'[5] but, 'Come unto these drab sands.' That is what they would be, without iron.

Iron is in some sort, therefore, the sunshine and light of landscape, so far as that light depends on the ground; but it is a source of another kind of sunshine, quite as important to us in the way we live at present – sunshine, not of landscape, but of dwelling-place.

In these days of swift locomotion I may doubtless assume that most of my audience have been somewhere out of England – have been in Scotland, or France, or Switzerland. Whatever may have been their impression, on returning to their own country, of its superiority or inferiority in other respects, they cannot but have felt one thing about it – the comfortable look of its towns and villages. Foreign towns are often very picturesque, very beautiful, but they never have quite that look of warm self-sufficiency and wholesome quiet with which our villages nestle themselves down among the green fields.[6] If you will take the trouble to examine into the sources of this impression, you will find that by far the greater part of that warm and satisfactory appearance depends upon the rich scarlet colour of the bricks and tiles. It does not belong to the neat building – very neat building has an uncomfortable rather than a comfortable look – but it depends on the *warm* building; our villages are dressed in red tiles as our old women are in red cloaks; and it does not matter how warm the cloaks, or how bent and bowed the roof may be, so long as there are no holes in either one or the other, and the sobered but unextinguishable colour still glows in the shadow of the hood, and burns among the green mosses of the gable. And what do you suppose dyes your tiles of cottage roof? You don't paint them. It is Nature who puts all that lovely vermilion into the clay for you; and all that lovely vermilion is this oxide of iron. Think, therefore, what your streets of towns would become – ugly enough, indeed, already, some of them, but still comfortable-looking – if instead of that warm brick red, the houses became all pepper-and-salt colour. Fancy your country villages changing from that homely scarlet of theirs which, in its sweet suggestion of laborious peace, is as honourable as the soldier's scarlet of laborious battle – suppose all those cottage roofs, I say, turned at once into the colour of unbaked clay, the colour of street gutters in rainy weather. That's what they would be without iron.

There is, however, yet another effect of colour in our English country towns, which, perhaps, you may not all yourselves have noticed, but for which you must take the word of a sketcher. They are not so often merely warm scarlet as they are warm purple; – a more beautiful colour still: and they owe this colour to a mingling with the vermilion of the deep grayish or purple hue of our fine Welsh slates on the more respectable roofs, made more blue still by the colour of intervening atmosphere. If you examine one of these Welsh slates freshly broken, you will find its purple colour clear and vivid; and although never strikingly so after it has been long exposed to weather, it always retains enough of the tint to give rich harmonies of distant purple in opposition to the green of our woods and fields. Whatever brightness or power there is in the hue is entirely owing to the oxide of iron. Without it the slates would either be pale stone colour, or cold gray, or black.

Thus far we have only been considering the use and pleasantness of iron in the common earth of clay. But there are three kinds of earth which, in mixed mass and prevalent quantity, form the world. Those are, in common language, the earths of clay, of lime, and of flint. Many other elements are mingled with these in sparing quantities; but the great frame and substance of the earth is made of these three, so that wherever you stand on solid ground, in any country of the globe, the thing that is mainly under your feet will be either clay, limestone, or some condition of the earth of flint, mingled with both.

These being what we have usually to deal with, Nature seems to have set herself to make these three substances as interesting to us, and as beautiful for us, as she can. The clay, being a soft and changeable substance, she doesn't take much pains about, as we have seen, till it is baked; she brings the colour into it only when it receives a permanent form. But the limestone and flint she paints, in her own way, in their native state: and her object in painting them seems to be much the same as in her painting of flowers; to draw us, careless and idle human creatures, to watch her a little, and see what she is about – that being on the whole good for us, – her children. For Nature is always carrying on very strange work with this limestone and flint of hers: laying down beds of them at the bottom of the sea; building islands out of the sea; filling chinks and veins in mountains with curious treasures; petrifying mosses, and trees, and shells; in fact, carrying on all sorts of business, subterranean or submarine, which it would be highly desirable for us, who profit and live by it, to notice as it goes on. And apparently to lead us to do this, she makes picture-books for us of limestone and flint; and tempts us, like foolish children as we are, to read her books by the pretty colours in them. The pretty colours in her limestone-books form those variegated marbles which all mankind have taken delight to polish and build with from the beginning of time; and the pretty colours in her flint-books form those agates, jaspers, cornelians, bloodstones, onyxes, cairngorms, chrysoprases, which men have in like manner taken delight to cut, and polish, and make ornaments of, from the beginning of time; and yet so much of babies are they, and so fond of looking at the pictures instead of reading the book, that I question whether, after six thousand years of cutting and polishing, there are above two or three people out of any given hundred who know, or care to know, how a bit of agate or a bit of marble was made, or painted.[7]

How it was made, may not be always very easy to say; but with what it was painted there is no manner of question. All those beautiful violet veinings and variegations of the marbles of Sicily and Spain, the glowing orange and amber colours of those of Siena, the deep russet of the Rosso antico, and the blood-colour of all the precious jaspers that enrich the temples of Italy; and, finally, all the lovely transitions of tint in the pebbles of Scotland and the Rhine, which form, though not the most precious, by far the most interesting portion of our modern jewellers' work; – all these are painted by Nature with this one material only, variously proportioned and applied – the oxide of iron that stains your Tunbridge springs.

But this is not all, nor the best part of the work of iron. Its service in producing these beautiful stones is only rendered to rich people, who can afford to quarry and polish them. But Nature paints for all the world, poor and rich together[8]; and while, therefore, she thus adorns the innermost rocks of her hills, to tempt your investigation, or indulge your luxury, – she paints, far more carefully, the outsides of the hills, which are for the eyes of the shepherd and the ploughman. I spoke just now of the effect in the roofs of our villages of their purple slates; but if the slates are beautiful even in their flat and formal rows on house-roofs, much more are they beautiful on the rugged crests and flanks of their native mountains. Have you ever considered, in speaking as we do so often of distant blue hills, what it is that makes them blue? To a certain extent it is distance; but distance alone will not do it. Many hills look white, however distant. That lovely dark purple colour of our Welsh and Highland hills is owing, not to their distance merely, but to their rocks. Some of their rocks are, indeed, too dark to be beautiful, being black or ashy gray; owing to imperfect and porous structure. But when you see this dark colour dashed with russet and blue, and coming out in masses among the green ferns, so purple that you can hardly tell at first whether it is rock or heather, then you must thank your old Tunbridge friend, the oxide of iron.

But this is not all. It is necessary for the beauty of hill scenery that Nature should colour not only her soft rocks, but her hard ones; and she colours them with the same thing, only more beautifully. Perhaps you have wondered at my use of the word 'purple,' so often of stones; but the Greeks, and still more the Romans, who had profound respect for purple,[9] used it of stone long ago. You have all heard of 'porphyry' as among the most precious of the harder massive stones. The colour which gave it that noble name, as well as that which gives the flush to all the rosy granite of Egypt – yes, and to the rosiest summits of the Alps themselves – is still owing to the same substance – your humble oxide of iron.

And last of all:

A nobler colour than all these – the noblest colour ever seen on this earth[10] – one which belongs to a strength greater than that of the Egyptian granite, and to a beauty greater than that of the sunset or the rose – is still mysteriously connected with the presence of this dark iron. I believe it is not ascertained on what the crimson of blood actually depends; but the colour is connected, of course, with its vitality, and that vitality with the existence of iron as one of its substantial elements.

Is it not strange to find this stern and strong metal mingled so delicately in our human life that we cannot even blush without its help? Think of it, my fair and gentle hearers; how terrible the alternative – sometimes you have actually no choice but to be brazen-faced, or iron-faced!

In this slight review of some of the functions of the metal, you observe that I confine myself strictly to its operations as a colouring element. I should only confuse your conception of the facts if I endeavoured to describe its uses as a substantial element, either in strengthening rocks or influencing vegetation by the decomposition of rocks. I have not, therefore, even glanced at any of the more serious uses of the metal in the economy of nature. But what I wish you to carry clearly away with you is the remembrance that in all these uses the metal would be nothing without the air. The pure metal has no power, and never occurs in nature at all, except in meteoric stones, whose fall no one can account for, and which are useless after they have fallen: in the necessary work of the world, the iron is invariably joined with the oxygen, and would be capable of no service or beauty whatever without it.

II. IRON IN ART. – Passing, then, from the offices of the metal in the operations of nature to its uses in the hands of man, you must remember, in the outset, that the type which has been thus given you, by the lifeless metal, of the action of body and soul together, has noble antitype[11] in the operation of all human power. All art worthy the name is the energy – neither of the human body alone, nor of the human soul alone, but of both united, one guiding the other: good craftsmanship and work of the fingers joined with good emotion and work of the heart.

There is no good art, nor possible judgment of art, when these two are not united; yet we are constantly trying to separate them. Our amateurs cannot be persuaded but that they may produce some kind of art by their fancy or sensibility, without going through the necessary manual toil. That is entirely hopeless. Without a certain number, and that a very great number, of steady acts of hand – a practice as careful and constant as would be necessary to learn any other manual business – no drawing is possible. On the other side, the workman, and those who employ him, are continually trying to produce art by trick or habit of fingers, without using their fancy or sensibility.[12] That also is hopeless. Without mingling of heart-passion with hand-power, no art is possible.[13] The highest art unites both in their intensest degrees: the action of the hand at its finest, with that of the heart at its fullest.

Hence it follows that the utmost power of art can only be given in a material capable of receiving and retaining the influence of the subtlest touch of the human hand. That hand is the most perfect agent of material power existing in the universe; and its full subtlety can only be shown when the material it works on, or with, is entirely yielding. The chords of a perfect instrument will receive it, but not of an imperfect one; the softly-bending point of the hair pencil, and soft melting of colour, will receive it, but not even the chalk or pen point, still less the steel point, chisel, or marble. The hand of a sculptor may, indeed, be as subtle as that of a painter, but all its subtlety is not bestowable nor expressible: the touch of Titian, Correggio, or Turner is a far more marvellous piece of nervous action than can be shown in anything but colour, or in the very highest conditions of executive expression in music. In proportion as the material worked upon is less delicate, the execution necessarily becomes lower, and the art with it. This is one main principle of all work. Another is, that whatever the material you choose to work with, your art is base if it does not bring out the distinctive qualities of that material.[14]

The reason of this second law is, that if you don't want the qualities of the substance you use, you ought to use some other substance: it can be only affectation, and desire to display your skill, that lead you to employ a refractory substance, and therefore your art will all be base. Glass, for instance, is eminently, in its nature, transparent. If you don't want transparency, let the glass alone. Do not try to make a window look like an opaque picture,[15] but take an opaque ground to begin with. Again, marble is eminently a solid and massive substance. Unless you want mass and solidity, don't work in marble. If you wish for lightness, take wood; if for freedom, take stucco; if for ductility, take glass. Don't try to carve feathers, or trees, or nets, or foam, out of marble. Carve white limbs and broad breasts only out of that.

So again, iron is eminently a ductile and tenacious substance – tenacious above all things, ductile more than most. When you want tenacity, therefore, and involved form, take iron. It is eminently made for that. It is the material given to the sculptor as the companion of marble, with a message, as plain as it can well be spoken, from the lips of the earth-mother, 'Here's for you to cut, and here's for you to hammer. Shape this, and twist that. What is solid and simple, carve out; what is thin and entangled, beat out. I give you all kinds of forms to be delighted in; fluttering leaves as well as fair bodies; twisted branches as well as open brows. The leaf and the branch you may beat and drag into their imagery: the body and brow you shall reverently touch into their imagery. And if you choose rightly and work rightly, what you do shall be safe afterwards. Your slender leaves shall not break off in my tenacious iron, though they may be rusted a little with an iron autumn. Your broad surfaces shall not be unsmoothed in my pure crystalline marble – no decay shall touch them. But if you carve in the marble what will break with a touch, or mould in the metal what a stain of rust or verdigris will spoil, it is your fault – not mine.'

These are the main principles in this matter; which, like nearly all other right principles in art, we moderns delight in contradicting as directly and specially as may be. We continually look for, and praise, in our exhibitions, the sculpture of veils, and lace, and thin leaves, and all kinds of impossible things pushed as far as possible in the fragile stone, for the sake of showing

the sculptor's dexterity.* On the other hand, we *cast* our iron into bars –
brittle, though an inch thick – sharpen them at the ends, and consider
fences, and other work, made of such materials, decorative! I do not believe
it would be easy to calculate the amount of mischief done to our taste in
England by that fence ironwork of ours alone. If it were asked of us, by a
single characteristic, to distinguish the dwellings of a country into two
broad sections; and to set, on one side, the places where people were, for the
most part, simple, happy, benevolent, and honest; and, on the other side,
the places where at least a great number of the people were sophisticated,
unkind, uncomfortable, and unprincipled, there is, I think, one feature that
you could fix upon as a positive test: the uncomfortable and unprincipled
parts of a country would be the parts where people lived among iron
railings, and the comfortable and principled parts where they had none. A
broad generalization, you will say! Perhaps a little too broad; yet, in all
sobriety, it will come truer than you think. Consider every other kind of
fence or defence, and you will find some virtue in it; but in the iron railing,
none. There is, first, your castle rampart of stone – somewhat too grand to
be considered here among our types of fencing; next, your garden or park
wall of brick, which has indeed often an unkind look on the outside, but
there is more modesty in it than unkindness. It generally means, not that
the builder of it wants to shut you out from the view of his garden, but from
the view of himself: it is a frank statement that as he needs a certain portion
of time to himself, so he needs a certain portion of ground to himself, and
must not be stared at when he digs there in his shirt-sleeves, or plays at
leapfrogs with his boys from school, or talks over old times with his wife,
walking up and down in the evening sunshine. Besides, the brick wall has
good practical service in it, and shelters you from the east wind, and ripens
your peaches and nectarines, and glows in autumn like a sunny bank. And,
moreover, your brick wall, if you build it properly, so that it shall stand long
enough, is a beautiful thing when it is old, and has assumed its grave purple
red, touched with mossy green.

---

* I do not mean to attach any degree of blame to the effort to represent leafage in
marble for certain expressive purposes. The later works of Mr Munro[16] have
depended for some of their most tender thoughts on a delicate and skilful use of such
accessories. And in general, leaf sculpture is good and admirable, if it renders, as in
Gothic work, the grace and lightness of the leaf by the arrangement of light and
shadow – supporting the masses well by strength of stone below; but all carving is
base which proposes to itself *slightness* as an aim, and tries to imitate the absolute
thinness of thin or slight things, as much modern wood-carving does. I saw in Italy, a
year or two ago, a marble sculpture of birds' nests.

Next to your lordly wall, in dignity of enclosure, comes your close-set wooden paling, which is more objectionable, because it commonly means enclosure on a larger scale than people want. Still it is significative of pleasant parks, and well-kept field walks, and herds of deer, and other such aristocratic pastoralisms, which have here and there their proper place in a country, and may be passed without any discredit.

Next to your paling comes your low stone dyke, your mountain fence, indicative at a glance either of wild hill country, or of beds of stone beneath the soil; the hedge of the mountains – delightful in all its associations, and yet more in the varied and craggy forms of the loose stones it is built of: and next to the low stone wall, your lowland hedge, either in trim line of massive green, suggestive of the pleasances[17] of old Elizabethan houses, and smooth alleys for aged feet, and quaint labyrinths for young ones, or else in fair entanglement of eglantine and virgin's bower, tossing its scented luxuriance along our country waysides: – how many such you have here among your pretty hills, fruitful with black clusters of the bramble for boys in autumn, and crimson hawthorn-berries for birds in winter. And then last, and most difficult to class among fences, comes your hand-rail, expressive of all sorts of things; sometimes having a knowing and vicious look, which it learns at race-courses; sometimes an innocent and tender look, which it learns at rustic bridges over cressy brooks; and sometimes a prudent and protective look, which it learns on passes of the Alps, where it has posts of granite and bars of pine, and guards the brows of cliffs and the banks of torrents. So that in all these kinds of defence there is some good, pleasant, or noble meaning. But what meaning has the iron railing? Either, observe, that you are living in the midst of such bad characters that you must keep them out by main force of bar, or that you are yourself of a character requiring to be kept inside in the same manner. Your iron railing always means thieves outside, or Bedlam inside; – it *can* mean nothing else than that. If the people outside were good for anything, a hint in the way of fence would be enough for them; but because they are violent and at enmity with you, you are forced to put the close bars and the spikes at the top. Last summer I was lodging for a little while in a cottage in the country, and in front of my low window there were, first, some beds of daisies, then a row of gooseberry and currant bushes, and then a low wall about three feet above the ground, covered with stone-cress; outside, a cornfield, with its green ears glistening in the sun, and a field path through it, just past the garden gate. From my window I could see every peasant of the village who passed that way, with basket on arm for market, or spade on shoulder for field. When I was inclined for society, I could lean over my wall, and talk to anybody; when I was inclined for science, I could botanize all along the top of my wall – there were four species of stone-cress alone growing on it; and when I was inclined for exercise, I could jump over my wall, backwards and forwards. That's the sort of fence to have in a Christian country; not a thing which you can't walk inside of without making yourself look like a wild beast, nor look at out of your window in the morning without expecting to see somebody impaled upon it in the night.

And yet farther, observe that the iron railing is a useless fence – it can shelter nothing, and support nothing; you can't nail your peaches to it, nor protect your flowers with it, nor make anything whatever out of its costly tyranny; and besides being useless, it is an insolent fence; – it says plainly to everybody who passes – 'You may be an honest person, – but, also, you may be a thief: honest or not, you shall not get in here, for I am a respectable person and much above you; you shall only see what a grand place I have got to keep you out of – look here, and depart in humiliation.'

This, however, being in the present state of civilization a frequent manner of discourse, and there being unfortunately many districts where the iron railing is unavoidable, it yet remains a question whether you need absolutely make it ugly, no less than significative of evil. You must have railings round your squares in London, and at the sides of your areas; but need you therefore have railings so ugly that the constant sight of them is enough to neutralise the effect of all the schools of art in the kingdom? You need not. Far from such necessity, it is even in your power to turn all your police force of iron bars actually into drawing masters, and natural historians. Not, of course, without some trouble and some expense; you can do nothing much worth doing, in this world, without trouble, you can get nothing much worth having, without expense. The main question is only – what is worth doing and having: – Consider, therefore, if this is not. Here is your iron railing, as yet, an uneducated monster; a sombre seneschal,[18] incapable of any words, except his perpetual 'Keep out!' and 'Away with you!' Would it not be worth some trouble and cost to turn this ungainly ruffian porter into a well-educated servant; who, while he was severe as ever in forbidding entrance to evilly disposed people, should yet have a kind word for well-disposed people, and a pleasant look, and a little useful information at his command, in case he should be asked a question by the passers-by?

We have not time to-night to look at many examples of ironwork; and those I happen to have by me are not the best; ironwork is not one of my special subjects of study[19]; so that I only have memoranda of bits that happened to come into picturesque subjects which I was drawing for other reasons. Besides, external ironwork is more difficult to find good than any other sort of ancient art; for when it gets rusty and broken, people are sure, if they can afford it, to send it to the old iron shop, and get a fine new grating instead; and in the great cities of Italy the old iron is thus nearly all gone: the best bits I remember in the open air were at Brescia; – fantastic sprays of laurel-like foliage rising over the garden gates; and there are a few fine fragments at Verona, and some good trellis-work enclosing the Scala tombs[20]; but on the whole, the most interesting pieces, though by no means the purest in style, are to be found in out-of-the-way provincial towns, where people do not care, or are unable, to make polite alterations. The little town of Bellinzona, for instance, on the south of the Alps, and that of Sion on the north, have both of them complete schools of ironwork in their balconies and vineyard gates. That of Bellinzona is the best, though not very old – I suppose most of it of the seventeenth century; still it is very quaint and beautiful. Here, for example, are two balconies,[21] from two different houses: one has been a cardinal's, and the hat is the principal ornament of the balcony, its tassels being wrought with delightful delicacy and freedom; and catching the eye clearly even among the mass of rich wreathed leaves. These tassels and strings are precisely the kind of subject fit for ironwork – noble in ironwork, they would have been entirely ignoble in marble, on the grounds above stated. The real plant of oleander standing in the window enriches the whole group of lines very happily.

The other balcony, from a very ordinary-looking house in the same street, is much more interesting in its details. It appeared last summer with convolvulus twined about the bars, the arrow-shaped living leaves mingled among the leaves of iron [. . .] It is composed of a large tulip in the centre; then two turkscap lilies; then two pinks, a little conventionalized; then two narcissi; then two nondescripts, or, at least, flowers I do not know; and then two dark buds, and a few leaves; I say *dark* buds, for all these flowers have been coloured in their original state. The plan of the group is exceedingly simple: it is all enclosed in a pointed arch, the large mass of the tulip forming the apex; a six-foiled star on each side; then a jagged star; then a five-foiled star; then an unjagged star or rose; finally a small bud, so as to establish relation and cadence through the whole group. The profile is very free and fine, and the upper bar of the balcony exceedingly beautiful in effect; – none the less so on account of the marvellously simple means employed. A thin strip of iron is bent over a square rod; out of the edge of this strip are cut a series of triangular openings – widest at top, leaving projecting teeth of iron; then each of these projecting pieces gets a little sharp tap with the hammer in front, which breaks its edge inwards, tearing it a little open at the same time, and the thing is done.

The common forms of Swiss ironwork are less naturalistic than these Italian balconies, depending more on beautiful arrangements of various curve; nevertheless there has been a rich naturalist school at Fribourg, where a few bell-handles are still left, consisting of rods branched into laurel and other leafage. At Geneva, modern improvements have left nothing; but at Annecy a little good work remains; the balcony of its old hôtel de ville especially, with a trout of the lake – presumably the town arms – forming its central ornament.

I might expatiate all night – if you would sit and hear me – on the treatment of such required subject, or introduction of pleasant caprice by the old workmen; but we have no more time to spare, and I must quit this part of our subject – the rather as I could not explain to you the intrinsic merit of such ironwork without going fully into the theory of curvilinear design; only let me leave with you this one distinct assertion – that the quaint beauty and character of many natural objects, such as intricate branches, grass, foliage (especially thorny branches and prickly foliage), as well as that of many animals, plumed, spined, or bristled, is sculpturally expressible in iron only, and in iron would be majestic and impressive in the highest degree; and that every piece of metal work you use might be, rightly treated, not only a superb decoration, but a most valuable abstract of portions of natural forms, holding in dignity precisely the same relation to the painted representation of plants that a statue does to the painted form of man. It is difficult to give you an idea of the grace and interest which the simplest objects possess when their forms are thus abstracted from among the surrounding of rich circumstance which in nature disturbs the feebleness of our attention. Every cluster of herbage would furnish fifty such groups, and every such group would work into iron (fitting it, of course, rightly to its service) with perfect ease, and endless grandeur of result.

III. IRON IN POLICY. – Having thus obtained some idea of the use of iron in art, as dependent on its ductility, I need not, certainly, say anything of its uses in manufacture and commerce; we all of us know enough – perhaps a little too much – about *them*. So I pass lastly to consider its uses in policy; dependent chiefly upon its tenacity – that is to say, on its power of bearing a pull, and receiving an edge. These powers, which enable it to pierce, to bind, and to smite, render it fit for the three great instruments by which its political action may be simply typified; namely, the Plough, the Fetter, and the Sword.

On our understanding the right use of these three instruments depends, of course, all our power as a nation, and all our happiness as individuals.

(1) THE PLOUGH. – I say, first, on our understanding the right use of the plough, with which, in justice to the fairest of our labourers, we must always associate that feminine plough – the needle. The first requirement for the happiness of a nation is that it should understand the function in this world of these two great instruments: a happy nation may be defined as one in which the husband's hand is on the plough, and the housewife's on the needle; so in due time reaping its golden harvest, and shining in golden vesture: and an unhappy nation is one which, acknowledging no use of plough nor needle, will assuredly at last find its storehouse empty in the famine, and its breast naked to the cold.

Perhaps you think this is a mere truism, which I am wasting your time in repeating. I wish it were.

By far the greater part of the suffering and crime which exist at this moment in civilized Europe, arises simply from people not understanding this truism – not knowing that produce or wealth is eternally connected by the laws of heaven and earth with resolute labour; but hoping in some way to cheat or abrogate this everlasting law of life,[22] and to feed where they have not furrowed, and be warm where they have not woven.

I repeat, nearly all our misery and crime result from this one misapprehension. The law of nature is, that a certain quantity of work is necessary to produce a certain quantity of good, of any kind whatever. If you want knowledge, you must toil for it: if food, you must toil for it: and if pleasure, you must toil for it. But men do not acknowledge this law; or strive to evade it, hoping to get their knowledge, and food, and pleasure for nothing: and in this effort they either fail of getting them, and remain ignorant and miserable, or they obtain them by making other men work for their benefit; and then they are tyrants and robbers. Yes, and worse than robbers. I am not one who in the least doubts or disputes the progress of this century in many things useful to mankind; but it seems to me a very dark sign respecting us that we look with so much indifference upon dishonesty and cruelty in the pursuit of wealth. In the dream of Nebuchadnezzar, it was only the *feet* that were part of iron and part of clay[23]; but many of us are now getting so cruel in our avarice that it seems as if, in us, the *heart* were part of iron, part of clay.

From what I have heard of the inhabitants of this town, I do not doubt but that I may be permitted to do here what I have found it usually thought elsewhere highly improper and absurd to do, namely, trace a few Bible sentences to their practical result.

You cannot but have noticed how often in those parts of the Bible which are likely to be oftenest opened when people look for guidance, comfort, or help in the affairs of daily life, – namely, the Psalms and Proverbs, – mention is made of the guilt attaching to the *Oppression* of the poor. Observe: not the neglect of them, but the *Oppression* of them: the word is as frequent as it is strange. You can hardly open either of those books, but somewhere in their pages you will find a description of the wicked man's attempts against the poor: such as, – 'He doth ravish the poor when he getteth him into his net.'

'He sitteth in the lurking places of the villages; his eyes are privily set against the poor.'

'In his pride he doth persecute the poor, and blesseth the covetous, whom God abhorreth.'

'His mouth is full of deceit and fraud; in the secret places doth he murder the innocent. Have the workers of iniquity no knowledge, who eat up my people as they eat bread? They have drawn out the sword, and bent the bow, to cast down the poor and needy.'

'They are corrupt, and speak wickedly concerning oppression.'

'Pride compasseth them about as a chain, and violence as a garment.'

'Their poison is like the poison of a serpent. Ye weigh the violence of your hands in the earth.'[24]

Yes: 'Ye weigh the violence of your hands:' – weigh these words as well. The last things we ever usually think of weighing are Bible words. We like to dream and dispute over them; but to weigh them, and see what their true contents are – anything but that.[25] Yet, weigh these; for I have purposely taken all these verses, perhaps more striking to you read in this connection than separately in their places, out of the Psalms, because, for all people belonging to the Established Church of this country, these Psalms are appointed lessons, portioned out to them by their clergy to be read once through every month. Presumably, therefore, whatever portions of Scripture we may pass by or forget, these, at all events, must be brought continually to our observance as useful for direction of daily life. Now, do we ever ask ourselves what the real meaning of these passages may be, and who these wicked people are, who are 'murdering the innocent'? You know it is rather singular language, this! – rather strong language, we might, perhaps, call it – hearing it for the first time. Murder! and murder of innocent people! – nay, even a sort of cannibalism. Eating people, – yes, and

God's people, too – eating *My* people as if they were bread! swords drawn, bows bent, poison of serpents mixed! violence of hands weighed, measured, and trafficked with as so much coin! – where is all this going on? Do you suppose it was only going on in the time of David, and that nobody but Jews ever murder the poor? If so, it would surely be wiser not to mutter and mumble for our daily lessons what does not concern us; but if there be any chance that it may concern us, and if this description, in the Psalms, of human guilt is at all generally applicable, as the descriptions in the Psalms of human sorrow are, may it not be advisable to know wherein this guilt is being committed round about us, or by ourselves? and when we take the words of the Bible into our mouths in a congregational way, to be sure whether we mean merely to chant a piece of melodious poetry relating to other people – (we know not exactly to whom) – or to assert our belief in facts bearing somewhat stringently on ourselves and our daily business. And if you make up your minds to do this no longer, and take pains to examine into the matter, you will find that these strange words, occurring as they do, not in a few places only, but almost in every alternate psalm and every alternate chapter of proverb or prophecy, with tremendous reiteration, were not written for one nation or one time only, but for all nations and languages, for all places and all centuries; and it is as true of the wicked man now as ever it was of Nabal or Dives,[26] that 'his eyes are set against the poor.'

Set *against* the poor, mind you. Not merely set *away* from the poor, so as to neglect or lose sight of them, but set against, so as to afflict and destroy them. This is the main point I want to fix your attention upon. You will often hear sermons about neglect or carelessness of the poor. But neglect and carelessness are not at all the points. The Bible hardly ever talks about neglect of the poor. It always talks of *oppression* of the poor – a very different matter. It does not merely speak of passing by on the other side, and binding up no wounds,[27] but of drawing the sword and ourselves smiting the men down. It does not charge us with being idle in the pest-house,[28] and giving no medicine, but with being busy in the pest-house, and giving much poison.

May we not advisedly look into this matter a little, even to-night, and ask first, Who are these poor?

No country is, or ever will be, without them: that is to say, without the class which cannot, on the average, do more by its labour than provide for its subsistence, and which has no accumulations of property laid by on any considerable scale. Now there are a certain number of this class whom we cannot oppress with much severity. An able-bodied and intelligent workman – sober, honest, and industrious, – will almost always command a fair price for his work, and lay by enough in a few years to enable him to hold his own in the labour market. But all men are not able-bodied, nor intelligent, nor industrious; and you cannot expect them to be. Nothing appears to me at once more ludicrous and more melancholy than the way the people of the present age usually talk about the morals of labourers. You hardly ever address a labouring man upon his prospects in life, without quietly assuming that he is to possess, at starting, as a small moral capital to begin with, the virtue of Socrates, the philosophy of Plato, and the heroism of Epaminondas.[29] 'Be assured, my good man,' – you say to him, – 'that if you work steadily for ten hours a day all your life long, and if you drink nothing but water, or the very mildest beer, and live on very plain food, and never lose your temper, and go to church every Sunday, and always remain content in the position in which Providence has placed you, and never grumble, nor swear; and always keep your clothes decent, and rise early, and use every opportunity of improving yourself, you will get on very well, and never come to the parish.'

All this is exceedingly true; but before giving the advice so confidently, it would be well if we sometimes tried it practically ourselves, and spent a year or so at some hard manual labour, not of an entertaining kind – ploughing or digging, for instance, with a very moderate allowance of beer; nothing but bread and cheese for dinner; no papers nor muffins in the morning; no sofas nor magazines at night; one small room for parlour and kitchen; and a large family of children always in the middle of the floor. If we think we could, under these circumstances, enact Socrates, or Epaminondas, entirely to our own satisfaction, we shall be somewhat justified in requiring the same behaviour from our poorer neighbours; but if not, we should surely consider a little whether among the various forms of the oppression of the poor, we may not rank as one of the first and likeliest – the oppression of expecting too much from them.

But let this pass; and let it be admitted that we never can be guilty of oppression towards the sober, industrious, intelligent, exemplary labourer. There will always be in the world some who are not altogether intelligent and exemplary; we shall, I believe, to the end of time find the majority somewhat unintelligent, a little inclined to be idle, and occasionally, on Saturday night, drunk; we must even be prepared to hear of reprobates who like skittles on Sunday morning better than prayers; and of unnatural parents who send their children out to beg instead of to go to school.

Now these are the kind of people whom you *can* oppress, and whom you do oppress, and that to purpose, – and with all the more cruelty and the greater sting, because it is just their own fault that puts them into your power. You know the words about wicked people are, 'He doth ravish the poor when he getteth him *into his net.*' This getting into the net is constantly the fault or folly of the sufferer – his own heedlessness or his own indolence; but after he is once in the net, the oppression of him, and making the most of his distress, are ours. The nets which we use against the poor are just those worldly embarrassments which either their ignorance or their improvidence are almost certain at some time or other to bring them into: then, just at the time when we ought to hasten to help them, and disentangle them, and teach them how to manage better in future, we rush forward to *pillage* them, and force all we can out of them in their adversity. For, to take one instance only, remember this is literally and simply what we do, whenever we buy, or try to buy, cheap goods – goods offered at a price which we know cannot be remunerative for the labour involved in them. Whenever we buy such goods, remember we are stealing somebody's labour.[30] Don't let us mince the matter. I say, in plain Saxon, STEALING – taking from him the proper reward of his work, and putting it into our own pocket. You know well enough that the thing could not have been offered you at that price, unless distress of some kind had forced the producer to part with it. You take advantage of this distress, and you force as much out of him as you can under the circumstances. The old barons of the Middle Ages used, in general, the thumbscrew to extort property; we moderns use, in preference, hunger, or domestic affliction: but the fact of extortion remains precisely the same. Whether we force the man's property from him by pinching his stomach, or pinching his fingers, makes some difference anatomically; – morally, none whatsoever: we use a form of torture of some sort in order to make him give up his property; we use, indeed, the man's own anxieties, instead of the rack; and his immediate peril of starvation, instead of the pistol at the head; but otherwise we differ from Front de Bœuf, or Dick Turpin,[31] merely in being less dexterous, more cowardly, and more cruel. More cruel, I say, because the fierce baron and the redoubted highwayman are reported to have robbed, at least by preference, only the rich; *we* steal habitually from the poor. We buy our liveries, and gild our prayer-books, with pilfered pence out of children's and sick men's wages, and thus ingeniously dispose a given quantity of Theft, so that it may produce the largest possible measure of delicately-distributed suffering.

But this is only one form of common oppression of the poor – only one way of taking our hands off the Plough-handle, and binding another's upon it. The first way of doing it is the economical way – the way preferred by prudent and virtuous people. The bolder way is the acquisitive way: – the way of speculation. You know we are considering at present the various modes in which a nation corrupts itself, by not acknowledging the eternal connection between its plough and its pleasure; – by striving to get pleasure, without working for it. Well, I say the first and commonest way of doing so is to try to get the product of other people's work, and enjoy it ourselves, by cheapening their labour in times of distress; then the second way is that grand one of watching the chances of the market; – the way of speculation. Of course there are some speculations that are fair and honest – speculations made with our own money, and which do not involve in their success the loss, by others, of what we gain. But generally modern speculation involves much risk to others, with chance of profit only to ourselves; even in its best conditions it is merely one of the forms of gambling or treasure-hunting: it is either leaving the steady plough and the steady pilgrimage of life, to look for silver mines beside the way; or else it is the full stop beside the dice-tables in Vanity Fair[32] – investing all the thoughts and passions of the soul in the fall of the cards, and choosing rather the wild accidents of idle fortune than the calm and accumulative rewards of toil. And this is destructive enough, at least to our peace and virtue. But it is usually destructive of far more than *our* peace, or *our* virtue. Have you ever deliberately set yourselves to imagine and measure the suffering, the guilt, and the mortality caused necessarily by the failure of any large-dealing merchant, or largely-branched bank? Take it at the lowest possible supposition – count, at the fewest you choose, the families whose means of support have been involved in the catastrophe. Then, on the morning after the intelligence of ruin, let us go forth amongst them in earnest thought; let us use that imagination which we waste so often on fictitious sorrow, to measure the stern facts of that multitudinous distress; strike open the private doors of their chambers,[33] and enter silently into the midst of the domestic misery; look upon the old men, who had reserved for their failing strength some remainder of rest in the evening-tide of life, cast helplessly back into its trouble and tumult; look upon the active strength of middle age suddenly blasted into incapacity – its hopes crushed, and its hardly-earned rewards snatched away in the same instant – at once the heart withered, and the right arm snapped; look upon the piteous children, delicately nurtured, whose soft eyes, now large with wonder at their parents' grief, must soon be set in the dimness of famine; and, far more than all this, look forward to the length of sorrow beyond – to the hardest labour of life, now to be undergone either in all the severity of unexpected and inexperienced trial, or else, more bitter still, to be begun again, and endured for the second time, amidst the ruins of cherished hopes and the feebleness of advancing years, embittered by the continual sting and taunt of the inner feeling that it has all been brought about, not by the fair course of appointed circumstance, but by miserable chance and wanton treachery; and, last of all, look beyond this – to the shattered destinies of those who have faltered under the trial, and sunk past recovery to despair. And then consider whether the hand which has poured this poison into all the springs of life be one whit less guiltily red with human blood than that which literally pours the hemlock into the cup, or guides the dagger to the heart? We read with horror of the crimes of a Borgia or a Tophana[34]; but there never lived Borgias such as live now in the midst of us. The cruel lady of Ferrara slew only in the strength of passion – she slew only a few, those who thwarted her purposes or who vexed her soul; she slew sharply and suddenly, embittering the fate of her victims with no foretastes of destruction, no prolongations of pain; and, finally and chiefly, she slew not without remorse nor without pity. But we, in no storm of passion, – in no blindness of wrath, – we, in calm and clear and untempted selfishness, pour our poison – not for a few only, but for multitudes; – not for those who have wronged us, or resisted, – but for those who have trusted us and aided; – we, not with sudden gift of merciful and unconscious death, but with slow waste of hunger and weary rack of disappointment and despair! – we, lastly and chiefly, do our murdering, not with any pauses of pity or scorching of conscience, but in facile and forgetful calm of mind – and so, forsooth, read day by day, complacently, as if they meant any one else than ourselves, the words that for ever describe the wicked: 'The *poison of asps* is under their lips, and their *feet are swift to shed blood*.'[35]

You may indeed, perhaps, think there is some excuse for many in this matter, just because the sin is so unconscious; that the guilt is not so great when it is unapprehended, and that it is much more pardonable to slay heedlessly than purposefully. I believe no feeling can be more mistaken; and that in reality, and in the sight of heaven, the callous indifference which pursues its own interests at any cost of life, though it does not definitely adopt the purpose of sin, is a state of mind at once more heinous and more hopeless than the wildest aberrations of ungoverned passion. There may be, in the last case, some elements of good and of redemption still mingled in the character; but, in the other, few or none. There may be hope for the man who has slain his enemy in anger; – hope even for the man who has betrayed his friend in fear; but what hope for him who trades in unregarded blood, and builds his fortune on unrepented treason?

But, however this may be, and wherever you may think yourselves bound in justice to impute the greater sin, be assured that the question is one of responsibilities only, not of facts. The definite result of all our modern haste to be rich is assuredly, and constantly, the murder of a certain number of persons by our hands every year. I have not time to go into the details of another – on the whole, the broadest and terriblest way in which we cause the destruction of the poor – namely, the way of luxury and waste, destroying, in improvidence, what might have been the support of thousands; but if you follow out the subject for yourselves at home – and what I have endeavoured to lay before you to-night will only be useful to you if you do – you will find that wherever and whenever men are endeavouring to *make money hastily*, and to avoid the labour which Providence has appointed to be the only source of honourable profit; – and also wherever and whenever they permit themselves to *spend it luxuriously*, without reflecting how far they are misguiding the labour of others; – there and then, in either case, they are literally and infallibly causing, for their own benefit or their own pleasure, a certain annual number of human deaths; that, therefore, the choice given to every man born into this world is, simply, whether he will be a labourer or an assassin; and that whosoever has not his hand on the Stilt of the plough, has it on the Hilt of the dagger.

It would also be quite vain for me to endeavour to follow out this evening the lines of thought which would be suggested by the other two great political uses of iron in the Fetter and the Sword: a few words only I must permit myself respecting both.

(2) THE FETTER. – As the plough is the typical instrument of industry, so the fetter is the typical instrument of the restraint or subjection necessary in a nation – either literally, for its evildoers, or figuratively, in accepted laws, for its wise and good men. You have to choose between this figurative and literal use; for depend upon it, the more laws you accept, the fewer penalties you will have to endure, and the fewer punishments to enforce. For wise laws and just restraints are to a noble nation not chains, but chain mail – strength and defence, though something also of an incumbrance. And this necessity of restraint, remember, is just as honourable to man as the necessity of labour. You hear every day greater numbers of foolish people speaking about liberty, as if it were such an honourable thing: so far from being that, it is on the whole, and in the broadest sense, dishonourable, and an attribute of the lower creatures. No human being, however great, or powerful, was ever so free as a fish.[36] There is always something that he must, or must not do; while the fish may do whatever he likes. All the kingdoms of the world put together are not half so large as the sea, and all the railroads and wheels that ever were, or will be, invented are not so easy as fins. You will find on fairly thinking of it, that it is his

Restraint which is honourable to man, not his Liberty; and, what is more, it is restraint which is honourable even in the lower animals. A butterfly is much more free than a bee; but you honour the bee more, just because it is subject to certain laws which fit it for orderly function in bee society. And throughout the world, of the two abstract things, liberty and restraint, restraint is always the more honourable. It is true, indeed, that in these and all other matters you never can reason finally from the abstraction, for both liberty and restraint are good when they are nobly chosen, and both are bad when they are basely chosen; but of the two, I repeat, it is restraint which characterizes the higher creature, and betters the lower creature: and, from the ministering of the archangel to the labour of the insect, – from the poising of the planets to the gravitation of a grain of dust, – the power and glory of all creatures, and all matter, consist in their obedience, not in their freedom. The Sun has no liberty – a dead leaf has much. The dust of which you are formed has no liberty. Its liberty will come – with its corruption.

And, therefore, I say boldly, though it seems a strange thing to say in England, that as the first power of a nation consists in knowing how to guide the Plough, its second power consists in knowing how to wear the Fetter: –

(3) THE SWORD. – And its third power, which perfects it as a nation, consists in knowing how to wield the sword, so that the three talismans of national existence are expressed in these three short words – Labour, Law, and Courage.

This last virtue we at least possess; and all that is to be alleged against us is that we do not honour it enough. I do not mean honour by acknowledgment of service, though sometimes we are slow in doing even that. But we do not honour it enough in consistent regard to the lives and souls of our soldiers. How wantonly we have wasted their lives you have seen lately in the reports of their mortality by disease, which a little care and science might have prevented[37]; but we regard their souls less than their lives, by keeping them in ignorance and idleness, and regarding them merely as instruments of battle. The argument brought forward for the maintenance of a standing army usually refers only to expediency in the case of unexpected war, whereas, one of the chief reasons for the maintenance of an army is the advantage of the military system as a method of education. The most fiery and headstrong, who are often also the most gifted and generous of your youths, have always a tendency both in the lower and upper classes to offer themselves for your soldiers: others, weak and unserviceable in the civil capacity, are tempted or entrapped into the army in a fortunate hour for them: out of this fiery or uncouth material, it is only soldier's discipline which can bring the full value and power. Even at present, by mere force of order and authority, the army is the salvation of myriads; and men who, under other circumstances, would have sunk into lethargy or dissipation, are redeemed into noble life by a service which at once summons and directs their energies. How much more than this, military education is capable of doing, you will find only when you make it education indeed. We have no excuse for leaving our private soldiers at their present level of ignorance and want of refinement, for we shall invariably find that, both among officers and men, the gentlest and best informed are the bravest; still less have we excuse for diminishing our army, either in the present state of political events,[38] or, as I believe, in any other conjunction of them that for many a year will be possible in this world.

You may, perhaps, be surprised at my saying this; perhaps surprised at my implying that war itself can be right, or necessary, or noble at all. Nor do I speak of all war as necessary, nor of all war as noble. Both peace and war are noble or ignoble according to their kind and occasion. No man has a profounder sense of the horror and guilt of ignoble war than I have: I have personally seen its effects,[39] upon nations, of unmitigated evil, on soul and body, with perhaps as much pity, and as much bitterness of indignation, as any of those whom you will hear continually declaiming in the cause of peace. But peace may be sought in two ways. One way is as Gideon sought it, when he built his altar in Ophrah, naming it, 'God send peace,' yet sought this peace that he loved, as he was ordered to seek it, and the peace was sent, in God's way: – 'the country was in quietness forty years in the days of Gideon.'[40] And the other way of seeking peace is as Menahem sought it, when he gave the King of Assyria a thousand talents of silver, that 'his hand might be with him.'[41] That is, you may either win your peace, or buy it: – win it, by resistance to evil; – buy it, by compromise with evil. You may buy your peace, with silenced consciences; – you may buy it, with broken vows, – buy it, with lying words, – buy it, with base connivances, – buy it, with the blood of the slain, and the cry of the captive, and the silence of lost souls – over hemispheres of the earth, while you sit smiling at your serene hearths, lisping comfortable prayers evening and morning, and counting your pretty Protestant beads (which are flat, and of gold, instead of round, and of ebony, as the monks' ones were), and so mutter continually to yourselves, 'Peace, peace,' when there is No peace[42]; but only captivity and death, for you, as well as for those you leave unsaved; – and yours darker than theirs.

I cannot utter to you what I would in this matter; we all see too dimly, as yet, what our great world-duties are, to allow any of us to try to outline their enlarging shadows. But think over what I *have* said; and as you return to your quiet homes to-night, reflect that their peace was not won for you by your own hands, but by theirs who long ago jeoparded their lives for you, their children; and remember that neither this inherited peace, nor any other, can be kept, but through the same jeopardy. No peace was ever won from Fate by subterfuge or agreement; no peace is ever in store for any of us, but that which we shall win by victory over shame or sin; – victory over the sin that oppresses, as well as over that which corrupts. For many a year to come, the sword of every righteous nation must be whetted to save or to subdue; nor will it be by patience of others' suffering, but by the offering of your own, that you will ever draw nearer to the time when the great change shall pass upon the iron of the earth; – when men shall beat their swords into ploughshares, and their spears into pruning-hooks; neither shall they learn war any more.[43]

from

Modern Painters

VOLUME V PART IX

Of Invention Spiritual

Published 1860

COMMENTARY

The final volume of *Modern Painters* is elegiac in tone. The brilliant word-painting of Volumes I and II is still in evidence, but the landscapes are mainly overcast, or lit by the tragic splendour of Turner's late sunsets. These sunsets represent the one possible hope for art, as Ruskin sees it, in an unjust social order and a cruel world: the hope that the artist may tell the truth by exposing the facts of the human condition, however painful, to the great light of nature.

'The Two Boyhoods' is concerned with the origins of Turner's art in the scenes of his childhood and youth. It thus exemplifies Ruskin's concern with subject-matter and its transformation at the hands of a great artist. The other boyhood of the title is that of the fifteenth-century Venetian painter, Giorgione. Ruskin sees the Arcadian serenity of Giorgione's art as a product of the ideal society depicted in *The Stones of Venice*. Whether Ruskin ever really believed in the idealized portrait of the Venetian Republic with which the chapter begins, it is impossible to say. In any event, against this imagined world he sets a real one: the London of Turner's boyhood (already the modern city) and the battlefields and seascapes of the Napoleonic Wars. The juxtaposition allows fantasy to criticize reality: evidence that Ruskin had now moved beyond the criticism of art to the criticism of society.

'The Two Boyhoods' occurs in the final Part of *Modern Painters*, 'Of Ideas of Relation – Of Invention Spiritual', which is mainly concerned with the painter's choice of subject and the overall moral effect of his treatment. In it Ruskin returns to the 'great classes' of painter defined in 'The Nature of Gothic' – purist, naturalist and sensualist – and examines the work of five painters to illustrate each class. Thus Salvator Rosa represents sensualism and Fra Angelico purism. Dürer is a naturalist whose work retains 'the marks of the contest' with evil, but the chapter preceding 'The Two Boyhoods' ends with a greater naturalist:

> In Giorgione, you have the same high spiritual power and practical sense [as in Dürer]; but now, with entirely perfect intellect, contending with evil; conquering it utterly, casting it away for ever, and rising beyond it into magnificence of rest.

THE
TWO BOYHOODS

BORN half-way between the mountains and the sea – that young George of Castelfranco – of the Brave Castle: – Stout George they called him, George of Georges, so goodly a boy he was – Giorgione.[1]

Have you ever thought what a world his eyes opened on – fair, searching eyes of youth? What a world of mighty life, from those mountain roots to the shore; – of loveliest life, when he went down, yet so young, to the marble city[2] – and became himself as a fiery heart to it?

A city of marble, did I say? nay, rather a golden city, paved with emerald. For truly, every pinnacle and turret glanced or glowed, overlaid with gold, or bossed with jasper. Beneath, the unsullied sea drew in deep breathing, to and fro, its eddies of green wave. Deep-hearted, majestic, terrible as the sea, – the men of Venice moved in sway of power and war; pure as her pillars of alabaster, stood her mothers and maidens; from foot to brow, all noble, walked her knights; the low bronzed gleaming of sea-rusted armour shot angrily under their blood-red mantle-folds. Fearless, faithful, patient, impenetrable, implacable, – every word a fate – sate her senate. In hope and honour, lulled by flowing of wave around their isles of sacred sand, each with his name written and the cross graved at his side, lay her dead. A wonderful piece of world. Rather, itself a world. It lay along the face of the waters, no larger, as its captains saw it from their masts at evening, than a bar of sunset that could not pass away; but for its power, it must have seemed to them as if they were sailing in the expanse of heaven, and this a great planet, whose orient edge widened through ether. A world from which all ignoble care and petty thoughts were banished, with all the common and poor elements of life. No foulness, nor tumult, in those tremulous streets, that filled, or fell, beneath the moon; but rippled music of majestic change, or thrilling silence. No weak walls could rise above them; no low-roofed cottage, nor straw-built shed. Only the strength as of rock, and the finished setting of stones most precious. And around them, far as the eye could reach, still the soft moving of stainless waters, proudly pure; as not the flower, so neither the thorn nor the thistle, could grow in the glancing fields. Ethereal strength of Alps, dreamlike, vanishing in high procession beyond the Torcellan shore; blue islands of Paduan hills, poised in the golden west. Above, free winds and fiery clouds ranging at their will;

– brightness out of the north, and balm from the south, and the stars of the evening and morning clear in the limitless light of arched heaven and circling sea.

Such was Giorgione's school – such Titian's home.

Near the south-west corner of Covent Garden, a square brick pit or well is formed by a close-set block of houses, to the back windows of which it admits a few rays of light. Access to the bottom of it is obtained out of Maiden Lane, through a low archway and an iron gate; and if you stand long enough under the archway to accustom your eyes to the darkness you may see on the left hand a narrow door, which formerly gave quiet access to a respectable barber's shop,[3] of which the front window, looking into Maiden Lane, is still extant, filled, in this year (1860), with a row of bottles, connected, in some defunct manner, with a brewer's business. A more fashionable neighbourhood, it is said, eighty years ago than now – never certainly a cheerful one – wherein a boy being born on St George's day, 1775, began soon after to take interest in the world of Covent Garden, and put to service such spectacles of life as it afforded.

No knights to be seen there, nor, I imagine, many beautiful ladies; their costume at least disadvantageous, depending much on incumbency of hat and feather, and short waists; the majesty of men founded similarly on shoebuckles and wigs; – impressive enough when Reynolds will do his best for it; but not suggestive of much ideal delight to a boy.

'Bello ovile dov' io dormii agnello';[4] of things beautiful, besides men and women, dusty sunbeams up or down the street on summer mornings; deep furrowed cabbage-leaves at the greengrocer's; magnificence of oranges in wheelbarrows round the corner; and Thames' shore within three minutes' race.

None of these things very glorious; the best, however, that England, it seems, was then able to provide for a boy of gift: who, such as they are, loves them – never, indeed, forgets them. The short waists modify to the last his visions of Greek ideal. His foregrounds had always a succulent cluster or two of greengrocery at the corners. Enchanted oranges gleam in Covent Gardens of the Hesperides; and great ships go to pieces in order to scatter chests of them on the waves.[5] That mist of early sunbeams in the London dawn crosses, many and many a time, the clearness of Italian air; and by Thames' shore, with its stranded barges and glidings of red sail, dearer to us than Lucerne lake or Venetian lagoon, – by Thames' shore we will die.[6]

With such circumstance round him in youth, let us note what necessary effects followed upon the boy. I assume him to have had Giorgione's sensibility (and more than Giorgione's, if that be possible) to colour and form. I tell you farther, and this fact you may receive trustfully, that his sensibility to human affection and distress was no less keen than even his sense for natural beauty – heart-sight deep as eyesight.

Consequently, he attaches himself with the faithfullest child-love to everything that bears an image of the place he was born in. No matter how ugly it is, – has it anything about it like Maiden Lane, or like Thames' shore? If so, it shall be painted for their sake. Hence, to the very close of life, Turner could endure ugliness which no one else, of the same sensibility, would have borne with for an instant. Dead brick walls, blank square windows, old clothes, market-womanly types of humanity – anything fishy and muddy, like Billingsgate or Hungerford Market, had great attraction for him; black barges, patched sails, and every possible condition of fog.

You will find these tolerations and affections guiding or sustaining him to the last hour of his life; the notablest of all such endurances being that of dirt. No Venetian ever draws anything foul; but Turner devoted picture after picture to the illustration of effects of dinginess, smoke, soot, dust, and dusty texture; old sides of boats, weedy roadside vegetation, dung-hills, straw-yards, and all the soilings and stains of every common labour.

And more than this, he not only could endure, but enjoyed and looked for *litter*, like Covent Garden wreck after the market. His pictures are often full of it, from side to side; their foregrounds differ from all others in the natural way that things have of lying about in them. Even his richest vegetation, in ideal work, is confused; and he delights in shingle, débris, and heaps of fallen stones. The last words he ever spoke to me about a picture were in gentle exultation about his St Gothard[7]: 'that *litter* of stones which I endeavoured to represent.'

The second great result of this Covent Garden training was, understanding of and regard for the poor, whom the Venetians, we saw, despised; whom, contrarily, Turner loved, and more than loved – understood. He got no romantic sight of them, but an infallible one, as he prowled about the end of his lane, watching night effects in the wintry streets; nor sight of the poor alone, but of the poor in direct relations with the rich. He knew, in good and evil, what both classes thought of, and how they dealt with, each other.

Reynolds and Gainsborough, bred in country villages, learned there the country boy's reverential theory of 'the squire,' and kept it. They painted the squire and the squire's lady as centres of the movements of the universe, to the end of their lives. But Turner perceived the younger squire in other aspects about his lane, occurring prominently in its night scenery, as a dark figure, or one of two, against the moonlight. He saw also the working of city commerce, from endless warehouse, towering over Thames, to the back shop in the lane, with its stale herrings – highly interesting these last; one of his father's best friends, whom he often afterwards visited affectionately at Bristol, being a fishmonger and glue-boiler; which gives us a friendly turn of mind towards herring-fishing, whaling, Calais poissardes,[8] and many other of our choicest subjects in after-life; all this being connected with that mysterious forest below London Bridge on one side; and, on the other, with these masses of human power and national wealth which weigh upon us, at Covent Garden here, with strange compression, and crush us into narrow Hand Court.

'That mysterious forest below London Bridge' – better for the boy than wood of pine, or grove of myrtle. How he must have tormented the watermen, beseeching them to let him crouch anywhere in the bows, quiet as a log, so only that he might get floated down there among the ships, and round and round the ships, and with the ships, and by the ships, and under the ships, staring, and clambering; – these the only quite beautiful things he can see in all the world, except the sky; but these, when the sun is on their sails, filling or falling, endlessly disordered by sway of tide and stress of anchorage, beautiful unspeakably; which ships also are inhabited by glorious creatures – red-faced sailors, with pipes, appearing over the gunwales, true knights, over their castle parapets – the most angelic beings in the whole compass of London world. And Trafalgar happening long before we can draw ships, we, nevertheless, coax all current stories out of the wounded sailors, do our best at present to show Nelson's funeral streaming up the Thames; and vow that Trafalgar shall have its tribute of memory some day. Which, accordingly, is accomplished – once, with all our might, for its death; twice, with all our might, for its victory; thrice, in pensive farewell to the old *Téméraire*, and with it, to that order of things.[9]

Now this fond companying with sailors must have divided his time, it appears to me, pretty equally between Covent Garden and Wapping (allowing for incidental excursions to Chelsea on one side, and Greenwich on the other), which time he would spend pleasantly, but not magnificently, being limited in pocket-money, and leading a kind of 'Poor Jack' life on the river.

In some respects, no life could be better for a lad. But it was not calculated to make his ear fine to the niceties of language, nor form his moralities on an entirely regular standard. Picking up his first scraps of vigorous English chiefly at Deptford and in the markets, and his first ideas of female tenderness and beauty among nymphs of the barge and the barrow, –

another boy might, perhaps, have become what people usually term 'vulgar.' But the original make and frame of Turner's mind being not vulgar, but as nearly as possible a combination of the minds of Keats and Dante, joining capricious waywardness, and intense openness to every fine pleasure of sense, and hot defiance of formal precedent, with a quite infinite tenderness, generosity, and desire of justice and truth – this kind of mind did not become vulgar, but very tolerant of vulgarity, even fond of it in some forms; and on the outside, visibly infected by it, deeply enough; the curious result, in its combination of elements, being to most people wholly incomprehensible. It was as if a cable had been woven of blood-crimson silk, and then tarred on the outside. People handled it, and the tar came off on their hands; red gleams were seen through the black underneath, at the places where it had been strained. Was it ochre? – said the world – or red lead?

Schooled thus in manners, literature, and general moral principles at Chelsea and Wapping, we have finally to inquire concerning the most important point of all. We have seen the principal differences between this boy and Giorgione, as respects sight of the beautiful, understanding of poverty, of commerce, and of order of battle; then follows another cause of difference in our training – not slight, – the aspect of religion, namely, in the neighbourhood of Covent Garden. I say the aspect; for that was all the lad could judge by. Disposed, for the most part, to learn chiefly by his eyes, in this special matter he finds there is really no other way of learning. His father had taught him 'to lay one penny upon another.' Of mother's teaching, we hear of none; of parish pastoral teaching, the reader may guess how much.

I chose Giorgione rather than Veronese to help me in carrying out this parallel; because I do not find in Giorgione's work any of the early Venetian monarchist element. He seems to me to have belonged more to an abstract contemplative school. I may be wrong in this; it is no matter; – suppose it were so, and that he came down to Venice somewhat recusant or insentient, concerning the usual priestly doctrines of his day, how would the Venetian religion, from an outer intellectual standing-point, have *looked* to him?

He would have seen it to be a religion indisputably powerful in human affairs; often very harmfully so; sometimes devouring widows' houses,[10] and consuming the strongest and fairest from among the young: freezing into merciless bigotry the policy of the old: also, on the other hand, animating national courage, and raising souls, otherwise sordid, into heroism: on the whole, always a real and great power; served with daily sacrifice of gold, time, and thought; putting forth its claims, if hypocritically, at least in bold hypocrisy, not waiving any atom of them in doubt or fear; and, assuredly, in large measure, sincere, believing in itself, and believed: a goodly system, moreover, in aspect; gorgeous, harmonious, mysterious; – a thing which had either to be obeyed or combated, but could not be scorned. A religion towering over all the city – many-buttressed – luminous in marble stateliness, as the dome of our Lady of Safety[11] shines over the sea; many-voiced, also, giving, over all the eastern seas, to the sentinel his watchword, to the soldier his war-cry; and, on the lips of all who died for Venice, shaping the whisper of death.[12]

I suppose the boy Turner to have regarded the religion of his city also from an external intellectual standing-point.

What did he see in Maiden Lane?

Let not the reader be offended with me: I am willing to let him describe, at his own pleasure, what Turner saw there; but to me, it seems to have been this. A religion maintained occasionally, even the whole length of the lane, at point of constable's staff; but, at other times, placed under the custody of the beadle, within certain black and unstately iron railings of St Paul's, Covent Garden. Among the wheelbarrows and over the vegetables, no perceptible dominance of religion; in the narrow, disquieted streets, none; in the tongues, deeds, daily ways of Maiden Lane, little. Some honesty, indeed, and English industry, and kindness of heart, and general idea of justice; but faith, of any national kind, shut up from one Sunday to the next, not artistically beautiful even in those Sabbatical exhibitions; its paraphernalia being chiefly of high pews, heavy elocution, and cold grimness of behaviour.

What chiaroscuro belongs to it – (dependent mostly on candlelight), – we will, however, draw, considerately; no goodliness of escutcheon, nor other respectability being omitted, and the best of their results confessed, a meek old woman and a child being let into a pew, for whom the reading by candlelight will be beneficial.*

For the rest, this religion seems to him discreditable – discredited – not believing in itself: putting forth its authority in a cowardly way, watching how far it might be tolerated, continually shrinking, disclaiming, fencing, finessing; divided against itself, not by stormy rents, but by thin fissures, and splittings of plaster from the walls. Not to be either obeyed, or

---

* Liber Studiorum.[13] 'Interior of a church.' It is worthy of remark that Giorgione and Titian are always delighted to have an opportunity of drawing priests. The English Church may, perhaps, accept it as matter of congratulation that this is the only instance in which Turner drew a clergyman.

combated, by an ignorant, yet clear-sighted youth! only to be scorned. And scorned not one whit the less, though also the dome dedicated to *it* looms high over distant winding of the Thames; as St Mark's campanile rose, for goodly landmark, over mirage of lagoon. For St Mark ruled over life; the Saint of London over death; St Mark over St Mark's Place, but St Paul over St Paul's Churchyard.

Under these influences pass away the first reflective hours of life, with such conclusion as they can reach. In consequence of a fit of illness, he was taken – I cannot ascertain in what year[14] – to live with an aunt, at Brentford; and here, I believe, received some schooling, which he seems to have snatched vigorously; getting knowledge, at least by translation, of the more picturesque classical authors, which he turned presently to use, as we shall see. Hence also, walks about Putney and Twickenham in the summer time acquainted him with the look of English meadow-ground in its restricted states of paddock and park; and with some round-headed appearances of trees, and stately entrances to houses of mark: the avenue at Bushey, and the iron gates and carved pillars of Hampton, impressing him apparently with great awe and admiration; so that in after-life his little country house is, – of all places in the world, – at Twickenham! Of swans and reedy shores he now learns the soft motion and the green mystery, in a way not to be forgotten.

And at last fortune wills that the lad's true life shall begin; and one summer's evening, after various wonderful stage-coach experiences on the north road, which gave him a love of stage-coaches ever after, he finds himself sitting alone among the Yorkshire hills*. For the first time, the silence of Nature round him, her freedom sealed to him, her glory opened to him. Peace at last; no roll of cart-wheel, nor mutter of sullen voices in the back shop; but curlew-cry in space of heaven, and welling of bell-toned streamlet by its shadowy rock. Freedom at last. Dead-wall, dark railing, fenced field, gated garden, all passed away like the dream of a prisoner; and behold, far as foot or eye can race or range, the moor, and cloud. Loveliness at last. It is here then, among these deserted vales! Not among men. Those pale, poverty-struck, or cruel faces; – that multitudinous, marred humanity – are not the only things that God has made. Here is something He has made which no one has marred. Pride of purple rocks, and river pools of blue, and tender wilderness of glittering trees, and misty lights of evening on immeasurable hills.

---

* I do not mean that this is his first acquaintance with the country, but the first impressive and touching one, after his mind was formed.

Beauty, and freedom, and peace; and yet another teacher, graver than these. Sound preaching at last here, in Kirkstall crypt, concerning fate and life. Here, where the dark pool reflects the chancel pillars, and the cattle lie in unhindered rest, the soft sunshine on their dappled bodies, instead of priests' vestments; their white furry hair ruffled a little, fitfully, by the evening wind deep-scented from the meadow thyme.[15]

Consider deeply the import to him of this, his first sight of ruin, and compare it with the effect of the architecture that was around Giorgione. There were indeed aged buildings, at Venice, in his time, but none in decay. All ruin was removed, and its place filled as quickly as in our London; but filled always by architecture loftier and more wonderful than that whose place it took, the boy himself happy to work upon the walls of it[16]; so that the idea of the passing away of the strength of men and beauty of their works never could occur to him sternly. Brighter and brighter the cities of Italy had been rising and broadening on hill and plain, for three hundred years. He saw only strength and immortality, could not but paint both; conceived the form of man as deathless, calm with power, and fiery with life.

Turner saw the exact reverse of this. In the present work of men, meanness, aimlessness, unsightliness: thin-walled, lath-divided, narrow-garreted houses of clay; booths of a darksome Vanity Fair, busily base.

But on Whitby Hill, and by Bolton Brook,[17] remained traces of other handiwork. Men who could build had been there; and who also had wrought, not merely for their own days. But to what purpose? Strong faith, and steady hands, and patient souls – can this, then, be all you have left? this the sum of your doing on the earth; – a nest whence the night-owl may whimper to the brook, and a ribbed skeleton of consumed arches, looming above the bleak banks of mist, from its cliff to the sea?

As the strength of men to Giorgione, to Turner their weakness and vileness, were alone visible. They themselves, unworthy or ephemeral; their work, despicable, or decayed. In the Venetian's eyes, all beauty depended on man's presence and pride; in Turner's, on the solitude he had left, and the humiliation he had suffered.

And thus the fate and issue of all his work were determined at once. He must be a painter of the strength of nature, there was no beauty elsewhere than in that; he must paint also the labour and sorrow and passing away of men: this was the great human truth visible to him.

Their labour, their sorrow, and their death. Mark the three. Labour; by sea and land, in field and city, at forge and furnace, helm and plough. No pastoral indolence nor classic pride shall stand between him and the troubling of the world; still less between him and the toil of his country, – blind, tormented, unwearied, marvellous England.

Also their Sorrow; Ruin of all their glorious work, passing away of their thoughts and their honour, mirage of pleasure, FALLACY OF HOPE[18]; gathering of weed on temple step; gaining of wave on deserted strand; weeping of the mother for the children, desolate by her breathless first-born in the streets of the city, desolate by her last sons slain, among the beasts of the field.[19]

And their Death. That old Greek question again[20]; – yet unanswered. The unconquerable spectre still flitting among the forest trees at twilight; rising ribbed out of the sea-sand; – white, a strange Aphrodite, – out of the sea-foam; stretching its gray, cloven wings among the clouds; turning the light of their sunsets into blood. This has to be looked upon, and in a more terrible shape than ever Salvator or Dürer[21] saw it. The wreck of one guilty country does not infer the ruin of all countries, and need not cause general terror respecting the laws of the universe. Neither did the orderly and narrow succession of domestic joy and sorrow in a small German community bring the question in its breadth, or in any unresolvable shape, before the mind of Dürer. But the English death – the European death of the nineteenth century – was of another range and power; more terrible a thousand-fold in its merely physical grasp and grief; more terrible, incalculably, in its mystery and shame. What were the robber's casual pang, or the range of the flying skirmish, compared to the work of the axe, and the sword, and the famine, which was done during this man's youth on all the hills and plains of the Christian earth, from Moscow to Gibraltar? He was eighteen years old when Napoleon came down on Arcola. Look on the map of Europe and count the blood-stains on it, between Arcola and Waterloo.

Not alone those blood-stains on the Alpine snow, and the blue of the Lombard plain. The English death was before his eyes also. No decent, calculable, consoled dying; no passing to rest like that of the aged burghers of Nuremberg town. No gentle processions to churchyards among the fields, the bronze crests bossed deep on the memorial tablets, and the skylark singing above them from among the corn. But the life trampled out in the slime of the street, crushed to dust amidst the roaring of the wheel, tossed countlessly away into howling winter wind along five hundred leagues of rock-fanged shore. Or, worst of all, rotted down to forgotten graves through years of ignorant patience, and vain seeking for help from man, for hope in God – infirm, imperfect yearning, as of motherless infants starving at the dawn; oppressed royalties of captive thought, vague ague-fits of bleak, amazed despair.

A goodly landscape this, for the lad to paint, and under a goodly light. Wide enough the light was, and clear; no more Salvator's lurid chasm on jagged horizon, nor Dürer's spotted rest of sunny gleam on hedgerow and field; but light over all the world. Full shone now its awful globe, one pallid charnel-house, – a ball strewn bright with human ashes, glaring in poised sway beneath the sun, all blinding-white with death from pole to pole, – death, not of myriads of poor bodies only, but of will, and mercy, and conscience; death, not once inflicted on the flesh, but daily fastening on the spirit; death, not silent or patient, waiting his appointed hour, but voiceful, venomous; death with the taunting word, and burning grasp, and infixed sting.

'Put ye in the sickle, for the harvest is ripe.'[22] The word is spoken in our ears continually to other reapers than the angels, – to the busy skeletons that never tire for stooping. When the measure of iniquity is full, and it seems that another day might bring repentance and redemption, – 'Put ye in the sickle.' When the young life has been wasted all away, and the eyes are just opening upon the tracks of ruin, and faint resolution rising in the heart for nobler things, – 'Put ye in the sickle.' When the roughest blows of fortune have been borne long and bravely, and the hand is just stretched to grasp its goal, – 'Put ye in the sickle.' And when there are but a few in the midst of a nation, to save it, or to teach, or to cherish; and all its life is bound up in those few golden ears, – 'Put ye in the sickle, pale reapers, and pour hemlock for your feast of harvest home.'

This was the sight which opened on the young eyes, this the watchword sounding within the heart of Turner in his youth.

So taught, and prepared for his life's labour, sate the boy at last alone among his fair English hills; and began to paint, with cautious toil, the rocks, and fields, and trickling brooks, and soft white clouds of heaven.

Unto this Last

FOUR ESSAYS

on the first principles of
Political Economy

Published 1862

COMMENTARY

Unto this Last is dealt with in detail in the general Introduction to this selection. I therefore confine myself here to an analysis of Ruskin's epigraphs. The first of these introduces the theme of the just wage, the second that of the just price.

Christ's Parable of the Vineyard is the source of the book's title. As the significance of the story is taken for granted by Ruskin, I quote it here in full:

> For the kingdom of heaven is like unto a man that is an householder, which went out early in the morning to hire labourers into his vineyard.
>
> And when he had agreed with the labourers for a penny a day, he sent them into his vineyard.
>
> And he went out about the third hour, and saw others standing idle in the marketplace,
>
> And said unto them; Go ye also into the vineyard, and whatsoever is right I will give you. And they went their way.
>
> Again he went out about the sixth and ninth hour, and did likewise.
>
> And about the eleventh hour he went out, and found others standing idle, and saith unto them, Why stand ye here all the day idle?
>
> They say unto him, Because no man hath hired us. He saith unto them, Go ye also into the vineyard; and whatsoever is right, that shall ye receive.
>
> So when even was come, the lord of the vineyard saith unto his steward, Call the labourers, and give them their hire, beginning from the last unto the first.
>
> And when they came that were hired about the eleventh hour, they received every man a penny.
>
> But when the first came, they supposed that they should have received more; and they likewise received every man a penny.
>
> And when they had received it, they murmured against the goodman of the house,
>
> Saying, these last have wrought but one hour, and thou hast made them equal unto us, which have borne the burden and the heat of the day.

But he answered one of them, and said, Friend, I do thee no wrong: didst not thou agree with me for a penny?

Take that thine is, and go thy way: I will give unto this last, even as unto thee.

(Matthew xx.1–14)

The spiritual meaning of this Ruskin takes for granted. What counts in *Unto this Last* is the economic significance of Christ's teaching. Ruskin's understanding of this is never directly stated, but a careful reading of the book will suggest two emphases. First, that the economic relationship between employer and employee should not be seen as a question of profit or advantage, but of justice. Thus we may take it that the householder pays all his workers the same, not in order to under-pay those who have borne 'the burden and the heat of the day', but because all men have equal needs. So justice is to be seen in the recognition of need and reciprocal responsibility. Secondly, the parable has bearing on what at the time seemed Ruskin's most eccentric proposal, that there should be a fixed rate of wages for any job of work, regardless of quality. (This proposal occurs on pp. 173–4.)

The significance of the second epigraph is less clear and less interesting. We know that one of the essays Ruskin had originally projected was to have been called 'Thirty Pieces' and that it was concerned with Price. Presumably much of the argument was crammed into 'Ad Valorem'. Certainly the discussion of pricing in that essay includes part of the epigraph (on p. 215) and goes some way towards explaining it. The quotation is from Zechariah xi.12 and occurs in the chapter where the Lord commands that 'the poor of the flock' be fed: 'Thus saith the Lord my God; Feed the flock of the slaughter; whose possessors slay thee, and hold themselves not guilty . . .' (xi.4–5). It seems unlikely that Ruskin was not also thinking of the thirty pieces of silver that were paid to Judas Iscariot and which, after his suicide, were used to buy 'the potter's field, to bury strangers in' (Matthew xxvii.3–7). This incident is alluded to on p. 187. There the silver stands for unjustly earned income, from which the unjust merchant's gain is death – in contrast to the just merchant who recognizes that 'There is no Wealth but Life'.

UNTO THIS LAST

'Friend, I do thee no wrong.
Didst not thou agree with me for a penny?
Take that thine is, and go thy way.
I will give unto this last even as unto thee.'

'If ye think good, give me my price;
And if not, forbear.
So they weighed for my price thirty pieces of silver.'

PREFACE

The four following essays were published eighteen months ago in the *Cornhill Magazine*, and were reprobated in a violent manner, as far as I could hear, by most of the readers they met with.

Not a whit the less, I believe them to be the best, that is to say, the truest, rightest-worded, and most serviceable things I have ever written; and the last of them, having had especial pains spent on it, is probably the best I shall ever write.

'This,' the reader may reply, 'it might be, yet not therefore well written.' Which, in no mock humility, admitting, I yet rest satisfied with the work, though with nothing else that I have done; and purposing shortly to follow out the subjects opened in these papers,[1] as I may find leisure, I wish the introductory statements to be within the reach of any one who may care to refer to them. So I republish the essays as they appeared. One word only is changed, correcting the estimate of a weight; and no word is added.

Although, however, I find nothing to modify in these papers, it is a matter of regret to me that the most startling of all the statements in them, – that respecting the necessity of the organization of labour, with fixed wages, – should have found its way into the first essay; it being quite one of the least important, though by no means the least certain, of the positions to be defended. The real gist of these papers, their central meaning and aim, is to give, as I believe for the first time in plain English, – it has often been incidentally given in good Greek by Plato and Xenophon, and good Latin by Cicero and Horace,[2] – a logical definition of W E A L T H : such definition being absolutely needed for a basis of economical science. The most reputed essay on that subject which has appeared in modern times,[3] after opening with the statement that 'writers on political economy profess to teach, or to investigate,* the nature of wealth,' thus follows up the declaration of its thesis – 'Every one has a notion, sufficiently correct for common purposes, of what is meant by wealth.' . . . 'It is no part of the design of this treatise to aim at metaphysical nicety of definition.'[4]

Metaphysical nicety, we assuredly do not need; but physical nicety, and logical accuracy, with respect to a physical subject, we as assuredly do.

Suppose the subject of inquiry, instead of being House-law (*Oikonomia*), had been Star-law (*Astronomia*),[5] and that, ignoring distinction between

---

* Which? for where investigation is necessary, teaching is impossible.

stars fixed and wandering, as here between wealth radiant and wealth reflective,[6] the writer had begun thus: 'Every one has a notion, sufficiently correct for common purposes, of what is meant by stars. Metaphysical nicety in the definition of a star is not the object of this treatise'; – the essay so opened might yet have been far more true in its final statements, and a thousand fold more serviceable to the navigator, than any treatise on wealth, which founds its conclusions on the popular conception of wealth, can ever become to the economist.

It was, therefore, the first object of these following papers to give an accurate and stable definition of wealth. Their second object was to show that the acquisition of wealth was finally possible only under certain moral conditions of society, of which quite the first was a belief in the existence, and even, for practical purposes, in the attainability of honesty.

Without venturing to pronounce – since on such a matter human judgment is by no means conclusive – what is, or is not, the noblest of God's works, we may yet admit so much of Pope's assertion[7] as that an honest man is among His best works presently visible, and, as things stand, a somewhat rare one; but not an incredible or miraculous work; still less an abnormal one. Honesty is not a disturbing force, which deranges the orbits of economy; but a consistent and commanding force, by obedience to which – and by no other obedience – those orbits can continue clear of chaos.

It is true, I have sometimes heard Pope condemned for the lowness, instead of the height, of his standard: – 'Honesty is indeed a respectable virtue; but how much higher may men attain! Shall nothing more be asked of us than that we be honest?'

For the present, good friends, nothing. It seems that in our aspirations to be more than that, we have to some extent lost sight of the propriety of being so much as that. What else we may have lost faith in, there shall be here no question; but assuredly we have lost faith in common honesty, and in the working power of it. And this faith, with the facts on which it may rest, it is quite our first business to recover and keep: not only believing, but even by experience assuring ourselves, that there are yet in the world men who can be restrained from fraud otherwise than by the fear of losing employment;*[8] nay, that it is even accurately in proportion to the number

* 'The effectual discipline which is exercised over a workman is not that of his corporation, but of his customers. It is the fear of losing their employment which restrains his frauds, and corrects his negligence.' (*Wealth of Nations*, Book I, chap. 10.)

Note to Second Edition. – The only addition I will make to the words of this book of such men in any State, that the said State does or can prolong its existence.

To these two points, then, the following essays are mainly directed. The subject of the organization of labour is only casually touched upon; because, if we once can get a sufficient quantity of honesty in our captains,[11] the organization of labour is easy, and will develop itself without quarrel or difficulty; but if we cannot get honesty in our captains, the organization of labour is for evermore impossible.

The several conditions of its possibility I purpose to examine at length in the sequel.[12] Yet, lest the reader should be alarmed by the hints thrown out during the following investigation of first principles, as if they were leading him into unexpectedly dangerous ground, I will, for his better assurance, state at once the worst of the political creed at which I wish him to arrive.[13]

(1.) First, – that there should be training schools for youth established, at Government cost,* and under Government discipline, over the whole country; that every child born in the country should, at the parent's wish, be permitted (and, in certain cases, be under penalty required) to pass through them; and that, in these schools, the child should (with other minor pieces of knowledge hereafter to be considered) imperatively be taught, with the best skill of teaching that the country could produce, the following three things: –

(*a*) The laws of health, and the exercises enjoined by them;

---

shall be a very earnest request to any Christian reader to think within himself what an entirely damned state of soul any human creature must have got into, who could read with acceptance such a sentence as this: much more, write it; and to oppose to it, the first commercial words of Venice, discovered by me in her first church[9]:

'Around this temple, let the Merchant's law be just, his weights true, and his contracts guileless.'

If any of my present readers think that my language in this note is either intemperate, or unbecoming, I will beg them to read with attention the Eighteenth paragraph of *Sesame and Lilies*[10]; and to be assured that I never, myself, now use, in writing, any word which is not, in my deliberate judgment, the fittest for the occasion.

VENICE,
Sunday, 18th March, 1877.

* It will probably be inquired by near-sighted persons, out of what funds such schools could be supported. The expedient modes of direct provision for them I will examine hereafter; indirectly, they would be far more than self-supporting. The economy in crime alone, (quite one of the most costly articles of luxury in the modern European market,) which such schools would induce, would suffice to support them ten times over. Their economy of labour would be pure gain, and that too large to be presently calculable.

(*b*) Habits of gentleness and justice; and

(*c*) The calling by which he is to live.

(2.) Secondly, – that, in connection with these training schools, there should be established, also entirely under Government regulation, manufactories and workshops for the production and sale of every necessary of life, and for the exercise of every useful art. And that, interfering no whit with private enterprise, nor setting any restraints or tax on private trade, but leaving both to do their best, and beat the Government if they could, – there should, at these Government manufactories and shops, be authoritatively good and exemplary work done, and pure and true substance sold; so that a man could be sure, if he chose to pay the Government price, that he got for his money bread that was bread, ale that was ale, and work that was work.

(3.) Thirdly, – that any man, or woman, or boy, or girl, out of employment, should be at once received at the nearest Government school, and set to such work as it appeared, on trial, they were fit for, at a fixed rate of wages determinable every year; – that, being found incapable of work through ignorance, they should be taught, or being found incapable of work through sickness, should be tended; but that being found objecting to work, they should be set, under compulsion of the strictest nature, to the more painful and degrading forms of necessary toil, especially to that in mines and other places of danger (such danger being, however, diminished to the utmost by careful regulation and discipline), and the due wages of such work be retained, cost of compulsion first abstracted – to be at the workman's command, so soon as he has come to sounder mind respecting the laws of employment.

(4.) Lastly, – that for the old and destitute, comfort and home should be provided; which provision, when misfortune had been by the working of such a system sifted from guilt, would be honourable instead of disgraceful to the receiver.[14] For (I repeat this passage out of my *Political Economy of Art*, to which the reader is referred for farther detail) 'a labourer serves his country with his spade, just as a man in the middle ranks of life serves it with sword, pen, or lancet. If the service be less, and, therefore, the wages during health less, then the reward when health is broken may be less, but not less honourable; and it ought to be quite as natural and straightforward a matter for a labourer to take his pension from his parish, because he has deserved well of his parish, as for a man in higher rank to take his pension from his country, because he has deserved well of his country.'[15]

To which statement, I will only add, for conclusion, respecting the discipline and pay of life and death, that, for both high and low, Livy's last words touching Valerius Publicola, '*de publico est elatus*,'*[16] ought not to be a dishonourable close of epitaph.

These things, then, I believe, and am about, as I find power, to explain and illustrate in their various bearings; following out also what belongs to them of collateral inquiry. Here I state them only in brief, to prevent the reader casting about in alarm for my ultimate meaning; yet requesting him, for the present, to remember, that in a science dealing with so subtle elements as those of human nature, it is only possible to answer for the final truth of principles, not for the direct success of plans: and that in the best of these last, what can be immediately accomplished is always questionable, and what can be finally accomplished, inconceivable.

DENMARK HILL,
10th May, 1862.

* P. Valerius, omnium consensu princeps belli pacisque artibus, anno post moritur; gloriâ ingenti, copiis, familiaribus adeo exiguis, ut funeri sumtus deesset: de publico est elatus. Luxere matronæ ut Brutum.' – Lib. ii. c. xvi.

ESSAY I

THE ROOTS OF HONOUR

AMONG the delusions which at different periods have possessed themselves of the minds of large masses of the human race, perhaps the most curious – certainly the least creditable – is the modern *soi-disant* science of political economy, based on the idea that an advantageous code of social action may be determined irrespectively of the influence of social affection.

Of course, as in the instances of alchemy, astrology, witchcraft, and other such popular creeds, political economy has a plausible idea at the root of it. 'The social affections,' says the economist, 'are accidental and disturbing elements in human nature; but avarice and the desire of progress are constant elements. Let us eliminate the inconstants, and, considering the human being merely as a covetous machine, examine by what laws of labour, purchase, and sale, the greatest accumulative result in wealth is obtainable. Those laws once determined, it will be for each individual afterwards to introduce as much of the disturbing affectionate element as he chooses, and to determine for himself the result on the new conditions supposed.'[17]

This would be a perfectly logical and successful method of analysis, if the accidentals afterwards to be introduced were of the same nature as the powers first examined. Supposing a body in motion to be influenced by constant and inconstant forces, it is usually the simplest way of examining its course to trace it first under the persistent conditions, and afterwards introduce the causes of variation. But the disturbing elements in the social problem are not of the same nature as the constant ones: they alter the essence of the creature under examination the moment they are added; they operate, not mathematically, but chemically, introducing conditions which render all our previous knowledge unavailable. We made learned experiments upon pure nitrogen, and have convinced ourselves that it is a very manageable gas: but, behold! the thing which we have practically to deal with is its chloride[18]; and this, the moment we touch it on our established principles, sends us and our apparatus through the ceiling.

Observe, I neither impugn nor doubt the conclusion of the science if its terms are accepted. I am simply uninterested in them, as I should be in those of a science of gymnastics which assumed that men had no skeletons. It might be shown, on that supposition, that it would be advantageous to roll the students up into pellets, flatten them into cakes, or stretch them into cables; and that when these results were effected, the re-insertion of the skeleton would be attended with various inconveniences to their constitution. The reasoning might be admirable, the conclusions true, and the science deficient only in applicability. Modern political economy stands on a precisely similar basis. Assuming, not that the human being has no skeleton, but that it is all skeleton, it founds an ossifiant theory of progress on this negation of a soul; and having shown the utmost that may be made of bones, and constructed a number of interesting geometrical figures with death's-head and humeri, successfully proves the inconvenience of the reappearance of a soul among these corpuscular structures. I do not deny the truth of this theory: I simply deny its applicability to the present phase of the world.

This inapplicability has been curiously manifested during the embarrassment caused by the late strikes of our workmen.[19] Here occurs one of the simplest cases, in a pertinent and positive form, of the first vital problem which political economy has to deal with (the relation between employer and employed); and, at a severe crisis, when lives in multitudes and wealth in masses are at stake, the political economists are helpless – practically mute: no demonstrable solution of the difficulty can be given by them, such as may convince or calm the opposing parties. Obstinately the masters take one view of the matter; obstinately the operatives another; and no political science can set them at one.

It would be strange if it could, it being not by 'science' of any kind that men were ever intended to be set at one. Disputant after disputant vainly strives to show that the interests of the masters are, or are not, antagonistic to those of the men: none of the pleaders ever seeming to remember that it does not absolutely or always follow that the persons must be antagonistic because their interests are. If there is only a crust of bread in the house, and mother and children are starving, their interests are not the same. If the mother eats it, the children want it; if the children eat it, the mother must go hungry to her work. Yet it does not necessarily follow that there will be 'antagonism' between them, that they will fight for the crust, and that the mother, being strongest, will get it, and eat it. Neither, in any other case, whatever the relations of the persons may be, can it be assumed for certain that, because their interests are diverse, they must necessarily regard each other with hostility, and use violence or cunning to obtain the advantage.

Even if this were so, and it were as just as it is convenient to consider men as actuated by no other moral influences than those which affect rats or swine, the logical conditions of the question are still indeterminable. It can never be shown generally either that the interests of master and labourer are alike, or that they are opposed; for, according to circumstances, they may be either. It is, indeed, always the interest of both that the work should be rightly done, and a just price obtained for it; but, in the division of profits, the gain of the one may or may not be the loss of the other. It is not the master's interest to pay wages so low as to leave the men sickly and depressed,[20] nor the workman's interest to be paid high wages if the smallness of the master's profit hinders him from enlarging his business, or conducting it in a safe and liberal way. A stoker ought not to desire high pay if the company is too poor to keep the engine-wheels in repair.

And the varieties of circumstance which influence these reciprocal interests are so endless, that all endeavour to deduce rules of action from balance of expediency is in vain. And it is meant to be in vain. For no human actions ever were intended by the Maker of men to be guided by balances of expediency, but by balances of justice.[21] He has therefore rendered all endeavours to determine expediency futile for evermore. No man ever knew, or can know, what will be the ultimate result to himself, or to others, of any given line of conduct. But every man may know, and most of us do know, what is a just and unjust act. And all of us may know also, that the consequences of justice will be ultimately the best possible, both to others and ourselves, though we can neither say what *is* best, or how it is likely to come to pass.

I have said balances of justice, meaning, in the term justice, to include affection, – such affection as one man *owes* to another. All right relations between master and operative, and all their best interests, ultimately depend on these.

We shall find the best and simplest illustration of the relations of master and operative in the position of domestic servants.

We will suppose that the master of a household desires only to get as much work out of his servants as he can, at the rate of wages he gives. He never allows them to be idle; feeds them as poorly and lodges them as ill as they will endure, and in all things pushes his requirements to the exact point beyond which he cannot go without forcing the servant to leave him. In doing this, there is no violation on his part of what is commonly called 'justice.' He agrees with the domestic for his whole time and service, and takes them; – the limits of hardship in treatment being fixed by the practice of other masters in his neighbourhood; that is to say, by the current rate of wages for domestic labour. If the servant can get a better place, he is free to take one, and the master can only tell what is the real market value of his labour, by requiring as much as he will give.

This is the politico-economical view of the case, according to the doctors of that science; who assert that by this procedure the greatest average of work will be obtained from the servant, and therefore the greatest benefit to the community, and through the community, by reversion, to the servant himself.[22]

That, however, is not so. It would be so if the servant were an engine of which the motive power was steam, magnetism, gravitation, or any other agent of calculable force. But he being, on the contrary, an engine whose motive power is a Soul, the force of this very peculiar agent, as an unknown quantity, enters into all the political economist's equations, without his knowledge, and falsifies every one of their results. The largest quantity of work will not be done by this curious engine for pay, or under pressure, or by help of any kind of fuel which may be supplied by the chaldron. It will be done only when the motive force, that is to say, the will or spirit of the creature, is brought to its greatest strength by its own proper fuel: namely, by the affections.

It may indeed happen, and does happen often, that if the master is a man of sense and energy, a large quantity of material work may be done under mechanical pressure, enforced by strong will and guided by wise method; also it may happen, and does happen often, that if the master is indolent and weak (however good-natured), a very small quantity of work, and that bad, may be produced by the servant's undirected strength, and contemptuous gratitude. But the universal law of the matter is that, assuming any given quantity of energy and sense in master and servant, the greatest material result obtainable by them will be, not through antagonism to each other, but through affection for each other; and that, if the master, instead of endeavouring to get as much work as possible from the servant, seeks rather to render his appointed and necessary work beneficial to him, and to forward his interests in all just and wholesome ways, the real amount of work ultimately done, or of good rendered, by the person so cared for, will indeed be the greatest possible.

Observe, I say, 'of good rendered,' for a servant's work is not necessarily or always the best thing he can give his master. But good of all kinds, whether in material service, in protective watchfulness of his master's interest and credit, or in joyful readiness to seize unexpected and irregular occasions of help.

Nor is this one whit less generally true because indulgence will be frequently abused, and kindness met with ingratitude. For the servant who, gently treated, is ungrateful, treated ungently, will be revengeful; and the man who is dishonest to a liberal master will be injurious to an unjust one.

In any case, and with any person, this unselfish treatment will produce the most effective return. Observe, I am here considering the affections wholly as a motive power; not at all as things in themselves desirable or noble, or in any other way abstractedly good. I look at them simply as an anomalous force, rendering every one of the ordinary political economist's calculations nugatory; while, even if he desired to introduce this new element into his estimates, he has no power of dealing with it; for the affections only become a true motive power when they ignore every other motive and condition of political economy. Treat the servant kindly, with the idea of turning his gratitude to account, and you will get, as you deserve, no gratitude, nor any value for your kindness; but treat him kindly without any economical purpose, and all economical purposes will be answered; in this, as in all other matters, whosoever will save his life shall lose it, whoso loses it shall find it. *[23]

* The difference between the two modes of treatment, and between their effective material results, may be seen very accurately by a comparison of the relations of Esther and Charlie in *Bleak House* with those of Miss Brass and the Marchioness in *Master Humphrey's Clock*.

The essential value and truth of Dickens's writings have been unwisely lost sight of by many thoughtful persons, merely because he presents his truth with some colour of caricature. Unwisely, because Dickens's caricature, though often gross, is never mistaken. Allowing for his manner of telling them, the things he tells us are always true. I wish that he could think it right to limit his brilliant exaggeration to works written only for public amusement; and when he takes up a subject of high national importance, such as that which he handled in *Hard Times*,[24] that he would use severer and more accurate analysis. The usefulness of that work (to my mind, in several respects the greatest he has written) is with many persons seriously diminished because Mr Bounderby is a dramatic monster, instead of a characteristic example of a worldly master; and Stephen Blackpool a dramatic perfection, instead of a characteristic example of an honest workman. But let us not lose the use of Dickens's wit and insight, because he chooses to speak in a circle of stage fire. He is entirely right in his main drift and purpose in every book he has written; and all of them, but especially *Hard Times*, should be studied with close and earnest care by persons interested in social questions. They will find much that is partial, and, because partial, apparently unjust; but if they examine all the evidence on the other side, which Dickens seems to overlook, it will appear, after all their trouble, that his view was the finally right one, grossly and sharply told.

The next clearest and simplest example of relation between master and operative is that which exists between the commander of a regiment and his men.

Supposing the officer only desires to apply the rules of discipline so as, with least trouble to himself, to make the regiment most effective, he will not be able, by any rules or administration of rules, on this selfish principle, to develop the full strength of his subordinates. If a man of sense and firmness, he may, as in the former instance, produce a better result than would be obtained by the irregular kindness of a weak officer; but let the sense and firmness be the same in both cases, and assuredly the officer who has the most direct personal relations with his men, the most care for their interests, and the most value for their lives, will develop their effective strength, through their affection for his own person, and trust in his character, to a degree wholly unattainable by other means. This law applies still more stringently as the numbers concerned are larger: a charge may often be successful, though the men dislike their officers; a battle has rarely been won, unless they loved their general.

Passing from these simple examples to the more complicated relations existing between a manufacturer and his workmen, we are met first by certain curious difficulties, resulting, apparently, from a harder and colder state of moral elements. It is easy to imagine an enthusiastic affection existing among soldiers for the colonel. Not so easy to imagine an enthusiastic affection among cotton-spinners for the proprietor of the mill. A body of men associated for purposes of robbery (as a Highland clan in ancient times) shall be animated by perfect affection, and every member of it be ready to lay down his life for the life of his chief. But a band of men associated for purposes of legal production and accumulation is usually animated, it appears, by no such emotions, and none of them are in any wise willing to give his life for the life of his chief. Not only are we met by this apparent anomaly, in moral matters, but by others connected with it, in administration of system. For a servant or a soldier is engaged at a definite rate of wages, for a definite period; but a workman at a rate of wages variable according to the demand for labour, and with the risk of being at any time thrown out of his situation by chances of trade. Now, as, under these contingencies, no action of the affections can take place, but only an explosive action of *dis*affections, two points offer themselves for consideration in the matter.

The first – How far the rate of wages may be so regulated as not to vary with the demand for labour.

The second – How far it is possible that bodies of workmen may be engaged and maintained at such fixed rate of wages (whatever the state of trade may be), without enlarging or diminishing their number,[25] so as to give them permanent interest in the establishment with which they are connected, like that of the domestic servants in an old family, or an *esprit de corps*, like that of the soldiers in a crack regiment.

The first question is, I say, how far it may be possible to fix the rate of wages, irrespectively of the demand for labour.

Perhaps one of the most curious facts in the history of human error is the denial by the common political economist of the possibility of thus regulating wages; while, for all the important, and much of the unimportant, labour, on the earth, wages are already so regulated.

We do not sell our prime-ministership by Dutch auction; nor, on the decease of a bishop, whatever may be the general advantages of simony, do we (yet) offer his diocese to the clergyman who will take the episcopacy at the lowest contract. We (with exquisite sagacity of political economy!) do indeed sell commissions; but not openly, generalships: sick, we do not inquire for a physician who takes less than a guinea; litigious, we never think of reducing six-and-eightpence[26] to four-and-sixpence; caught in a shower, we do not canvass the cabmen, to find one who values his driving at less than sixpence a mile.

It is true that in all these cases there is, and in every conceivable case there must be, ultimate reference to the presumed difficulty of the work, or number of candidates for the office. If it were thought that the labour necessary to make a good physician would be gone through by a sufficient number of students with the prospect of only half-guinea fees, public consent would soon withdraw the unnecessary half-guinea. In this ultimate sense, the price of labour is indeed always regulated by the demand for it; but, so far as the practical and immediate administration of the matter is regarded, the best labour always has been, and is, as *all* labour ought to be, paid by an invariable standard.

'What!' the reader perhaps answers amazedly: 'pay good and bad workmen alike?'

Certainly. The difference between one prelate's sermons and his successor's – or between one physician's opinion and another's, – is far greater, as respects the qualities of mind involved, and far more important in result to you personally, than the difference between good and bad laying of bricks (though that is greater than most people suppose). Yet you pay with equal fee, contentedly, the good and bad workmen upon your soul, and the good and bad workmen upon your body; much more may you pay, contentedly, with equal fees, the good and bad workmen upon your house.

'Nay, but I choose my physician, and (?) my clergyman, thus indicating my sense of the quality of their work.' By all means, also, choose your bricklayer; that is the proper reward of the good workman, to be 'chosen.' The natural and right system respecting all labour is, that it should be paid at a fixed rate, but the good workman employed, and the bad workman unemployed. The false, unnatural, and destructive system is when the bad workman is allowed to offer his work at half-price, and either take the place of the good, or force him by his competition to work for an inadequate sum.

This equality of wages, then, being the first object towards which we have to discover the directest available road, the second is, as above stated, that of maintaining constant numbers of workmen in employment, whatever may be the accidental demand for the article they produce.

I believe the sudden and extensive inequalities of demand, which necessarily arise in the mercantile operations of an active nation, constitute the only essential difficulty which has to be overcome in a just organization of labour.

The subject opens into too many branches to admit of being investigated in a paper of this kind; but the following general facts bearing on it may be noted.

The wages which enable any workman to live are necessarily higher, if his work is liable to intermission, than if it is assured and continuous; and however severe the struggle for work may become, the general law will always hold, that men must get more daily pay if, on the average, they can only calculate on work three days a week than they would require if they were sure of work six days a week. Supposing that a man cannot live on less than a shilling a day, his seven shillings he must get, either for three days' violent work, or six days' deliberate work. The tendency of all modern mercantile operations is to throw both wages and trade into the form of a lottery, and to make the workman's pay depend on intermittent exertion, and the principal's profit on dexterously used chance.

In what partial degree, I repeat, this may be necessary in consequence of the activities of modern trade, I do not here investigate; contenting myself with the fact that in its fatallest aspects it is assuredly unnecessary, and results merely from love of gambling on the part of the masters, and from ignorance and sensuality in the men. The masters cannot bear to let any opportunity of gain escape them, and frantically rush at every gap and breach in the walls of Fortune, raging to be rich, and affronting, with impatient covetousness, every risk of ruin, while the men prefer three days of violent labour, and three days of drunkenness, to six days of moderate work and wise rest. There is no way in which a principal, who really desires to help his workmen, may do it more effectually than by checking these disorderly habits both in himself and them; keeping his own business operations on a scale which will enable him to pursue them securely, not yielding to temptations of precarious gain; and at the same time, leading his workmen into regular habits of labour and life, either by inducing them rather to take low wages, in the form of a fixed salary, than high wages, subject to the chance of their being thrown out of work; or, if this be impossible, by discouraging the system of violent exertion for nominally high day wages, and leading the men to take lower pay for more regular labour.

In effecting any radical changes of this kind, doubtless there would be great inconvenience and loss incurred by all the originators of the movement. That which can be done with perfect convenience and without loss, is not always the thing that most needs to be done, or which we are most imperatively required to do.

I have already alluded to the difference hitherto existing between regiments of men associated for purposes of violence, and for purposes of manufacture; in that the former appear capable of self-sacrifice – the latter, not; which singular fact is the real reason of the general lowness of estimate in which the profession of commerce is held, as compared with that of arms. Philosophically, it does not, at first sight, appear reasonable (many writers have endeavoured to prove it unreasonable) that a peaceable and rational person, whose trade is buying and selling, should be held in less honour than an unpeaceable and often irrational person, whose trade is slaying. Nevertheless, the consent of mankind has always, in spite of the philosophers, given precedence to the soldier.

And this is right.

For the soldier's trade, verily and essentially, is not slaying, but being slain. This, without well knowing its own meaning, the world honours it for. A bravo's trade is slaying; but the world has never respected bravos more than merchants: the reason it honours the soldier is, because he holds his life at the service of the State. Reckless he may be – fond of pleasure or of adventure – all kinds of bye-motives and mean impulses may have determined the choice of his profession, and may affect (to all appearance exclusively) his daily conduct in it; but our estimate of him is based on this ultimate fact – of which we are well assured – that put him in a fortress breach, with all the pleasures of the world behind him, and only death and his duty in front of him, he will keep his face to the front; and he knows that his choice may be put to him at any moment – and has beforehand taken his part – virtually takes such part continually – does, in reality, die daily.[27]

Not less is the respect we pay to the lawyer and physician, founded ultimately on their self-sacrifice. Whatever the learning or acuteness of a great lawyer, our chief respect for him depends on our belief that, set in a judge's seat, he will strive to judge justly, come of it what may. Could we suppose that he would take bribes, and use his acuteness and legal knowledge to give plausibility to iniquitous decisions, no degree of intellect would win for him our respect. Nothing will win it, short of our tacit conviction, that in all important acts of his life justice is first with him; his own interest, second.

In the case of a physician, the ground of the honour we render him is clearer still. Whatever his science, we would shrink from him in horror if we found him regard his patients merely as subjects to experiment upon; much more, if we found that, receiving bribes from persons interested in their deaths, he was using his best skill to give poison in the mask of medicine.

Finally, the principle holds with utmost clearness as it respects clergymen. No goodness of disposition will excuse want of science in a physician, or of shrewdness in an advocate; but a clergyman, even though his power of intellect be small, is respected on the presumed ground of his unselfishness and serviceableness.

Now, there can be no question but that the tact, foresight, decision, and other mental powers, required for the successful management of a large mercantile concern, if not such as could be compared with those of a great lawyer, general, or divine, would at least match the general conditions of mind required in the subordinate officers of a ship, or of a regiment, or in the curate of a country parish. If, therefore, all the efficient members of the so-called liberal professions are still, somehow, in public estimate of honour, preferred before the head of a commercial firm, the reason must lie deeper than in the measurement of their several powers of mind.

And the essential reason for such preference will be found to lie in the fact that the merchant is presumed to act always selfishly. His work may be very necessary to the community; but the motive of it is understood to be wholly personal. The merchant's first object in all his dealings must be (the public believe) to get as much for himself, and leave as little to his neighbour (or customer) as possible. Enforcing this upon him, by political statute, as the necessary principle of his action; recommending it to him on all occasions, and themselves reciprocally adopting it, proclaiming vociferously, for law of the universe, that a buyer's function is to cheapen, and a seller's to cheat, – the public, nevertheless, involuntarily condemn the man of commerce for his compliance with their own statement, and stamp him for ever as belonging to an inferior grade of human personality.

This they will find, eventually, they must give up doing. They must not cease to condemn selfishness; but they will have to discover a kind of commerce which is not exclusively selfish. Or, rather, they will have to discover that there never was, or can be, any other kind of commerce; that this which they have called commerce was not commerce at all, but cozening; and that a true merchant differs as much from a merchant according to laws of modern political economy, as the hero of the *Excursion* from Autolycus.[28] They will find that commerce is an occupation which gentlemen will every day see more need to engage in, rather than in the businesses of talking to men, or slaying them; that, in true commerce, as in true preaching, or true fighting, it is necessary to admit the idea of occasional voluntary loss; – that sixpences have to be lost, as well as lives, under a sense of duty; that the market may have its martyrdoms as well as the pulpit; and trade its heroisms as well as war.

May have – in the final issue, must have – and only has not had yet, because men of heroic temper have always been misguided in their youth into other fields; not recognizing what is in our days, perhaps, the most important of all fields; so that, while many a zealous person loses his life in trying to teach the form of a gospel, very few will lose a hundred pounds in showing the practice of one.

The fact is, that people never have had clearly explained to them the true functions of a merchant with respect to other people. I should like the reader to be very clear about this.

Five great intellectual professions, relating to daily necessities of life, have hitherto existed – three exist necessarily, in every civilized nation:

The Soldier's profession is to *defend* it.

The Pastor's to *teach* it.

The Physician's to *keep it in health*.

The Lawyer's to *enforce justice* in it.

The Merchant's to *provide* for it.

And the duty of all these men is, on due occasion, to *die* for it.

'On due occasion,' namely: –

The Soldier, rather than leave his post in battle.

The Physician, rather than leave his post in plague.

The Pastor, rather than teach Falsehood.

The Lawyer, rather than countenance Injustice.

The Merchant – what is *his* 'due occasion' of death?

It is the main question for the merchant, as for all of us. For, truly, the man who does not know when to die, does not know how to live.

Observe, the merchant's function (or manufacturer's, for in the broad sense in which it is here used the word must be understood to include both) is to provide for the nation. It is no more his function to get profit for himself out of that provision than it is a clergyman's function to get his stipend. This stipend is a due and necessary adjunct, but not the object of his life, if he be a true clergyman, any more than his fee (or honorarium) is the object of life to a true physician. Neither is his fee the object of life to a true merchant. All three, if true men, have a work to be done irrespective of fee — to be done even at any cost, or for quite the contrary of fee; the pastor's function being to teach, the physician's to heal, and the merchant's, as I have said, to provide. That is to say, he has to understand to their very root the qualities of the thing he deals in, and the means of obtaining or producing it; and he has to apply all his sagacity and energy to the producing or obtaining it in perfect state, and distributing it at the cheapest possible price where it is most needed.

And because the production or obtaining of any commodity involves necessarily the agency of many lives and hands, the merchant becomes in the course of his business the master and governor of large masses of men in a more direct, though less confessed way, than a military officer or pastor; so that on him falls, in great part, the responsibility for the kind of life they lead: and it becomes his duty, not only to be always considering how to produce what he sells, in the purest and cheapest forms, but how to make the various employments involved in the production, or transference of it, most beneficial to the men employed.

And as into these two functions, requiring for their right exercise the highest intelligence, as well as patience, kindness, and tact, the merchant is bound to put all his energy, so for their just discharge he is bound, as soldier or physician is bound, to give up, if need be, his life, in such way as it may be demanded of him. Two main points he has in his providing function to maintain: first, his engagements (faithfulness to engagements being the real root of all possibilities, in commerce); and, secondly, the perfectness and purity of the thing provided; so that, rather than fail in any engagement, or consent to any deterioration, adulteration, or unjust and exorbitant price of that which he provides, he is bound to meet fearlessly any form of distress, poverty, or labour, which may, through maintenance of these points, come upon him.

Again: in his office as governor of the men employed by him, the merchant or manufacturer is invested with a distinctly paternal authority and responsibility.[29] In most cases, a youth entering a commercial establishment is withdrawn altogether from home influence; his master must become his father, else he has, for practical and constant help, no father at hand: in all cases the master's authority, together with the general tone and atmosphere of his business, and the character of the men with whom the youth is compelled in the course of it to associate, have more immediate and pressing weight than the home influence, and will usually neutralize it either for good or evil; so that the only means which the master has of doing justice to the men employed by him is to ask himself sternly whether he is dealing with such subordinate as he would with his own son, if compelled by circumstances to take such a position.

Supposing the captain of a frigate saw it right, or were by any chance obliged, to place his own son in the position of a common sailor: as he would then treat his son, he is bound always to treat every one of the men under him. So, also, supposing the master of a manufactory saw it right, or were by any chance obliged, to place his own son in the position of an ordinary workman; as he would then treat his son, he is bound always to treat every one of his men. This is the only effective, true, or practical RULE which can be given on this point of political economy.

And as the captain of a ship is bound to be the last man to leave his ship in case of wreck, and to share his last crust with the sailors in case of famine, so the manufacturer, in any commercial crisis or distress, is bound to take the suffering of it with his men, and even to take more of it for himself than he allows his men to feel; as a father would in a famine, shipwreck, or battle, sacrifice himself for his son.

All which sounds very strange: the only real strangeness in the matter being, nevertheless, that it should so sound. For all this is true, and that not partially nor theoretically, but everlastingly and practically: all other doctrine than this respecting matters political being false in premises, absurd in deduction, and impossible in practice, consistently with any progressive state of national life; all the life which we now possess as a nation showing itself in the resolute denial and scorn, by a few strong minds and faithful hearts, of the economic principles taught to our multitudes, which principles, so far as accepted, lead straight to national destruction. Respecting the modes and forms of destruction to which they lead, and, on the other hand, respecting the farther practical working of true polity, I hope to reason farther in a following paper.

ESSAY II

THE VEINS OF WEALTH

THE answer which would be made by any ordinary political economist to the statements contained in the preceding paper, is in few words as follows: –

'It is indeed true that certain advantages of a general nature may be obtained by the development of social affections. But political economists never professed, nor profess, to take advantages of a general nature into consideration. Our science is simply the science of getting rich. So far from being a fallacious or visionary one, it is found by experience to be practically effective. Persons who follow its precepts do actually become rich, and persons who disobey them become poor. Every capitalist of Europe has acquired his fortune by following the known laws of our science, and increases his capital daily by an adherence to them. It is vain to bring forward tricks of logic, against the force of accomplished facts. Every man of business knows by experience how money is made, and how it is lost.'

Pardon me. Men of business do indeed know how they themselves made their money, or how, on occasion, they lost it. Playing a long-practised game, they are familiar with the chances of its cards, and can rightly explain their losses and gains. But they neither know who keeps the bank of the gambling-house, nor what other games may be played with the same cards, nor what other losses and gains, far away among the dark streets, are essentially, though invisibly, dependent on theirs in the lighted rooms. They have learned a few, and only a few, of the laws of mercantile economy; but not one of those of political economy.[30]

Primarily, which is very notable and curious, I observe that men of business rarely know the meaning of the word 'rich.' At least, if they know, they do not in their reasonings allow for the fact, that it is a relative word, implying its opposite 'poor' as positively as the word 'north' implies its opposite 'south.' Men nearly always speak and write as if riches were absolute, and it were possible, by following certain scientific precepts, for everybody to be rich. Whereas riches are a power like that of electricity, acting only through inequalities or negations of itself. The force of the guinea you have in your pocket depends wholly on the default of a guinea in your neighbour's pocket. If he did not want it, it would be of no use to you; the degree of power it possesses depends accurately upon the need or desire he has for it, – and the art of making yourself rich, in the ordinary mercantile economist's sense, is therefore equally and necessarily the art of keeping your neighbour poor.

I would not contend in this matter (and rarely in any matter) for the acceptance of terms. But I wish the reader clearly and deeply to understand the difference between the two economies, to which the terms 'Political' and 'Mercantile' might not unadvisedly be attached.

Political economy (the economy of a State, or of citizens) consists simply in the production, preservation, and distribution, at fittest time and place, of useful or pleasurable things. The farmer who cuts his hay at the right time; the shipwright who drives his bolts well home in sound wood; the builder who lays good bricks in well-tempered mortar; the housewife who takes care of her furniture in the parlour, and guards against all waste in her kitchen; and the singer who rightly disciplines, and never overstrains her voice, are all political economists in the true and final sense: adding continually to the riches and well-being of the nation to which they belong.

But mercantile economy, the economy of 'merces' or of 'pay,' signifies the accumulation, in the hands of individuals, of legal or moral claim upon, or power over, the labour of others; every such claim implying precisely as much poverty or debt on one side, as it implies riches or right on the other.

It does not, therefore, necessarily involve an addition to the actual property, or well-being of the State in which it exists. But since this commercial wealth, or power over labour, is nearly always convertible at once into real property, while real property is not always convertible at once into power over labour,[31] the idea of riches among active men in civilized nations generally refers to commercial wealth; and in estimating their possessions, they rather calculate the value of their horses and fields by the number of guineas they could get for them, than the value of their guineas by the number of horses and fields they could buy with them.

There is, however, another reason for this habit of mind: namely, that an accumulation of real property is of little use to its owner, unless, together with it, he has commercial power over labour. Thus, suppose any person to be put in possession of a large estate of fruitful land, with rich beds of gold in its gravel; countless herds of cattle in its pastures; houses, and gardens, and storehouses full of useful stores: but suppose, after all, that he could get no servants? In order that he may be able to have servants, some one in his neighbourhood must be poor, and in want of his gold – or his corn. Assume that no one is in want of either, and that no servants are to be had. He must, therefore, bake his own bread, make his own clothes, plough his own ground, and shepherd his own flocks. His gold will be as useful to him as any other yellow pebbles on his estate. His stores must rot, for he cannot consume them. He can eat no more than another man could eat, and wear no more than another man could wear. He must lead a life of severe and common labour to procure even ordinary comforts; he will be ultimately unable to keep either houses in repair, or fields in cultivation; and forced to content himself with a poor man's portion of cottage and garden, in the midst of a desert of waste land, trampled by wild cattle, and encumbered by ruins of palaces, which he will hardly mock at himself by calling 'his own.'

The most covetous of mankind would, with small exultation, I presume, accept riches of this kind on these terms. What is really desired, under the name of riches, is, essentially, power over men; in its simplest sense, the power of obtaining for our own advantage the labour of servant, tradesman, and artist; in wider sense, authority of directing large masses of the nation to various ends (good, trivial, or hurtful, according to the mind of the rich person). And this power of wealth of course is greater or less in direct proportion to the poverty of the men over whom it is exercised, and in inverse proportion to the number of persons who are as rich as ourselves, and who are ready to give the same price for an article of which the supply is limited. If the musician is poor, he will sing for small pay, as long as there is only one person who can pay him; but if there be two or three, he will sing for the one who offers him most. And thus the power of the riches of the patron (always imperfect and doubtful, as we shall see presently,[32] even when most authoritative) depends first on the poverty of the artist, and then on the limitation of the number of equally wealthy persons, who also want seats at the concert. So that, as above stated, the art of becoming 'rich,' in the common sense, is not absolutely nor finally the art of accumulating much money for ourselves, but also of contriving that our neighbours shall have less. In accurate terms, it is 'the art of establishing the maximum inequality in our own favour.'

Now, the establishment of such inequality cannot be shown in the abstract to be either advantageous or disadvantageous to the body of the nation. The rash and absurd assumption that such inequalities are necessarily advantageous, lies at the root of most of the popular fallacies on the subject of political economy. For the eternal and inevitable law in this matter is, that the beneficialness of the inequality[33] depends, first, on the methods by which it was accomplished; and, secondly, on the purposes to which it is applied. Inequalities of wealth, unjustly established, have assuredly injured the nation in which they exist during their establishment; and, unjustly directed, injure it yet more during their existence. But inequalities of wealth, justly established, benefit the nation in the course of their establishment; and, nobly used, aid it yet more by their existence. That is to say, among every active and well-governed people, the various strength of individuals, tested by full exertion and specially applied to various need, issues in unequal, but harmonious results, receiving reward or authority according to its class and service;* while, in the inactive or ill-governed nation, the gradations of decay and the victories of treason work out also their own rugged system of subjection and success; and substitute, for the melodious inequalities of concurrent power, the iniquitous dominances and depressions of guilt and misfortune.

Thus the circulation of wealth in a nation resembles that of the blood in the natural body. There is one quickness of the current which comes of cheerful emotion or wholesome exercise; and another which comes of shame or of fever. There is a flush of the body which is full of warmth and life; and another which will pass into putrefaction.

The analogy will hold down even to minute particulars. For as diseased local determination of the blood involves depression of the general health of

---

* I have been naturally asked several times with respect to the sentence in the first of these papers, 'the bad workmen unemployed,' 'But what are you to do with your bad unemployed workmen?' Well, it seems to me the question might have occurred to you before. Your housemaid's place is vacant – you give twenty pounds a year – two girls come for it, one neatly dressed, the other dirtily; one with good recommendations, the other with none. You do not, under these circumstances, usually ask the dirty one if she will come for fifteen pounds, or twelve; and, on her consenting, take her instead of the well-recommended one. Still less do you try to beat both down by making them bid against each other, till you can hire both, one at twelve pounds a year, and the other at eight. You simply take the one fittest for the place, and send away the other, not perhaps concerning yourself quite as much as you should with the question which you now impatiently put to me, 'What is to become of her?' For, all that I advise you to do, is to deal with workmen as with servants; and verily the question is of weight: 'Your bad workman, idler, and rogue – what are you to do with him?'

We will consider of this presently: remember that the administration of a complete system of national commerce and industry cannot be explained in full detail within the space of twelve pages. Meantime, consider whether, there being confessedly some difficulty in dealing with rogues and idlers, it may not be advisable to produce as few of them as possible. If you examine into the history of rogues, you will find they are as truly manufactured articles as anything else, and it is just because our present system of political economy gives so large a stimulus to that manufacture that you may know it to be a false one. We had better seek for a system which will develop honest men, than for one which will deal cunningly with vagabonds. Let us reform our schools, and we shall find little reform needed in our prisons.

the system, all morbid local action of riches will be found ultimately to involve a weakening of the resources of the body politic.

The mode in which this is produced may be at once understood by examining one or two instances of the development of wealth in the simplest possible circumstances.

Suppose two sailors cast away[34] on an uninhabited coast, and obliged to maintain themselves there by their own labour for a series of years.

If they both kept their health, and worked steadily and in amity with each other, they might build themselves a convenient house, and in time come to possess a certain quantity of cultivated land, together with various stores laid up for future use. All these things would be real riches or property; and, supposing the men both to have worked equally hard, they would each have right to equal share or use of it. Their political economy would consist merely in careful preservation and just division of these possessions. Perhaps, however, after some time one or other might be dissatisfied with the results of their common farming; and they might in consequence agree to divide the land they had brought under the spade into equal shares, so that each might thenceforward work in his own field, and live by it. Suppose that after this arrangement had been made, one of them were to fall ill, and be unable to work on his land at a critical time – say of sowing or harvest.

He would naturally ask the other to sow or reap for him.

Then his companion might say, with perfect justice, 'I will do this additional work for you; but if I do it, you must promise to do as much for me at another time. I will count how many hours I spend on your ground, and you shall give me a written promise to work for the same number of hours on mine, whenever I need your help, and you are able to give it.'

Suppose the disabled man's sickness to continue, and that under various circumstances, for several years, requiring the help of the other, he on each occasion gave a written pledge to work, as soon as he was able, at his companion's orders, for the same number of hours which the other had given up to him. What will the positions of the two men be when the invalid is able to resume work?

Considered as a 'Polis,' or state, they will be poorer than they would have been otherwise: poorer by the withdrawal of what the sick man's labour would have produced in the interval. His friend may perhaps have toiled with an energy quickened by the enlarged need, but in the end his own land and property must have suffered by the withdrawal of so much of his time and thought from them: and the united property of the two men will be certainly less than it would have been if both had remained in health and activity.

But the relations in which they stand to each other are also widely altered. The sick man has not only pledged his labour for some years, but will probably have exhausted his own share of the accumulated stores, and will be in consequence for some time dependent on the other for food, which he can only 'pay' or reward him for by yet more deeply pledging his own labour.

Supposing the written promises to be held entirely valid (among civilized nations their validity is secured by legal measures*), the person who had hitherto worked for both might now, if he chose, rest altogether, and pass his time in idleness, not only forcing his companion to redeem all the engagements he had already entered into, but exacting from him pledges for further labour, to an arbitrary amount, for what food he had to advance to him.

There might not, from first to last, be the least illegality (in the ordinary sense of the word) in the arrangement; but if a stranger arrived on the coast at this advanced epoch of their political economy, he would find one man commercially Rich; the other commercially Poor. He would see, perhaps, with no small surprise, one passing his days in idleness; the other labouring for both, and living sparely, in the hope of recovering his independence at some distant period.

This is, of course, an example of one only out of many ways in which inequality of possession may be established between different persons, giving rise to the Mercantile forms of Riches and Poverty. In the instance before us, one of the men might from the first have deliberately chosen to be idle, and to put his life in pawn for present ease; or he might have mismanaged his land, and been compelled to have recourse to his neighbour for food and help, pledging his future labour for it. But what I want the reader to note especially is the fact, common to a large number of typical cases of this kind, that the establishment of the mercantile wealth which

---

* The disputes which exist respecting the real nature of money arise more from the disputants examining its functions on different sides, than from any real dissent in their opinions. All money, properly so called, is an acknowledgment of debt; but as such, it may either be considered to represent the labour and property of the creditor, or the idleness and penury of the debtor. The intricacy of the question has been much increased by the (hitherto necessary) use of marketable commodities, such as gold, silver, salt, shells, etc., to give intrinsic value or security to currency; but the final and best definition of money is that it is a documentary promise ratified and guaranteed by the nation to give or find a certain quantity of labour on demand. A man's labour for a day is a better standard of value than a measure of any produce, because no produce ever maintains a consistent rate of productibility.

consists in a claim upon labour, signifies a political diminution of the real wealth which consists in substantial possessions.[35]

Take another example, more consistent with the ordinary course of affairs of trade. Suppose that three men, instead of two, formed the little isolated republic, and found themselves obliged to separate, in order to farm different pieces of land at some distance from each other along the coast: each estate furnishing a distinct kind of produce, and each more or less in need of the material raised on the other. Suppose that the third man, in order to save the time of all three, undertakes simply to superintend the transference of commodities from one farm to the other[36]; on condition of receiving some sufficiently remunerative share of every parcel of goods conveyed, or of some other parcel received in exchange for it.

If this carrier or messenger always brings to each estate, from the other, what is chiefly wanted, at the right time, the operations of the two farmers will go on prosperously, and the largest possible result in produce, or wealth, will be attained by the little community. But suppose no inter-course between the landowners is possible, except through the travelling agent; and that, after a time, this agent, watching the course of each man's agriculture, keeps back the articles with which he has been entrusted until there comes a period of extreme necessity for them, on one side or other, and then exacts in exchange for them all that the distressed farmer can spare of other kinds of produce: it is easy to see that by ingeniously watching his opportunities, he might possess himself regularly of the greater part of the superfluous produce of the two estates, and at last, in some year of severest trial or scarcity, purchase both for himself and maintain the former proprietors thenceforward as his labourers or servants.

This would be a case of commercial wealth acquired on the exactest principles of modern political economy. But more distinctly even than in the former instance, it is manifest in this that the wealth of the State, or of the three men considered as a society, is collectively less than it would have been had the merchant been content with juster profit. The operations of the two agriculturists have been cramped to the utmost; and the continual limitations of the supply of things they wanted at critical times, together with the failure of courage consequent on the prolongation of a struggle for mere existence, without any sense of permanent gain, must have seriously diminished the effective results of their labour; and the stores finally accumulated in the merchant's hands will not in any wise be of equivalent value to those which, had his dealings been honest, would have filled at once the granaries of the farmers and his own.

The whole question, therefore, respecting not only the advantage, but even the quantity, of national wealth, resolves itself finally into one of abstract justice.[37] It is impossible to conclude, of any given mass of acquired wealth, merely by the fact of its existence, whether it signifies good or evil to the nation in the midst of which it exists. Its real value depends on the moral sign attached to it, just as sternly as that of a mathematical quantity depends on the algebraical sign attached to it. Any given accumulation of commercial wealth may be indicative, on the one hand, of faithful industries, progressive energies, and productive ingenuities: or, on the other, it may be indicative of mortal luxury, merciless tyranny, ruinous chicane. Some treasures are heavy with human tears, as an ill-stored harvest with untimely rain; and some gold is brighter in sunshine than it is in substance.

And these are not, observe, merely moral or pathetic[38] attributes of riches, which the seeker of riches may, if he chooses, despise; they are, literally and sternly, material attributes of riches, depreciating or exalting, incalculably, the monetary signification of the sum in question. One mass of money is the outcome of action which has created, – another, of action which has annihilated, – ten times as much in the gathering of it; such and such strong hands have been paralyzed, as if they had been numbed by nightshade: so many strong men's courage broken, so many productive operations hindered; this and the other false direction given to labour, and lying image of prosperity set up, on Dura plains[39] dug into seven-times-heated furnaces. That which seems to be wealth may in verity be only the gilded index of far-reaching ruin; a wrecker's handful of coin gleaned from the beach to which he has beguiled an argosy; a camp-follower's bundle of rags unwrapped from the breasts of goodly soldiers dead; the purchase-pieces of potter's fields, wherein shall be buried together the citizen and the stranger.[40]

And therefore, the idea that directions can be given for the gaining of wealth, irrespectively of the consideration of its moral sources, or that any general and technical law of purchase and gain can be set down for national practice, is perhaps the most insolently futile of all that ever beguiled men through their vices. So far as I know, there is not in history record of anything so disgraceful to the human intellect as the modern idea that the commercial text, 'Buy in the cheapest market and sell in the dearest,' represents, or under any circumstances could represent, an available principle of national economy. Buy in the cheapest market? – yes; but what made your market cheap? Charcoal may be cheap among your roof timbers after a fire, and bricks may be cheap in your streets after an earthquake; but fire and earthquake may not therefore be national benefits. Sell in the dearest? – yes, truly; but what made your market dear? You sold your bread well to-day: was it to a dying man who gave his last coin for it, and will never need bread more; or to a rich man who to-morrow will buy your farm over your head; or to a soldier on his way to pillage the bank in which you have put your fortune?

None of these things you can know. One thing only you can know: namely, whether this dealing of yours is a just and faithful one, which is all you need concern yourself about respecting it; sure thus to have done your own part in bringing about ultimately in the world a state of things which will not issue in pillage or in death. And thus every question concerning these things merges itself ultimately in the great question of justice, which, the ground being thus far cleared for it, I will enter upon in the next paper, leaving only, in this, three final points for the reader's consideration.

It has been shown that the chief value and virtue of money consists in its having power over human beings; that, without this power, large material possessions are useless, and to any person possessing such power, comparatively unnecessary. But power over human beings is attainable by other means than by money. As I said a few pages back, the money power is always imperfect and doubtful; there are many things which cannot be reached with it, others which cannot be retained by it. Many joys may be given to men which cannot be bought for gold, and many fidelities found in them which cannot be rewarded with it.

Trite enough, – the reader thinks. Yes: but it is not so trite, – I wish it were, – that in this moral power, quite inscrutable and immeasurable though it be, there is a monetary value just as real as that represented by more ponderous currencies. A man's hand may be full of invisible gold, and the wave of it, or the grasp, shall do more than another's with a shower of bullion. This invisible gold, also, does not necessarily diminish in spending. Political economists will do well some day to take heed of it, though they cannot take measure.

But farther. Since the essence of wealth consists in its authority over men, if the apparent or nominal wealth fail in this power, it fails in essence; in fact, ceases to be wealth at all. It does not appear lately in England, that our authority over men is absolute. The servants show some disposition to rush riotously upstairs, under an impression that their wages are not regularly paid.[41] We should augur ill of any gentleman's property to whom this happened every other day in his drawing-room.

So, also, the power of our wealth seems limited as respects the comfort of the servants, no less than their quietude. The persons in the kitchen appear to be ill-dressed, squalid, half-starved. One cannot help imagining that the riches of the establishment must be of a very theoretical and documentary character.

Finally. Since the essence of wealth consists in power over men, will it not follow that the nobler and the more in number the persons are over whom it has power, the greater the wealth? Perhaps it may even appear, after some consideration, that the persons themselves *are* the wealth – that these pieces of gold with which we are in the habit of guiding them, are, in fact, nothing more than a kind of Byzantine harness or trappings, very glittering and beautiful in barbaric sight, wherewith we bridle the creatures; but that if these same living creatures could be guided without the fretting and jingling of the Byzants[42] in their mouths and ears, they might themselves be more valuable than their bridles. In fact, it may be discovered that the true veins of wealth are purple – and not in Rock, but in Flesh – perhaps even that the final outcome and consummation of all wealth is in the producing as many as possible full-breathed, bright-eyed, and happy-hearted human creatures. Our modern wealth, I think, has rather a tendency the other way; – most political economists appearing to consider multitudes of human creatures not conducive to wealth, or at best conducive to it only by remaining in a dim-eyed and narrow-chested state of being.

Nevertheless, it is open, I repeat, to serious question, which I leave to the reader's pondering, whether, among national manufactures, that of Souls of a good quality may not at last turn out a quite leadingly lucrative one? Nay, in some far-away and yet undreamt-of hour, I can even imagine that England may cast all thoughts of possessive wealth back to the barbaric nations among whom they first arose; and that, while the sands of the Indus and adamant of Golconda[43] may yet stiffen the housings of the charger, and flash from the turban of the slave, she, as a Christian mother, may at last attain to the virtues and the treasures of a Heathen one, and be able to lead forth her Sons, saying, –

'These are MY Jewels.'[44]

ESSAY III

QUI JUDICATIS TERRAM

SOME centuries before the Christian era, a Jew merchant,[45] largely engaged in business on the Gold Coast,[46] and reported to have made one of the largest fortunes of his time (held also in repute for much practical sagacity), left among his ledgers some general maxims concerning wealth, which have been preserved, strangely enough, even to our own days. They were held in considerable respect by the most active traders of the Middle Ages, especially by the Venetians, who even went so far in their admiration as to place a statue of the old Jew on the angle of one of their principal public buildings.[47] Of late years these writings have fallen into disrepute, being opposed in every particular to the spirit of modern commerce. Nevertheless I shall reproduce a passage or two from them here, partly because they may interest the reader by their novelty; and chiefly because they will show him that it is possible for a very practical and acquisitive tradesman to hold, through a not unsuccessful career, that principle of distinction between well-gotten and ill-gotten wealth, which, partially insisted on in my last paper, it must be our work more completely to examine in this.

He says, for instance, in one place: 'The getting of treasures by a lying tongue is a vanity tossed to and fro of them that seek death'[48]; adding in another, with the same meaning (he has a curious way of doubling his sayings): 'Treasures of wickedness profit nothing: but justice delivers from death.'[49] Both these passages are notable for their assertions of death as the only real issue and sum of attainment by any unjust scheme of wealth. If we read, instead of 'lying tongue,' 'lying label, title, pretence, or advertisement,'[50] we shall more clearly perceive the bearing of the words on modern business. The seeking of death is a grand expression of the true course of men's toil in such business. We usually speak as if death pursued us, and we fled from him; but that is only so in rare instances. Ordinarily he masks himself – makes himself beautiful – all-glorious; not like the King's daughter, all glorious within,[51] but outwardly: his clothing of wrought gold. We pursue him frantically all our days, he flying or hiding from us. Our crowning success at three-score and ten is utterly and perfectly to seize, and hold him in his eternal integrity – robes, ashes, and sting.

Again: the merchant says, 'He that oppresseth the poor to increase his riches, shall surely come to want.'[52] And again, more strongly: 'Rob not the poor because he is poor; neither oppress the afflicted in the place of business. For God shall spoil the soul of those that spoiled them.'[53]

This 'robbing the poor because he is poor,' is especially the mercantile form of theft, consisting in taking advantage of a man's necessities in order to obtain his labour or property at a reduced price. The ordinary highwayman's opposite form of robbery – of the rich, because he is rich – does not appear to occur so often to the old merchant's mind; probably because, being less profitable and more dangerous than the robbery of the poor, it is rarely practised by persons of discretion.

But the two most remarkable passages in their deep general significance are the following: –

'The rich and the poor have met. God is their maker.'

'The rich and the poor have met. God is their light.'[54]

They 'have met': more literally, have stood in each other's way (*obviaverunt*). That is to say, as long as the world lasts, the action and counteraction of wealth and poverty, the meeting, face to face, of rich and poor, is just as appointed and necessary a law of that world as the flow of stream to sea, or the interchange of power among the electric clouds: – 'God is their maker.' But, also, this action may be either gentle and just, or convulsive and destructive: it may be by rage of devouring flood, or by lapse of serviceable wave; – in blackness of thunderstroke, or continual force of vital fire, soft, and shapeable into love-syllables from far away. And which of these it shall be, depends on both rich and poor knowing that God is their light; that in the mystery of human life, there is no other light than this by which they can see each other's faces, and live; – light, which is called in another of the books among which the merchant's maxims have been preserved, the 'sun of justice,'*[55] of which it is promised that it shall rise at

---

* More accurately, Sun of Justness; but, instead of the harsh word 'Justness,' the old English 'Righteousness' being commonly employed, has, by getting confused with 'godliness,' or attracting about it various vague and broken meanings, prevented most persons from receiving the force of the passage in which it occurs. The word 'righteousness' properly refers to the justice of rule, or right, as distinguished from 'equity,' which refers to the justice of balance. More broadly, Righteousness is King's justice; and Equity Judge's justice; the King guiding or ruling all, the Judge dividing or discerning between opposites (therefore, the double question, 'Man, who made me a ruler – δικαστὴς – or a divider – μεριστὴς – over you?'[56]) Thus, with respect to the Justice of Choice (selection, the feebler and passive justice), we have from lego, – lex, legal, loi, and loyal; and with respect to the Justice of Rule (direction, the stronger and active justice), we have from rego, – rex, regal, roi, and royal.

last with 'healing' (health-giving or helping, making whole or setting at one) in its wings. For truly this healing is only possible by means of justice; no love, no faith, no hope will do it; men will be unwisely fond – vainly faithful, – unless primarily they are just; and the mistake of the best men through generation after generation, has been that great one of thinking to help the poor by almsgiving, and by preaching of patience or of hope, and by every other means, emollient or consolatory, except the one thing which God orders for them, justice. But this justice, with its accompanying holiness or helpfulness, being even by the best man denied in its trial time, is by the mass of men hated wherever it appears: so that, when the choice was one day fairly put to them, they denied the Helpful One and the Just;*[57] and desired a murderer, sedition-raiser, and robber, to be granted to them[59]; – the murderer instead of the Lord of Life, the sedition-raiser instead of the Prince of Peace, and the robber instead of the Just Judge of all the world.

I have just spoken of the flowing of streams to the sea as a partial image of the action of wealth. In one respect it is not a partial, but a perfect image. The popular economist thinks himself wise in having discovered that wealth, or the forms of property in general, must go where they are required; that where demand is, supply must follow.[60] He farther declares that this course of demand and supply cannot be forbidden by human laws. Precisely in the same sense, and with the same certainty, the waters of the world go where they are required. Where the land falls, the water flows. The course neither of clouds nor rivers can be forbidden by human will. But the disposition and administration of them can be altered by human forethought. Whether the stream shall be a curse or a blessing, depends upon man's labour, and administering intelligence. For centuries after centuries, great districts of the world, rich in soil, and favoured in climate, have lain desert under the rage of their own rivers; nor only desert, but plague-struck.[61] The stream which, rightly directed, would have flowed in soft irrigation from field to field – would have purified the air, given food to man and beast, and carried their burdens for them on its bosom – now overwhelms the plain and poisons the wind; its breath pestilence, and its work famine. In like manner this wealth 'goes where it is required.' No human laws can withstand its flow. They can only guide it: but this, the leading trench and limiting mound can do so thoroughly, that it shall become water of life – the riches of the hand of wisdom;† or, on the

---

* In another place written with the same meaning, 'Just, and having salvation.'[58]
† 'Length of days in her right hand; in her left, riches and honour.'[62]

contrary, by leaving it to its own lawless flow, they may make it, what it has been too often, the last and deadliest of national plagues: water of Marah[63] – the water which feeds the roots of all evil.

The necessity of these laws of distribution or restraint is curiously overlooked in the ordinary political economist's definition of his own 'science.' He calls it, shortly, the 'science of getting rich.' But there are many sciences, as well as many arts, of getting rich. Poisoning people of large estates, was one employed largely in the Middle Ages; adulteration of food of people of small estates, is one employed largely now. The ancient and honourable Highland method of black mail[64]; the more modern and less honourable system of obtaining goods on credit, and the other variously improved methods of appropriation – which, in major and minor scales of industry, down to the most artistic pocket-picking, we owe to recent genius, – all come under the general head of sciences, or arts, of getting rich.

So that it is clear the popular economist, in calling his science the science par excellence of getting rich, must attach some peculiar ideas of limitation to its character. I hope I do not misrepresent him, by assuming that he means *his* science to be the science of 'getting rich by legal or just means.' In this definition, is the word 'just,' or 'legal,' finally to stand? For it is possible among certain nations, or under certain rulers, or by help of certain advocates, that proceedings may be legal which are by no means just. If, therefore, we leave at last only the word 'just' in that place of our definition, the insertion of this solitary and small word will make a notable difference in the grammar of our science. For then it will follow that in order to grow rich scientifically, we must grow rich justly; and, therefore, know what is just; so that our economy will no longer depend merely on prudence, but on jurisprudence – and that of divine, not human law. Which prudence is indeed of no mean order, holding itself, as it were, high in the air of heaven, and gazing for ever on the light of the sun of justice; hence the souls which have excelled in it are represented by Dante[65] as stars forming in heaven for ever the figure of the eye of an eagle; they having been in life the discerners of light from darkness; or to the whole human race, as the light of the body, which is the eye[66]; while those souls which form the wings of the bird (giving power and dominion to justice, 'healing in its wings') trace also in light the inscription in heaven: 'DILIGITE JUSTITIAM QUI JUDICATIS TERRAM.' 'Ye who judge the earth, give' (not, observe, merely love, but) 'diligent love to justice': the love which seeks diligently, that is to say, choosingly, and by preference to all things else. Which judging or doing judgment in the earth is, according to their capacity and position, required not of judges only, nor of rulers only, but of all men:* a truth sorrowfully lost sight of even by those who are ready enough to apply to themselves passages in which Christian men are spoken of as called to be 'saints' (*i.e.*, to helpful or healing functions); and 'chosen to be kings'[67] (*i.e.*, to knowing or directing functions); the true meaning of these titles having been long lost through the pretences of unhelpful and unable persons to saintly and kingly character; also through the once popular idea that both the sanctity and royalty are to consist in wearing long robes and high crowns, instead of in mercy and judgment[68]; whereas all true sanctity is saving power, as all true royalty is ruling power; and injustice is part and parcel of the denial of such power, which 'makes men as the creeping things, as the fishes of the sea, that have no ruler over them.'†[69]

Absolute justice is indeed no more attainable than absolute truth; but the righteous man is distinguished from the unrighteous by his desire and hope of justice, as the true man from the false by his desire and hope of truth. And though absolute justice be unattainable, as much justice as we need for all practical use is attainable by all those who make it their aim.

We have to examine, then, in the subject before us, what are the laws of justice respecting payment of labour – no small part, these, of the foundations of all jurisprudence.

I reduced, in my last paper, the idea of money payment to its simplest or radical terms. In those terms its nature, and the conditions of justice respecting it, can be best ascertained.

Money payment, as there stated, consists radically in a promise to some person working for us, that for the time and labour he spends in our service to-day we will give or procure equivalent time and labour[70] in his service at any future time when he may demand it.‡

---

* I hear that several of our lawyers have been greatly amused by the statement in the first of these papers that a lawyer's function was to do justice. I did not intend it for a jest; nevertheless it will be seen that in the above passage neither the determination nor doing of justice are contemplated as functions wholly peculiar to the lawyer. Possibly, the more our standing armies, whether of soldiers, pastors, or legislators (the generic term 'pastor' including all teachers, and the generic term 'lawyer' including makers as well as interpreters of law), can be superseded by the force of national heroism, wisdom, and honesty, the better it may be for the nation.

† It being the privilege of the fishes, as it is of rats and wolves, to live by the laws of demand and supply; but the distinction of humanity, to live by those of right.

‡ It might appear at first that the market price of labour expressed such an exchange: but this is a fallacy, for the market price is the momentary price of the kind of labour required, but the just price is its equivalent of the productive labour of mankind. This difference will be analyzed in its place.[71] It must be noted also that I

If we promise to give him less labour than he has given us, we under-pay him. If we promise to give him more labour than he has given us, we over-pay him. In practice, according to the laws of demand and supply, when two men are ready to do the work, and only one man wants to have it done, the two men underbid each other for it; and the one who gets it to do, is under-paid. But when two men want the work done, and there is only one man ready to do it, the two men who want it done overbid each other, and the workman is over-paid.

I will examine these two points of injustice in succession; but first I wish the reader to clearly understand the central principle, lying between the two, of right or just payment.

When we ask a service of any man, he may either give it us freely, or demand payment for it. Respecting free gift of service, there is no question at present, that being a matter of affection – not of traffic. But if he demand payment for it, and we wish to treat him with absolute equity, it is evident that this equity can only consist in giving time for time, strength for strength, and skill for skill. If a man works an hour for us, and we only promise to work half an hour for him in return, we obtain an unjust advantage. If, on the contrary, we promise to work an hour and a half for him in return, he has an unjust advantage. The justice consists in absolute exchange; or, if there be any respect to the stations of the parties, it will not be in favour of the employer: there is certainly no equitable reason in a man's being poor, that if he give me a pound of bread to-day, I should return him less than a pound of bread to-morrow; or any equitable reason in a man's being uneducated, that if he uses a certain quantity of skill and knowledge in my service, I should use a less quantity of skill and knowledge in his. Perhaps, ultimately, it may appear desirable, or, to say the least, gracious, that I should give in return somewhat more than I received. But at present, we are concerned on the law of justice only,[72] which is that of perfect and accurate exchange; – one circumstance only interfering with the simplicity of this radical idea of just payment – that inasmuch as labour (rightly directed) is fruitful just as seed is, the fruit (or 'interest,'[73] as it is called) of the labour first given, or 'advanced,' ought to be taken into account, and balanced by an additional quantity of labour in the subsequent repayment. Supposing the repayment to take place at the end of the year, or

speak here only of the exchangeable value of labour, not of that of commodities. The exchangeable value of a commodity is that of the labour required to produce it, multiplied into the force of the demand for it. If the value of the labour $= x$ and the force of demand $= y$, the exchangeable value of the commodity is xy, in which if either $x = 0$, or $y = 0$, $xy = 0$.

of any other given time, this calculation could be approximately made, but as money (that is to say, cash) payment involves no reference to time (it being optional with the person paid to spend what he receives at once or after any number of years), we can only assume, generally, that some slight advantage must in equity be allowed to the person who advances the labour, so that the typical form of bargain will be: If you give me an hour to-day, I will give you an hour and five minutes on demand. If you give me a pound of bread to-day, I will give you seventeen ounces on demand, and so on. All that is necessary for the reader to note is, that the amount returned is at least in equity not to be *less* than the amount given.

The abstract idea, then, of just or due wages, as respects the labourer, is that they will consist in a sum of money which will at any time procure for him at least as much labour as he has given, rather more than less. And this equity or justice of payment is, observe, wholly independent of any reference to the number of men who are willing to do the work. I want a horseshoe for my horse. Twenty smiths, or twenty thousand smiths,[74] may be ready to forge it; their number does not in one atom's weight affect the question of the equitable payment of the one who *does* forge it. It costs him a quarter of an hour of his life, and so much skill and strength of arm, to make that horseshoe for me. Then at some future time I am bound in equity to give a quarter of an hour, and some minutes more, of my life (or of some other person's at my disposal), and also as much strength of arm and skill, and a little more, in making or doing what the smith may have need of.

Such being the abstract theory of just remunerative payment, its application is practically[75] modified by the fact that the order for labour, given in payment, is general, while the labour received is special. The current coin or document is practically an order on the nation for so much work of any kind; and this universal applicability to immediate need renders it so much more valuable than special labour can be, that an order for a less quantity of this general toil will always be accepted as a just equivalent for a greater quantity of special toil. Any given craftsman will always be willing to give an hour of his own work in order to receive command over half an hour, or even much less, of national work. This source of uncertainty, together with the difficulty of determining the monetary value of skill,* render the

---

* Under the term 'skill' I mean to include the united force of experience, intellect, and passion, in their operation on manual labour: and under the term 'passion' to include the entire range and agency of the moral feelings; from the simple patience and gentleness of mind which will give continuity and fineness to the touch, or enable one person to work without fatigue, and with good effect, twice as long as another, up to the qualities of character which render science possible – (the retardation of science

ascertainment (even approximate) of the proper wages of any given labour in terms of a currency, matter of considerable complexity. But they do not affect the principle of exchange. The worth of the work may not be easily known; but it *has* a worth, just as fixed and real as the specific gravity of a substance, though such specific gravity may not be easily ascertainable when the substance is united with many others. Nor is there so much difficulty or chance in determining it, as in determining the ordinary maxima and minima of vulgar political economy. There are few bargains in which the buyer can ascertain with anything like precision that the seller would have taken no less; – or the seller acquire more than a comfortable faith that the purchaser would have given no more. This impossibility of precise knowledge prevents neither from striving to attain the desired point of greatest vexation and injury to the other, nor from accepting it for a scientific principle that he is to buy for the least and sell for the most possible, though what the real least or most may be he cannot tell. In like manner, a just person lays it down for a scientific principle that he is to pay a just price, and, without being able precisely to ascertain the limits of such a price, will nevertheless strive to attain the closest possible approximation to them. A practically serviceable approximation he *can* obtain. It is easier to

by envy is one of the most tremendous losses in the economy of the present century) – and to the incommunicable emotion and imagination which are the first and mightiest sources of all value in art.

It is highly singular that political economists should not yet have perceived, if not the moral, at least the passionate element, to be an inextricable quantity in every calculation. I cannot conceive, for instance, how it was possible that Mr Mill should have followed the true clue so far as to write, – 'No limit can be set to the importance – even in a purely productive and material point of view – of mere thought,' without seeing that it was logically necessary to add also, 'and of mere feeling.' And this the more, because in his first definition of labour[76] he includes in the idea of it 'all feelings of a disagreeable kind connected with the employment of one's thoughts in a particular occupation.' True; but why not also, 'feelings of an agreeable kind'? It can hardly be supposed that the feelings which retard labour are more essentially a part of the labour than those which accelerate it. The first are paid for as pain, the second as power. The workman is merely indemnified for the first; but the second both produce a part of the exchangeable value of the work, and materially increase its actual quantity.[77]

'Fritz is with us. *He* is worth fifty thousand men.' Truly, a large addition to the material force; – consisting, however, be it observed, not more in operations carried on in Fritz's head, than in operations carried on in his armies' heart. 'No limit can be set to the importance of *mere* thought.' Perhaps not! Nay, suppose some day it should turn out that 'mere' thought was in itself a recommendable object of production, and that all Material production was only a step towards this more precious Immaterial one?

determine scientifically what a man ought to have for his work, than what his necessities will compel him to take for it.[78] His necessities can only be ascertained by empirical, but his due by analytical, investigation. In the one case, you try your answer to the sum like a puzzled schoolboy – till you find one that fits; in the other, you bring out your result within certain limits, by process of calculation.

Supposing, then, the just wages of any quantity of given labour to have been ascertained, let us examine the first results of just and unjust payment, when in favour of the purchaser or employer: *i.e.*, when two men are ready to do the work, and only one wants to have it done.

The unjust purchaser forces the two to bid against each other till he has reduced their demand to its lowest terms. Let us assume that the lowest bidder offers to do the work at half its just price.

The purchaser employs him, and does not employ the other. The first or *apparent* result is, therefore, that one of the two men is left out of employ, or to starvation, just as definitely as by the just procedure of giving fair price to the best workman. The various writers who endeavoured to invalidate the positions of my first paper never saw this, and assumed that the unjust hirer employed *both*. He employs both no more than the just hirer. The only difference (in the outset) is that the just man pays sufficiently, the unjust man insufficiently, for the labour of the single person employed.

I say, 'in the outset'; for this first or apparent difference is not the actual difference. By the unjust procedure, half the proper price of the work is left in the hands of the employer. This enables him to hire another man at the same unjust rate, on some other kind of work; and the final result is that he has two men working for him at half-price, and two are out of employ.

By the just procedure, the whole price of the first piece of work goes into the hands of the man who does it. No surplus being left in the employer's hands, *he* cannot hire another man for another piece of labour. But by precisely so much as his power is diminished, the hired workman's power is increased: that is to say, by the additional half of the price he has received; which additional half *he* has the power of using to employ another man in *his* service. I will suppose, for the moment, the least favourable, though quite probable, case – that, though justly treated himself, he yet will act unjustly to his subordinate; and hire at half-price if he can. The final result will then be, that one man works for the employer, at just price; one for the workman, at half-price; and two, as in the first case, are still out of employ. These two, as I said before, are out of employ in *both* cases. The difference between the just and unjust procedure does not lie in the number of men hired, but in the price paid to them, and the *persons by whom* it is paid. The essential difference, that which I want the reader to see clearly, is, that in the unjust case, two men work for one, the first hirer. In the just case, one man works for the first hirer, one for the person hired, and so on, down or up through the various grades of service; the influence being carried forward by justice, and arrested by injustice. The universal and constant action of justice in this matter is therefore to diminish the power of wealth, in the hands of one individual, over masses of men, and to distribute it through a chain of men. The actual power exerted by the wealth is the same in both cases; but by injustice it is put all into one man's hands, so that he directs at once and with equal force the labour of a circle of men about him; by the just procedure, he is permitted to touch the nearest only, through whom, with diminished force, modified by new minds, the energy of the wealth passes on to others, and so till it exhausts itself.

The immediate operation of justice in this respect is therefore to diminish the power of wealth, first, in acquisition of luxury, and secondly, in exercise of moral influence. The employer cannot concentrate so multitudinous labour on his own interests, nor can he subdue so multitudinous mind to his own will. But the secondary operation of justice is not less important. The insufficient payment of the group of men working for one, places each under a maximum of difficulty in rising above his position. The tendency of the system is to check advancement. But the sufficient or just payment, distributed through a descending series of offices or grades of labour,* gives each subordinated person fair and sufficient means of rising in the social

---

* I am sorry to lose time by answering, however curtly, the equivocations of the writers who sought to obscure the instances given of regulated labour in the first of these papers, by confusing kinds, ranks, and quantities of labour with its qualities. I never said that a colonel should have the same pay as a private, nor a bishop the same pay as a curate. Neither did I say that more work ought to be paid as less work (so that the curate of a parish of two thousand souls should have no more than the curate of a parish of five hundred). But I said that, so far as you employ it at all, bad work should be paid no less than good work; as a bad clergyman yet takes his tithes, a bad physician takes his fee, and a bad lawyer his costs. And this, as will be farther shown in the conclusion, I said, and say, partly because the best work never was, nor ever will be, done for money at all; but chiefly because, the moment people know they have to pay the bad and good alike, they will try to discern the one from the other, and not use the bad. A sagacious writer in the *Scotsman* asks me if I should like any common scribbler to be paid by Messrs Smith, Elder and Co. as their good authors are. I should, if they employed him – but would seriously recommend them, for the scribbler's sake as well as their own, *not* to employ him. The quantity of its money which the country at present invests in scribbling is not, in the outcome of it, economically spent; and even the highly ingenious person to whom this question occurred, might perhaps have been more beneficially employed than in printing it.

scale, if he chooses to use them; and thus not only diminishes the immediate power of wealth, but removes the worst disabilities of poverty.

It is on this vital problem that the entire destiny of the labourer is ultimately dependent. Many minor interests may sometimes appear to interfere with it, but all branch from it. For instance, considerable agitation is often caused in the minds of the lower classes when they discover the share which they nominally, and to all appearance, actually, pay out of their wages in taxation (I believe thirty-five or forty per cent[79]). This sounds very grievous; but in reality the labourer does not pay it, but his employer. If the workman had not to pay it, his wages would be less by just that sum; competition would still reduce them to the lowest rate at which life was possible. Similarly the lower orders agitated for the repeal of the corn laws,*[80] thinking they would be better off if bread were cheaper; never perceiving that as soon as bread was permanently cheaper, wages would permanently fall[82] in precisely that proportion. The corn laws were rightly

---

* I have to acknowledge an interesting communication on the subject of free trade from Paisley (for a short letter from 'A Well-wisher' at —, my thanks are yet more due). But the Scottish writer will, I fear, be disagreeably surprised to hear, that I am, and always have been, an utterly fearless and unscrupulous free-trader. Seven years ago, speaking of the various signs of infancy in the European mind (*Stones of Venice*, vol. iii, p. 168), I wrote: 'The first principles of commerce were acknowledged by the English parliament only a few months ago, in its free-trade measures, and are still so little understood by the million, that *no nation dares to abolish its custom-houses.*'

It will be observed that I do not admit even the idea of reciprocity. Let other nations, if they like, keep their ports shut; every wise nation will throw its own open. It is not the opening them, but a sudden, inconsiderate, and blunderingly experimental manner of opening them, which does harm. If you have been protecting a manufacture for a long series of years, you must not take the protection off in a moment, so as to throw every one of its operatives at once out of employ, any more than you must take all its wrappings off a feeble child at once in cold weather, though the cumber of them may have been radically injuring its health. Little by little, you must restore it to freedom and to air.

Most people's minds are in curious confusion on the subject of free-trade, because they suppose it to imply enlarged competition. On the contrary, free-trade puts an end to all competition. 'Protection' (among various other mischievous functions) endeavours to enable one country to compete with another in the production of an article at a disadvantage. When trade is entirely free, no country can be competed with in the articles for the production of which it is naturally calculated; nor can it compete with any other, in the production of articles for which it is not naturally calculated. Tuscany, for instance, cannot compete with England in steel, nor England with Tuscany in oil. They must exchange their steel and oil. Which exchange should be as frank and free as honesty and the sea-winds can make it. Competition, indeed, arises at first, and sharply, in order to prove which is strongest in any given manufacture possible to both; this point once ascertained, competition is at an end.[81]

repealed; not, however, because they directly oppressed the poor, but because they indirectly oppressed them in causing a large quantity of their labour to be consumed unproductively.[83] So also unnecessary taxation oppresses them, through destruction of capital; but the destiny of the poor depends primarily always on this one question of dueness of wages. Their distress (irrespectively of that caused by sloth, minor error, or crime) arises on the grand scale from the two reacting forces of competition and oppression. There is not yet, nor will yet for ages be, any real over-population in the world[84]; but a local over-population, or, more accurately, a degree of population locally unmanageable under existing circumstances for want of forethought and sufficient machinery, necessarily shows itself by pressure of competition; and the taking advantage of this competition by the purchaser to obtain their labour unjustly cheap, consummates at once their suffering and his own; for in this (as I believe in every other kind of slavery) the oppressor suffers at last more than the oppressed, and those magnificent lines of Pope,[85] even in all their force, fall short of the truth: —

> 'Yet, to be just to these poor men of pelf,
> Each does but HATE HIS NEIGHBOUR AS HIMSELF:
> Damned to the mines, an equal fate betides
> The slave that digs it, and the slave that hides.'

The collateral and reversionary operations of justice in this matter I shall examine hereafter[86] (it being needful first to define the nature of value); proceeding then to consider within what practical terms a juster system may be established; and ultimately the vexed question of the destinies of the unemployed workmen.* Lest, however, the reader should be alarmed at

---

* I should be glad if the reader would first clear the ground for himself so far as to determine whether the difficulty lies in getting the work or getting the pay for it. Does he consider occupation itself to be an expensive luxury, difficult of attainment, of which too little is to be found in the world? or is it rather that, while in the enjoyment even of the most athletic delight, men must nevertheless be maintained, and this maintenance is not always forthcoming? We must be clear on this head before going farther, as most people are loosely in the habit of talking of the difficulty of 'finding employment.' Is it employment that we want to find, or support during employment? Is it idleness we wish to put an end to, or hunger? We have to take up both questions in succession, only not both at the same time. No doubt that work *is* a luxury, and a very great one. It is, indeed, at once a luxury and a necessity; no man can retain either health of mind or body without it. So profoundly do I feel this, that, as will be seen in the sequel,[87] one of the principal objects I would recommend to benevolent and practical persons, is to induce rich people to seek for a larger quantity of this luxury than they at present possess. Nevertheless, it appears by experience that even this healthiest of pleasures may be indulged in to excess, and that human

some of the issues to which our investigations seem to be tending, as if in their bearing against the power of wealth they had something in common with those of socialism, I wish him to know, in accurate terms, one or two of the main points which I have in view.

Whether socialism has made more progress among the army and navy (where payment is made on my principles), or among the manufacturing operatives (who are paid on my opponents' principles), I leave it to those opponents to ascertain and declare. Whatever their conclusion may be, I think it necessary to answer for myself only this: that if there be any one point insisted on throughout my works more frequently than another, that one point is the impossibility of Equality. My continual aim has been to show the eternal superiority of some men to others, sometimes even of one man to all others,[88] and to show also the advisability of appointing such persons or person to guide, to lead, or on occasion even to compel and subdue, their inferiors according to their own better knowledge and wiser will. My principles of Political Economy were all involved in a single phrase spoken three years ago at Manchester: 'Soldiers of the Ploughshare as well as Soldiers of the Sword'[89]: and they were all summed in a single sentence in the last volume of *Modern Painters*[90] – 'Government and co-operation are in all things the Laws of Life; Anarchy and competition the Laws of Death.'

And with respect to the mode in which these general principles affect the secure possession of property, so far am I from invalidating such security, that the whole gist of these papers will be found ultimately to aim at an extension in its range; and whereas it has long been known and declared that the poor have no right to the property of the rich, I wish it also to be known and declared that the rich have no right to the property of the poor.

But that the working of the system which I have undertaken to develop would in many ways shorten the apparent and direct, though not the unseen and collateral, power, both of wealth, as the Lady of Pleasure, and of capital as the Lord of Toil, I do not deny: on the contrary, I affirm it in all joyfulness; knowing that the attraction of riches is already too strong, as their authority is already too weighty, for the reason of mankind. I said in my last paper[91] that nothing in history had ever been so disgraceful to human intellect as the acceptance among us of the common doctrines of political economy as a science. I have many grounds for saying this, but one

---

beings are just as liable to surfeit of labour as to surfeit of meat; so that, as on the one hand, it may be charitable to provide, for some people, lighter dinner, and more work, – for others, it may be equally expedient to provide lighter work, and more dinner.

of the chief may be given in few words. I know no previous instance in history of a nation's establishing a systematic disobedience to the first principles of its professed religion. The writings which we (verbally) esteem as divine, not only denounce the love of money as the source of all evil,[92] and as an idolatry abhorred of the Deity, but declare mammon service[93] to be the accurate and irreconcileable opposite of God's service: and, whenever they speak of riches absolute, and poverty absolute, declare woe to the rich, and blessing to the poor. Whereupon we forthwith investigate a science of becoming rich, as the shortest road to national prosperity.

> 'Tai Cristian dannerà l'Etiòpe,
> Quando si partiranno i due collegi,
> L'UNO IN ETERNO RICCO, E L'ALTRO INÒPE.'[94]

In the last paper we saw that just payment of labour consisted in a sum of money which would approximately obtain equivalent labour at a future time: we have now to examine the means of obtaining such equivalence. Which question involves the definition of Value, Wealth, Price, and Produce.

None of these terms are yet defined so as to be understood by the public.[95] But the last, Produce, which one might have thought the clearest of all, is, in use, the most ambiguous; and the examination of the kind of ambiguity attendant on its present employment will best open the way to our work.

In his chapter on Capital,* Mr J. S. Mill instances, as a capitalist, a hardware manufacturer, who, having intended to spend a certain portion of the proceeds of his business in buying plate and jewels, changes his mind, and 'pays it as wages to additional workpeople.' The effect is stated by Mr Mill to be, that 'more food is appropriated to the consumption of productive labourers.'

Now I do not ask, though, had I written this paragraph, it would surely have been asked of me, What is to become of the silversmiths? If they are truly unproductive persons, we will acquiesce in their extinction. And though in another part of the same passage, the hardware merchant is supposed also to dispense with a number of servants, whose 'food is thus set free for productive purposes,' I do not inquire what will be the effect, painful or otherwise, upon the servants, of this emancipation of their food. But I very seriously inquire why ironware is produce, and silverware is not? That the merchant consumes the one, and sells the other, certainly does not constitute the difference, unless it can be shown (which, indeed, I perceive it to be becoming daily more and more the aim of tradesmen to show) that commodities are made to be sold, and not to be consumed. The merchant is an agent of conveyance to the consumer in one case, and is himself the

---

* Book I. chap. iv.s.1. To save space, my future references to Mr Mill's work will be by numerals only, as in this instance, I.iv.1. Ed. in 2 vols. 8vo, Parker, 1848.[96]

consumer in the other:* but the labourers are in either case equally productive, since they have produced goods to the same value, if the hardware and the plate are both goods.

And what distinction separates them? It is indeed possible that in the 'comparative estimate of the moralist,'[97] with which Mr Mill says political economy has nothing to do (III.i.2), a steel fork might appear a more substantial production than a silver one: we may grant also that knives, no less than forks, are good produce; and scythes and ploughshares serviceable articles. But, how of bayonets? Supposing the hardware merchant to effect large sales of *these*, by help of the 'setting free' of the food of his servants and his silversmith, – is he still employing productive labourers, or, in Mr Mill's words, labourers who increase 'the stock of permanent means of enjoyment'[98] (I.iii.4)? Or if, instead of bayonets, he supply bombs, will not the absolute and final 'enjoyment' of even these energetically productive articles (each of which costs ten pounds†) be dependent on a proper choice of time and place for their *enfantement*; choice, that is to say, depending on those philosophical considerations with which political economy has nothing to do?‡

I should have regretted the need of pointing out inconsistency in any portion of Mr Mill's work, had not the value of his work proceeded from its inconsistencies. He deserves honour among economists by inadvertently disclaiming the principles which he states, and tacitly introducing the moral considerations with which he declares his science has no connection. Many of his chapters are, therefore, true and valuable; and the only conclusions

* If Mr Mill had wished to show the difference in result between consumption and sale, he should have represented the hardware merchant as consuming his own goods instead of selling them; similarly, the silver merchant as consuming his own goods instead of selling them. Had he done this, he would have made his position clearer, though less tenable; and perhaps this was the position he really intended to take, tacitly involving his theory, elsewhere stated, and shown in the sequel of this paper to be false, that demand for commodities is not demand for labour. But by the most diligent scrutiny of the paragraph now under examination, I cannot determine whether it is a fallacy pure and simple, or the half of one fallacy supported by the whole of a greater one; so that I treat it here on the kinder assumption that it is one fallacy only.

† I take Mr Helps' estimate in his essay on War.[99]

‡ Also, when the wrought silver vases of Spain were dashed to fragments by our custom-house officers because bullion might be imported free of duty, but not brains, was the axe that broke them productive? – the artist who wrought them unproductive? Or again. If the woodman's axe is productive, is the executioner's? as also, if the hemp of a cable be productive, does not the productiveness of hemp in a halter depend on its moral more than on its material application?

of his which I have to dispute are those which follow from his premises.

Thus, the idea which lies at the root of the passage we have just been examining, namely, that labour applied to produce luxuries will not support so many persons as labour applied to produce useful articles, is entirely true; but the instance given fails – and in four directions of failure at once – because Mr Mill has not defined the real meaning of usefulness. The definition which he has given – 'capacity to satisfy a desire, or serve a purpose' (III.i.2) – applies equally to the iron and silver; while the true definition – which he has not given, but which nevertheless underlies the false verbal definition in his mind, and comes out once or twice by accident (as in the words 'any support to life or strength'[100] in I.iii.5) – applies to some articles of iron, but not to others, and to some articles of silver, but not to others. It applies to ploughs, but not to bayonets; and to forks, but not to filigree.*

The eliciting of the true definitions will give us the reply to our first question, 'What is value?' respecting which, however, we must first hear the popular statements.

'The word "value," when used without adjunct, always means, in political economy, value in exchange'[101] (Mill, III.i.2). So that, if two ships cannot exchange their rudders, their rudders are, in politico-economic language, of no value to either.[102]

But 'the subject of political economy is wealth.' – (Preliminary remarks, page 1.)

And wealth 'consists of all useful and agreeable objects which possess exchangeable value.' – (Preliminary remarks, page 10.)

It appears, then, according to Mr Mill, that usefulness and agreeableness underlie the exchange value, and must be ascertained to exist in the thing, before we can esteem it an object of wealth.

Now, the economical usefulness of a thing depends not merely on its own nature, but on the number of people who can and will use it. A horse is useless, and therefore unsaleable, if no one can ride, – a sword, if no one can strike, and meat, if no one can eat. Thus every material utility depends on its relative human capacity.

Similarly: The agreeableness of a thing depends not merely on its own likeableness, but on the number of people who can be got to like it. The relative agreeableness, and therefore saleableness, of 'a pot of the smallest ale,' and of 'Adonis painted by a running brook,' depends virtually on the

---

* Filigree; that is to say, generally, ornament dependent on complexity, not on art.

opinion of Demos, in the shape of Christopher Sly.[103] That is to say, the agreeableness of a thing depends on its relatively human disposition.* Therefore, political economy, being a science of wealth, must be a science respecting human capacities and dispositions. But moral considerations have nothing to do with political economy (III.i.2). Therefore, moral considerations have nothing to do with human capacities and dispositions.

I do not wholly like the look of this conclusion from Mr Mill's statements: – let us try Mr Ricardo's.

'Utility is not the measure of exchangeable value, though it is absolutely essential to it.'[105] – (Chap. I. sect. i.) Essential in what degree, Mr Ricardo? There may be greater and less degrees of utility. Meat, for instance, may be so good as to be fit for any one to eat, or so bad as to be fit for no one to eat. What is the exact degree of goodness which is 'essential' to its exchangeable value, but not 'the measure' of it? How good must the meat be, in order to possess any exchangeable value? and how bad must it be – (I wish this were a settled question in London markets) – in order to possess none?

There appears to be some hitch, I think, in the working even of Mr Ricardo's principles; but let him take his own example. 'Suppose that in the early stages of society the bows and arrows of the hunter were of equal value with the implements of the fisherman. Under such circumstances the value of the deer, the produce of the hunter's day's labour, would be *exactly*' (italics mine) 'equal to the value of the fish, the product of the fisherman's day's labour. The comparative value of the fish and game would be *entirely* regulated by the quantity of labour realized in each.'[106] (Ricardo, chap. iii. On Value.)

Indeed! Therefore, if the fisherman catches one sprat, and the huntsman one deer, one sprat will be equal in value to one deer; but if the fisherman

* These statements sound crude in their brevity; but will be found of the utmost importance when they are developed. Thus, in the above instance, economists have never perceived that disposition to buy is a wholly *moral* element in demand: that is to say, when you give a man half a crown, it depends on his disposition whether he is rich or poor with it – whether he will buy disease, ruin, and hatred, or buy health, advancement, and domestic love. And thus the agreeableness or exchange value of every offered commodity depends on production, not merely of the commodity, but of buyers of it; therefore on the education of buyers, and on all the moral elements by which their disposition to buy this, or that, is formed. I will illustrate and expand into final consequences every one of these definitions in its place: at present they can only be given with extremest brevity; for in order to put the subject at once in a connected form before the reader, I have thrown into one, the opening definitions of four chapters[104]: namely, of that on Value ('Ad Valorem'); on Price ('Thirty Pieces'); on Production ('Demeter'); and on Economy ('The Law of the House').

catches no sprat and the huntsman two deer, no sprat will be equal in value to two deer?

Nay; but – Mr Ricardo's supporters may say – he means, on an average; – if the average product of a day's work of fisher and hunter be one fish and one deer, the one fish will always be equal in value to the one deer.

Might I inquire the species of fish? Whale? or whitebait?*

It would be waste of time to pursue these fallacies farther; we will seek for a true definition.

Much store has been set for centuries upon the use of our English classical education. It were to be wished that our well-educated merchants recalled to mind always this much of their Latin schooling, – that the nominative of *valorem* (a word already sufficiently familiar to them) is *valor*; a word which, therefore, ought to be familiar to them. *Valor*, from *valere*, to be

---

* Perhaps it may be said, in farther support of Mr Ricardo, that he meant, 'when the utility is constant or given, the price varies as the quantity of labour.' If he meant this, he should have said it; but, had he meant it, he could have hardly missed the necessary result, that utility would be one measure of price (which he expressly denies it to be); and that, to prove saleableness, he had to prove a given quantity of utility, as well as a given quantity of labour; to wit, in his own instance, that the deer and fish would each feed the same number of men, for the same number of days, with equal pleasure to their palates. The fact is, he did not know what he meant himself. The general idea which he had derived from commercial experience, without being able to analyze it, was that when the demand is constant, the price varies as the quantity of labour required for production; or, using the formula I gave in the last paper – when y is constant, xy varies as x. But demand never is nor can be ultimately constant, if x varies distinctly; for, as price rises, consumers fall away; and as soon as there is a monopoly (and all scarcity is a form of monopoly, so that every commodity is affected occasionally by some colour of monopoly), y becomes the most influential condition of the price. Thus the price of a painting depends less on its merit than on the interest taken in it by the public; the price of singing less on the labour of the singer than the number of persons who desire to hear him; and the price of gold less on the scarcity which affects it in common with cerium or iridium, than on the sunlight colour and unalterable purity by which it attracts the admiration and answers the trust of mankind.

It must be kept in mind, however, that I use the word 'demand' in a somewhat different sense from economists usually. They mean by it 'the quantity of a thing sold.' I mean by it 'the force of the buyer's capable intention to buy.' In good English, a person's 'demand' signifies, not what he gets, but what he asks for.

Economists also do not notice that objects are not valued by absolute bulk or weight, but by such bulk and weight as is necessary to bring them into use. They say, for instance, that water bears no price in the market. It is true that a cupful does not, but a lake does; just as a handful of dust does not, but an acre does. And were it possible to make even the possession of a cupful or handful permanent (*i.e.*, to find a place for them), the earth and sea would be bought up by handfuls and cupfuls.

well or strong (ὑγιαίνω); – strong, *in* life (if a man), or valiant; strong, *for* life (if a thing), or valuable. To be 'valuable,' therefore, is to 'avail towards life.' A truly valuable or availing thing is that which leads to life with its whole strength. In proportion as it does not lead to life, or as its strength is broken, it is less valuable; in proportion as it leads away from life, it is unvaluable or malignant.

The value of a thing, therefore, is independent of opinion, and of quantity. Think what you will of it, gain how much you may of it, the value of the thing itself is neither greater nor less. For ever it avails, or avails not; no estimate can raise, no disdain repress, the power which it holds from the Maker of things and of men. [107]

The real science of political economy, which has yet to be distinguished from the bastard science, as medicine from witchcraft, and astronomy from astrology, is that which teaches nations to desire and labour for the things that lead to life: and which teaches them to scorn and destroy the things that lead to destruction. And if, in a state of infancy, they supposed indifferent things, such as excrescences of shell-fish, and pieces of blue and red stone, to be valuable, and spent large measures of the labour which ought to be employed for the extension and ennobling of life, in diving or digging for them, and cutting them into various shapes, – or if, in the same state of infancy, they imagine precious and beneficent things, such as air, light, and cleanliness, to be valueless, – or if, finally, they imagine the conditions of their own existence, by which alone they can truly possess or use anything, such, for instance, as peace, trust, and love, to be prudently exchangeable, when the markets offer, for gold, iron, or excrescences of shells – the great and only science of Political Economy teaches them, in all these cases, what is vanity, and what substance; and how the service of Death, the Lord of Waste, and of eternal emptiness, differs from the service of Wisdom, the Lady of Saving, and of eternal fulness; she who has said, 'I will cause those that love me to inherit SUBSTANCE; and I will FILL their treasuries.' [108]

The 'Lady of Saving,' in a profounder sense than that of the savings bank, though that is a good one: Madonna della Salute, [109] – Lady of Health, – which, though commonly spoken of as if separate from wealth, is indeed a part of wealth. This word, 'wealth,' it will be remembered, is the next we have to define.

'To be wealthy,' says Mr Mill, 'is to have a large stock of useful articles.'

I accept this definition. Only let us perfectly understand it. My opponents often lament my not giving them enough logic: I fear I must at present use a little more than they will like; but this business of Political Economy is no light one, and we must allow no loose terms in it.

We have, therefore, to ascertain in the above definition, first, what is the meaning of 'having,' or the nature of Possession. Then what is the meaning of 'useful,' or the nature of Utility.

And first of possession. At the crossing of the transepts of Milan Cathedral has lain, for three hundred years, the embalmed body of St Carlo Borromeo. It holds a golden crosier, and has a cross of emeralds on its breast. Admitting the crosier and emeralds to be useful articles, is the body to be considered as 'having' them? Do they, in the politico-economical sense of property, belong to it? If not, and if we may, therefore, conclude generally that a dead body cannot possess property, what degree and period of animation in the body will render possession possible?

As thus: lately in a wreck of a Californian ship, one of the passengers fastened a belt about him with two hundred pounds of gold in it, with which he was found afterwards at the bottom. Now, as he was sinking – had he the gold? or had the gold him?*

And if, instead of sinking him in the sea by its weight, the gold had struck him on the forehead, and thereby caused incurable disease – suppose palsy or insanity, – would the gold in that case have been more a 'possession' than in the first? Without pressing the inquiry up through instances of gradually increasing vital power over the gold (which I will, however, give, if they are asked for), I presume the reader will see that possession, or 'having,' is not an absolute, but a gradated, power; and consists not only in the quantity or nature of the thing possessed, but also (and in a greater degree) in its suitableness to the person possessing it and in his vital power to use it.

And our definition of Wealth, expanded, becomes: 'The possession of useful articles, *which we can use*.' This is a very serious change. For wealth, instead of depending merely on a 'have,' is thus seen to depend on a 'can.' Gladiator's death, on a 'habet'[111]; but soldier's victory, and State's salvation, on a 'quo plurimum posset.'[112] (Liv. VII.6.) And what we reasoned of only as accumulation of material, is seen to demand also accumulation of capacity.

So much for our verb. Next for our adjective. What is the meaning of 'useful'?

The inquiry is closely connected with the last. For what is capable of use in the hands of some persons, is capable, in the hands of others, of the opposite of use, called commonly 'from-use,' or 'ab-use.' And it depends on the person, much more than on the article, whether its usefulness or ab-usefulness will be the quality developed in it. Thus, wine, which the Greeks, in their Bacchus, made rightly the type of all passion, and which,

---

* Compare GEORGE HERBERT, *The Church Porch*, Stanza 28.[110]

when used, 'cheereth god and man'[113] (that is to say, strengthens both the divine life, or reasoning power, and the earthly, or carnal power, of man); yet, when abused, becomes 'Dionusos,' hurtful[114] especially to the divine part of man, or reason. And again, the body itself, being equally liable to use and to abuse, and, when rightly disciplined, serviceable to the State, both for war and labour; – but when not disciplined, or abused, valueless to the State, and capable only of continuing the private or single existence of the individual (and that but feebly) – the Greeks called such a body an 'idiotic' or 'private' body, from their word signifying a person employed in no way directly useful to the State; whence finally, our 'idiot,' meaning a person entirely occupied with his own concerns.

Hence, it follows that if a thing is to be useful, it must be not only of an availing nature, but in availing hands. Or, in accurate terms, usefulness is value in the hands of the valiant; so that this science of wealth being, as we have just seen, when regarded as the science of Accumulation, accumulative of capacity as well as of material, – when regarded as the Science of Distribution, is distribution not absolute, but discriminate; not of every thing to every man, but of the right thing to the right man. A difficult science, dependent on more than arithmetic.

Wealth, therefore, is 'THE POSSESSION OF THE VALUABLE BY THE VALIANT'[115]; and in considering it as a power existing in a nation, the two elements, the value of the thing, and the valour of its possessor, must be estimated together. Whence it appears that many of the persons commonly considered wealthy, are in reality no more wealthy than the locks of their own strong boxes are, they being inherently and eternally incapable of wealth; and operating for the nation, in an economical point of view, either as pools of dead water, and eddies in a stream (which, so long as the stream flows, are useless, or serve only to drown people, but may become of importance in a state of stagnation should the stream dry); or else, as dams in a river, of which the ultimate service depends not on the dam, but the miller; or else, as mere accidental stays and impediments, acting not as wealth, but (for we ought to have a correspondent term) as 'illth,' causing various devastation and trouble around them in all directions; or lastly, act not at all, but are merely animated conditions of delay, (no use being possible of anything they have until they are dead,) in which last condition they are nevertheless often useful *as* delays, and 'impedimenta,' if a nation is apt to move too fast.

This being so, the difficulty of the true science of Political Economy lies not merely in the need of developing manly character to deal with material value, but in the fact, that while the manly character and material value only form wealth by their conjunction, they have nevertheless a mutually destructive operation on each other. For the manly character is apt to ignore, or even cast away, the material value: – whence that of Pope[116]: –

> 'Sure, of qualities demanding praise,
> More go to ruin fortunes, than to raise.'

And on the other hand, the material value is apt to undermine the manly character; so that it must be our work, in the issue, to examine what evidence there is of the effect of wealth on the minds of its possessors; also, what kind of person it is who usually sets himself to obtain wealth, and succeeds in doing so; and whether the world owes more gratitude to rich or to poor men, either for their moral influence upon it, or for chief goods, discoveries, and practical advancements. I may, however, anticipate future conclusions, so far as to state that in a community regulated only by laws of demand and supply, but protected from open violence, the persons who become rich are, generally speaking, industrious, resolute, proud, covetous, prompt, methodical, sensible, unimaginative, insensitive, and ignorant. The persons who remain poor are the entirely foolish, the entirely wise,* the idle, the reckless, the humble, the thoughtful, the dull, the imaginative, the sensitive, the well-informed, the improvident, the irregularly and impulsively wicked, the clumsy knave, the open thief, and the entirely merciful, just, and godly person.

Thus far, then, of wealth. Next, we have to ascertain the nature of Price; that is to say, of exchange value, and its expression by currencies.

Note first, of exchange, there can be no *profit* in it. It is only in labour there can be profit – that is to say, a 'making in advance,' or 'making in favour of' (from *proficio*). In exchange, there is only advantage, *i.e.*, a bringing of vantage or power to the exchanging persons. Thus, one man, by sowing and reaping, turns one measure of corn into two measures. That is Profit. Another, by digging and forging, turns one spade into two spades. That is Profit. But the man who has two measures of corn wants sometimes to dig; and the man who has two spades wants sometimes to eat: – They exchange the gained grain for the gained tool; and both are the better for the exchange; but though there is much advantage in the transaction, there is no profit. Nothing is constructed or produced. Only that which had been before constructed is given to the person by whom it can be used. If labour is necessary to effect the exchange, that labour is in reality involved in the

---

* 'ὁ Ζεὺς δήπου πένεται.' – Arist. *Plut.* 582.[117] It would but weaken the grand words to lean on the preceding ones: – 'ὅτι τοῦ Πλούτου παρέχω βελτίονας, ἄνδρας, καὶ τὴν γνώμην, καὶ τὴν ἰδέαν.'

production, and, like all other labour, bears profit. Whatever number of men are concerned in the manufacture, or in the conveyance, have share in the profit; but neither the manufacture nor the conveyance are the exchange, and in the exchange itself there is no profit.

There may, however, be acquisition, which is a very different thing. If, in the exchange, one man is able to give what cost him little labour for what has cost the other much, he 'acquires' a certain quantity of the produce of the other's labour. And precisely what he acquires, the other loses. In mercantile language, the person who thus acquires is commonly said to have 'made a profit'; and I believe that many of our merchants are seriously under the impression that it is possible for everybody, somehow, to make a profit in this manner. Whereas, by the unfortunate constitution of the world we live in, the laws both of matter and motion have quite rigorously forbidden universal acquisition of this kind. Profit, or material gain, is attainable only by construction or by discovery; not by exchange. Whenever material gain follows exchange, for every *plus* there is a precisely equal *minus*.

Unhappily for the progress of the science of Political Economy, the plus quantities, or – if I may be allowed to coin an awkward plural – the pluses, make a very positive and venerable appearance in the world, so that every one is eager to learn the science which produces results so magnificent; whereas the minuses have, on the other hand, a tendency to retire into back streets, and other places of shade, – or even to get themselves wholly and finally put out of sight in graves: which renders the algebra of this science peculiar, and difficultly legible; a large number of its negative signs being written by the account-keeper in a kind of red ink, which starvation thins, and makes strangely pale, or even quite invisible ink, for the present.

The Science of Exchange, or, as I hear it has been proposed to call it, of 'Catallactics,'[118] considered as one of gain, is, therefore, simply nugatory; but considered as one of acquisition, it is a very curious science, differing in its data and basis from every other science known. Thus: – If I can exchange a needle with a savage for a diamond, my power of doing so depends either on the savage's ignorance of social arrangements in Europe, or on his want of power to take advantage of them, by selling the diamond to any one else for more needles. If, farther, I make the bargain as completely advantageous to myself as possible, by giving to the savage a needle with no eye in it (reaching, thus, a sufficiently satisfactory type of the perfect operation of catallactic science), the advantage to me in the entire transaction depends wholly upon the ignorance, powerlessness, or heedlessness of the person dealt with. Do away with these, and catallactic advantage becomes impossible. So far, therefore, as the science of exchange relates to the advantage of one of the exchanging persons only, it is founded on the ignorance or incapacity of the opposite person. Where these vanish, it also vanishes. It is therefore a science founded on nescience, and an art founded on artlessness. But all other sciences and arts, except this, have for their object the doing away with their opposite nescience and artlessness. *This* science, alone of sciences, must, by all available means, promulgate and prolong its opposite nescience; otherwise the science itself is impossible. It is, therefore, peculiarly and alone the science of darkness; probably a bastard science – not by any means a *divina scientia*, but one begotten of another father, that father who, advising his children to turn stones into bread,[119] is himself employed in turning bread into stones, and who, if you ask a fish of him (fish not being producible on his estate), can but give you a serpent.[120]

The general law, then, respecting just or economical exchange, is simply this: – There must be advantage on both sides (or if only advantage on one, at least no disadvantage on the other) to the persons exchanging; and just payment for his time, intelligence, and labour, to any intermediate person effecting the transaction (commonly called a merchant); and whatever advantage there is on either side, and whatever pay is given to the intermediate person, should be thoroughly known to all concerned. All attempt at concealment implies some practice of the opposite, or undivine science, founded on nescience. Whence another saying of the Jew merchant's – 'As a nail between the stone joints, so doth sin stick fast between buying and selling.'[121] Which peculiar riveting of stone and timber, in men's dealings with each other, is again set forth in the house which was to be destroyed – timber and stones together – when Zechariah's roll[122] (more probably 'curved sword') flew over it: 'the curse that goeth forth over all the earth upon every one that stealeth and holdeth himself guiltless,' instantly followed by the vision of the Great Measure; – the measure 'of the injustice of them in all the earth' (αὕτη ἡ ἀδικία αὐτῶν ἐν πάσῃ τῇ γῇ), with the weight of lead for its lid, and the woman, the spirit of wickedness, within it; – that is to say, Wickedness hidden by dulness, and formalized, outwardly, into ponderously established cruelty. 'It shall be set upon its own base in the land of Babel.'*

I have hitherto carefully restricted myself, in speaking of exchange, to the use of the term 'advantage'; but that term includes two ideas: the advantage, namely, of getting what we *need*, and that of getting what we *wish for*. Three-fourths of the demands existing in the world are romantic;

---

* Zech. v.11. See note on the passage, at p. 219.

founded on visions, idealisms, hopes, and affections; and the regulation of the purse is, in its essence, regulation of the imagination and the heart. Hence, the right discussion of the nature of price is a very high metaphysical and psychical problem; sometimes to be solved only in a passionate manner, as by David in his counting the price of the water of the well by the gate of Bethlehem; [123] but its first conditions are the following: – The price of anything is the quantity of labour [124] given by the person desiring it, in order to obtain possession of it. This price depends on four variable quantities. *A*. The quantity of wish the purchaser has for the thing; opposed to α, the quantity of wish the seller has to keep it. *B*. The quantity of labour the purchaser can afford, to obtain the thing; opposed to β, the quantity of labour the seller can afford, to keep it. These quantities are operative only in excess: *i.e.*, the quantity of wish (*A*) means the quantity of wish for this thing, above wish for other things; and the quantity of work (*B*) means the quantity which can be spared to get this thing from the quantity needed to get other things.

Phenomena of price, therefore, are intensely complex, curious, and interesting – too complex, however, to be examined yet; every one of them, when traced far enough, showing itself at last as a part of the bargain of the Poor of the Flock (or 'flock of slaughter'[125]), 'If ye think good, give M E my price, and if not, forbear' – Zech. xi.12; but as the price of everything is to be calculated finally in labour, it is necessary to define the nature of that standard.

Labour is the contest of the life of man with an opposite; – the term 'life' including his intellect, soul, and physical power, contending with question, difficulty, trial, or material force.

Labour is of a higher or lower order, as it includes more or fewer of the elements of life: and labour of good quality, in any kind, includes always as much intellect and feeling as will fully and harmoniously regulate the physical force.

In speaking of the value and price of labour, it is necessary always to understand labour of a given rank and quality, as we should speak of gold or silver of a given standard. Bad (that is, heartless, inexperienced, or senseless) labour cannot be valued; it is like gold of uncertain alloy, or flawed iron. *

* Labour which is entirely good of its kind, that is to say, effective, or efficient, the Greeks called 'weighable,' or ἄξιος, translated usually 'worthy,' and because thus substantial and true, they called its price τιμή, the 'honourable estimate' of it (honorarium): this word being founded on their conception of true labour as a divine thing, to be honoured with the kind of honour given to the gods; whereas the price of

The quality and kind of labour being given, its value, like that of all other valuable things, is invariable. But the quantity of it which must be given for other things is variable: and in estimating this variation, the price of other things must always be counted by the quantity of labour; not the price of labour by the quantity of other things.

Thus, if we want to plant an apple sapling in rocky ground, it may take two hours' work; in soft ground, perhaps only half an hour. Grant the soil equally good for the tree in each case. Then the value of the sapling planted by two hours' work is nowise greater than that of the sapling planted in half an hour. One will bear no more fruit than the other. Also, one half-hour of work is as valuable as another half-hour; nevertheless, the one sapling has cost four such pieces of work, the other only one. Now, the proper statement of this fact is, not that the labour on the hard ground is cheaper than on the soft; but that the tree is dearer. The exchange value may, or may not, afterwards depend on this fact. If other people have plenty of soft ground to plant in, they will take no cognizance of our two hours' labour in the price they will offer for the plant on the rock. And if, through want of sufficient botanical science, we have planted an upas-tree[127] instead of an apple, the exchange value will be a negative quantity; still less proportionate to the labour expended.

What is commonly called cheapness of labour, signifies, therefore, in reality, that many obstacles have to be overcome by it; so that much labour is required to produce a small result. But this should never be spoken of as cheapness of labour, but as dearness of the object wrought for. It would be just as rational to say that walking was cheap, because we had ten miles to walk home to our dinner, as that labour was cheap, because we had to work ten hours to earn it.

The last word which we have to define is 'Production.'

I have hitherto spoken of all labour as profitable; because it is impossible to consider under one head the quality or value of labour, and its aim. But labour of the best quality may be various in aim. It may be either constructive ('gathering,' from con and struo), as agriculture; nugatory, as jewel-cutting; or destructive ('scattering,' from de and struo), as war. It is not, however, always easy to prove labour, apparently nugatory, to be

---

false labour, or of that which led away from life, was to be, not honour, but vengeance; for which they reserved another word,[126] attributing the exaction of such price to a peculiar goddess, called Tisiphone, the 'requiter (or quittance-taker) of death'; a person versed in the highest branches of arithmetic, and punctual in her habits; with whom accounts current have been opened also in modern days.

actually so;* generally, the formula holds good: 'he that gathereth not, scattereth'[128]; thus, the jeweller's art is probably very harmful in its ministering to a clumsy and inelegant pride. So that, finally, I believe nearly all labour may be shortly divided into positive and negative labour: positive, that which produces life; negative, that which produces death; the most directly negative labour being murder, and the most directly positive, the bearing and rearing of children: so that in the precise degree in which murder is hateful, on the negative side of idleness, in that exact degree child-rearing is admirable, on the positive side of idleness. For which reason, and because of the honour that there is in rearing† children, while the wife is said to be as the vine (for cheering), the children are as the olive branch,[129] for praise: nor for praise only, but for peace (because large families can only be reared in times of peace): though since, in their spreading and voyaging in various directions, they distribute strength, they are, to the home strength, as arrows in the hand of the giant[131] – striking here and there far away.

Labour being thus various in its result, the prosperity of any nation is in exact proportion to the quantity of labour which it spends in obtaining and employing means of life. Observe, – I say, obtaining and employing; that is to say, not merely wisely producing, but wisely distributing and consuming. Economists usually speak as if there were no good in consumption absolute.‡ So far from this being so, consumption absolute is the end, crown, and perfection of production; and wise consumption is a far more difficult art than wise production. Twenty people can gain money for one

---

* The most accurately nugatory labour is, perhaps, that of which not enough is given to answer a purpose effectually, and which, therefore, has all to be done over again. Also, labour which fails of effect through non-co-operation. The curé of a little village near Bellinzona, to whom I had expressed wonder that the peasants allowed the Ticino to flood their fields, told me that they would not join to build an effectual embankment high up the valley, because everybody said 'that would help his neighbours as much as himself.' So every proprietor built a bit of low embankment about his own field; and the Ticino, as soon as it had a mind, swept away and swallowed all up together.

† Observe, I say, 'rearing,' not 'begetting.' The praise is in the seventh season,[130] not in σπορητός, nor in φυταλία, but in ὀπώρα. It is strange that men always praise enthusiastically any person who, by a momentary exertion, saves a life; but praise very hesitatingly a person who, by exertion and self-denial prolonged through years, creates one. We give the crown 'ob civem servatum'; – why not 'ob civem natum'? Born, I mean, to the full, in soul as well as body. England has oak enough, I think, for both chaplets.

‡ When Mr Mill speaks of productive consumption, he only means consumption which results in increase of capital, or material wealth. See I.iii.4, and I.iii.5.

who can use it; and the vital question, for individual and for nation, is, never 'how much do they make?' but 'to what purpose do they spend?'

The reader may, perhaps, have been surprised at the slight reference I have hitherto made to 'capital,' and its functions. It is here the place to define them.

Capital[132] signifies 'head, or source, or root material' – it is material by which some derivative or secondary good is produced. It is only capital proper (caput vivum, not caput mortuum[133]) when it is thus producing something different from itself. It is a root, which does not enter into vital function till it produces something else than a root: namely, fruit. That fruit will in time again produce roots; and so all living capital issues in reproduction of capital; but capital which produces nothing but capital is only root producing root; bulb issuing in bulb, never in tulip; seed issuing in seed, never in bread. The Political Economy of Europe has hitherto devoted itself wholly to the multiplication, or (less even) the aggregation, of bulbs. It never saw, nor conceived, such a thing as a tulip. Nay, boiled bulbs they might have been – glass bulbs – Prince Rupert's drops,[134] consummated in powder (well, if it were glass-powder and not gunpowder), for any end or meaning the economists had in defining the laws of aggregation. We will try and get a clearer notion of them.

The best and simplest general type of capital is a well-made ploughshare. Now, if that ploughshare did nothing but beget other ploughshares, in a polypous manner, – however the great cluster of polypous plough might glitter in the sun, it would have lost its function of capital. It becomes true capital only by another kind of splendour, – when it is seen 'splendescere sulco,'[135] to grow bright in the furrow; rather with diminution of its substance, than addition, by the noble friction. And the true home question, to every capitalist and to every nation, is not, 'how many ploughs have you?' but, 'where are your furrows?' not – 'how quickly will this capital reproduce itself?' – but, 'what will it do during reproduction?' What substance will it furnish, good for life? what work construct, protective of life? if none, its own reproduction is useless – if worse than none, – (for capital may destroy life as well as support it), its own reproduction is worse than useless; it is merely an advance from Tisiphone, on mortgage – not a profit by any means.

Not a profit, as the ancients truly saw, and showed in the type of Ixion[136]; – for capital is the head, or fountain head, of wealth – the 'well-head' of wealth, as the clouds are the well-heads of rain: but when clouds are without water,[137] and only beget clouds, they issue in wrath at last, instead of rain, and in lightning instead of harvest; whence Ixion is said first to have invited his guests to a banquet, and then made them fall into a pit filled with fire; which is the type of the temptation of riches issuing in imprisoned torment, – torment in a pit, (as also Demas' silver mine,[138]) after which, to show the rage of riches passing from lust of pleasure to lust of power, yet power not truly understood, Ixion is said to have desired Juno, and instead, embracing a cloud (or phantasm),[139] to have begotten the Centaurs; the power of mere wealth being, in itself, as the embrace of a shadow, – comfortless, (so also 'Ephraim feedeth on wind and followeth after the east wind'[140]; or 'that which is not' – Prov. xxiii.5; and again Dante's Geryon, the type of avaricious fraud, as he flies, gathers the *air* up with retractile claws, – 'l'aer a se raccolse,'*[141]) but in its offspring, a mingling of the brutal with the human nature: human in sagacity – using both intellect and arrow; but brutal in its body and hoof, for consuming, and trampling down. For which sin Ixion is at last bound upon a wheel – fiery and toothed, and rolling perpetually in the air; – the type of human labour when selfish and fruitless (kept far into the Middle Ages in their wheel of fortune); the wheel which has in it no breath or spirit, but is whirled by chance only; whereas of all true work the Ezekiel vision is true; that the Spirit of the living creature is in the wheels, and where the angels go, the wheels go by them[144]; but move no otherwise.

This being the real nature of capital, it follows that there are two kinds of true production, always going on in an active State: one of seed, and one of food; or production for the Ground, and for the Mouth; both of which are by covetous persons thought to be production only for the granary; whereas the function of the granary is but intermediate and conservative, fulfilled in distribution; else it ends in nothing but mildew, and nourishment of rats and worms. And since production for the Ground is only useful with future hope of harvest, all *essential* production is for the Mouth; and is finally measured by the mouth; hence, as I said above, consumption is the

---

* So also in the vision of the women bearing the ephah, before quoted,[142] 'the wind was in their wings,' not wings 'of a stork,' as in our version; but *'milvi,'* of a kite, in the Vulgate, or perhaps more accurately still in the Septuagint, 'hoopoe,' a bird connected typically with the power of riches by many traditions, of which that of its petition for a crest of gold is perhaps the most interesting. The 'Birds' of Aristophanes, in which its part is principal, are full of them; note especially the 'fortification of the air with baked bricks, like Babylon,' L. 550; and, again, compare the Plutus of Dante,[143] who (to show the influence of riches in destroying the reason) is the only one of the powers of the Inferno who cannot speak intelligibly; and also the cowardliest; he is not merely quelled or restrained, but literally 'collapses' at a word; the sudden and helpless operation of mercantile panic being all told in the brief metaphor, 'as the sails, swollen with the wind, fall, when the mast breaks.'

crown of production; and the wealth of a nation is only to be estimated by
what it consumes.

The want of any clear sight of this fact is the capital error, issuing in rich
interest and revenue of error among the political economists. Their minds
are continually set on money-gain, not on mouth-gain; and they fall into
every sort of net and snare, dazzled by the coin-glitter as birds by the
fowler's glass; or rather (for there is not much else like birds in them) they
are like children trying to jump on the heads of their own shadows; the
money-gain being only the shadow of the true gain, which is humanity.

The final object of political economy, therefore, is to get good method of
consumption, and great quantity of consumption: in other words, to use
everything, and to use it nobly; whether it be substance, service, or service
perfecting substance. The most curious error in Mr Mill's entire work,
(provided for him originally by Ricardo,) is his endeavour to distinguish
between direct and indirect service, and consequent assertion that a demand
for commodities is not demand for labour[145] (I.v.9, *et seq.*). He distinguishes between labourers employed to lay out pleasure grounds, and to
manufacture velvet; declaring that it makes material difference to the
labouring classes in which of these two ways a capitalist spends his money;
because the employment of the gardeners is a demand for labour, but the
purchase of velvet is not.*[146] Error colossal, as well as strange. It will,
indeed, make a difference to the labourer whether we bid him swing his
scythe in the spring winds, or drive the loom in pestilential air; but, so far as
his pocket is concerned, it makes to him absolutely no difference whether
we order him to make green velvet, with seed and a scythe, or red velvet,
with silk and scissors. Neither does it anywise concern him whether, when
the velvet is made, we consume it by walking on it, or wearing it, so long as

---

* The value of raw material, which has, indeed, to be deducted from the price of
the labour, is not contemplated in the passages referred to, Mr Mill having fallen
into the mistake solely by pursuing the collateral results of the payment of wages to
middlemen. He says – 'The consumer does not, with his own funds, pay the weaver
for his day's work.' Pardon me: the consumer of the velvet pays the weaver with his
own funds as much as he pays the gardener. He pays, probably, an intermediate
ship-owner, velvet merchant, and shopman; pays carriage money, shop rent, damage
money, time money, and care money; all these are above and beside the velvet price,
(just as the wages of a head gardener would be above the grass price); but the velvet is
as much produced by the consumer's capital, though he does not pay for it till six
months after production, as the grass is produced by his capital, though he does not
pay the man who rolled and mowed it on Monday, till Saturday afternoon. I do not
know if Mr Mill's conclusion, – 'the capital cannot be dispensed with, the purchasers
can' (p. 98), has yet been reduced to practice in the City on any large scale.

our consumption of it is wholly selfish. But if our consumption is to be in anywise unselfish, not only our mode of consuming the articles we require interests him, but also the *kind* of article we require with a view to consumption. As thus (returning for a moment to Mr Mill's great hardware theory*[147]): it matters, so far as the labourer's immediate profit is concerned, not an iron filing whether I employ him in growing a peach, or forging a bombshell; but my probable mode of consumption of those articles matters seriously. Admit that it is to be in both cases 'unselfish,' and the difference, to him, is final, whether when his child is ill, I walk into his cottage and give it the peach, or drop the shell down his chimney, and blow his roof off.

The worst of it, for the peasant, is, that the capitalist's consumption of the peach is apt to be selfish, and of the shell, distributive;† but, in all cases, this is the broad and general fact, that on due catallactic commercial principles, *somebody's* roof must go off in fulfilment of the bomb's destiny. You may grow for your neighbour, at your liking, grapes or grape-shot; he will also, catallactically, grow grapes or grape-shot for you, and you will each reap what you have sown.[150]

It is, therefore, the manner and issue of consumption which are the real tests of production. Production does not consist in things laboriously made, but in things serviceably consumable; and the question for the nation is not how much labour it employs, but how much life it produces. For as

---

* Which, observe, is the precise opposite of the one under examination. The hardware theory required us to discharge our gardeners and engage manufacturers; the velvet theory requires us to discharge our manufacturers and engage gardeners.

† It is one very awful form of the operation of wealth in Europe that it is entirely capitalists' wealth[148] which supports unjust wars. Just wars do not need so much money to support them; for most of the men who wage such, wage them gratis; but for an unjust war, men's bodies and souls have both to be bought; and the best tools of war for them besides; which makes such war costly to the maximum; not to speak of the cost of base fear, and angry suspicion, between nations which have not grace nor honesty enough in all their multitudes to buy an hour's peace of mind with: as, at present, France and England, purchasing of each other ten millions sterling worth of consternation annually,[149] (a remarkably light crop, half thorns and half aspen leaves, – sown, reaped, and granaried by the 'science' of the modern political economist, teaching covetousness instead of truth). And all unjust war being supportable, if not by pillage of the enemy, only by loans from capitalists, these loans are repaid by subsequent taxation of the people, who appear to have no will in the matter, the capitalists' will being the primary root of the war; but its real root is the covetousness of the whole nation, rendering it incapable of faith, frankness, or justice, and bringing about, therefore, in due time, his own separate loss and punishment to each person.

consumption is the end and aim of production, so life is the end and aim of consumption.

I left this question to the reader's thought two months ago,[151] choosing rather that he should work it out for himself than have it sharply stated to him. But now, the ground being sufficiently broken (and the details into which the several questions, here opened, must lead us, being too complex for discussion in the pages of a periodical, so that I must pursue them elsewhere[152]), I desire, in closing the series of introductory papers, to leave this one great fact clearly stated. THERE IS NO WEALTH BUT LIFE. Life, including all its powers of love, of joy, and of admiration. That country is the richest which nourishes the greatest number of noble and happy human beings[153]; that man is richest who, having perfected the functions of his own life to the utmost, has also the widest helpful influence, both personal, and by means of his possessions, over the lives of others.

A strange political economy; the only one, nevertheless, that ever was or can be: all political economy founded on self-interest* being but the fulfilment of that which once brought schism into the Policy of angels, and ruin into the Economy of Heaven.[154]

'The greatest number of human beings noble and happy.' But is the nobleness consistent with the number?[155] Yes, not only consistent with it, but essential to it. The maximum of life can only be reached by the maximum of virtue. In this respect the law of human population differs wholly from that of animal life. The multiplication of animals is checked only by want of food, and by the hostility of races; the population of the gnat is restrained by the hunger of the swallow, and that of the swallow by the scarcity of gnats. Man, considered as an animal, is indeed limited by the same laws: hunger, or plague, or war, are the necessary and only restraints upon his increase, – effectual restraints hitherto, – his principal study having been how most swiftly to destroy himself, or ravage his dwelling-places, and his highest skill directed to give range to the famine, seed to the plague, and sway to the sword. But, considered as other than an animal, his increase is not limited by these laws. It is limited only by the limits of his courage and his love. Both of these *have* their bounds; and ought to have; his race has its bounds also; but these have not yet been reached, nor will be reached for ages.

In all the ranges of human thought I know none so melancholy as the speculations of political economists on the population question. It is

---

* 'In all reasoning about prices, the proviso must be understood, "supposing all parties to take care of their own interest." ' – Mill, III.i.5.

proposed to better the condition of the labourer by giving him higher waves. 'Nay,' says the economist, – 'if you raise his wages, he will either people down to the same point of misery[156] at which you found him, or drink your wages away.' He will. I know it. Who gave him this will? Suppose it were your own son[157] of whom you spoke, declaring to me that you dared not take him into your firm, nor even give him his just labourer's wages, because if you did he would die of drunkenness, and leave half a score of children to the parish. 'Who gave your son these dispositions?' – I should enquire. Has he them by inheritance or by education? By one or other they *must* come; and as in him, so also in the poor. Either these poor are of a race essentially different from ours, and unredeemable (which, however often implied, I have heard none yet openly say), or else by such care as we have ourselves received, we may make them continent and sober as ourselves – wise and dispassionate as we are – models arduous of imitation. 'But,' it is answered, 'they cannot receive education.'[158] Why not? That is precisely the point at issue. Charitable persons suppose the worst fault of the rich is to refuse the people meat; and the people cry for their meat, kept back by fraud, to the Lord of Multitudes.* Alas! it is not meat of which the refusal is cruelest, or to which the claim is validest. The life is more than the meat.[161] The rich not only refuse food to the poor; they refuse wisdom; they refuse virtue; they refuse salvation. Ye sheep without

* James v.4. Observe, in these statements I am not taking up, nor countenancing one whit, the common socialist idea of division of property: division of property is its destruction; and with it the destruction of all hope, all industry, and all justice: it is simply chaos – a chaos towards which the believers in modern political economy are fast tending, and from which I am striving to save them. The rich man does not keep back meat from the poor by retaining his riches; but by basely using them. Riches are a form of strength; and a strong man does not injure others by keeping his strength, but by using it injuriously. The socialist, seeing a strong man oppress a weak one, cries out – 'Break the strong man's arms;' but I say, 'Teach him to use them to better purpose.' The fortitude and intelligence which acquire riches are intended, by the Giver of both, not to scatter, nor to give away, but to employ those riches in the service of mankind; in other words, in the redemption of the erring and aid of the weak – that is to say, there is first to be the work to gain money; then the Sabbath of use for it – the Sabbath, whose law is, not to lose life, but to save.[159] It is continually the fault or the folly of the poor that they are poor,[160] as it is usually a child's fault if it falls into a pond, and a cripple's weakness that slips at a crossing; nevertheless, most passers-by would pull the child out, or help up the cripple. Put it at the worst, that all the poor of the world are but disobedient children, or careless cripples, and that all rich people are wise and strong, and you will see at once that neither is the socialist right in desiring to make everybody poor, powerless, and foolish as he is himself, nor the rich man right in leaving the children in the mire.

shepherd,[162] it is not the pasture that has been shut from you, but the Presence. Meat! perhaps your right to that may be pleadable; but other rights have to be pleaded first. Claim your crumbs from the table if you will; but claim them as children, not as dogs; claim your right to be fed, but claim more loudly your right to be holy, perfect, and pure.

Strange words to be used of working people! 'What! holy; without any long robes or anointing oils; these rough-jacketed, rough-worded persons; set to nameless, dishonoured service? Perfect! – these, with dim eyes and cramped limbs, and slowly wakening minds? Pure! – these, with sensual desire and grovelling thought; foul of body and coarse of soul?' It may be so; nevertheless, such as they are, they are the holiest, perfectest, purest persons the earth can at present show. They may be what you have said; but if so, they yet are holier than we who have left them thus.

But what can be done for them? Who can clothe – who teach – who restrain their multitudes? What end can there be for them at last, but to consume one another?

I hope for another end, though not, indeed, from any of the three remedies for over-population commonly suggested by economists.

These three are, in brief – Colonization; Bringing in of waste lands; or Discouragement of Marriage.

The first and second of these expedients merely evade or delay the question. It will, indeed, be long before the world has been all colonized, and its deserts all brought under cultivation. But the radical question is, not how much habitable land is in the world, but how many human beings ought to be maintained on a given space of habitable land.

Observe, I say, *ought* to be, not how many *can* be. Ricardo, with his usual inaccuracy, defines what he calls the 'natural rate of wages' as 'that which will maintain the labourer.'[163] Maintain him! yes; but how? – the question was instantly thus asked of me by a working girl, to whom I read the passage. I will amplify her question for her. 'Maintain him, how?' As, first, to what length of life? Out of a given number of fed persons, how many are to be old – how many young? that is to say, will you arrange their maintenance so as to kill them early – say at thirty or thirty-five on the average, including deaths of weakly or ill-fed children? – or so as to enable them to live out a natural life? You will feed a greater number, in the first case,* by rapidity of succession; probably a happier number in the second: which does Mr Ricardo mean to be their natural state, and to which state belongs the natural rate of wages?

---

* The quantity of life is the same in both cases; but it is differently allotted.

Again: A piece of land which will only support ten idle, ignorant, and improvident persons, will support thirty or forty intelligent and industrious ones. Which of these is their natural state, and to which of them belongs the natural rate of wages?

Again: If a piece of land support forty persons in industrious ignorance; and if, tired of this ignorance, they set apart ten of their number to study the properties of cones, and the sizes of stars; the labour of these ten being withdrawn from the ground, must either tend to the increase of food in some transitional manner, or the persons set apart for sidereal and conic purposes must starve, or some one else starve instead of them. What is, therefore, the natural rate of wages of the scientific persons, and how does this rate relate to, or measure, their reverted or transitional productiveness?

Again: If the ground maintains, at first, forty labourers in a peaceable and pious state of mind, but they become in a few years so quarrelsome and impious that they have to set apart five, to meditate upon and settle their disputes; – ten, armed to the teeth with costly instruments, to enforce the decisions; and five to remind everybody in an eloquent manner of the existence of a God; – what will be the result upon the general power of production, and what is the 'natural rate of wages' of the meditative, muscular, and oracular labourers?[164]

Leaving these questions to be discussed, or waived, at their pleasure, by Mr Ricardo's followers, I proceed to state the main facts bearing on that probable future of the labouring classes which has been partially glanced at by Mr Mill. That chapter and the preceding one[165] differ from the common writing of political economists in admitting some value in the aspect of nature, and expressing regret at the probability of the destruction of natural scenery. But we may spare our anxieties on this head. Men can neither drink steam, nor eat stone. The maximum of population on a given space of land implies also the relative maximum of edible vegetable, whether for men or cattle; it implies a maximum of pure air; and of pure water. Therefore: a maximum of wood, to transmute the air, and of sloping ground, protected by herbage from the extreme heat of the sun, to feed the streams. All England may, if it so chooses, become one manufacturing town; and Englishmen, sacrificing themselves to the good of general humanity, may live diminished lives in the midst of noise, of darkness, and of deadly exhalation. But the world cannot become a factory nor a mine. No amount of ingenuity will ever make iron digestible by the million, nor substitute hydrogen for wine. Neither the avarice nor the rage of men will ever feed them; and however the apple of Sodom and the grape of Gomorrah[166] may spread their table for a time with dainties of ashes, and nectar of asps, – so long as men live by bread, the far away valleys must laugh as they are covered with the gold of God, and the shouts of His happy multitudes ring round the wine-press and the well.

Nor need our more sentimental economists fear the too wide spread of the formalities of a mechanical agriculture. The presence of a wise population implies the search for felicity as well as for food; nor can any population reach its maximum but through that wisdom which 'rejoices' in the habitable parts of the earth.[167] The desert has its appointed place and work; the eternal engine, whose beam is the earth's axle, whose beat is its year, and whose breath is its ocean, will still divide imperiously to their desert kingdoms bound with unfurrowable rock, and swept by unarrested sand, their powers of frost and fire: but the zones and lands between, habitable, will be loveliest in habitation. The desire of the heart is also the light of the eyes.[168] No scene is continually and untiringly loved, but one rich by joyful human labour; smooth in field; fair in garden; full in orchard; trim, sweet, and frequent in homestead; ringing with voices of vivid existence. No air is sweet that is silent; it is only sweet when full of low currents of under sound – triplets of birds, and murmur and chirp of insects, and deep-toned words of men, and wayward trebles of childhood. As the art of life is learned, it will be found at last that all lovely things are also necessary; – the wild flower by the wayside, as well as the tended corn; and the wild birds and creatures of the forest, as well as the tended cattle; because man doth not live by bread only, but also by the desert manna; by every wondrous word and unknowable work of God.[169] Happy, in that he knew them not, nor did his fathers know; and that round about him reaches yet into the infinite, the amazement of his existence.

Note, finally, that all effectual advancement towards this true felicity of the human race must be by individual, not public effort. Certain general measures may aid, certain revised laws guide, such advancement; but the measure and law which have first to be determined are those of each man's home. We continually hear it recommended by sagacious people to complaining neighbours (usually less well placed in the world than themselves), that they should 'remain content in the station in which Providence has placed them.'[170] There are perhaps some circumstances of life in which Providence has no intention that people *should* be content. Nevertheless, the maxim is on the whole a good one; but it is peculiarly for home use. That your neighbour should, or should not, remain content with *his* position, is not your business; but it is very much your business to remain content with your own. What is chiefly needed in England at the present day is to show the quantity of pleasure that may be obtained by a consistent, well-administered competence, modest, confessed, and laborious. We need examples of people who, leaving Heaven to decide whether they are to rise in the world, decide for themselves that they will be happy in it, and have resolved to seek – not greater wealth, but simpler pleasure; not higher fortune, but deeper felicity; making the first of possessions, self-possession; and honouring themselves in the harmless pride and calm pursuits of peace.

Of which lowly peace it is written that 'justice and peace have kissed each other'[171]; and that the fruit of justice is 'sown in peace of them that make peace'[172]; not 'peace-makers' in the common understanding – reconcilers of quarrels; (though that function also follows on the greater one;) but peace-Creators; Givers of Calm. Which you cannot give, unless you first gain; nor is this gain one which will follow assuredly on any course of business, commonly so called. No form of gain is less probable, business being (as is shown in the language of all nations[173] – πωλεῖν from πέλω, πρᾶσις from περάω, venire, vendre, and venal, from venio, etc.) essentially restless – and probably contentious; – having a raven-like mind to the motion to and fro, as to the carrion food; whereas the olive-feeding and bearing birds look for rest for their feet[174]; thus it is said of Wisdom that she 'hath builded her house, and hewn out her seven pillars'[175]; and even when, though apt to wait long at the doorposts, she has to leave her house and go abroad, her paths are peace[176] also.

For us, at all events, her work must begin at the entry of the doors: all true economy is 'Law of the house.' Strive to make that law strict, simple, generous: waste nothing, and grudge nothing. Care in nowise to make more of money, but care to make much of it; remembering always the great, palpable, inevitable fact – the rule and root of all economy – that what one person has, another cannot have; and that every atom of substance, of whatever kind, used or consumed, is so much human life spent; which, if it issue in the saving present life, or gaining more, is well spent, but if not is either so much life prevented, or so much slain. In all buying, consider, first, what condition of existence you cause in the producers of what you buy; secondly, whether the sum you have paid is just to the producer, and in due proportion, lodged in his hands;* thirdly, to how much clear use, for food, knowledge, or joy, this that you have bought can be put; and fourthly, to whom and in what way it can be most speedily and serviceably

---

* The proper offices of middlemen, namely, overseers (or authoritative workmen), conveyancers (merchants, sailors, retail dealers, etc.), and order-takers (persons employed to receive directions from the consumer), must, of course, be examined before I can enter farther into the question of just payment of the first

distributed; in all dealings whatsoever insisting on entire openness and stern fulfilment; and in all doings, on perfection and loveliness of accomplishment; especially on fineness and purity of all marketable commodity: watching at the same time for all ways of gaining, or teaching, powers of simple pleasure; and of showing 'ὅσον ἐν ἀσφοδέλῳ μέγ ὄνειαρ'[177] – the sum of enjoyment depending not on the quantity of things tasted, but on the vivacity and patience of taste.

And if, on due and honest thought over these things, it seems that the kind of existence to which men are now summoned by every plea of pity and claim of right, may, for some time at least, not be a luxurious one; – consider whether, even supposing it guiltless, luxury would be desired by any of us, if we saw clearly at our sides the suffering which accompanies it in the world. Luxury is indeed possible in the future – innocent and exquisite; luxury for all, and by the help of all; but luxury at present can only be enjoyed by the ignorant; the cruelest man living could not sit at his feast, unless he sat blindfold. Raise the veil boldly; face the light; and if, as yet, the light of the eye can only be through tears, and the light of the body[178] through sackcloth, go thou forth weeping, bearing precious seed, until the time come, and the kingdom, when Christ's gift of bread, and bequest of peace, shall be 'Unto this last as unto thee'; and when, for earth's severed multitudes of the wicked and the weary, there shall be holier reconciliation than that of the narrow home, and calm economy, where the Wicked cease – not from trouble, but from troubling – and the Weary are at rest.[179]

---

producer. But I have not spoken of them in these introductory papers, because the evils attendant on the abuse of such intermediate functions result not from any alleged principle of modern political economy, but from private carelessness or iniquity.

from
The Crown of Wild Olive

FOUR LECTURES
on Industry and War

Published 1866

COMMENTARY

The Crown of Wild Olive and *Sesame and Lilies* consist, in their first editions, of lectures delivered by Ruskin in the years 1864 and 1865. They may be taken as characteristic of Ruskin's work between *Unto this Last* and *Fors Clavigera*.

The Crown of Wild Olive was published in 1866. The 'Crown' of the title is one of the emblems of Athene, Goddess of Wisdom, a key figure in Ruskin's personal mythology – and one to whom a whole book was soon to be devoted, *The Queen of the Air* (1869). The significance of the Crown is touched upon in 'Traffic', but Ruskin's Introduction indicates wider implications than are apparent in that context alone. The lectures all directly or indirectly grow out of the question, exceptionally troubling to a man who has lost his faith in eternal life, of the ultimate goal of our labours here on earth. The Greeks, says Ruskin, though they lacked the consolations promised by Christianity, saw the end of their activity as honour alone – not riches, nor the promise of a future life. The earth itself with its natural riches was sufficient. 'They knew that life brought its contest, but they expected from it also the crown of all contest: No proud one! no jewelled circlet flaming through Heaven above the height of the unmerited throne; only some few leaves of wild olive, cool to the tired brow, through a few years of peace. It should have been of gold, they thought; but Jupiter was poor; this was the best the god could give them.' If such a reward was adequate to pagans, Ruskin suggests, how much more so ought it to be to Christians – and to those who, though they can no longer believe in eternal reward, still live according to the Christian ethic.

The lecture on 'Traffic' was delivered at Bradford Town Hall in 1864. Its interest lies in the encounter between Ruskin's ideas on architecture and his more recently formulated social views. A new Exchange was to be built in Bradford; a committee of citizens had asked him to come and advise them on the style of architecture they should choose for it. It was a subject close to Ruskin's heart, and the invitation must have appealed to his vanity, but, in the lecture, he refuses to do what he has been asked to on the grounds that good architecture cannot come out of an unjust social and economic situation. Moreover, he was already disenchanted with the practical results of his architectural advocacy. E. T. Cook suggests, in the *Library Edition*, that Ruskin probably rewrote his opening paragraphs in order to harshen still further what must have been in any case a disturbingly outspoken piece of public speaking. This was because, when he gave the lecture, the design had not yet been chosen. By the time the book was prepared, it had been, and Ruskin found that his worst fears had been only too well justified: the building was to be Venetian Gothic and, as Cook puts it, 'of ambitious design but feeble execution'.

TRAFFIC

Delivered in the Town Hall, Bradford
[April 21, 1864]

MY good Yorkshire friends, you asked me down here among your hills that I might talk to you about this Exchange you are going to build: but, earnestly and seriously asking you to pardon me, I am going to do nothing of the kind. I cannot talk, or at least can say very little, about this same Exchange. I must talk of quite other things, though not willingly; – I could not deserve your pardon, if, when you invited me to speak on one subject, I *wilfully* spoke on another. But I cannot speak, to purpose, of anything about which I do not care; and most simply and sorrowfully I have to tell you, in the outset, that I do *not* care about this Exchange of yours.

If, however, when you sent me your invitation, I had answered, 'I won't come, I don't care about the Exchange of Bradford,' you would have been justly offended with me, not knowing the reasons of so blunt a carelessness. So I have come down, hoping that you will patiently let me tell you why, on this, and many other such occasions, I now remain silent, when formerly I should have caught at the opportunity of speaking to a gracious audience.

In a word, then, I do not care about this Exchange – because *you* don't; and because you know perfectly well I cannot make you. Look at the essential conditions of the case, which you, as business men, know perfectly well, though perhaps you think I forget them. You are going to spend £30,000, which to you, collectively, is nothing; the buying a new coat is, as to the cost of it, a much more important matter of consideration to me, than building a new Exchange is to you. But you think you may as well have the right thing for your money. You know there are a great many odd styles of architecture about; you don't want to do anything ridiculous; you hear of me, among others, as a respectable architectural man-milliner; and you send for me, that I may tell you the leading fashion; and what is, in our shops, for the moment, the newest and sweetest thing in pinnacles.

Now, pardon me for telling you frankly, you cannot have good architecture merely by asking people's advice on occasion. All good architecture is the expression of national life and character[1]; and it is produced by a prevalent and eager national taste, or desire for beauty. And I want you to think a little of the deep significance of this word 'taste'; for no statement of mine has been more earnestly or oftener controverted than that good taste is essentially a moral quality.[2] 'No,' say many of my antagonists, 'taste is one thing, morality is another. Tell us what is pretty: we shall be glad to know that; but we need no sermons – even were you able to preach them, which may be doubted.'

Permit me, therefore, to fortify this old dogma of mine somewhat. Taste is not only a part and an index of morality; – it is the ONLY morality. The first, and last, and closest trial question to any living creature is, 'What do you like?' Tell me what you like, and I'll tell you what you are. Go out into the street, and ask the first man or woman you meet, what their 'taste' is; and if they answer candidly, you know them, body and soul. 'You, my friend in the rags, with the unsteady gait, what do *you* like?' 'A pipe, and a quartern of gin.' I know you. 'You, good woman, with the quick step and tidy bonnet, what do you like?' 'A swept hearth, and a clean tea-table; and my husband opposite me, and a baby at my breast.' Good, I know you also. 'You, little girl with the golden hair and the soft eyes, what do you like?' 'My canary, and a run among the wood hyacinths.' 'You, little boy with the dirty hands, and the low forehead, what do you like?' 'A shy at the sparrows, and a game at pitch farthing.' Good; we know them all now. What more need we ask?

'Nay,' perhaps you answer; 'we need rather to ask what these people and children do, than what they like. If they *do* right, it is no matter that they like what is wrong; and if they *do* wrong, it is no matter that they like what is right. Doing is the great thing; and it does not matter that the man likes drinking, so that he does not drink; nor that the little girl likes to be kind to her canary, if she will not learn her lessons; nor that the little boy likes throwing stones at the sparrows, if he goes to the Sunday school.' Indeed, for a short time, and in a provisional sense, this is true. For if, resolutely, people do what is right, in time to come they like doing it. But they only are in a right moral state when they *have* come to like doing it; and as long as they don't like it, they are still in a vicious state. The man is not in health of body who is always thinking of the bottle in the cupboard, though he bravely bears his thirst; but the man who heartily enjoys water in the morning, and wine in the evening, each in its proper quantity and time. And the entire object of true education is to make people not merely *do* the right things, but *enjoy* the right things: – not merely industrious, but to love industry – not merely learned, but to love knowledge – not merely pure, but to love purity – not merely just, but to hunger and thirst after justice.[3]

But you may answer or think, 'Is the liking for outside ornaments, – for pictures, or statues, or furniture, or architecture, a moral quality?' Yes, most surely, if a rightly set liking. Taste for *any* pictures or statues is not a moral quality, but taste for good ones is. Only here again we have to define the word 'good.' I don't mean by 'good,' clever – or learned – or difficult in the doing. Take a picture by Teniers, of sots quarrelling over their dice; it is an entirely clever picture; so clever that nothing in its kind has ever been done equal to it; but it is also an entirely base and evil picture. It is an expression of delight in the prolonged contemplation of a vile thing, and delight in that is an 'unmannered,' or 'immoral' quality. It is 'bad taste' in the profoundest sense – it is the taste of the devils.[4] On the other hand, a picture of Titian's, or a Greek statue, or a Greek coin, or a Turner landscape, expresses delight in the perpetual contemplation of a good and perfect thing. That is an entirely moral quality – it is the taste of the angels. And all delight in fine art, and all love of it, resolve themselves into simple love of that which deserves love. That deserving is the quality which we call 'loveliness' – (we ought to have an opposite word, hateliness, to be said of the things which deserve to be hated); and it is not an indifferent nor optional thing whether we love this or that; but it is just the vital function of all our being. What we *like* determines what we *are*, and is the sign of what we are; and to teach taste is inevitably to form character.

As I was thinking over this, in walking up Fleet Street the other day, my eye caught the title of a book standing open in a bookseller's window. It was – *On the necessity of the diffusion of taste among all classes*.[5] 'Ah,' I thought to myself, 'my classifying friend, when you have diffused your taste, where will your classes be? The man who likes what you like, belongs to the same class with you, I think. Inevitably so. You may put him to other work if you choose; but, by the condition you have brought him into, he will dislike the work as much as you would yourself. You get hold of a scavenger or a costermonger, who enjoyed the Newgate Calendar[6] for literature, and 'Pop goes the Weasel' for music. You think you can make him like Dante and Beethoven? I wish you joy of your lessons; but if you do, you have made a gentleman of him: – he won't like to go back to his costermongering.'

And so completely and unexceptionally is this so, that, if I had time to-night, I could show you that a nation cannot be affected by any vice, or weakness, without expressing it, legibly, and for ever, either in bad art, or by want of art; and that there is no national virtue, small or great, which is not manifestly expressed in all the art which circumstances enable the people possessing that virtue to produce. Take, for instance, your great English virtue of enduring and patient courage. You have at present in England only one art of any consequence – that is, iron-working. You know thoroughly well how to cast and hammer iron. Now, do you think, in those masses of lava which you build volcanic cones to melt, and which you forge at the mouths of the Infernos you have created; do you think, on those iron plates, your courage and endurance are not written for ever, – not merely with an iron pen, but on iron parchment? And take also your great English vice – European vice – vice of all the world – vice of all other worlds that roll or shine in heaven, bearing with them yet the atmosphere of hell – the vice of jealousy, which brings competition into your commerce, treachery into your councils, and dishonour into your wars – that vice which has rendered for you, and for your next neighbouring nation, the daily occupations of existence no longer possible, but with the mail upon your breasts and the sword loose in its sheath; so that at last, you have realised for all the multitudes of the two great peoples who lead the so-called civilization of the earth, – you have realised for them all, I say, in person and in policy, what was once true only of the rough Border riders of your Cheviot hills –

> 'They carved at the meal
> With gloves of steel,
> And they drank the red wine through the helmet barr'd;'[7] –

do you think that this national shame and dastardliness of heart are not written as legibly on every rivet of your iron armour as the strength of the right hands that forged it?

Friends, I know not whether this thing be the more ludicrous or the more melancholy. It is quite unspeakably both. Suppose, instead of being now sent for by you, I had been sent for by some private gentleman, living in a suburban house, with his garden separated only by a fruit wall from his next door neighbour's; and he had called me to consult with him on the furnishing of his drawing-room. I begin looking about me, and find the walls rather bare; I think such and such a paper might be desirable – perhaps a little fresco here and there on the ceiling – a damask curtain or so at the windows. 'Ah,' says my employer, 'damask curtains, indeed! That's all very fine, but you know I can't afford that kind of thing just now!' 'Yet the world credits you with a splendid income!' 'Ah, yes,' says my friend, 'but do you know, at present I am obliged to spend it nearly all in steel-traps?' 'Steel-traps! for whom?' 'Why, for that fellow on the other side the wall, you know: we're very good friends, capital friends; but we are obliged to keep our traps set on both sides of the wall; we could not possibly keep on friendly terms without them, and our spring guns. The worst of it is, we are both clever fellows enough; and there's never a day passes that we don't find out a new trap, or a new gun-barrel, or something; we spend about fifteen millions a year each in our traps, take it altogether; and I don't see how we're to do with less.' A highly comic state of life for two private gentlemen! but for two nations, it seems to me, not wholly comic. Bedlam would be comic, perhaps, if there were only one madman in it; and your Christmas pantomime is comic, when there is only one clown in it; but when the whole world turns clown, and paints itself red with its own heart's blood instead of vermilion, it is something else than comic, I think.

Mind, I know a great deal of this is play, and willingly allow for that. You don't know what to do with yourselves for a sensation: fox-hunting and cricketing will not carry you through the whole of this unendurably long mortal life: you liked pop-guns when you were schoolboys, and rifles and Armstrongs[8] are only the same things better made: but then the worst of it is, that what was play to you when boys, was not play to the sparrows; and what is play to you now, is not play to the small birds of State neither; and for the black eagles, you are somewhat shy of taking shots at them, if I mistake not.[9]

I must get back to the matter in hand, however. Believe me, without farther instance, I could show you, in all time, that every nation's vice, or virtue, was written in its art: the soldiership of early Greece; the sensuality of late Italy; the visionary religion of Tuscany; the splendid human energy of Venice. I have no time to do this to-night (I have done it elsewhere before now[10]); but I proceed to apply the principle to ourselves in a more searching manner.

I notice that among all the new buildings which cover your once wild hills, churches and schools are mixed in due, that is to say, in large proportion, with your mills and mansions; and I notice also that the churches and schools are almost always Gothic, and the mansions and mills are never Gothic. May I ask the meaning of this? for, remember, it is peculiarly a modern phenomenon. When Gothic was invented, houses were Gothic as well as churches; and when the Italian style superseded the Gothic, churches were Italian as well as houses. If there is a Gothic spire to the cathedral of Antwerp, there is a Gothic belfry to the Hôtel de Ville at Brussels; if Inigo Jones builds an Italian Whitehall, Sir Christopher Wren builds an Italian St Paul's. But now you live under one school of architecture, and worship under another. What do you mean by doing this? Am I to understand that you are thinking of changing your architecture back to Gothic; and that you treat your churches experimentally, because it does not matter what mistakes you make in a church? Or am I to understand that you consider Gothic a pre-eminently sacred and beautiful mode of building, which you think, like the fine frankincense, should be mixed for the tabernacle only, and reserved for your religious services? For if this be the feeling, though it may seem at first as if it were graceful and reverent, at the root of the matter, it signifies neither more nor less than that you have separated your religion from your life.

For consider what a wide significance this fact has; and remember that it is not you only, but all the people of England, who are behaving thus, just now.

You have all got into the habit of calling the church 'the house of God.' I have seen, over the doors of many churches, the legend actually carved, '*This* is the house of God and this is the gate of heaven.'[11] Now, note where that legend comes from, and of what place it was first spoken. A boy leaves his father's house to go on a long journey on foot, to visit his uncle: he has to cross a wild hill-desert; just as if one of your own boys had to cross the wolds to visit an uncle at Carlisle. The second or third day your boy finds himself somewhere between Hawes and Brough, in the midst of the moors, at sunset. It is stony ground, and boggy; he cannot go one foot farther that night. Down he lies, to sleep, on Wharnside, where best he may, gathering a few of the stones together to put under his head; – so wild the place is, he cannot get anything but stones. And there, lying under the broad night, he has a dream; and he sees a ladder set up on the earth, and the top of it reaches to heaven, and the angels of God are seen ascending and descending upon it. And when he wakes out of his sleep, he says, 'How dreadful is this place; surely this is none other than the house of God, and this is the gate of heaven.' This PLACE, observe; not this church; not this city; not this stone, even, which he puts up for a memorial – the piece of flint on which his head was lain. But this *place*; this windy slope of Wharnside; this moorland hollow, torrent-bitten, snow-blighted! this *any* place where God lets down the ladder. And how are you to know where that will be? or how are you to determine where it may be, but by being ready for it always? Do you know where the lightning is to fall next? You *do* know that, partly; you can guide the lightning; but you cannot guide the going forth of the Spirit, which is as that lightning when it shines from the east to the west.[12]

But the perpetual and insolent warping of that strong verse to serve a merely ecclesiastical purpose, is only one of the thousand instances in which we sink back into gross Judaism. We call our churches 'temples.' Now, you know perfectly well they are *not* temples. They have never had, never can have, anything whatever to do with temples. They are 'synagogues' – 'gathering places' – where you gather yourselves together as an assembly; and by not calling them so, you again miss the force of another mighty text – 'Thou, when thou prayest, shalt not be as the hypocrites are; for they love to pray standing in the *churches*' [we should translate it], 'that they may be seen of men. But thou, when thou prayest, enter into thy closet, and when thou hast shut thy door, pray to thy Father,' – which is, not in chancel nor in aisle, but 'in secret.'[13]

Now, you feel, as I say this to you – I know you feel – as if I were trying to take away the honour of your churches. Not so; I am trying to prove to you the honour of your houses and your hills; not that the Church is not sacred – but that the whole Earth is. I would have you feel what careless, what constant, what infectious sin there is in all modes of thought, whereby, in calling your churches only 'holy,' you call your hearths and homes 'profane'; and have separated yourselves from the heathen by casting all your household gods to the ground, instead of recognizing, in the places of their many and feeble Lares, the presence of your One and Mighty Lord and Lar.[14]

'But what has all this to do with our Exchange?' you ask me, impatiently. My dear friends, it has just everything to do with it; on these inner and great questions depend all the outer and little ones; and if you have asked me down here to speak to you, because you had before been interested in anything I have written, you must know that all I have yet said about architecture was to show this. The book I called *The Seven Lamps* was to show that certain right states of temper and moral feeling were the magic powers by which all good architecture, without exception, had been produced. *The Stones of Venice* had, from beginning to end, no other aim than to show that the Gothic architecture of Venice had arisen out of, and indicated in all its features, a state of pure national faith, and of domestic virtue; and that its Renaissance architecture had arisen out of, and in all its features indicated, a state of concealed national infidelity, and of domestic corruption. And now, you ask me what style is best to build in, and how can I answer, knowing the meaning of the two styles, but by another question – do you mean to build as Christians or as infidels?[15] And still more – do you mean to build as honest Christians or as honest Infidels? as thoroughly and confessedly either one or the other? You don't like to be asked such rude questions. I cannot help it; they are of much more importance than this Exchange business; and if they can be at once answered, the Exchange business settles itself in a moment. But before I press them farther, I must ask leave to explain one point clearly.

In all my past work, my endeavour has been to show that good architecture is essentially religious – the production of a faithful and virtuous, not of an infidel and corrupted people. But in the course of doing this, I have had also to show that good architecture is not *ecclesiastical*.[16]

People are so apt to look upon religion as the business of the clergy, not their own, that the moment they hear of anything depending on 'religion,' they think it must also have depended on the priesthood; and I have had to take what place was to be occupied between these two errors, and fight both, often with seeming contradiction. Good architecture is the work of good and believing men; therefore, you say, at least some people say, 'Good architecture must essentially have been the work of the clergy, not of the laity.' No – a thousand times no; good architecture has always been the work of the commonalty, *not* of the clergy. 'What,' you say, 'those glorious cathedrals – the pride of Europe – did their builders not form Gothic architecture?' No; they corrupted Gothic architecture. Gothic was formed in the baron's castle, and the burgher's street. It was formed by the thoughts, and hands, and powers of labouring citizens and warrior kings. By the monk it was used as an instrument for the aid of his superstition: when that superstition became a beautiful madness, and the best hearts of Europe vainly dreamed and pined in the cloister, and vainly raged and perished in the crusade, – through that fury of perverted faith and wasted war, the Gothic rose also to its loveliest, most fantastic, and, finally, most foolish dreams; and in those dreams was lost.

I hope, now, that there is no risk of your misunderstanding me when I come to the gist of what I want to say to-night; – when I repeat, that every great national architecture has been the result and exponent of a great national religion. You can't have bits of it here, bits there – you must have it everywhere or nowhere. It is not the monopoly of a clerical company – it is not the exponent of a theological dogma – it is not the hieroglyphic writing of an initiated priesthood; it is the manly language of a people inspired by resolute and common purpose, and rendering resolute and common fidelity to the legible laws of an undoubted God.

Now there have as yet been three distinct schools of European architecture. I say, European, because Asiatic and African architectures belong so entirely to other races and climates, that there is no question of them here; only, in passing, I will simply assure you that whatever is good or great in Egypt, and Syria, and India, is just good or great for the same reasons as the buildings on our side of the Bosphorus. We Europeans, then, have had three great religions: the Greek, which was the worship of the God of Wisdom and Power; the Mediæval, which was the worship of the God of Judgment and Consolation; the Renaissance, which was the worship of the God of Pride and Beauty: these three we have had – they are past, – and now, at last, we English have got a fourth religion, and a God of our own, about which I want to ask you. But I must explain these three old ones first.

I repeat, first, the Greeks essentially worshipped the God of Wisdom; so that whatever contended against their religion, – to the Jews a stumbling-block, – was, to the Greeks – *Foolishness*.[17]

The first Greek idea of deity was that expressed in the word, of which we keep the remnant in our words '*Di*-urnal' and '*Di*-vine' – the god of *Day*, Jupiter the revealer.[18] Athena is his daughter, but especially daughter of the Intellect, springing armed from the head. We are only with the help of recent investigation beginning to penetrate the depth of meaning couched under the Athenaic symbols: but I may note rapidly, that her ægis, the mantle with the serpent fringes, in which she often, in the best statues, is represented as folding up her left hand, for better guard; and the Gorgon, on her shield, are both representative mainly of the chilling horror and sadness (turning men to stone, as it were,) of the outmost and superficial spheres of knowledge – that knowledge which separates, in bitterness, hardness, and sorrow, the heart of the full-grown man from the heart of the child. For out of imperfect knowledge spring terror, dissension, danger, and disdain; but from perfect knowledge, given by the full-revealed Athena, strength and peace, in sign of which she is crowned with the olive spray,[19] and bears the resistless spear.

This, then, was the Greek conception of purest Deity; and every habit of life, and every form of his art developed themselves from the seeking this bright, serene, resistless wisdom; and setting himself, as a man, to do things evermore rightly and strongly;* not with any ardent affection or ultimate hope; but with a resolute and continent energy of will, as knowing that for failure there was no consolation, and for sin there was no remission. And the Greek architecture rose unerring, bright, clearly defined, and self-contained.

Next followed in Europe the great Christian faith, which was essentially the religion of Comfort. Its great doctrine is the remission of sins; for which cause, it happens, too often, in certain phases of Christianity, that sin and sickness themselves are partly glorified, as if, the more you had to be healed of, the more divine was the healing. The practical result of this doctrine, in

---

* It is an error to suppose that the Greek worship, or seeking, was chiefly of Beauty. It was essentially of rightness and strength, founded on Forethought: the principal character of Greek art is not beauty, but design: and the Dorian Apollo-worship and Athenian Virgin-worship are both expressions of adoration of divine wisdom and purity. Next to these great deities, rank, in power over the national mind, Dionysus and Ceres, the givers of human strength and life; then, for heroic examples, Hercules. There is no Venus-worship among the Greeks in the great times: and the Muses are essentially teachers of Truth, and of its harmonies.

art, is a continual contemplation of sin and disease, and of imaginary states of purification from them; thus we have an architecture conceived in a mingled sentiment of melancholy and aspiration, partly severe, partly luxuriant, which will bend itself to every one of our needs, and every one of our fancies, and be strong or weak with us, as we are strong or weak ourselves. It is, of all architecture, the basest, when base people build it – of all, the noblest, when built by the noble.[20]

And now note that both these religions – Greek and Mediæval – perished by falsehood in their own main purpose. The Greek religion of Wisdom perished in a false philosophy – 'Oppositions of science, falsely so called.'[21] The Mediæval religion of Consolation perished in false comfort; in remission of sins given lyingly. It was the selling of absolution that ended the Mediæval faith; and I can tell you more, it is the selling of absolution which, to the end of time, will mark false Christianity. Pure Christianity gives her remission of sins only by *ending* them; but false Christianity gets her remission of sins by *compounding for* them. And there are many ways of compounding for them. We English have beautiful little quiet ways of buying absolution, whether in low Church or high, far more cunning than any of Tetzel's trading.[22]

Then, thirdly, there followed the religion of Pleasure, in which all Europe gave itself to luxury, ending in death. First, *bals masqués* in every saloon, and then guillotines in every square. And all these three worships issue in vast temple building. Your Greek worshipped Wisdom, and built you the Parthenon – the Virgin's temple. The Mediæval worshipped Consolation, and built you Virgin temples also – but to our Lady of Salvation. Then the Revivalist worshipped beauty, of a sort, and built you Versailles and the Vatican. Now, lastly, will you tell me what *we* worship, and what *we* build?

You know we are speaking always of the real, active, continual, national worship; that by which men act, while they live; not that which they talk of, when they die. Now, we have, indeed, a nominal religion, to which we pay tithes of property and sevenths of time; but we have also a practical and earnest religion, to which we devote nine-tenths of our property, and six-sevenths of our time. And we dispute a great deal about the nominal religion: but we are all unanimous about this practical one; of which I think you will admit that the ruling goddess may be best generally described as the 'Goddess of Getting-on,' or 'Britannia of the Market.' The Athenians had an 'Athena Agoraia,' or Athena of the Market; but she was a subordinate type of their goddess, while our Britannia Agoraia is the principal type of ours. And all your great architectural works are, of course, built to her. It is long since you built a great cathedral; and how you would laugh at me if I proposed building a cathedral on the top of one of these hills of yours, to make it an Acropolis! But your railroad mounds, vaster than the walls of Babylon; your railroad stations, vaster than the temple of Ephesus, and innumerable; your chimneys, how much more mighty and costly than cathedral spires! your harbour-piers; your warehouses; your exchanges! – all these are built to your great Goddess of 'Getting-on'; and she has formed, and will continue to form, your architecture, as long as you worship her; and it is quite vain to ask me to tell you how to build to *her*; you know far better than I.

There might, indeed, on some theories, be a conceivably good architecture for Exchanges – that is to say, if there were any heroism in the fact or deed of exchange, which might be typically carved on the outside of your building. For, you know, all beautiful architecture must be adorned with sculpture or painting; and for sculpture or painting, you must have a subject. And hitherto it has been a received opinion among the nations of the world that the only right subjects for either, were *heroisms* of some sort. Even on his pots and his flagons, the Greek put a Hercules slaying lions, or an Apollo slaying serpents, or Bacchus slaying melancholy giants, and earthborn despondencies. On his temples, the Greek put contests of great warriors in founding states, or of gods with evil spirits. On his houses and temples alike, the Christian put carvings of angels conquering devils; or of hero-martyrs exchanging this world for another: subject inappropriate, I think, to our direction of exchange here. And the Master of Christians not only left His followers without any orders as to the sculpture of affairs of exchange on the outside of buildings, but gave some strong evidence of His dislike of affairs of exchange within them. And yet there might surely be a heroism in such affairs; and all commerce become a kind of selling of doves, not impious.[23] The wonder has always been great to me, that heroism has never been supposed to be in anywise consistent with the practice of supplying people with food, or clothes[24]; but rather with that of quartering one's self upon them for food, and stripping them of their clothes. Spoiling of armour is an heroic deed in all ages; but the selling of clothes, old, or new, has never taken any colour of magnanimity. Yet one does not see why feeding the hungry and clothing the naked should ever become base businesses, even when engaged in on a large scale. If one could contrive to attach the notion of conquest to them anyhow! so that, supposing there were anywhere an obstinate race, who refused to be comforted, one might take some pride in giving them compulsory comfort!* and, as it were,

---

* Quite serious, all this, though it reads like jest. [1873.]

'*occupying* a country' with one's gifts, instead of one's armies? If one could only consider it as much a victory to get a barren field sown, as to get an eared field stripped; and contend who should build villages, instead of who should 'carry' them! Are not all forms of heroism conceivable in doing these serviceable deeds? You doubt who is strongest? It might be ascertained by push of spade, as well as push of sword. Who is wisest? There are witty things to be thought of in planning other business than campaigns. Who is bravest? There are always the elements to fight with, stronger than men; and nearly as merciless.

The only absolutely and unapproachably heroic element in the soldier's work seems to be – that he is paid little for it – and regularly: while you traffickers, and exchangers, and others occupied in presumably benevolent business, like to be paid much for it – and by chance. I never can make out how it is that a *knight*-errant does not expect to be paid for his trouble, but a *pedlar*-errant always does; – that people are willing to take hard knocks for nothing, but never to sell ribands cheap; that they are ready to go on fervent crusades, to recover the tomb of a buried God, but never on any travels to fulfil the orders of a living one; – that they will go anywhere barefoot to preach their faith, but must be well bribed to practise it, and are perfectly ready to give the Gospel gratis, but never the loaves and fishes.*

If you chose to take the matter up on any such soldierly principle; to do your commerce, and your feeding of nations, for fixed salaries; and to be as particular about giving people the best food, and the best cloth, as soldiers are about giving them the best gunpowder, I could carve something for you on your exchange worth looking at. But I can only at present suggest decorating its frieze with pendant purses; and making its pillars broad at the base, for the sticking of bills. And in the innermost chambers of it there might be a statue of Britannia of the Market,[25] who may have, perhaps advisably, a partridge for her crest, typical at once of her courage in fighting for noble ideas, and of her interest in game; and round its neck, the inscription in golden letters, 'Perdix fovit quæ non peperit.'† Then, for her spear, she might have a weaver's beam; and on her shield, instead of St George's Cross, the Milanese boar, semi-fleeced, with the town of Gennesaret proper, in the field; and the legend, 'In the best market,'‡ and

---

* Please think over this paragraph, too briefly and antithetically put, but one of those which I am happiest in having written. [1873.]

† Jerem. xvii.11, (best in Septuagint and Vulgate). 'As the partridge, fostering what she brought not forth, so he that getteth riches, not by right, shall leave them in the midst of his days, and at his end shall be a fool.'

‡ Meaning, fully, 'We have brought our pigs to it.' [1873.]

her corslet, of leather, folded over her heart in the shape of a purse, with thirty slits in it, for a piece of money to go in at, on each day of the month. And I doubt not but that people would come to see your exchange, and its goddess, with applause.

Nevertheless, I want to point out to you certain strange characters in this goddess of yours. She differs from the great Greek and Mediæval deities essentially in two things – first, as to the continuance of her presumed power; secondly, as to the extent of it.

1st, as to the Continuance.

The Greek Goddess of Wisdom gave continual increase of wisdom, as the Christian Spirit of Comfort (or Comforter) continual increase of comfort. There was no question, with these, of any limit or cessation of function. But with your Agora Goddess, that is just the most important question. Getting on – but where to? Gathering together – but how much? Do you mean to gather always – never to spend? If so, I wish you joy of your goddess, for I am just as well off as you, without the trouble of worshipping her at all. But if you do not spend, somebody else will – somebody else must. And it is because of this (among many other such errors) that I have fearlessly declared your so-called science of Political Economy to be no science; because, namely, it has omitted the study of exactly the most important branch of the business – the study of *spending*.[26] For spend you must, and as much as you make, ultimately. You gather corn: – will you bury England under a heap of grain; or will you, when you have gathered, finally eat? You gather gold: – will you make your house-roofs of it, or pave your streets with it? That is still one way of spending it. But if you keep it, that you may get more, I'll give you more; I'll give you all the gold you want – all you can imagine – if you can tell me what you'll do with it. You shall have thousands of gold pieces; – thousands of thousands – millions – mountains, of gold: where will you keep them? Will you put an Olympus of silver upon a golden Pelion – make Ossa like a wart?[27] Do you think the rain and dew would then come down to you, in the streams from such mountains, more blessedly than they will down the mountains which God has made for you, of moss and whinstone? But it is not gold that you want to gather! What is it? greenbacks? No; not those neither. What is it then – is it ciphers after a capital I? Cannot you practise writing ciphers, and write as many as you want! Write ciphers for an hour every morning, in a big book, and say every evening, I am worth all those noughts more than I was yesterday. Won't that do? Well, what in the name of Plutus[28] is it you want? Not gold, not greenbacks, not ciphers after a capital I? You will have to answer, after all, 'No; we want, somehow or other, money's *worth*.' Well, what is that? Let your Goddess of Getting-on discover it, and let her learn to stay therein.

II. But there is yet another question to be asked respecting this Goddess of Getting-on. The first was of the continuance of her power; the second is of its extent.

Pallas[29] and the Madonna were supposed to be all the world's Pallas, and all the world's Madonna. They could teach all men, and they could comfort all men. But, look strictly into the nature of the power of your Goddess of Getting-on; and you will find she is the Goddess – not of everybody's getting on – but only of somebody's getting on. This is a vital, or rather deathful, distinction. Examine it in your own ideal of the state of national life which this Goddess is to evoke and maintain. I asked you what it was, when I was last here[30]; – you have never told me. Now, shall I try to tell you?

Your ideal of human life then is, I think, that it should be passed in a pleasant undulating world, with iron and coal everywhere underneath it. On each pleasant bank of this world is to be a beautiful mansion, with two wings; and stables, and coach-houses; a moderately-sized park; a large garden and hot-houses; and pleasant carriage drives through the shrubberies. In this mansion are to live the favoured votaries of the Goddess; the English gentleman, with his gracious wife, and his beautiful family; he always able to have the boudoir and the jewels for the wife, and the beautiful ball dresses for the daughters, and hunters for the sons, and a shooting in the Highlands for himself. At the bottom of the bank, is to be the mill; not less than a quarter of a mile long, with one steam engine at each end, and two in the middle, and a chimney three hundred feet high. In this mill are to be in constant employment from eight hundred to a thousand workers, who never drink, never strike, always go to church on Sunday, and always express themselves in respectful language.

Is not that, broadly, and in the main features, the kind of thing you propose to yourselves? It is very pretty indeed, seen from above; not at all so pretty, seen from below. For, observe, while to one family this deity is indeed the Goddess of Getting-on, to a thousand families she is the Goddess of *not* Getting-on. 'Nay,' you say, 'they have all their chance.' Yes, so has every one in a lottery, but there must always be the same number of blanks. 'Ah! but in a lottery it is not skill and intelligence which take the lead, but blind chance.' What then! do you think the old practice, that 'they should take who have the power, and they should keep who can,'[31] is less iniquitous, when the power has become power of brains instead of fist? and that, though we may not take advantage of a child's or a woman's weakness, we may of a man's foolishness? 'Nay, but finally, work must be done, and some one must be at the top, some one at the bottom.' Granted, my friends. Work must always be, and captains of work must always be; and if you in the least remember the tone of any of my writings, you must know that they are thought unfit for this age, because they are always insisting on need of government, and speaking with scorn of liberty. But I beg you to observe that there is a wide difference between being captains or governors of work, and taking the profits of it. It does not follow, because you are general of an army, that you are to take all the treasure, or land, it wins; (if it fight for treasure or land;) neither, because you are king of a nation, that you are to consume all the profits of the nation's work. Real kings, on the contrary, are known invariably by their doing quite the reverse of this, – by their taking the least possible quantity of the nation's work for themselves. There is no test of real kinghood so infallible as that. Does the crowned creature live simply, bravely, unostentatiously? probably he *is* a King. Does he cover his body with jewels, and his table with delicates? in all probability he is *not* a King. It is possible he may be, as Solomon was; but that is when the nation shares his splendour with him. Solomon made gold, not only to be in his own palace as stones, but to be in Jerusalem as stones. [32] But, even so, for the most part, these splendid kinghoods expire in ruin, and only the true kinghoods live, which are of royal labourers governing loyal labourers; who, both leading rough lives, establish the true dynasties. Conclusively you will find that because you are king of a nation, it does not follow that you are to gather for yourself all the wealth of that nation; neither, because you are king of a small part of the nation, and lord over the means of its maintenance – over field, or mill, or mine, – are you to take all the produce of that piece of the foundation of national existence for yourself.

You will tell me I need not preach against these things, for I cannot mend them. No, good friends, I cannot; but you can, and you will; or something else can and will. Even good things have no abiding power – and shall these evil things persist in victorious evil? All history shows, on the contrary, that to be the exact thing they never can do. Change *must* come; but it is ours to determine whether change of growth, or change of death. Shall the Parthenon be in ruins on its rock, and Bolton priory in its meadow, but these mills of yours be the consummation of the buildings of the earth, and their wheels be as the wheels of eternity? Think you that 'men may come, and men may go,' but – mills – go on for ever? [33] Not so; out of these, better or worse shall come; and it is for you to choose which.

I know that none of this wrong is done with deliberate purpose. I know, on the contrary, that you wish your workmen well; that you do much for them, and that you desire to do more for them, if you saw your way to such benevolence safely. I know that even all this wrong and misery are brought about by a warped sense of duty, each of you striving to do his best; but, unhappily, not knowing for whom this best should be done. And all our hearts have been betrayed by the plausible impiety of the modern economist, telling us that, 'To do the best for ourselves, is finally to do the best for others.' Friends, our great Master said not so; and most absolutely we shall find this world is not made so. Indeed, to do the best for others, is finally to do the best for ourselves; but it will not do to have our eyes fixed on that issue. The Pagans had got beyond that. Hear what a Pagan says of this matter; hear what were, perhaps, the last written words of Plato, – if not the last actually written (for this we cannot know), yet assuredly in fact and power his parting words – in which, endeavouring to give full crowning and harmonious close to all his thoughts, and to speak the sum of them by the imagined sentence of the Great Spirit, his strength and his heart fail him, and the words cease, broken off for ever.

They are at the close of the dialogue called *Critias*, in which he describes, partly from real tradition, partly in ideal dream, the early state of Athens; and the genesis, and order, and religion, of the fabled isle of Atlantis; in which genesis he conceives the same first perfection and final degeneracy of man, which in our own Scriptural tradition is expressed by saying that the Sons of God inter-married with the daughters of men,[34] for he supposes the earliest race to have been indeed the children of God; and to have corrupted themselves, until 'their spot was not the spot of his children.'[35] And this, he says, was the end; that indeed[36] 'through many generations, so long as the God's nature in them yet was full, they were submissive to the sacred laws, and carried themselves lovingly to all that had kindred with them in divineness; for their uttermost spirit was faithful and true, and in every wise great; so that, in *all meekness of wisdom, they dealt with each other*, and took all the chances of life; and despising all things except virtue, they cared little what happened day by day, and *bore lightly the burden* of gold and of possessions[37]; for they saw that, if *only their common love and virtue increased, all these things would be increased together with them*; but to set their esteem and ardent pursuit upon material possession would be to lose that first, and their virtue and affection together with it. And by such reasoning, and what of the divine nature remained in them, they gained all this greatness of which we have already told; but when the God's part of them faded and became extinct,[38] being mixed again and again, and effaced by the prevalent mortality; and the human nature at last exceeded, they then became unable to endure the courses of fortune; and fell into shapelessness of life, and baseness in the sight of him who could see, having lost everything that was fairest of their honour; while to the blind hearts which could not discern the true life, tending to happiness, it seemed that they were then chiefly noble and happy, being filled with all iniquity of inordinate possession and power. Whereupon, the God of Gods, whose Kinghood is in laws, beholding a once just nation thus cast into misery, and desiring to lay such punishment upon them as might make them repent into restraining, gathered together all the gods into his dwelling place, which from heaven's centre overlooks whatever has part in creation; and having assembled them, he said'—

The rest is silence.[39] Last words of the chief wisdom of the heathen, spoken of this idol of riches; this idol of yours; this golden image, high by measureless cubits, set up where your green fields of England are furnace-burnt into the likeness of the plain of Dura[40]: this idol, forbidden to us, first of all idols, by our own Master and faith; forbidden to us also by every human lip that has ever, in any age or people, been accounted of as able to speak according to the purposes of God. Continue to make that forbidden deity your principal one, and soon no more art, no more science, no more pleasure will be possible. Catastrophe will come; or, worse than catastrophe, slow mouldering and withering into Hades. But if you can fix some conception of a true human state of life to be striven for – life, good for all men, as for yourselves; if you can determine some honest and simple order of existence; following those trodden ways of wisdom, which are pleasantness, and seeking her quiet and withdrawn paths, which are peace[41];* – then, and so sanctifying wealth into 'commonwealth,' all your art, your literature, your daily labours, your domestic affection, and citizen's duty, will join and increase into one-magnificent harmony. You will know then how to build, well enough; you will build with stone well, but with flesh better; temples not made with hands,[42] but riveted of hearts; and that kind of marble, crimson-veined, is indeed eternal.

---

* I imagine the Hebrew chant merely intends passionate repetition, and not a distinction of this somewhat fanciful kind; yet we may profitably make it in reading the English.

COMMENTARY

Sesame and Lilies, first published in 1865, originally consisted of two long lectures. 'Sesame' refers to the first lecture, 'Of Kings' Treasuries', which is reprinted here. 'Lilies' refers to the second, 'Of Queens' Gardens'. The book was, in its day, the most popular of all Ruskin's works; 160,000 copies were printed during his lifetime alone, which accounts for its frequency in second-hand bookshops today.

'Of Kings' Treasuries' was delivered at Rusholme Town Hall, near Manchester, in 1864. It was given in aid of a fund for the setting up of a library connected with the Rusholme Institute. This explains the direction of the argument, which Ruskin summarizes in his Preface: 'that valuable books should, in a civilized country, be within the reach of every one, printed in excellent form, for a just price . . .' It is mainly a plea for the introduction of public libraries 'in every considerable city' in the kingdom. This proposal, which may strike the modern reader as both sensible and characteristically Victorian, was felt at the time to be impracticable and was thus associated with Ruskin's other 'sentimentalities'.

The title, which seems both decorative and cryptic, is exceptionally rich in implication. The lilies are the 'sceptres' of queens: in other words, they represent the power and influence of women. Appropriately enough, 'Of Queens' Gardens' is concerned with female education. 'Sesame' is more complex. At the close of the lecture, Ruskin alludes to the story of Ali Baba and the potent injunction, 'Open Sesame': as E. T. Cook puts it, the lecture deals 'with the cultivation of the spirit which opens the door to the secrets of good literature'. The Kings' Treasuries, therefore, are primarily books; right education gives us the power to draw on their inexhaustible wealth. But Ruskin also extends the significance of this image. The treasuries of real kings and governors, he says, are 'the streets of their cities', their true wealth being, as in *Unto this Last*, the happiness and well-being of the subjects who inhabit those streets. In 'Of Queens' Gardens' he takes the argument further: true kingship 'consists in a stronger moral state, and a truer thoughtful state than that of others'. This moral and intellectual power over men is impossible without good education. It is this interconnection of Ruskin's literary argument with his moral and social one that makes it possible for him to analyse, in one and the same lecture, both

from
Sesame and Lilies

TWO LECTURES

Published 1865

Milton's *Lycidas* and a coroner's report from a daily newspaper. The 'sesame' has a further significance, which is located in the epigraph from the Greek satirist Lucian. A sesame cake was a delicacy much prized by the Greeks, and in Lucian's dialogue *The Fisherman* it is given as a prize to those philosophers who are willing to have their arguments judged by Philosophy in person. In other words, true riches are Wisdom.

OF KINGS' TREASURIES

'You shall each have a cake of sesame, – and ten pound.'
LUCIAN: *The Fisherman.*

My first duty this evening is to ask your pardon for the ambiguity of title under which the subject of lecture has been announced: for indeed I am not going to talk of kings, known as regnant, nor of treasuries, understood to contain wealth; but of quite another order of royalty, and another material of riches, than those usually acknowledged. I had even intended to ask your attention for a little while on trust, and (as sometimes one contrives, in taking a friend to see a favourite piece of scenery) to hide what I wanted most to show, with such imperfect cunning as I might, until we unexpectedly reached the best point of view by winding paths. But – and as also I have heard it said, by men practised in public address, that hearers are never so much fatigued as by the endeavour to follow a speaker who gives them no clue to his purpose, – I will take the slight mask off at once, and tell you plainly that I want to speak to you about the treasures hidden in books; and about the way we find them, and the way we lose them. A grave subject, you will say; and a wide one! Yes; so wide that I shall make no effort to touch the compass of it. I will try only to bring before you a few simple thoughts about reading, which press themselves upon me every day more deeply, as I watch the course of the public mind with respect to our daily enlarging means of education; and the answeringly wider spreading on the levels, of the irrigation of literature.

It happens that I have practically some connection with schools for different classes of youth[1]; and I receive many letters from parents respecting the education of their children. In the mass of these letters I am always struck by the precedence which the idea of a 'position in life' takes above all other thoughts in the parents' – more especially in the mothers' – minds. 'The education befitting such and such a *station in life*' – this is the phrase, this the object, always. They never seek, as far as I can make out, an education good in itself; even the conception of abstract rightness in training rarely seems reached by the writers. But, an education 'which shall keep a good coat on my son's back; – which shall enable him to ring with confidence the visitors' bell at double-belled doors; which shall result ultimately in establishment of a double-belled door to his own house; – in a word, which shall lead to advancement in life; – *this* we pray for on bent

knees – and this is *all* we pray for.' It never seems to occur to the parents
that there may be an education which, in itself, *is* advancement in Life; –
that any other than that may perhaps be advancement in Death; and that
this essential education might be more easily got, or given, than they fancy,
if they set about it in the right way; while it is for no price, and by no favour,
to be got, if they set about it in the wrong.

Indeed, among the ideas most prevalent and effective in the mind of this
busiest of countries, I suppose the first – at least that which is confessed with
the greatest frankness, and put forward as the fittest stimulus to youthful
exertion – is this of 'Advancement in life.' May I ask you to consider with
me, what this idea practically includes, and what it should include?

Practically, then, at present, 'advancement in life' means, becoming
conspicuous in life; obtaining a position which shall be acknowledged by
others to be respectable or honourable. We do not understand by this
advancement, in general, the mere making of money, but the being known
to have made it; not the accomplishment of any great aim, but the being
seen to have accomplished it. In a word, we mean the gratification of our
thirst for applause. That thirst, if the last infirmity of noble minds,[2] is also
the first infirmity of weak ones; and, on the whole, the strongest impulsive
influence of average humanity: the greatest efforts of the race have always
been traceable to the love of praise, as its greatest catastrophes to the love of
pleasure.

I am not about to attack or defend this impulse. I want you only to feel
how it lies at the root of effort; especially of all modern effort. It is the
gratification of vanity which is, with us, the stimulus of toil and balm of
repose; so closely does it touch the very springs of life that the wounding of
our vanity is always spoken of (and truly) as in its measure *mortal*; we call it
'mortification,' using the same expression which we should apply to a
gangrenous and incurable bodily hurt. And although a few of us may be
physicians enough to recognise the various effect of this passion upon
health and energy, I believe most honest men know, and would at once
acknowledge, its leading power with them as a motive. The seaman does not
commonly desire to be made captain only because he knows he can manage
the ship better than any other sailor on board. He wants to be made captain
that he may be *called* captain. The clergyman does not usually want to be
made a bishop only because he believes that no other hand can, as firmly as
his, direct the diocese through its difficulties. He wants to be made bishop
primarily that he may be called 'My Lord.' And a prince does not usually
desire to enlarge, or a subject to gain, a kingdom, because he believes no one
else can as well serve the State, upon its throne; but, briefly, because he

wishes to be addressed as 'Your Majesty,' by as many lips as may be brought to such utterance.

This, then, being the main idea of 'advancement in life,' the force of it applies, for all of us, according to our station, particularly to that secondary result of such advancement which we call 'getting into good society.' We want to get into good society, not that we may have it, but that we may be seen in it; and our notion of its goodness depends primarily on its conspicuousness.

Will you pardon me if I pause for a moment to put what I fear you may think an impertinent question? I never can go on with an address unless I feel, or know, that my audience are either with me or against me: I do not much care which, in beginning; but I must know where they are; and I would fain find out, at this instant, whether you think I am putting the motives of popular action too low. I am resolved, to-night, to state them low enough to be admitted as probable; for whenever, in my writings on Political Economy, I assume that a little honesty, or generosity, – or what used to be called 'virtue,' – may be calculated upon as a human motive of action, people always answer me, saying, 'You must not calculate on that: that is not in human nature: you must not assume anything to be common to men but acquisitiveness and jealousy; no other feeling ever has influence on them, except accidentally, and in matters out of the way of business.' I begin, accordingly, to-night low in the scale of motives; but I must know if you think me right in doing so. Therefore, let me ask those who admit the love of praise to be usually the strongest motive in men's minds in seeking advancement, and the honest desire of doing any kind of duty to be an entirely secondary one, to hold up their hands. (*About a dozen hands held up – the audience, partly, not being sure the lecturer is serious, and, partly, shy of expressing opinion.*) I am quite serious – I really do want to know what you think; however, I can judge by putting the reverse question. Will those who think that duty is generally the first, and love of praise the second, motive, hold up their hands? (*One hand reported to have been held up behind the lecturer.*) Very good: I see you are with me, and that you think I have not begun too near the ground. Now, without teasing you by putting farther question, I venture to assume that you will admit duty as at least a secondary or tertiary motive. You think that the desire of doing something useful, or obtaining some real good, is indeed an existent collateral idea, though a secondary one, in most men's desire of advancement. You will grant that moderately honest men desire place and office, at least in some measure for the sake of beneficent power; and would wish to associate rather with sensible and well-informed persons than with fools and ignorant persons, whether they are seen in the company of the sensible ones or not. And finally, without being troubled by repetition of any common truisms about the preciousness of friends, and the influence of companions, you will admit, doubtless, that according to the sincerity of our desire that our friends may be true, and our companions wise, – and in proportion to the earnestness and discretion with which we choose both, – will be the general chances of our happiness and usefulness.

But, granting that we had both the will and the sense to choose our friends well, how few of us have the power! or, at least, how limited, for most, is the sphere of choice! Nearly all our associations are determined by chance or necessity; and restricted within a narrow circle. We cannot know whom we would; and those whom we know, we cannot have at our side when we most need them. All the higher circles of human intelligence are, to those beneath, only momentarily and partially open. We may, by good fortune, obtain a glimpse of a great poet, and hear the sound of his voice; or put a question to a man of science, and be answered good-humouredly. We may intrude ten minutes' talk on a cabinet minister, answered probably with words worse than silence, being deceptive; or snatch, once or twice in our lives, the privilege of throwing a bouquet in the path of a princess, or arresting the kind glance of a queen. And yet these momentary chances we covet; and spend our years, and passions, and powers, in pursuit of little more than these; while, meantime, there is a society continually open to us, of people who will talk to us as long as we like, whatever our rank or occupation; – talk to us in the best words they can choose, and of the things nearest their hearts. And this society, because it is so numerous and so gentle, and can be kept waiting round us all day long, – kings and statesmen lingering patiently, not to grant audience, but to gain it! – in those plainly furnished and narrow ante-rooms, our bookcase shelves, – we make no account of that company, – perhaps never listen to a word they would say, all day long!

You may tell me, perhaps, or think within yourselves, that the apathy with which we regard this company of the noble, who are praying us to listen to them; and the passion with which we pursue the company, probably of the ignoble, who despise us, or who have nothing to teach us, are grounded in this, – that we can see the faces of the living men, and it is themselves, and not their sayings, with which we desire to become familiar. But it is not so. Suppose you never were to see their faces; – suppose you could be put behind a screen in the statesman's cabinet, or the prince's chamber, would you not be glad to listen to their words, though you were forbidden to advance beyond the screen? And when the screen is only a little less, folded in two instead of four, and you can be hidden behind the cover of the two boards that bind a book, and listen all day long, not to the casual talk, but to the studied, determined, chosen addresses of the wisest of men; – this station of audience, and honourable privy council, you despise!

But perhaps you will say that it is because the living people talk of things that are passing, and are of immediate interest to you, that you desire to hear them. Nay; that cannot be so, for the living people will themselves tell you about passing matters much better in their writings than in their careless talk. Yet I admit that this motive does influence you, so far as you prefer those rapid and ephemeral writings to slow and enduring writings – books, properly so called. For all books are divisible into two classes, the books of the hour, and the books of all time. Mark this distinction – it is not one of quality only. It is not merely the bad book that does not last, and the good one that does. It is a distinction of species. There are good books for the hour, and good ones for all time; bad books for the hour, and bad ones for all time. I must define the two kinds before I go farther.

The good book of the hour, then, – I do not speak of the bad ones, – is simply the useful or pleasant talk of some person whom you cannot otherwise converse with, printed for you. Very useful often, telling you what you need to know; very pleasant often, as a sensible friend's present talk would be. These bright accounts of travels; good-humoured and witty discussions of question; lively or pathetic story-telling in the form of novel; firm fact-telling, by the real agents concerned in the events of passing history; – all these books of the hour, multiplying among us as education becomes more general, are a peculiar possession of the present age: we ought to be entirely thankful for them, and entirely ashamed of ourselves if we make no good use of them. But we make the worst possible use if we allow them to usurp the place of true books: for, strictly speaking, they are not books at all, but merely letters or newspapers in good print. Our friend's letter may be delightful, or necessary, to-day: whether worth keeping or not, is to be considered. The newspaper may be entirely proper at breakfast time, but assuredly it is not reading for all day. So, though bound up in a volume, the long letter which gives you so pleasant an account of the inns, and roads, and weather, last year at such a place, or which tells you that amusing story, or gives you the real circumstances of such and such events, however valuable for occasional reference, may not be, in the real sense of the word, a 'book' at all, nor, in the real sense, to be 'read.' A book is essentially not a talking thing, but a written thing; and written, not with a view of mere communication, but of permanence. The book of talk is printed only because its author cannot speak to thousands of people at once;

if he could, he would – the volume is mere *multiplication* of his voice. You cannot talk to your friend in India; if you could, you would; you write instead: that is mere *conveyance* of voice. But a book is written, not to multiply the voice merely, not to carry it merely, but to perpetuate it. The author has something to say which he perceives to be true and useful, or helpfully beautiful. So far as he knows, no one has yet said it; so far as he knows, no one else can say it. He is bound to say it, clearly and melodiously if he may; clearly at all events. In the sum of his life he finds this to be the thing, or group of things, manifest to him; – this, the piece of true knowledge, or sight, which his share of sunshine and earth has permitted him to seize. He would fain set it down for ever; engrave it on rock, if he could; saying, 'This is the best of me; for the rest, I ate, and drank, and slept, loved, and hated, like another; my life was as the vapour,[3] and is not; but this I saw and knew: this, if anything of mine, is worth your memory.' That is his 'writing'; it is, in his small human way, and with whatever degree of true inspiration is in him, his inscription, or scripture. That is a 'Book.'

Perhaps you think no books were ever so written?

But, again, I ask you, do you at all believe in honesty, or at all in kindness, or do you think there is never any honesty or benevolence in wise people? None of us, I hope, are so unhappy as to think that. Well, whatever bit of a wise man's work is honestly and benevolently done, that bit is his book or his piece of art. It is mixed always with evil fragments – ill-done, redundant, affected work. But if you read rightly, you will easily discover the true bits, and those *are* the book.

Now books of this kind have been written in all ages by their greatest men: – by great leaders, great statesmen, and great thinkers. These are all at your choice; and Life is short. You have heard as much before; – yet have you measured and mapped out this short life and its possibilities? Do you know, if you read this, that you cannot read that – that what you lose to-day you cannot gain to-morrow? Will you go and gossip with your housemaid, or your stable-boy, when you may talk with queens and kings; or flatter yourself that it is with any worthy consciousness of your own claims to respect, that you jostle with the hungry and common crowd for *entrée* here, and audience there, when all the while this eternal court is open to you, with its society, wide as the world, multitudinous as its days, the chosen, and the mighty, of every place and time? Into that you may enter always; in that you may take fellowship and rank according to your wish; from that, once entered into it, you can never be outcast but by your own fault; by your aristocracy of companionship there, your own inherent aristocracy will be assuredly tested, and the motives with which you strive to take high place in the society of the living, measured, as to all the truth and sincerity that are in them, by the place you desire to take in this company of the Dead.

'The place you desire,' and the place you *fit yourself for*, I must also say; because, observe, this court of the past differs from all living aristocracy in this: – it is open to labour and to merit, but to nothing else. No wealth will bribe, no name overawe, no artifice deceive, the guardian of those Elysian gates. In the deep sense, no vile or vulgar person ever enters there. At the portières of that silent Faubourg St Germain, there is but brief question: – 'Do you deserve to enter? Pass. Do you ask to be the companion of nobles? Make yourself noble, and you shall be. Do you long for the conversation of the wise? Learn to understand it, and you shall hear it. But on other terms? – no. If you will not rise to us, we cannot stoop to you. The living lord may assume courtesy, the living philosopher explain his thought to you with considerate pain; but here we neither feign nor interpret; you must rise to the level of our thoughts if you would be gladdened by them, and share our feelings, if you would recognise our presence.'

This, then, is what you have to do, and I admit that it is much. You must, in a word, love these people, if you are to be among them. No ambition is of any use. They scorn your ambition. You must love them, and show your love in these two following ways.

(1) First, by a true desire to be taught by them, and to enter into their thoughts. To enter into theirs, observe; not to find your own expressed by them. If the person who wrote the book is not wiser than you, you need not read it; if he be, he will think differently from you in many respects.

(2) Very ready we are to say of a book, 'How good this is – that's exactly what I think!' But the right feeling is, 'How strange that is! I never thought of that before, and yet I see it is true; or if I do not now, I hope I shall, some day.' But whether thus submissively or not, at least be sure that you go to the author to get at *his* meaning, not to find yours. Judge it afterwards if you think yourself qualified to do so; but ascertain it first. And be sure, also, if the author is worth anything, that you will not get at his meaning all at once; – nay, that at his whole meaning you will not for a long time arrive in any wise. Not that he does not say what he means, and in strong words too; but he cannot say it all; and what is more strange, *will* not, but in a hidden way and in parables,[4] in order that he may be sure you want it. I cannot quite see the reason of this, nor analyse that cruel reticence in the breasts of wise men which makes them always hide their deeper thought. They do not give it you by way of help, but of reward; and will make themselves sure that you deserve it before they allow you to reach it. But it is the same with the physical type of wisdom, gold. There seems, to you and me, no reason

why the electric forces of the earth should not carry whatever there is of gold within it at once to the mountain tops, so that kings and people might know that all the gold they could get was there; and without any trouble of digging, or anxiety, or chance, or waste of time, cut it away, and coin as much as they needed. But Nature does not manage it so. She puts it in little fissures in the earth, nobody knows where: you may dig long and find none; you must dig painfully to find any.

And it is just the same with men's best wisdom. When you come to a good book, you must ask yourself, 'Am I inclined to work as an Australian miner would? Are my pickaxes and shovels in good order, and am I in good trim myself, my sleeves well up to the elbow, and my breath good, and my temper?' And, keeping the figure a little longer, even at cost of tiresomeness, for it is a thoroughly useful one, the metal you are in search of being the author's mind or meaning, his words are as the rock which you have to crush and smelt in order to get at it. And your pickaxes are your own care, wit, and learning; your smelting furnace is your own thoughtful soul. Do not hope to get at any good author's meaning without those tools and that fire; often you will need sharpest, finest chiselling, and patientest fusing, before you can gather one grain of the metal.

And, therefore, first of all, I tell you earnestly and authoritatively (I *know* I am right in this), you must get into the habit of looking intensely at words, and assuring yourself of their meaning, syllable by syllable – nay, letter by letter. For though it is only by reason of the opposition of letters in the function of signs, to sounds in the function of signs, that the study of books is called 'literature,' and that a man versed in it is called, by the consent of nations, a man of letters instead of a man of books, or of words, you may yet connect with that accidental nomenclature this real fact: – that you might read all the books in the British Museum (if you could live long enough), and remain an utterly 'illiterate,' uneducated person; but that if you read ten pages of a good book, letter by letter, – that is to say, with real accuracy, – you are for evermore in some measure an educated person. The entire difference between education and non-education (as regards the merely intellectual part of it), consists in this accuracy. A well-educated gentleman may not know many languages, – may not be able to speak any but his own, – may have read very few books. But whatever language he knows, he knows precisely; whatever word he pronounces, he pronounces rightly; above all, he is learned in the *peerage* of words[5]; knows the words of true descent and ancient blood, at a glance, from words of modern canaille; remembers all their ancestry, their intermarriages, distant relationships, and the extent to which they were admitted, and offices they held, among the national noblesse of words at any time, and in any country. But an uneducated person may know, by memory, many languages, and talk them all, and yet truly know not a word of any, – not a word even of his own. An ordinarily clever and sensible seaman will be able to make his way ashore at most ports; yet he has only to speak a sentence of any language to be known for an illiterate person: so also the accent, or turn of expression of a single sentence, will at once mark a scholar. And this is so strongly felt, so conclusively admitted, by educated persons, that a false accent or a mistaken syllable is enough, in the parliament of any civilized nation, to assign to a man a certain degree of inferior standing for ever.

And this is right; but it is a pity that the accuracy insisted on is not greater, and required to a serious purpose. It is right that a false Latin quantity[6] should excite a smile in the House of Commons; but it is wrong that a false English *meaning* should *not* excite a frown there. Let the accent of words be watched; and closely: let their meaning be watched more closely still, and fewer will do the work. A few words well chosen, and distinguished, will do work that a thousand cannot, when every one is acting, equivocally, in the function of another. Yes; and words, if they are not watched, will do deadly work sometimes. There are masked words droning and skulking about us in Europe just now, – (there never were so many, owing to the spread of a shallow, blotching, blundering, infectious 'information,' or rather deformation, everywhere, and to the teaching of catechisms and phrases at school instead of human meanings) – there are masked words abroad, I say, which nobody understands, but which every-body uses, and most people will also fight for, live for, or even die for, fancying they mean this or that, or the other, of things dear to them: for such words wear chameleon cloaks – 'ground-lion'[7] cloaks, of the colour of the ground of any man's fancy: on that ground they lie in wait, and rend them with a spring from it. There never were creatures of prey so mischievous, never diplomatists so cunning, never poisoners so deadly, as these masked words; they are the unjust stewards of all men's ideas: whatever fancy or favourite instinct a man most cherishes, he gives to his favourite masked word to take care of for him; the word at last comes to have an infinite power over him, – you cannot get at him but by its ministry.

And in languages so mongrel in breed as the English, there is a fatal power of equivocation put into men's hands, almost whether they will or no, in being able to use Greek or Latin words for an idea when they want it to be awful; and Saxon or otherwise common words when they want it to be vulgar. What a singular and salutary effect, for instance, would be produced on the minds of people who are in the habit of taking the Form of the 'Word' they live by, for the Power of which that Word tells them, if we always either retained, or refused, the Greek form 'biblos,' or 'biblion,' as the right expression for 'book' – instead of employing it only in the one instance in which we wish to give dignity to the idea, and translating it into English everywhere else. How wholesome it would be for many simple persons if, in such places (for instance) as Acts xix.19, we retained the Greek expression, instead of translating it, and they had to read – 'Many of them also which used curious arts, brought their bibles together, and burnt them before all men; and they counted the price of them, and found it fifty thousand pieces of silver'! Or if, on the other hand, we translated where we retain it, and always spoke of 'The Holy Book,' instead of 'Holy Bible,' it might come into more heads than it does at present, that the Word of God, by which the heavens were, of old, and by which they are now kept in store,* cannot be made a present of to anybody in morocco binding; nor sown on any wayside by help either of steam plough or steam press; but is nevertheless being offered to us daily, and by us with contumely refused; and sown in us daily, and by us, as instantly as may be, choked.[8]

So, again, consider what effect has been produced on the English vulgar mind by the use of the sonorous Latin form 'damno,' in translating the Greek κατακρίνω, when people charitably wish to make it forcible; and the substitution of the temperate 'condemn' for it, when they choose to keep it gentle; and what notable sermons have been preached by illiterate clergymen on – 'He that believeth not shall be damned'[9]; though they would shrink with horror from translating Heb. xi.7, 'The saving of his house, by which he damned the world,' or John viii.10–11, 'Woman, hath no man damned thee? She saith, No man, Lord. Jesus answered her, Neither do I damn thee: go and sin no more.' And divisions in the mind of Europe, which have cost seas of blood, and in the defence of which the noblest souls of men have been cast away in frantic desolation, countless as forest-leaves – though, in the heart of them, founded on deeper causes – have nevertheless been rendered practically possible, mainly, by the European adoption of the Greek word for a public meeting, 'ecclesia,' to give peculiar respectability to such meetings, when held for religious purposes; and other collateral equivocations, such as the vulgar English one of using the word 'priest' as a contraction for 'presbyter.'

Now, in order to deal with words rightly, this is the habit you must form.

* 2 Peter iii.5–7.

Nearly every word in your language has been first a word of some other language – of Saxon, German, French, Latin, or Greek; (not to speak of eastern and primitive dialects). And many words have been all these – that is to say, have been Greek first, Latin next, French or German next, and English last: undergoing a certain change of sense and use on the lips of each nation; but retaining a deep vital meaning, which all good scholars feel in employing them, even at this day. If you do not know the Greek alphabet, learn it; young or old – girl or boy – whoever you may be, if you think of reading seriously (which, of course, implies that you have some leisure at command), learn your Greek alphabet; then get good dictionaries of all these languages, and whenever you are in doubt about a word, hunt it down patiently. Read Max Müller's lectures[10] thoroughly, to begin with; and, after that, never let a word escape you that looks suspicious. It is severe work; but you will find it, even at first, interesting, and at last endlessly amusing. And the general gain to your character, in power and precision, will be quite incalculable.

Mind, this does not imply knowing, or trying to know, Greek or Latin, or French. It takes a whole life to learn any language perfectly. But you can easily ascertain the meanings through which the English word has passed; and those which in a good writer's work it must still bear.

And now, merely for example's sake, I will, with your permission, read a few lines of a true book with you, carefully; and see what will come out of them. I will take a book perfectly known to you all. No English words are more familiar to us, yet few perhaps have been read with less sincerity. I will take these few following lines of *Lycidas*: –

> 'Last came, and last did go,
> The pilot of the Galilean lake.
> Two massy keys he bore of metals twain,
> (The golden opes, the iron shuts amain,)
> He shook his mitred locks, and stern bespake,
> "How well could I have spared for thee, young swain,
> Enow of such as for their bellies' sake
> Creep, and intrude, and climb into the fold!
> Of other care they little reckoning make,
> Than how to scramble at the shearers' feast,
> And shove away the worthy bidden guest;
> Blind mouths! that scarce themselves know how to hold
> A sheep-hook, or have learn'd aught else, the least
> That to the faithful herdman's art belongs!

What recks it them? What need they? They are sped;
And when they list, their lean and flashy songs
Grate on their scrannel pipes of wretched straw;
The hungry sheep look up, and are not fed,
But, swoln with wind, and the rank mist they draw,
Rot inwardly, and foul contagion spread;
Besides what the grim wolf with privy paw
Daily devours apace, and nothing said." '

Let us think over this passage, and examine its words.

First, is it not singular to find Milton assigning to St Peter, not only his full episcopal function, but the very types of it which Protestants usually refuse most passionately? His 'mitred' locks! Milton was no Bishop-lover; how comes St Peter to be 'mitred'? 'Two massy keys he bore.' Is this, then, the power of the keys claimed by the Bishops of Rome? and is it acknowledged here by Milton only in a poetical licence, for the sake of its picturesqueness, that he may get the gleam of the golden keys to help his effect?

Do not think it. Great men do not play stage tricks with the doctrines of life and death: only little men do that. Milton means what he says; and means it with his might too – is going to put the whole strength of his spirit presently into the saying of it. For though not a lover of false bishops, he *was* a lover of true ones; and the Lake-pilot is here, in his thoughts, the type and head of true episcopal power. For Milton reads that text, 'I will give unto thee the keys of the kingdom of heaven,' quite honestly.[11] Puritan though he be, he would not blot it out of the book because there have been bad bishops; nay, in order to understand *him*, we must understand that verse first; it will not do to eye it askance, or whisper it under our breath, as if it were a weapon of an adverse sect. It is a solemn, universal assertion, deeply to be kept in mind by all sects. But perhaps we shall be better able to reason on it if we go on a little farther, and come back to it. For clearly this marked insistence on the power of the true episcopate is to make us feel more weightily what is to be charged against the false claimants of episcopate; or generally, against false claimants of power and rank in the body of the clergy; they who, 'for their bellies' sake, creep, and intrude, and climb into the fold.'

Never think Milton uses those three words to fill up his verse, as a loose writer would. He needs all the three; – especially those three, and no more than those – 'creep,' and 'intrude,' and 'climb'; no other words would or could serve the turn, and no more could be added. For they exhaustively comprehend the three classes, correspondent to the three characters, of men who dishonestly seek ecclesiastical power. First, those who '*creep*' into the fold; who do not care for office, nor name, but for secret influence, and do all things occultly and cunningly, consenting to any servility of office or conduct, so only that they may intimately discern, and unawares direct, the minds of men. Then those who 'intrude' (thrust, that is) themselves into the fold, who by natural insolence of heart, and stout eloquence of tongue, and fearlessly perseverant self-assertion, obtain hearing and authority with the common crowd. Lastly, those who 'climb,' who, by labour and learning, both stout and sound, but selfishly exerted in the cause of their own ambition, gain high dignities and authorities, and become 'lords over the heritage,' though not 'ensamples to the flock.'

Now go on: –

> 'Of other care they little reckoning make,
> Than how to scramble at the shearers' feast.
> *Blind mouths* –'

I pause again, for this is a strange expression; a broken metaphor, one might think, careless and unscholarly.

Not so: its very audacity and pithiness are intended to make us look close at the phrase and remember it. Those two monosyllables express the precisely accurate contraries of right character, in the two great offices of the Church – those of bishop and pastor.

A 'Bishop' means 'a person who sees.'

A 'Pastor' means 'a person who feeds.'

The most unbishoply character a man can have is therefore to be Blind.

The most unpastoral is, instead of feeding, to want to be fed, – to be a Mouth.

Take the two reverses together, and you have 'blind mouths.' We may advisably follow out this idea a little. Nearly all the evils in the Church have arisen from bishops desiring *power* more than *light*. They want authority, not outlook. Whereas their real office is not to rule; though it may be vigorously to exhort and rebuke: it is the king's office to rule; the bishop's office is to *oversee* the flock; to number it, sheep by sheep; to be ready always to give full account of it. Now it is clear he cannot give account of the souls, if he has not so much as numbered the bodies, of his flock. The first thing, therefore, that a bishop has to do is at least to put himself in a position in which, at any moment, he can obtain the history, from childhood, of every living soul in his diocese, and of its present state. Down in that back street, Bill and Nancy, knocking each other's teeth out![12] – Does the bishop know all about it? Has he his eye upon them? Has he *had* his eye upon them? Can he circumstantially explain to us how Bill got into the habit of beating Nancy about the head? If he cannot, he is no bishop, though he had a mitre as high as Salisbury steeple; he is no bishop, – he has sought to be at the helm instead of the mast-head; he has no sight of things. 'Nay,' you say, 'it is not his duty to look after Bill in the back street.' What! the fat sheep that have full fleeces – you think it is only those he should look after while (go back to your Milton) 'the hungry sheep look up, and are not fed, besides what the grim wolf, with privy paw' (bishops knowing nothing about it), 'daily devours apace, and nothing said'?

'But that's not our idea of a bishop.' Perhaps not; but it was St Paul's[13]; and it was Milton's. They may be right, or we may be; but we must not think we are reading either one or the other by putting our meaning into their words.

I go on.

> 'But swoln with wind, and the rank mist they draw.'

This is to meet the vulgar answer that 'if the poor are not looked after in their bodies, they are in their souls; they have spiritual food.'

And Milton says, 'They have no such thing as spiritual food; they are only swollen with wind.' At first you may think that is a coarse type, and an obscure one. But again, it is a quite literally accurate one. Take up your Latin and Greek dictionaries, and find out the meaning of 'Spirit.' It is only a contraction of the Latin word 'breath,' and an indistinct translation of the Greek word for 'wind.' The same word is used in writing, 'The wind bloweth where it listeth'; and in writing, 'So is every one that is born of the Spirit'[14]; born of the *breath*, that is; for it means the breath of God, in soul and body. We have the true sense of it in our words 'inspiration' and 'expire.' Now, there are two kinds of breath with which the flock may be filled, – God's breath, and man's. The breath of God is health, and life, and peace to them, as the air of heaven is to the flocks on the hills; but man's breath – the word which *he* calls spiritual – is disease and contagion to them, as the fog of the fen. They rot inwardly with it; they are puffed up by it, as a dead body by the vapours of its own decomposition. This is literally true of all false religious teaching; the first and last, and fatalest sign of it, is that 'puffing up.'[15] Your converted children, who teach their parents; your converted convicts, who teach honest men; your converted dunces, who, having lived in cretinous stupefaction half their lives, suddenly awaking to the fact of there being a God, fancy themselves therefore His peculiar people and messengers; your sectarians of every species, small and great, Catholic or Protestant, of high church or low, in so far as they think themselves exclusively in the right and others wrong; and, pre-eminently, in every sect, those who hold that men can be saved by thinking rightly instead of doing rightly, by word instead of act, and wish instead of work; – these are the true fog children – clouds, these, without water[16]; bodies, these, of putrescent vapour and skin, without blood or flesh: blown bagpipes for the fiends to pipe with – corrupt, and corrupting, – 'Swollen with wind, and the rank mist they draw.'

Lastly, let us return to the lines respecting the power of the keys, for now we can understand them. Note the difference between Milton and Dante in their interpretation of this power[17]: for once, the latter is weaker in thought; he supposes *both* the keys to be of the gate of heaven; one is of gold, the other of silver: they are given by St Peter to the sentinel angel; and it is not easy to determine the meaning either of the substances of the three steps of the gate, or of the two keys. But Milton makes one, of gold, the key of heaven; the other, of iron, the key of the prison in which the wicked teachers are to be bound who 'have taken away the key of knowledge, yet entered not in themselves.'[18]

We have seen that the duties of bishop and pastor are to see, and feed; and of all who do so it is said, 'He that watereth, shall be watered also himself.'[19] But the reverse is truth also. He that watereth not, shall be *withered* himself; and he that seeth not, shall himself be shut out of sight – shut into the perpetual prison-house. And that prison opens here, as well as here-after: he who is to be bound in heaven must first be bound on earth. That command to the strong angels, of which the rock-apostle is the image, 'Take him, and bind him hand and foot, and cast him out,'[20] issues, in its measure, against the teacher, for every help withheld, and for every truth refused, and for every falsehood enforced; so that he is more strictly fettered the more he fetters, and farther outcast as he more and more misleads, till at last the bars of the iron cage close upon him, and as 'the golden opes, the iron shuts amain.'

We have got something out of the lines, I think, and much more is yet to be found in them; but we have done enough by way of example of the kind of word-by-word examination of your author which is rightly called 'reading'; watching every accent and expression, and putting ourselves always in the author's place, annihilating our own personality, and seeking to enter into his, so as to be able assuredly to say, 'Thus Milton thought,' not 'Thus *I* thought, in mis-reading Milton.' And by this process you will gradually come to attach less weight to your own 'Thus I thought' at other times. You will begin to perceive that what *you* thought was a matter of no serious importance; – that your thoughts on any subject are not perhaps the clearest and wisest that could be arrived at thereupon: – in fact, that unless you are a very singular person, you cannot be said to have any 'thoughts' at all; that you have no materials for them, in any serious matters; * – no right to 'think,' but only to try to learn more of the facts. Nay, most probably all your life (unless, as I said, you are a singular person) you will have no legitimate right to an 'opinion' on any business, except that instantly under your hand. What must of necessity be done, you can always find out, beyond question, how to do. Have you a house to keep in order, a commodity to sell, a field to plough, a ditch to cleanse? There need be no two opinions about these proceedings; it is at your peril if you have not much more than an 'opinion' on the way to manage such matters. And also, outside of your own business, there are one or two subjects on which you are bound to have but one opinion. That roguery and lying are objectionable, and are instantly to be flogged out of the way whenever discovered; – that covetousness and love of quarrelling are dangerous dispositions even in children, and deadly dispositions in men and nations; – that, in the end, the God of heaven and earth loves active, modest, and kind people, and hates idle, proud, greedy, and cruel ones; – on these general facts you are bound to have but one, and that a very strong, opinion. For the rest, respecting religions, governments, sciences, arts, you will find that, on the whole, you can know NOTHING, – judge nothing; that the best you can do, even though you may be a well-educated person, is to be silent, and strive to be wiser every day, and to understand a little more of the thoughts of others, which so soon as you try to do honestly, you will discover that the thoughts even of the wisest are very little more than pertinent questions. To put the difficulty into a clear shape, and exhibit to you the grounds for *in*decision, that is all they can generally do for you! – and well for them and for us, if indeed they are able 'to mix the music with our thoughts and sadden us with heavenly doubts.'[21] This writer, from whom I have been reading to you, is not among the first or wisest: he sees shrewdly as far as he sees, and therefore it is easy to find out its full meaning; but with the greater men, you cannot fathom their meaning; they do not even wholly measure it themselves, – it is so wide. Suppose I had asked you, for instance, to seek for Shakespeare's opinion, instead of Milton's, on this matter of Church authority? – or for Dante's? Have any of you, at this instant, the least idea what either thought about it? Have you ever balanced the scene with the

---

* Modern 'Education' for the most part signifies giving people the faculty of thinking wrong on every conceivable subject of importance to them.

bishops in *Richard III* against the character of Cranmer?[22] the description of St Francis and St Dominic against that of him who made Virgil wonder to gaze upon him, – 'disteso, tanto vilmente, nell' eterno esilio': or of him whom Dante stood beside, 'come 'l frate che confessa lo perfido assassin'?[23] Shakespeare and Alighieri knew men better than most of us, I presume! They were both in the midst of the main struggle between the temporal and spiritual powers. They had an opinion, we may guess. But where is it? Bring it into court! Put Shakespeare's or Dante's creed into articles, and send *it* up for trial by the Ecclesiastical Courts![24]

You will not be able, I tell you again, for many and many a day, to come at the real purposes and teaching of these great men; but a very little honest study of them will enable you to perceive that what you took for your own 'judgment' was mere chance prejudice, and drifted, helpless, entangled weed of castaway thought; nay, you will see that most men's minds are indeed little better than rough heath wilderness, neglected and stubborn, partly barren, partly overgrown with pestilent brakes, and venomous, wind-sown herbage of evil surmise; that the first thing you have to do for them, and yourself, is eagerly and scornfully to set fire to *this*; burn all the jungle into wholesome ash-heaps, and then plough and sow. All the true literary work before you, for life, must begin with obedience to that order, 'Break up your fallow ground, and *sow not among thorns.'*[25]

(II.) Having then faithfully listened to the great teachers, that you may enter into their Thoughts, you have yet this higher advance to make; – you have to enter into their Hearts. As you go to them first for clear sight, so you must stay with them, that you may share at last their just and mighty Passion. Passion, or 'sensation.' I am not afraid of the word; still less of the thing. You have heard many outcries against sensation lately[26]; but, I can tell you, it is not less sensation we want, but more. The ennobling difference between one man and another, – between one animal and another, – is precisely in this, that one feels more than another. If we were sponges, perhaps sensation might not be easily got for us; if we were earth-worms, liable at every instant to be cut in two by the spade, perhaps too much sensation might not be good for us. But being human creatures, it *is* good for us; nay, we are only human in so far as we are sensitive, and our honour is precisely in proportion to our passion.

You know I said of that great and pure society of the Dead, that it would allow 'no vain or vulgar person to enter there.' What do you think I meant by a 'vulgar' person? What do you yourselves mean by 'vulgarity'? You will find it a fruitful subject of thought; but, briefly, the essence of all vulgarity lies in want of sensation. Simple and innocent vulgarity is merely an untrained and undeveloped bluntness of body and mind; but in true inbred vulgarity, there is a dreadful callousness, which, in extremity, becomes capable of every sort of bestial habit and crime, without fear, without pleasure, without horror, and without pity. It is in the blunt hand and the dead heart, in the diseased habit, in the hardened conscience, that men become vulgar; they are for ever vulgar, precisely in proportion as they are incapable of sympathy, – of quick understanding, – of all that, in deep insistence on the common, but most accurate term, may be called the 'tact' or 'touch-faculty,' of body and soul: that tact which the Mimosa has in trees, which the pure woman has above all creatures; – fineness and ful-ness of sensation, beyond reason; – the guide and sanctifier of reason itself. Reason can but determine what is true: – it is the God-given passion of humanity which alone can recognise what God has made good.

We come then to that great concourse of the Dead, not merely to know from them what is True, but chiefly to feel with them what is just. Now, to feel with them, we must be like them; and none of us can become that without pains. As the true knowledge is disciplined and tested knowledge, – not the first thought that comes, so the true passion is disciplined and tested passion, – not the first passion that comes. The first that come are the vain, the false, the treacherous; if you yield to them they will lead you wildly and far, in vain pursuit, in hollow enthusiasm, till you have no true purpose and no true passion left. Not that any feeling possible to humanity is in itself wrong, but only wrong when undisciplined. Its nobility is in its force and justice; it is wrong when it is weak, and felt for paltry cause. There is a mean wonder, as of a child who sees a juggler tossing golden balls; and this is base, if you will. But do you think that the wonder is ignoble, or the sensation less, with which every human soul is called to watch the golden balls of heaven tossed through the night by the Hand that made them? There is a mean curiosity, as of a child opening a forbidden door, or a servant prying into her master's business; – and a noble curiosity, questioning, in the front of danger, the source of the great river beyond the sand, – the place of the great continents beyond the sea; – a nobler curiosity still, which questions of the source of the River of Life, and of the space of the Continent of Heaven, – things which 'the angels desire to look into.'[27] So the anxiety is ignoble, with which you linger over the course and catastrophe of an idle tale; but do you think the anxiety is less, or greater, with which you watch, or *ought* to watch, the dealings of fate and destiny with the life of an agonized nation? Alas! it is the narrowness, selfishness, minuteness, of your sensation that you have to deplore in England at this day; – sensation which spends itself in bouquets and speeches: in revellings and junketings;

in sham fights and gay puppet shows, while you can look on and see noble nations murdered, man by man, without an effort or a tear.[28]

I said 'minuteness' and 'selfishness' of sensation, but it would have been enough to have said 'injustice' or 'unrighteousness' of sensation.[29] For as in nothing is a gentleman better to be discerned from a vulgar person, so in nothing is a gentle nation (such nations have been) better to be discerned from a mob, than in this, – that their feelings are constant and just, results of due contemplation, and of equal thought. You can talk a mob into anything; its feelings may be – usually are – on the whole, generous and right; but it has no foundation for them, no hold of them; you may tease or tickle it into any, at your pleasure; it thinks by infection, for the most part, catching an opinion like a cold, and there is nothing so little that it will not roar itself wild about, when the fit is on; – nothing so great but it will forget in an hour, when the fit is past. But a gentleman's, or a gentle nation's, passions are just, measured, and continuous. A great nation, for instance, does not spend its entire national wits for a couple of months in weighing evidence of a single ruffian's having done a single murder[30]; and for a couple of years see its own children murder each other by their thousands or tens of thousands a day, considering only what the effect is likely to be on the price of cotton, and caring no wise to determine which side of battle is in the wrong.[31] Neither does a great nation send its poor little boys to jail for stealing six walnuts; and allow its bankrupts to steal their hundreds of thousands with a bow, and its bankers, rich with poor men's savings, to close their doors 'under circumstances over which they have no control,' with a 'by your leave'; and large landed estates to be bought by men who have made their money by going with armed steamers up and down the China Seas, selling opium at the cannon's mouth,[32] and altering, for the benefit of the foreign nation, the common highwayman's demand of 'your money *or* your life,' into that of 'your money *and* your life.' Neither does a great nation allow the lives of its innocent poor to be parched out of them by fog fever, and rotted out of them by dunghill plague, for the sake of sixpence a life extra per week to its landlords; and then debate, with drivelling tears, and diabolical sympathies, whether it ought not piously to save, and nursingly cherish, the lives of its murderers.[33] Also, a great nation having made up its mind that hanging is quite the wholesomest process for its homicides in general, can yet with mercy distinguish between the degrees of guilt in homicides; and does not yelp like a pack of frost-pinched wolf-cubs on the blood-track of an unhappy crazed boy, or grey-haired clodpate Othello, 'perplexed i' the extreme,'[34] at the very moment that it is sending a Minister of the Crown to make polite speeches to a man who is bayoneting young girls in their fathers' sight, and killing noble youths in cool blood, faster than a country butcher kills lambs in spring.[35] And, lastly, a great nation does not mock Heaven and its Powers, by pretending belief in a revelation which asserts the love of money to be the root of *all* evil,[36] and declaring, at the same time, that it is actuated, and intends to be actuated, in all chief national deeds and measures, by no other love.

My friends, I do not know why any of us should talk about reading. We want some sharper discipline than that of reading; but, at all events, be assured, we cannot read. No reading is possible for a people with its mind in this state. No sentence of any great writer is intelligible to them. It is simply and sternly impossible for the English public, at this moment, to understand any thoughtful writing, – so incapable of thought has it become in its insanity of avarice. Happily, our disease is, as yet, little worse than this incapacity of thought; it is not corruption of the inner nature; we ring true still, when anything strikes home to us; and though the idea that everything should 'pay' has infected our every purpose so deeply, that even when we would play the good Samaritan, we never take out our two pence and give them to the host, without saying, 'When I come again, thou shalt give me fourpence,'[37] there is a capacity of noble passion left in our hearts' core. We show it in our work – in our war, – even in those unjust domestic affections which make us furious at a small private wrong, while we are polite to a boundless public one: we are still industrious to the last hour of the day, though we add the gambler's fury to the labourer's patience; we are still brave to the death, though incapable of discerning true cause for battle; and are still true in affection to our own flesh, to the death, as the sea-monsters are, and the rock-eagles. And there is hope for a nation while this can be still said of it. As long as it holds its life in its hand, ready to give it for its honour (though a foolish honour), for its love (though a selfish love), and for its business (though a base business), there is hope for it. But hope only; for this instinctive, reckless virtue cannot last. No nation can last, which has made a mob of itself, however generous at heart. It must discipline its passions, and direct them, or they will discipline *it*, one day, with scorpion whips.[38] Above all, a nation cannot last as a money-making mob: it cannot with impunity, – it cannot with existence, – go on despising literature, despising science, despising art, despising nature, despising compassion, and concentrating its soul on Pence. Do you think these are harsh or wild words? Have patience with me but a little longer. I will prove their truth to you, clause by clause.

(I.) I say first we have despised literature. What do we, as a nation, care about books? How much do you think we spend altogether on our libraries, public or private, as compared with what we spend on our horses? If a man spends lavishly on his library, you call him mad – a bibliomaniac. But you never call any one a horsemaniac, though men ruin themselves every day by their horses, and you do not hear of people ruining themselves by their books. Or, to go lower still, how much do you think the contents of the book-shelves of the United Kingdom, public and private, would fetch, as compared with the contents of its wine-cellars? What position would its expenditure on literature take, as compared with its expenditure on luxurious eating? We talk of food for the mind, as of food for the body: now a good book contains such food inexhaustibly; it is a provision for life, and for the best part of us; yet how long most people would look at the best book before they would give the price of a large turbot for it? Though there have been men who have pinched their stomachs and bared their backs to buy a book, whose libraries were cheaper to them, I think, in the end, than most men's dinners are. We are few of us put to such trial, and more the pity; for, indeed, a precious thing is all the more precious to us if it has been won by work or economy; and if public libraries were half so costly as public dinners, or books cost the tenth part of what bracelets do, even foolish men and women might sometimes suspect there was good in reading, as well as in munching and sparkling: whereas the very cheapness of literature is making even wise people forget that if a book is worth reading, it is worth buying. No book is worth anything which is not worth *much*; nor is it serviceable, until it has been read, and re-read, and loved, and loved again; and marked, so that you can refer to the passages you want in it, as a soldier can seize the weapon he needs in an armoury, or a housewife bring the spice she needs from her store. Bread of flour is good; but there is bread, sweet as honey, if we would eat it, in a good book; and the family must be poor indeed, which, once in their lives, cannot, for such multipliable barley-loaves,[39] pay their baker's bill. We call ourselves a rich nation, and we are filthy and foolish enough to thumb each other's books out of circulating libraries!

(II.) I say we have despised science. 'What!' you exclaim, 'are we not foremost in all discovery,* and is not the whole world giddy by reason, or unreason, of our inventions?' Yes; but do you suppose that is national work? That work is all done *in spite of* the nation; by private people's zeal and money. We are glad enough, indeed, to make our profit of science; we

---

* Since this was written, the answer has become definitely – No; we having surrendered the field of Arctic discovery to the Continental nations, as being ourselves too poor to pay for ships.[40]

snap up anything in the way of a scientific bone that has meat on it, eagerly enough; but if the scientific man comes for a bone or a crust to *us*, that is another story. What have we publicly done for science? We are obliged to know what o'clock it is, for the safety of our ships, and therefore we pay for an observatory; and we allow ourselves, in the person of our Parliament, to be annually tormented into doing something, in a slovenly way, for the British Museum; sullenly apprehending that to be a place for keeping stuffed birds in, to amuse our children. If anybody will pay for their own telescope, and resolve another nebula, we cackle over the discernment as if it were our own; if one in ten thousand of our hunting squires suddenly perceives that the earth was indeed made to be something else than a portion for foxes,[41] and burrows in it himself, and tells us where the gold is, and where the coals, we understand that there is some use in that; and very properly knight him: but is the accident of his having found out how to employ himself usefully any credit to *us*? (The negation of such discovery among his brother squires may perhaps be some *dis*credit to us, if we would consider of it.) But if you doubt these generalities, here is one fact for us all to meditate upon, illustrative of our love of science. Two years ago there was a collection of the fossils of Solenhofen to be sold in Bavaria; the best in existence, containing many specimens unique for perfectness, and one unique as an example of a species (a whole kingdom of unknown living creatures being announced by that fossil[42]). This collection, of which the mere market worth, among private buyers, would probably have been some thousand or twelve hundred pounds, was offered to the English nation for seven hundred: but we would not give seven hundred, and the whole series would have been in the Munich Museum at this moment, if Professor Owen had not, with loss of his own time, and patient tormenting of the British public in person of its representatives, got leave to give four hundred pounds at once, and himself became answerable for the other three! which the said public will doubtless pay him eventually, but sulkily, and caring nothing about the matter all the while; only always ready to cackle if any credit comes of it. Consider, I beg of you, arithmetically, what this fact means. Your annual expenditure for public purposes, (a third of it for military apparatus,) is at least 50 millions. Now £700 is to £50,000,000 roughly, as seven pence to two thousand pounds. Suppose, then, a gentleman of unknown income, but whose wealth was to be conjectured from the fact that he spent two thousand a year on his park-walls and footmen only, professes himself fond of science; and that one of his servants comes eagerly to tell him that an unique collection of fossils, giving clue to a new era of creation, is to be had for a sum of seven pence sterling; and that the gentleman who is fond of science, and spends two thousand a year on his park, answers, after keeping his servant waiting several months, 'Well! I'll give you fourpence for them, if you will be answerable for the extra threepence yourself, till next year!'

(III.) I say you have despised Art! 'What!' you again answer, 'have we not Art exhibitions, miles long? and do we not pay thousands of pounds for single pictures? and have we not Art schools and institutions, more than ever nation had before?' Yes, truly, but all that is for the sake of the shop. You would fain sell canvas as well as coals, and crockery as well as iron; you would take every other nation's bread out of its mouth if you could; not being able to do that, your ideal of life is to stand in the thoroughfares of the world, like Ludgate apprentices, screaming to every passer-by, 'What d'ye lack?'[43] You know nothing of your own faculties or circumstances; you fancy that, among your damp, flat, fat fields of clay, you can have as quick art-fancy as the Frenchman among his bronzed vines, or the Italian under his volcanic cliffs; – that Art may be learned, as book-keeping is, and when learned, will give you more books to keep. You care for pictures, absolutely, no more than you do for the bills pasted on your dead walls. There is always room on the walls for the bills to be read, – never for the pictures to be seen. You do not know what pictures you have (by repute) in the country, nor whether they are false or true, nor whether they are taken care of or not; in foreign countries, you calmly see the noblest existing pictures in the world rotting in abandoned wreck – (in Venice you saw the Austrian guns deliberately pointed at the palaces containing them[44]), and if you heard that all the fine pictures in Europe were made into sand-bags to-morrow on the Austrian forts, it would not trouble you so much as the chance of a brace or two of game less in your own bags, in a day's shooting. That is your national love of Art.

(IV.) You have despised Nature; that is to say, all the deep and sacred sensations of natural scenery. The French revolutionists made stables of the cathedrals of France; you have made race-courses of the cathedrals of the earth. Your *one* conception of pleasure is to drive in railroad carriages round their aisles, and eat off their altars.* You have put a railroad-bridge over the falls of Schaffhausen. You have tunnelled the cliffs of Lucerne by Tell's chapel; you have destroyed the Clarens shore of the Lake of Geneva; there is not a quiet valley in England that you have not filled with bellowing fire;

* I meant that the beautiful places of the world – Switzerland, Italy, South Germany, and so on – are, indeed, the truest cathedrals – places to be reverent in, and to worship in; and that we only care to drive through them: and to eat and drink at their most sacred places.

there is no particle left of English land which you have not trampled coal ashes into* – nor any foreign city in which the spread of your presence is not marked among its fair old streets and happy gardens by a consuming white leprosy of new hotels and perfumers' shops: the Alps themselves, which your own poets used to love so reverently, you look upon as soaped poles in a bear-garden, which you set yourselves to climb and slide down again, with 'shrieks of delight.' When you are past shrieking, having no human articulate voice to say you are glad with, you fill the quietude of their valleys with gunpowder blasts, and rush home, red with cutaneous eruption of conceit, and voluble with convulsive hiccough of self-satisfaction. I think nearly the two sorrowfullest spectacles I have ever seen in humanity, taking the deep inner significance of them, are the English mobs in the valley of Chamouni, amusing themselves with firing rusty howitzers; and the Swiss vintagers of Zurich expressing their Christian thanks for the gift of the vine, by assembling in knots in the 'towers of the vineyards,'[45] and slowly loading and firing horse-pistols from morning till evening. It is pitiful, to have dim conceptions of duty; more pitiful, it seems to me, to have conceptions like these, of mirth.

Lastly. You despise compassion. There is no need of words of mine for proof of this. I will merely print one of the newspaper paragraphs which I am in the habit of cutting out and throwing into my store-drawer; here is one from a *Morning Post* of an early date this year (1865); [. . .] it relates only one of such facts as happen now daily; this by chance having taken a form in which it came before the coroner. I will print the paragraph in red.[46] Be sure, the facts themselves are written in that colour, in a book which we shall all of us, literate or illiterate, have to read our page of, some day.

'An inquiry was held on Friday by Mr Richards, deputy coroner, at the White Horse Tavern, Christ Church, Spitalfields, respecting the death of Michael Collins, aged 58 years. Mary Collins, a miserable-looking woman, said that she lived with the deceased and his son in a room at 2, Cobb's Court, Christ Church. Deceased was a "translator" of boots. Witness went out and bought old boots; deceased and his son made them into good ones, and then witness sold them for what she could get at the shops, which was very little indeed. Deceased and his son used to work night and day to try and get a little bread and tea, and pay for the room (2s. a week), so as to keep the home together. On Friday-night-week

---

* I was singularly struck, some years ago, by finding all the river shore at Richmond, in Yorkshire, black in its earth, from the mere drift of soot-laden air from places many miles away.

deceased got up from his bench and began to shiver. He threw down the boots, saying, "Somebody else must finish them when I am gone, for I can do no more." There was no fire, and he said, "I would be better if I was warm." Witness therefore took two pairs of translated boots to sell at the shop, but she could only get 14d. for the two pairs, for the people at the shop said, "We must have our profit." Witness got 14 lb. of coal, and a little tea and bread. Her son sat up the whole night to make the "translations," to get money, but deceased died on Saturday morning. The family never had enough to eat. – Coroner: "It seems to me deplorable that you did not go into the workhouse." Witness: "We wanted the comforts of our little home." A juror asked what the comforts were, for he only saw a little straw in the corner of the room, the windows of which were broken. The witness began to cry, and said that they had a quilt and other little things. The deceased said he never would go into the workhouse. In summer, when the season was good, they sometimes made as much as 10s. profit in the week. They then always saved towards the next week, which was generally a bad one. In winter they made not half so much. For three years they had been getting from bad to worse. – Cornelius Collins said that he had assisted his father since 1847. They used to work so far into the night that both nearly lost their eyesight. Witness now had a film over his eyes. Five years ago deceased applied to the parish for aid. The relieving officer gave him a 4 lb. loaf, and told him if he came again he should "get the stones."* That disgusted deceased, and he would have nothing to do with them since. They got worse and worse until last Friday week, when they had not even a halfpenny to buy a candle. Deceased then lay down on the straw, and said he could not live till morning. – A juror: "You are dying of starvation yourself, and you ought to go into the house until the summer." – Witness: "If we went in we should die. When we come

---

* This abbreviation of the penalty of useless labour is curiously coincident in verbal form with a certain passage which some of us may remember.[47] It may perhaps be well to preserve beside this paragraph another cutting out of my store-drawer, from the *Morning Post*, of about a parallel date, Friday, March 10th, 1865: – 'The *salons* of Mme. C—, who did the honours with clever imitative grace and elegance, were crowded with princes, dukes, marquises, and counts – in fact, with the same *male* company as one meets at the parties of the Princess Metternich and Madame Drouyn de Lhuys. Some English peers and members of Parliament were present, and appeared to enjoy the animated and dazzlingly improper scene. On the second floor the supper tables were loaded with every delicacy of the season. That your readers may form some idea of the dainty fare of the Parisian demi-monde, I copy the menu of the supper, which was served to all the guests (about 200) seated at four

out in the summer we should be like people dropped from the sky. No one would know us, and we would not have even a room. I could work now if I had food, for my sight would get better.' Dr G. P. Walker said deceased died from syncope, from exhaustion from want of food. The deceased had had no bedclothes. For four months he had had nothing but bread to eat. There was not a particle of fat in the body. There was no disease, but, if there had been medical attendance, he might have survived the syncope or fainting. The Coroner having remarked upon the painful nature of the case, the jury returned the following verdict: "That deceased died from exhaustion from want of food and the common necessaries of life; also through want of medical aid."'

'Why would witness not go into the workhouse?' you ask. Well, the poor seem to have a prejudice against the workhouse which the rich have not; for of course everyone who takes a pension from Government goes into the workhouse on a grand scale:* only the workhouses for the rich do not involve the idea of work, and should be called play-houses. But the poor like to die independently, it appears; perhaps if we made the play-houses for them pretty and pleasant enough, or gave them their pensions at home, and allowed them a little introductory peculation with the public money, their minds might be reconciled to the conditions.[49] Meantime, here are the facts: we make our relief either so insulting to them, or so painful, that they rather die than take it at our hands; or, for third alternative, we leave them so untaught and foolish that they starve like brute creatures, wild and dumb, not knowing what to do, or what to ask. I say, you despise compassion; if you did not, such a newspaper paragraph would be as impossible in a Christian country as a deliberate assassination permitted in

---

o'clock. Choice Yquem, Johannisberg, Laffitte, Tokay, and champagne of the finest vintages were served most lavishly throughout the morning. After supper dancing was resumed with increased animation, and the ball terminated with a *chaîne diabolique* and a *cancan d'enfer* at seven in the morning. (Morning service – 'Ere the fresh lawns appeared, under the opening eyelids of the Morn. –'[48]) Here is the menu: – "Consommé de volaille à la Bagration: 16 hors-d'œuvres variés. Bouchées à la Talleyrand. Saumons froids, sauce Ravigote. Filets de bœuf en Bellevue, timbales milanaises, chaudfroid de gibier. Dindes truffées. Pâtés de foies gras, buissons d'écrevisses, salades vénétiennes, gelées blanches aux fruits, gâteaux mancini, parisiens et parisiennes. Fromages glacés. Ananas. Dessert."'

* Please observe this statement, and think of it, and consider how it happens that a poor old woman will be ashamed to take a shilling a week from the country – but no one is ashamed to take a pension of a thousand a year.

its public streets. 'Christian,' did I say? Alas! if we were but wholesomely *un*-Christian, it would be impossible: it is our imaginary Christianity that helps us to commit these crimes, for we revel and luxuriate in our faith, for the lewd sensation of it; dressing *it* up, like everything else, in fiction. The dramatic Christianity of the organ and aisle, of dawn-service and twilight-revival – the Christianity, which we do not fear to mix the mockery of, pictorially, with our play about the devil, in our Satanellas, – Roberts, – Fausts;[50] chanting hymns through traceried windows for background effect, and artistically modulating the "Dio" through variation on variation of mimicked prayer: (while we distribute tracts, next day, for the benefit of uncultivated swearers, upon what we suppose to be the signification of the Third Commandment; –) this gas-lighted, and gas-inspired Christianity, we are triumphant in, and draw back the hem of our robes from the touch of the heretics who dispute it. But to do a piece of common Christian righteousness in a plain English word or deed; to make Christian law any rule of life, and found one National act or hope thereon, – we know too well what our faith comes to for that! You might sooner get lightning out of incense smoke than true action or passion out of your modern English religion. You had better get rid of the smoke, and the organ pipes, both: leave them, and the Gothic windows, and the painted glass, to the property man; give up your carburetted hydrogen ghost[51] in one healthy expiration, and look after Lazarus at the doorstep.[52] For there is a true Church wherever one hand meets another helpfully, and that is the only holy or Mother Church which ever was, or ever shall be.[53]

All these pleasures then, and all these virtues, I repeat, you nationally despise. You have, indeed, men among you who do not; by whose work, by whose strength, by whose life, by whose death, you live, and never thank them. Your wealth, your amusement, your pride, would all be alike impossible, but for those whom you scorn or forget. The policeman, who is walking up and down the black lane all night to watch the guilt you have created there; and may have his brains beaten out, and be maimed for life, at any moment, and never be thanked; the sailor wrestling with the sea's rage; the quiet student poring over his book or his vial; the common worker, without praise, and nearly without bread, fulfilling his task as your horses drag your carts, hopeless, and spurned of all: these are the men by whom England lives; but they are not the nation; they are only the body and nervous force of it, acting still from old habit in a convulsive perseverance, while the mind is gone. Our National wish and purpose are only to be amused; our National religion is the performance of church ceremonies, and preaching of soporific truths (or untruths) to keep the mob quietly at work, while we amuse ourselves; and the necessity for this amusement is fastening on us, as a feverous disease of parched throat and wandering eyes – senseless, dissolute, merciless. How literally that word *Dis*-Ease, the Negation and impossibility of Ease, expressed the entire moral state of our English Industry and its Amusements!

When men are rightly occupied, their amusement grows out of their work, as the colour-petals out of a fruitful flower; – when they are faithfully helpful and compassionate, all their emotions become steady, deep, perpetual, and vivifying to the soul as the natural pulse to the body. But now, having no true business, we pour our whole masculine energy into the false business of money-making; and having no true emotion, we must have false emotions dressed up for us to play with, not innocently, as children with dolls, but guiltily and darkly, as the idolatrous Jews with their pictures on cavern walls, which men had to dig to detect.[54] The justice we do not execute, we mimic in the novel and on the stage; for the beauty we destroy in nature, we substitute the metamorphosis of the pantomime, and (the human nature of us imperatively requiring awe and sorrow of *some* kind) for the noble grief we should have borne with our fellows, and the pure tears we should have wept with them, we gloat over the pathos of the police court, and gather the night-dew of the grave.

It is difficult to estimate the true significance of these things; the facts are frightful enough; – the measure of national fault involved in them is perhaps not as great as it would at first seem. We permit, or cause, thousands of deaths daily, but we mean no harm; we set fire to houses, and ravage peasants' fields, yet we should be sorry to find we had injured anybody. We are still kind at heart; still capable of virtue, but only as children are. Chalmers,[55] at the end of his long life, having had much power with the public, being plagued in some serious matter by a reference to 'public opinion,' uttered the impatient exclamation, 'The public is just a great baby!' And the reason that I have allowed all these graver subjects of thought to mix themselves up with an inquiry into methods of reading, is that, the more I see of our national faults or miseries, the more they resolve themselves into conditions of childish illiterateness and want of education in the most ordinary habits of thought. It is, I repeat, not vice, not selfishness, not dulness of brain, which we have to lament; but an unreachable schoolboy's recklessness, only differing from the true schoolboy's in its incapacity of being helped, because it acknowledges no master.

There is a curious type of us given in one of the lovely, neglected works of the last of our great painters.[56] It is a drawing of Kirkby Lonsdale churchyard, and of its brook, and valley, and hills, and folded morning sky beyond. And unmindful alike of these, and of the dead who have left these for other valleys and for other skies, a group of schoolboys have piled their little books upon a grave, to strike them off with stones. So, also, we play with the words of the dead that would teach us, and strike them far from us with our bitter, reckless will; little thinking that those leaves which the wind scatters had been piled, not only upon a gravestone, but upon the seal of an enchanted vault – nay, the gate of a great city of sleeping kings, who would awake for us and walk with us, if we knew but how to call them by their names. How often, even if we lift the marble entrance gate, do we but wander among those old kings in their repose, and finger the robes they lie in, and stir the crowns on their foreheads; and still they are silent to us, and seem but a dusty imagery; because we know not the incantation of the heart that would wake them; – which, if they once heard, they would start up to meet us in their power of long ago, narrowly to look upon us, and consider us; and, as the fallen kings of Hades meet the newly fallen, saying, 'Art thou also become weak as we – art thou also become one of us?'[57] so would these kings, with their undimmed, unshaken diadems, meet us, saying, 'Art thou also become pure and mighty of heart as we – art thou also become one of us?'

Mighty of heart, mighty of mind – 'magnanimous' – to be this, is indeed to be great in life; to become this increasingly, is, indeed, to 'advance in life,' – in life itself – not in the trappings of it. My friends, do you remember that old Scythian custom, when the head of a house died?[58] How he was dressed in his finest dress, and set in his chariot, and carried about to his friends' houses; and each of them placed him at his table's head, and all feasted in his presence? Suppose it were offered to you in plain words, as it *is* offered to you in dire facts, that you should gain this Scythian honour, gradually, while you yet thought yourself alive. Suppose the offer were this: You shall die slowly; your blood shall daily grow cold, your flesh petrify, your heart beat at last only as a rusted group of iron valves. Your life shall fade from you, and sink through the earth into the ice of Caina[59]; but, day by day, your body shall be dressed more gaily, and set in higher chariots, and have more orders on its breast – crowns on its head, if you will. Men shall bow before it, stare and shout round it, crowd after it up and down the streets; build palaces for it, feast with it at their tables' heads all the night long; your soul shall stay enough within it to know what they do, and feel the weight of the golden dress on its shoulders, and the furrow of the crown-edge on the skull; – no more. Would you take the offer, verbally made by the death-angel? Would the meanest among us take it, think you? Yet practically and verily we grasp at it, every one of us, in a measure; many of us grasp at it in its fulness of horror. Every man accepts it, who desires to advance in life without knowing what life is; who means only that he is to get more horses, and more footmen, and more fortune, and more public honour, and – *not* more personal soul. He only is advancing in life, whose heart is getting softer, whose blood warmer, whose brain quicker, whose spirit is entering into Living peace.[60] And the men who have this life in them are the true lords or kings of the earth – they, and they only. All other kingships, so far as they are true, are only the practical issue and expression of theirs; if less than this, they are either dramatic royalties, – costly shows, set off, indeed, with real jewels, instead of tinsel – but still only the toys of nations; or else they are no royalties at all, but tyrannies, or the mere active and practical issue of national folly; for which reason I have said of them elsewhere, 'Visible governments are the toys of some nations, the diseases of others, the harness of some, the burdens of more.'[61]

But I have no words for the wonder with which I hear Kinghood still spoken of, even among thoughtful men, as if governed nations were a personal property, and might be bought and sold, or otherwise acquired, as sheep, of whose flesh their king was to feed, and whose fleece he was to gather; as if Achilles' indignant epithet of base kings, 'people-eating,'[62] were the constant and proper title of all monarchs; and the enlargement of a king's dominion meant the same thing as the increase of a private man's estate! Kings who think so, however powerful, can no more be the true kings of the nation than gadflies are the kings of a horse; they suck it, and may drive it wild, but do not guide it. They, and their courts, and their armies are, if one could see clearly, only a large species of marsh mosquito, with bayonet proboscis and melodious, band-mastered trumpeting, in the summer air; the twilight being, perhaps, sometimes fairer, but hardly more wholesome, for its glittering mists of midge companies. The true kings, meanwhile, rule quietly, if at all, and hate ruling[63]; too many of them make 'il gran rifiuto'; and if they do not, the mob, as soon as they are likely to become useful to it, is pretty sure to make *its* 'gran rifiuto'[64] of *them*.

Yet the visible king may also be a true one, some day, if ever day comes when he will estimate his dominion by the *force* of it, – not the geographical boundaries. It matters very little whether Trent cuts you a cantel out here,[65] or Rhine rounds you a castle less there. But it does matter to you, king of men, whether you can verily say to this man, 'Go,' and he goeth; and to another, 'Come,' and he cometh.[66] Whether you can turn your people, as you can Trent – and where it is that you bid them come, and where go. It matters to you, king of men, whether your people hate you, and die by you, or love you, and live by you. You may measure your dominion by multitudes, better than by miles; and count degrees of love-latitude, not from, but to, a wonderfully warm and infinite equator.

Measure! – nay, you cannot measure. Who shall measure the difference between the power of those who 'do and teach,'[67] and who are greatest in the kingdoms of earth, as of heaven – and the power of those who undo, and consume – whose power, at the fullest, is only the power of the moth and the rust?[68] Strange! to think how the Moth-kings lay up treasures for the moth; and the Rust-kings, who are to their peoples' strength as rust to armour, lay up treasures for the rust; and the Robber-kings, treasures for the robber; but how few kings have ever laid up treasures that needed no guarding – treasures of which, the more thieves there were, the better! Broidered robe, only to be rent; helm and sword, only to be dimmed; jewel and gold, only to be scattered; – there have been three kinds of kings who have gathered these. Suppose there ever should arise a Fourth order of kings, who had read, in some obscure writing of long ago, that there was a Fourth kind of treasure, which the jewel and gold could not equal, neither should it be valued with pure gold.[69] A web made fair in the weaving, by Athena's shuttle; an armour, forged in divine fire by Vulcanian force; a gold to be mined in the very sun's red heart, where he sets over the Delphian cliffs; – deep-pictured tissue; – impenetrable armour; – potable gold![70] – the three great Angels of Conduct, Toil, and Thought,[71] still calling to us, and waiting at the posts of our doors, to lead us, with their winged power, and guide us, with their unerring eyes, by the path which no fowl knoweth, and which the vulture's eye has not seen![72] Suppose kings should ever arise, who heard and believed this word, and at last gathered and brought forth treasures of – Wisdom – for their people?

Think what an amazing business *that* would be! How inconceivable, in the state of our present national wisdom! That we should bring up our peasants to a book exercise instead of a bayonet exercise! – organise, drill, maintain with pay, and good generalship, armies of thinkers, instead of armies of stabbers! – find national amusement in reading-rooms as well as rifle-grounds; give prizes for a fair shot at a fact, as well as for a leaden splash on a target. What an absurd idea it seems, put fairly in words, that the wealth of the capitalists of civilised nations should ever come to support literature instead of war!

Have yet patience with me, while I read you a single sentence out of the only book, properly to be called a book, that I have yet written myself, the one that will stand (if anything stand), surest and longest of all work of mine.[73]

'It is one very awful form of the operation of wealth in Europe that it is entirely capitalists' wealth which supports unjust wars. Just wars do not need so much money to support them; for most of the men who wage such, wage them gratis; but for an unjust war, men's bodies and souls have both to be bought; and the best tools of war for them besides, which make such war costly to the maximum; not to speak of the cost of base fear, and angry suspicion, between nations which have not grace nor honesty enough in all their multitudes to buy an hour's peace of mind with; as, at present, France and England, purchasing of each other ten millions sterling worth of consternation, annually (a remarkably light crop, half thorns and half aspen leaves, sown, reaped, and granaried by the "science" of the modern political economist, teaching covetousness instead of truth). And, all unjust war being supportable, if not by pillage of the enemy, only by loans from capitalists, these loans are repaid by subsequent taxation of the people, who appear to have no will in the matter, the capitalists' will being the primary root of the war; but its real root is the covetousness of the whole nation, rendering it incapable of faith, frankness, or justice, and bringing about, therefore, in due time, his own separate loss and punishment to each person.'

France and England literally, observe, buy *panic* of each other; they pay, each of them, for ten thousand-thousand-pounds'-worth of terror, a year. Now suppose, instead of buying these ten millions' worth of panic annually, they made up their minds to be at peace with each other, and buy ten millions' worth of knowledge annually; and that each nation spent its ten thousand thousand pounds a year in founding royal libraries, royal art galleries, royal museums, royal gardens, and places of rest. Might it not be better somewhat for both French and English?

It will be long, yet, before that comes to pass.[74] Nevertheless, I hope it will not be long before royal or national libraries will be founded in every considerable city, with a royal series of books in them[75]; the same series in every one of them, chosen books, the best in every kind, prepared for that national series in the most perfect way possible; their text printed all on leaves of equal size, broad of margin, and divided into pleasant volumes, light in the hand, beautiful, and strong, and thorough as examples of binders' work; and that these great libraries will be accessible to all clean and orderly persons at all times of the day and evening; strict law being enforced for this cleanliness and quietness.

I could shape for you other plans, for art-galleries, and for natural history galleries, and for many precious – many, it seems to me, needful – things;

but this book plan is the easiest and needfullest, and would prove a considerable tonic to what we call our British constitution, which has fallen dropsical of late, and has an evil thirst, and evil hunger, and wants healthier feeding. You have got its corn laws repealed for it; try if you cannot get corn laws established for it, dealing in a better bread; – bread made of that old enchanted Arabian grain, the Sesame, which opens doors; – doors not of robbers', but of Kings' Treasuries.

from
Fors Clavigera

LETTERS

to the Workmen and Labourers
of Great Britain

Published 1871–1884

COMMENTARY

Fors Clavigera consists of ninety-six open letters addressed 'to the Workmen and Labourers of Great Britain'. They were published as monthly periodicals between 1871 and 1878, and then intermittently between 1880 and 1884.

'Workmen and Labourers' means those who, like Ruskin himself, find themselves toiling in the vineyard in the heat of the day – with hand, mind, or both. Inevitably, though, the reader anticipates letters to the working *class* and, since it is with their welfare (economic and spiritual) that Ruskin is most deeply concerned, it seems probable that this ambiguity was intended. All forms of labour are seen as rooted in nature and having a common purpose – that of promoting the wealth that is life. The sickness of modern society is usury, a name Ruskin now gives to interest of any kind. The usurer alone is idle. Those who make money out of money, not out of their labour, live off the labour of others.

So the letters are about work, but work seen in the perspective of human destiny. This is the primary meaning of this most complex of Ruskin's titles. A simple translation of *Fors Clavigera* would be 'Fortune the Nail-bearer'. The immediate source of the phrase is in Horace, *Odes*, I.xxv: 'Ever before you stalks Necessity, the grim goddess with nails and wedges in her brazen hand; the strict hook and molten lead are also there.' The figure of Fortune, or Chance, or Necessity, is derived from various mythologies: 'she offers to men the conditions of prosperity', says Ruskin; 'and as these conditions are accepted or refused, nails down and fastens their fate for ever . . .' This lesson applies first of all to England: the richest and most powerful nation in the world, yet riddled with poverty, starvation and injustice. The letters are an attempt to awaken England to her own good fortune and to show her 'How you make your fortune or mar it'. But the title was also meant 'to indicate the desultory and accidental character of the work' itself: so Fortune in the role of Chance presided over its composition. In other words, the letters were written much as any extended correspondence is – topically, taking up the hints chance offers, weaving disparate matter into a single integrated text, referring back and forth from letter to letter. And the title applies to Ruskin himself: first, because he sees *Fors* as a task imposed on him by destiny and necessity; and secondly, because he is aware of impending crisis and the role of fortune in his own life. This last point explains why the letters are so personal, even confessional.

These are still not the only significances. ' "Fors" is the best part of three good English words, Force, Fortitude, and Fortune.' The Latin *clavus* means a nail, but *clavis* means a key and *clava* a club (*-gera* means bearer). So different archetypes can be drawn from the phrase. Force is the Club-bearer, typified by Hercules (and other monster-slaying heroes who figure in the letters, notably St George, the patron of England and therefore of Ruskin's Guild): this is 'the power of doing good work'. Fortitude is the Key-bearer, typified by Ulysses, and stands for 'the power of bearing necessary pain, or trial of patience'. Fortune the Nail-bearer is typified by the legendary law-maker of ancient Sparta, Lycurgus, and as such stands for necessary law and unchangeable fate. In this last sense it is important to realize that fortune can be a matter of accident or destiny or providence. These are all different, but, as Ruskin often implies, they are connected. Thus, man may be the victim of fate but also the maker of his own good fortune.

In spite of its fragmentary nature, it is almost impossible to select satisfactorily from *Fors*, since each letter depends for its effect on our sense of it as part of a series. Running through the book are a number of disparate themes that intermesh in unexpected ways, so that each letter contains echoes of others. The reader soon develops expectations of the different elements that will combine within them. I have selected Letters 7 and 10, not because they are the best, but because taken together they effectively illustrate the book's character. For instance, both of them attempt political self-definitions, and it is only through their juxtaposition that the necessary irony is achieved – for in one of them Ruskin is a Tory and in the other a Communist. Moreover, Ruskin's contempt for political partisanship is one of the work's minor themes. Most of the letters also draw attention to current events. The first year of *Fors*, for instance, is dominated by political upheavals in France. (The events referred to are summarized in my notes.) Against this topical news, Ruskin sets the evidence of 'authorities' – cultural heroes of past and present, many of whom make frequent appearances from letter to letter: examples of these in the numbers selected are Scott and Carlyle, Dante and Giotto. Extended quotation is another feature of the work, whether from the daily papers or from classic texts (such as More's *Utopia*). And Ruskin now makes use of his personal history. Letter 10, for example, includes a passage that later appeared in *Praeterita*. This was partly because, in a state of crisis, he felt impelled to do so. But his conscious intention was to show his readers something of the early experiences that first shaped the values he sought to teach – in particular, the habit of admiration. In its use of juxtaposition, the contingent charged with significance, and the fragmentary, *Fors* is technically innovative and anticipates much of the literature of our century.

LETTER SEVEN
CHARITAS

DENMARK HILL,
1st July, 1871.

MY FRIENDS, – It seldom chances, my work lying chiefly among stones, clouds, and flowers, that I am brought into any freedom of intercourse with my fellow-creatures; but since the fighting in Paris[1] I have dined out several times, and spoken to the persons who sat next me, and to others when I went upstairs; and done the best I could to find out what people thought about the fighting, or thought they ought to think about it, or thought they ought to say. I had, of course, no hope of finding any one thinking what they ought to do. But I have not yet, a little to my surprise, met with any one who either appeared to be sadder, or professed himself wiser for anything that has happened.

It is true that I am neither sadder nor wiser, because of it, myself. But then I was so sad before, that nothing could make me sadder; and getting wiser has always been to me a very slow process (sometimes even quite stopping for whole days together), so that if two or three new ideas fall in my way at once, it only puzzles me; and the fighting in Paris has given me more than two or three.

The newest of all these new ones, and, in fact, quite a glistering and freshly minted idea to me, is the Parisian notion of Communism, as far as I understand it (which I don't profess to do altogether, yet, or I should be wiser than I was, with a vengeance).

For, indeed, I am myself a Communist of the old school[2] – reddest also of the red; and was on the very point of saying so at the end of my last letter; only the telegram about the Louvre's being on fire stopped me, because I thought the Communists of the new school, as I could not at all understand them, might not quite understand me. For we Communists of the old school think that our property belongs to everybody, and everybody's property to us; so of course I thought the Louvre belonged to me as much as to the Parisians, and expected they would have sent word over to me, being an Art Professor, to ask whether I wanted it burnt down. But no message or intimation to that effect ever reached me.

Then the next bit of new coinage in the way of notion which I have picked up in Paris streets, is the present meaning of the French word 'Ouvrier,' which in my time the dictionaries used to give as 'Workman,' or 'Working-man.' For again, I have spent many days, not to say years, with the working-men of our English school myself[3]; and I know that, with the more advanced of them, the gathering word is that which I gave you at the end of my second number – 'To do good work, whether we live or die.'[4] Whereas I perceive the gathering, or rather scattering, word of the French 'ouvrier' is, 'To *undo* good work, whether we live or die.'

And this is the third, and the last, I will tell you for the present, of my new ideas, but a troublesome one: namely, that we are henceforward to have a duplicate power of political economy; and that the new Parisian expression for its first principle is not to be 'laissez faire,' but 'laissez *re*faire.'

I cannot, however, make anything of these new French fashions of thought till I have looked at them quietly a little; so to-day I will content myself with telling you what we Communists of the old school meant by Communism; and it will be worth your hearing, for – I tell you simply in my 'arrogant' way[5] – we know, and have known, what Communism is – for our fathers knew it, and told us, three thousand years ago[6]; while you baby Communists do not so much as know what the name means, in your own English or French – no, not so much as whether a House of Commons implies, or does not imply, also a House of Uncommons; nor whether the Holiness of the Commune, which Garibaldi came to fight for,[7] had any relation to the Holiness of the 'Communion' which he came to fight against.

Will you be at the pains, now, however, to learn rightly, and once for all, what Communism is? First, it means that everybody must work in common, and do common or simple work for his dinner[8]; and that if any man will not do it, he must not have his dinner. That much, perhaps, you thought you knew? – but you did not think we Communists of the old school knew it also? You shall have it, then, in the words of the Chelsea farmer and stout Catholic, I was telling you of, in last number.[9] He was born in Milk Street, London, three hundred and ninety-one years ago, [. . .] and he planned a Commune flowing with milk and honey, and otherwise Elysian; and called it the 'Place of Wellbeing,' or Utopia[10]; which is a word you perhaps have occasionally used before now, like others, without understanding it [. . .] You shall use it in that stupid way no more, if I can help it. Listen how matters really are managed there.

'The chief, and almost the only business of the government,* is to take care that no man may live idle, but that every one may follow his trade diligently: yet they do not wear themselves out with perpetual toil from morning till night, as if they were beasts of burden, which, as it is indeed a heavy slavery, so it is everywhere the common course of life amongst all mechanics except the Utopians; but they, dividing the day and night into twenty-four hours, appoint six of these for work, three of which are before dinner and three after; they then sup, and, at eight o'clock, counting from noon, go to bed and sleep eight hours: the rest of their time, besides that taken up in work, eating, and sleeping, is left to every man's discretion; yet they are not to abuse that interval to luxury and idleness, but must employ it in some proper exercise, according to their various inclinations, which is, for the most part, reading.

'But the time appointed for labour is to be narrowly examined, otherwise, you may imagine that, since there are only six hours appointed for work, they may fall under a scarcity of necessary provisions: but it is so far from being true that this time is not sufficient for supplying them with plenty of all things, either necessary or convenient, that it is rather too much; and this you will easily apprehend, if you consider how great a part of all other nations is quite idle. First, women generally do little, who are the half of mankind; and, if some few women are diligent, their husbands are idle: then, – . . .'

What then?

We will stop a minute, friends, if you please, for I want you before you read what then, to be once more made fully aware that this farmer who is speaking to you is one of the sternest Roman Catholics of his stern time; and at the fall of Cardinal Wolsey, became Lord High Chancellor of England in his stead.

'– then, consider the great company of idle priests, and of those that are called religious men; add to these, all rich men, chiefly those that have estates in land, who are called noblemen and gentlemen, together with their families, made up of idle persons, that are kept more for show than use; add to these, all those strong and lusty beggars that go about, pretending some disease in excuse for their begging; and, upon the whole account, you will find that the number of those by whose labours

---

* I spare you, for once, a word for 'government' used by this old author, which would have been unintelligible to you, and is so, except in its general sense, to me, too.[11]

mankind is supplied is much less than you, perhaps, imagined: then, consider how few of those that work are employed in labours that are of real service! for we, who measure all things by money, give rise to many trades that are both vain and superfluous, and serve only to support riot and luxury: for if those who work were employed only in such things as the conveniences of life require, there would be such an abundance of them, *that the prices of them would so sink that tradesmen could not be maintained by their gains;'*

– (italics mine – Fair and softly, Sir Thomas! we must have a shop round the corner, and a pedlar or two on fair-days, yet); –

'if all those who labour about useless things were set to more profitable employments, and if all that languish out their lives in sloth and idleness (every one of whom consumes as much as any two of the men that are at work) were forced to labour, you may easily imagine that a small proportion of time would serve for doing all that is either necessary, profitable, or pleasant to mankind, especially while pleasure is kept within its due bounds: this appears very plainly in Utopia; for there, in a great city, and in all the territory that lies round it, you can scarce find five hundred, either men or women, by their age and strength capable of labour, that are not engaged in it! even the heads of government, though excused by the law, yet do not excuse themselves, but work, that, by their examples, they may excite the industry of the rest of the people.'

You see, therefore, that there is never any fear, among us of the old school, of being out of work; but there is great fear, among many of us, lest we should not do the work set us well; for, indeed, we thorough-going Communists make it a part of our daily duty to consider how common we are; and how few of us have any brains or souls worth speaking of, or fit to trust to; – that being the, alas, almost unexceptionable lot of human creatures. Not that we think ourselves (still less, call ourselves without thinking so) miserable sinners, for we are not in anywise miserable, but quite comfortable for the most part; and we are not sinners, that we know of; but are leading godly, righteous, and sober lives, to the best of our power, since last Sunday (on which day some of us were, we regret to be informed, drunk); but we are of course common creatures enough, the most of us, and thankful if we may be gathered up in St Peter's sheet, so as not to be uncivilly or unjustly called unclean too.[12] And therefore our chief concern is to find out any among us wiser and of better make than the rest, and to get them, if they will for any persuasion take the trouble, to rule over us, and teach us how to behave, and make the most of what little good is in us.

So much for the first law of old Communism, respecting work. Then the second respects property, and it is that the public, or common, wealth, shall be more and statelier in all its substance than private or singular wealth; that is to say (to come to my own special business for a moment) that there shall be only cheap and few pictures, if any, in the insides of houses, where nobody but the owner can see them; but costly pictures, and many, on the outsides of houses, where the people can see them[13]: also that the Hôtel-de-Ville,[14] or Hotel of the whole Town, for the transaction of its common business, shall be a magnificent building, much rejoiced in by the people, and with its tower seen far away through the clear air; but that the hotels for private business or pleasure, cafés, taverns, and the like, shall be low, few, plain, and in back streets; more especially such as furnish singular and uncommon drinks and refreshments; but that the fountains which furnish the people's common drink shall be very lovely and stately, and adorned with precious marbles, and the like.[15] Then farther, according to old Communism, the private dwellings of uncommon persons – dukes and lords – are to be very simple, and roughly put together, – such persons being supposed to be above all care for things that please the commonalty; but the buildings for public or common service, more especially schools, alms-houses, and workhouses, are to be externally of a majestic character, as being for noble purposes and charities; and in their interiors furnished with many luxuries for the poor and sick. And, finally and chiefly, it is an absolute law of old Communism that the fortunes of private persons should be small, and of little account in the State; but the common treasure of the whole nation should be of superb and precious things in redundant quantity, as pictures, statues, precious books; gold and silver vessels, preserved from ancient times; gold and silver bullion laid up for use, in case of any chance need of buying anything suddenly from foreign nations; noble horses, cattle, and sheep, on the public lands; and vast spaces of land for culture, exercise, and garden, round the cities, full of flowers, which, being everybody's property, nobody could gather; and of birds which, being everybody's property, nobody could shoot. And, in a word, that instead of a common poverty, or national debt, which every poor person in the nation is taxed annually to fulfil his part of, there should be a common wealth, or national reverse of debt, consisting of pleasant things, which every poor person in the nation should be summoned to receive his dole of, annually[16]; and of pretty things, which every person capable of admiration, foreigners as well as natives, should unfeignedly admire, in an æsthetic, and not a covetous manner (though for my own part I can't understand what it is that I am taxed now to defend, or what foreign nations are supposed to covet, here). But truly, a nation that has got anything to defend of real public interest, can usually hold it; and a fat Latin Communist gave for sign of the strength of his commonalty, in its strongest time, –

'Privatus illis census erat brevis,
Commune magnum;'[17]

which you may get any of your boys or girls to translate for you, and remember; remembering, also, that the commonalty or publicity depends for its goodness on the nature of the *thing* that is common, and that is public. When the French cried, 'Vive la République!' after the battle of Sedan, they were thinking only of the Publique, in the word, and not of the Re in it.[18] But that is the essential part of it, for that 'Re' is not like the mischievous Re in Reform, and Refaire, which the words had better be without; but it is short for *res*, which means 'thing'; and when you cry, 'Live the Republic,' the question is mainly, what thing it is you wish to be publicly alive, and whether you are striving for a Common-Wealth, and Public-Thing; or, as too plainly in Paris, for a Common-Illth,[19] and Public-Nothing, or even Public-Less-than-nothing and Common Deficit.

Now all these laws respecting public and private property, are accepted in the same terms by the entire body of us Communists of the old school; but with respect to the management of both, we old Reds fall into two classes, differing, not indeed in colour of redness, but in depth of tint of it – one class being, as it were, only of a delicately pink, peach-blossom, or dog-rose redness; but the other, to which I myself do partly, and desire wholly, to belong, as I told you, reddest of the red – that is to say, full crimson, or even dark crimson, passing into that deep colour of the blood which made the Spaniards call it blue, instead of red, and which the Greeks call φοινίκεος, being an intense phœnix or flamingo colour[20]: and this not merely, as in the flamingo feathers, a colour on the outside, but going through and through, ruby-wise; so that Dante, who is one of the few people who have ever beheld our queen full in the face, says of her that, if she had been in a fire, he could not have seen her at all, so fire-colour she was, all through.[*21]

And between these two sects or shades of us, there is this difference in our way of holding our common faith (that our neighbour's property is ours, and ours his), namely, that the rose-red division of us are content in their diligence of care to preserve or guard from injury or loss their neighbours'

---

* 'Tanto rossa, ch' appena fora dentro al fuoco nota.' – *Purg.*, xxix.122.

property, as their own; so that they may be called, not merely dog-rose red, but even 'watch-dog-rose' red; being, indeed, more careful and anxious for the safety of the possessions of other people (especially their masters) than for any of their own; and also more sorrowful for any wound or harm suffered by any creature in their sight, than for hurt to themselves. So that they are Communists, even less in their having part in all common well-being of their neighbours, than part in all common pain: being yet, on the whole, infinite gainers; for there is in this world infinitely more joy than pain to be shared, if you will only take your share when it is set for you.

The vermilion, or Tyrian-red[22] sect of us, however, are not content merely with this carefulness and watchfulness over our neighbours' goods, but we cannot rest unless we are giving what we can spare of our own; and the more precious it is, the more we want to divide it with somebody. So that above all things, in what we value most of possessions, pleasant sights, and true knowledge, we cannot relish seeing any pretty things unless other people see them also; neither can we be content to know anything for ourselves, but must contrive, somehow, to make it known to others.

And as thus especially we like to give knowledge away, so we like to have it good to give (for, as for selling knowledge, thinking it comes by the spirit of Heaven, we hold the selling of it to be only a way of selling God again, and utterly Iscariot's business); also, we know that the knowledge made up for sale is apt to be watered and dusted, or even itself good for nothing; and we try, for our part, to get it, and give it, pure: the mere fact that it is to be given away at once to anybody who asks to have it, and immediately wants to use it, is a continual check upon us. For instance, when Colonel North, in the House of Commons, on the 20th of last month (as reported in the *Times*), 'would simply observe, in conclusion, that it was impossible to tell how many thousands of the young men who were to be embarked for India next September, would be marched, not to the hills, but to their graves;'[23] any of us Tyrian-reds 'would simply observe' that the young men themselves ought to be constantly, and on principle, informed of their destination before embarking; and that this pleasant communicativeness of what knowledge on the subject was to be got, would soon render quite possible the attainment of more. So also, in abstract science, the instant habit of making true discoveries common property, cures us of a bad trick which one may notice to have much hindered scientific persons lately, of rather spending their time in hiding their neighbours' discoveries, than improving their own: whereas, among us, scientific flamingoes are not only openly graced for discoveries, but openly disgraced for coveries; and that sharply and permanently; so that there is rarely a hint or thought among them of each other's being wrong, but quick confession of whatever is found out rightly.

But the point in which we dark-red Communists differ most from other people is, that we dread, above all things, getting miserly of virtue; and if there be any in us, or among us, we try forthwith to get it made common, and would fain hear the mob crying for some of that treasure, where it seems to have accumulated. I say, 'seems,' only: for though, at first, all the finest virtue looks as if it were laid up with the rich (so that, generally, a millionaire would be much surprised at hearing that his daughter had made a *petroleuse*[24] of herself, or that his son had murdered anybody for the sake of their watch and cravat), – it is not at all clear to us dark-reds that this virtue, proportionate to income, is of the right sort; and we believe that even if it were, the people who keep it thus all to themselves, and leave the so-called *canaille*[25] without any, vitiate what they keep by keeping it, so that it is like manna laid up through the night, which breeds worms in the morning.[26]

You see, also, that we dark-red Communists, since we exist only in giving, must, on the contrary, hate with a perfect hatred all manner of thieving: even to Cœur-de-Lion's tar-and-feather extreme[27]; and of all thieving, we dislike thieving on trust most (so that, if we ever get to be strong enough to do what we want, and chance to catch hold of any failed bankers, their necks will not be worth half-an-hour's purchase). So also, as we think virtue diminishes in the honour and force of it in proportion to income, we think vice increases in the force and shame of it, and is worse in kings and rich people than in poor[28]; and worse on a large scale than on a narrow one; and worse when deliberate than hasty. So that we can understand one man's coveting a piece of vineyard-ground for a garden of herbs, and stoning the master of it (both of them being Jews); – and yet the dogs ate queen's flesh for that, and licked king's blood![29] but for two nations – both Christian – to covet their neighbours' vineyards, all down beside the River of their border, and slay until the River itself runs red! The little pool of Samaria! – shall all the snows of the Alps, or the salt pool of the Great Sea, wash their armour, for these?

I promised in my last letter that I would tell you the main meaning and bearing of the war, and its results to this day: – now that you know what Communism is, I can tell you these briefly, and, what is more to the purpose, how to bear yourself in the midst of them.

The first reason for all wars, and for the necessity of national defences, is that the majority of persons, high and low, in all European nations, are

Thieves, and, in their hearts, greedy of their neighbours' goods, land, and fame.

But besides being Thieves, they are also fools, and have never yet been able to understand that if Cornish men want pippins cheap, they must not ravage Devonshire – that the prosperity of their neighbours is, in the end, their own also[30]; and the poverty of their neighbours, by the communism of God, becomes also in the end their own. 'Invidia,' jealousy of your neighbour's good, has been, since dust was first made flesh, the curse of man; and 'Charitas,'[31] the desire to do your neighbour grace, the one source of all human glory, power, and material Blessing.

[. . .] war between nations (fools and thieves though they be) is not necessarily in all respects evil [. . .]

But Occult Theft, – Theft which hides itself even from itself, and is legal, respectable, and cowardly, – corrupts the body and soul of man, to the last fibre of them. And the guilty Thieves of Europe, the real sources of all deadly war in it, are the Capitalists[32] – that is to say, people who live by percentages on the labour of others; instead of by fair wages for their own. The *Real* war in Europe, of which this fighting in Paris is the Inauguration, is between these and the workman, such as these have made him. They have kept him poor, ignorant, and sinful, that they might, without his knowledge, gather for themselves the produce of his toil. At last, a dim insight into the fact of this dawns on him; and such as they have made him he meets them, and *will* meet.

Nay, the time is even come when he will study that Meteorological question, suggested by the *Spectator*, formerly quoted, of the Filtration of Money from above downwards.[33]

'It was one of the many delusions of the Commune' (says to-day's *Telegraph*, 24th June) 'that it could do without rich consumers.' Well, such unconsumed existence would be very wonderful! Yet it is, to me also, conceivable. Without the riches, – no; but without the consumers? – possibly! It is occurring to the minds of the workmen that these Golden Fleeces must get their dew from somewhere. 'Shall there be dew upon the fleece only?'[34] they ask: – and will be answered. They cannot do without these long purses, say you? No; but they want to find where the long purses are filled. Nay, even their trying to burn the Louvre, without reference to Art Professors, had a ray of meaning in it – quite Spectatorial.

'If we must choose between a Titian and a Lancashire cotton-mill' (wrote the *Spectator* of August 6th, last year, instructing me in political economy, just as the war was beginning), 'in the name of manhood and morality, give us the cotton-mill.'

So thinks the French workman also, energetically; only *his* mill is not to be in Lancashire. Both French and English agree to have no more Titians, – it is well, – but which is to have the Cotton-Mill?

Do you see in the *Times* of yesterday and the day before, 22nd and 23rd June, that the Minister of France dares not, even in this her utmost need, put on an income-tax; and do you see why he dares not?[35]

Observe, such a tax is the only honest and just one; because it tells on the rich in true proportion to the poor, and because it meets necessity in the shortest and bravest way, and without interfering with any commercial operation.

All rich people object to income-tax, of course; – they like to pay as much as a poor man pays on their tea, sugar, and tobacco, – nothing on their incomes.

Whereas, in true justice, the only honest and wholly right tax is one not merely on income, but property; increasing in percentage as the property is greater. And the main virtue of such a tax is that it makes publicly known what every man has, and how he gets it.[36]

For every kind of Vagabonds, high and low, agree in their dislike to give an account of the way they get their living; still less, of how much they have got sewn up in their breeches. It does not, however, matter much to a country that it should know how its poor Vagabonds live; but it is of vital moment that it should know how its rich Vagabonds live; and that much of knowledge, it seems to me, in the present state of our education, is quite attainable. But that, when you have attained it, you may act on it wisely, the first need is that you should be sure you are living honestly yourselves. That is why I told you, in my second letter, you must learn to obey good laws before you seek to alter bad ones: – I will amplify now a little the three promises I want you to make. Look back at them.[37]

(I.) You are to do good work, whether you live or die. It may be you will have to die; – well, men have died for their country often, yet doing her no good; be ready to die for her in doing her assured good: her, and all other countries with her. Mind your own business with your absolute heart and soul; but see that it is a good business first. That it *is* corn and sweet pease you are producing, – not gunpowder and arsenic. And be sure of this, literally: – *you must simply rather die than make any destroying mechanism or compound*. You are to be *literally* employed in cultivating the ground, or making useful things, and carrying them where they are wanted. Stand in the streets, and say to all who pass by: Have you any vineyard we can work in, – *not* Naboth's? In your powder and petroleum manufactory, we work no more.

I have said little to you yet of any of the pictures engraved – you perhaps think, not to the ornament of my book.

Be it so. You will find them better than ornaments in time. Notice, however, in the one I give you with this letter – the 'Charity' of Giotto[38] – the Red Queen of Dante, and ours also, – how different his thought of her is from the common one.

Usually she is nursing children, or giving money. Giotto thinks there is little charity in nursing children; – bears and wolves do that for their little ones; and less still in giving money.

His Charity tramples upon bags of gold – has no use for them. She gives only corn and flowers; and God's angel gives *her*, not even these – but a Heart.*

Giotto is quite literal in his meaning, as well as figurative. Your love is to give food and flowers, and to labour for them only.

But what are we to do against powder and petroleum, then? What men may do; not what poisonous beasts may. If a wretch spit in your face, will you answer by spitting in his? – if he throw vitriol at you, will you go to the apothecary for a bigger bottle?

There is no physical crime at this day, so far beyond pardon, – so without parallel in its untempted guilt, as the making of war-machinery, and invention of mischievous substance. Two nations may go mad, and fight like harlots – God have mercy on them; – you, who hand them carving-knives off the table, for leave to pick up a dropped six-pence, what mercy is there for *you*? We are so humane, forsooth, and so wise; and our ancestors had tar-barrels for witches; *we* will have them for everybody else, and drive the witches' trade ourselves, by daylight; we will have our cauldrons, please Hecate, cooled (according to the Darwinian theory) with baboon's blood,[39] and enough of it, and sell hell-fire in the open street.

(II.) Seek to revenge no injury. You see now – do not you – a little more clearly why I wrote that? what strain there is on the untaught masses of you to revenge themselves, even with insane fire?

Alas, the Taught masses are strained enough also; – have you not just seen a great religious and reformed nation, with its goodly Captains, – philosophical, sentimental, domestic, evangelical-angelical-minded altogether, and with its Lord's Prayer really quite vital to it, – come and take its neighbour nation by the throat, saying, 'Pay me that thou owest'?[40]

Seek to revenge no injury: I do not say, seek to punish no crime: look what I hinted about failed bankers [. . .]

---

* I do not doubt I read the action wrong; she is *giving* her heart to God, while she gives gifts to men. – *Author's Index to Vols. I and II.*

(III.) Learn to obey good laws; and in a little while you will reach the better learning – how to obey good Men, who are living, breathing, unblinded law; and to subdue base and disloyal ones, recognizing in these the light, and ruling over those in the power of the Lord of Light and Peace, whose Dominion is an everlasting Dominion, and His Kingdom from generation to generation.[41]

> Ever faithfully yours,
> JOHN RUSKIN.

LETTER TEN

THE BARON'S GATE

DENMARK HILL
7th September, 1871.

MY FRIENDS, – For the last two or three days, the papers have been full of articles on a speech of Lord Derby's,[42] which, it seems, has set the public mind on considering the land question. My own mind having long ago been both set, and entirely made up, on that question, I have read neither the speech nor the articles on it; but my eye being caught this morning, fortunately, by the words 'Doomsday Book' in my *Daily Telegraph*, and presently looking up the column, by 'stalwart arms and heroic souls of free resolute Englishmen,' I glanced down the space between, and found this, to me, remarkable passage: –

> 'The upshot is, that, looking at the question from a purely mechanical point of view, we should seek the *beau idéal* in a landowner cultivating huge farms for himself, with abundant machinery and a few well-paid labourers to manage the mechanism, or delegating the task to the smallest possible number of tenants with capital. But when we bear in mind the origin of landlordism, of our national needs, and the real interests of the great body of English tenantry, we see how advisable it is to retain intelligent yeomen as part of our means of cultivating the soil.'

This is all, then, is it, that your Liberal paper[43] ventures to say for you? It is *advisable* to retain a *few* intelligent yeomen in the island. I don't mean to find fault with the *Daily Telegraph*: I think it always means well on the whole, and deals fairly; which is more than can be said for its highly toned and delicately perfumed opponent, the *Pall Mall Gazette*.[44] But I think a 'Liberal' paper might have said more for the 'stalwart arms and heroic souls' than this. I am going myself to say a great deal more for them, though I am not a Liberal – quite the polar contrary of that.

You, perhaps, have been provoked, in the course of these letters, by not being able to make out *what* I was. It is time you should know, and I will tell you plainly.[45] I am, and my father was before me, a violent Tory of the old school[46] (Walter Scott's school, that is to say, and Homer's). I name these two out of the numberless great Tory writers, because they were my own two masters. I had Walter Scott's novels, and the *Iliad* (Pope's translation), for my only reading when I was a child, on weekdays: on Sundays their effect was tempered by *Robinson Crusoe* and the *Pilgrim's Progress*; my mother having it deeply in her heart to make an evangelical clergyman of me. Fortunately, I had an aunt more evangelical than my mother; and my aunt gave me cold mutton for Sunday's dinner, which – as I much preferred it hot – greatly diminished the influence of the *Pilgrim's Progress*; and the end of the matter was, that I got all the noble imaginative teaching of Defoe and Bunyan, and yet – am not an evangelical clergyman.

I had, however, still better teaching than theirs, and that compulsorily, and every day of the week. (Have patience with me in this egotism; it is necessary for many reasons that you should know what influences have brought me into the temper in which I write to you.)

Walter Scott and Pope's *Homer* were reading of my own election, but my mother forced me, by steady daily toil, to learn long chapters of the Bible by heart; as well as to read it every syllable through, aloud, hard names and all, from Genesis to the Apocalypse, about once a year; and to that discipline – patient, accurate, and resolute – I owe not only a knowledge of the book, which I find occasionally serviceable, but much of my general power of taking pains, and the best part of my taste in literature. From Walter Scott's novels I might easily, as I grew older, have fallen to other people's novels; and Pope might, perhaps, have led me to take Johnson's English, or Gibbon's, as types of language; but, once knowing the 32nd of Deuteronomy, the 119th Psalm, the 15th of 1st Corinthians, the Sermon on the Mount, and most of the Apocalypse, every syllable by heart, and having always a way of thinking with myself what words meant, it was not possible for me, even in the foolishest times of youth, to write entirely superficial or formal English, and the affectation to write like Hooker and George Herbert, which I now with shame confess of having long tried,[47] was the most innocent I could have fallen into.

From my own masters, then, Scott and Homer, I learned the Toryism which my best after-thought has only served to confirm.

That is to say a most sincere love of kings, and dislike of everybody who attempted to disobey them. Only, both by Homer and Scott, I was taught strange ideas about kings, which I find, for the present, much obsolete; for, I perceived that both the author of the *Iliad* and the author of *Waverley* made their kings, or king-loving persons, do harder work than anybody else. Tydides or Idomeneus[48] always killed twenty Trojans to other people's one, and Redgauntlet[49] speared more salmon than any of the Solway fishermen, and – which was particularly a subject of admiration to me, – I observed that they not only did more, but in proportion to their doings, got less, than other people – nay, that the best of them were even ready to govern for nothing, and let their followers divide any quantity of spoil or profit. Of late if has seemed to me that the idea of a king has become exactly the contrary of this, and that it has been supposed the duty of superior persons generally to do less, and to get more than anybody else; so that it was, perhaps, quite as well that in those early days my contemplation of existent kingship was a very distant one, and my childish eyes wholly unacquainted with the splendour of courts.

The aunt who gave me cold mutton on Sundays was my father's sister: she lived at Bridge-end, in the town of Perth, and had a garden full of gooseberry-bushes, sloping down to the Tay, with a door opening to the water, which ran past it clear-brown over the pebbles three or four feet deep; an infinite thing for a child to look down into.

My father began business as a wine-merchant, with no capital, and a considerable amount of debts bequeathed him by my grandfather. He accepted the bequest, and paid them all before he began to lay by anything for himself, for which his best friends called him a fool, and I, without expressing any opinion as to his wisdom, which I knew in such matters to be at least equal to mine, have written on the granite slab over his grave that he was 'an entirely honest merchant.'[50] As days went on he was able to take a house in Hunter Street, Brunswick Square, No. 54 (the windows of it, fortunately for me, commanded a view of a marvellous iron post, out of which the water-carts were filled through beautiful little trap-doors, by pipes like boa-constrictors; and I was never weary of contemplating that mystery, and the delicious dripping consequent): and as years went on, and I came to be four or five years old, he could command a post-chaise and pair for two months in the summer, by help of which, with my mother and me, he went the round of his country customers (who liked to see the principal of the house his own traveller); so that, at a jog-trot pace, and through the panoramic opening of the four windows of a post-chaise, made more panoramic still to me because my seat was a little bracket in front (for we used to hire the chaise regularly for the two months out of Long Acre, and so could have it bracketed and pocketed as we liked), I saw all the high-roads, and most of the cross ones, of England and Wales, and great part of lowland Scotland, as far as Perth, where every other year we spent the whole summer; and I used to read the *Abbot* at Kinross, and the *Monastery* in Glen Farg, which I confused with 'Glendearg,' and thought that the White

Lady had as certainly lived by the streamlet in that glen of the Ochils, as the Queen of Scots in the island of Loch Leven.[51]

It happened also, which was the real cause of the bias of my after life, that my father had a rare love of pictures. I use the word 'rare' advisedly, having never met with another instance of so innate a faculty for the discernment of true art, up to the point possible without actual practice. Accordingly, wherever there was a gallery to be seen, we stopped at the nearest town for the night and in reverentest manner I thus saw nearly all the noblemen's houses in England; not indeed myself at that age caring for the pictures, but much for castles and ruins, feeling more and more, as I grew older, the healthy delight of uncovetous admiration, and perceiving, as soon as I could perceive any political truth at all, that it was probably much happier to live in a small house, and have Warwick Castle to be astonished at, than to live in Warwick Castle, and have nothing to be astonished at; but that, at all events, it would not make Brunswick Square in the least more pleasantly habitable, to pull Warwick Castle down. And, at this day, though I have kind invitations enough to visit America, I could not, even for a couple of months, live in a country so miserable as to possess no castles.

Nevertheless, having formed my notion of kinghood chiefly from the FitzJames of the *Lady of the Lake*, and of noblesse from the Douglas there, and the Douglas in *Marmion*, a painful wonder soon arose in my child-mind, why the castles should now be always empty. Tantallon was there; but no Archibald of Angus: – Stirling, but no Knight of Snowdoun.[52] The galleries and gardens of England were beautiful to see – but his Lordship and her Ladyship were always in town, said the housekeepers and gardeners. Deep yearning took hold of me for a kind of 'Restoration,' which I began slowly to feel that Charles the Second had not altogether effected, though I always wore a gilded oak-apple very reverently in my button-hole on the 29th of May.[53] It seemed to me that Charles the Second's Restoration had been, as compared with the Restoration I wanted, much as that gilded oak-apple to a real apple. And as I grew older, the desire for red pippins instead of brown ones, and Living Kings instead of dead ones, appeared to me rational as well as romantic; and gradually it has become the main purpose of my life to grow pippins, and its chief hope, to see Kings.

Hope, this last, for others much more than for myself. I can always behave as if I had a King, whether I have one or not; but it is otherwise with some unfortunate persons. Nothing has ever impressed me so much with the power of kingship, and the need of it, as the declamation of the French Republicans against the Emperor before his fall.[54]

He did not, indeed, meet my old Tory notion of a King; and in my own business of architecture he was doing, I saw, nothing but mischief; pulling down lovely buildings, and putting up frightful ones carved all over with L. N.'s[55]: but the intense need of France for a governor of some kind was made chiefly evident to me by the way the Republicans confessed themselves paralyzed by him. Nothing could be done in France, it seemed, because of the Emperor: they could not drive an honest trade; they could not keep their houses in order; they could not study the sun and moon; they could not eat a comfortable déjeûner à la fourchette[56]; they could not sail in the Gulf of Lyons, nor climb on the Mont d'Or; they could not, in fine (so they said), so much as walk straight, nor speak plain, because of the Emperor. On this side of the water, moreover, the Republicans were all in the same tale. Their opinions, it appeared, were not printed to their minds in the Paris journals, and the world must come to an end therefore. So that, in fact, here was all the Republican force of France and England, confessing itself paralyzed, not so much by a real King, as by the shadow of one. All the harm the extant and visible King did was, to encourage the dressmakers and stone-masons in Paris, – to pay some idle people very large salaries, – and to make some, perhaps agreeably talkative, people, hold their tongues. That, I repeat, was all the harm he did, or could do; he corrupted nothing but what was voluntarily corruptible, – crushed nothing but what was essentially not solid: and it remained open to these Republican gentlemen to do anything they chose that was useful to France, or honourable to themselves, between earth and heaven, except only – print violent abuse of this shortish man, with a long nose, who stood, as they would have it, between them and heaven. But there they stood, spell-bound; the one thing suggesting itself to their frantic impotence as feasible, being to get this one shortish man assassinated. Their children would not grow, their corn would not ripen, and the stars would not roll, till they had got this one short man blown into shorter pieces.

If the shadow of a King can thus hold (how many?) millions of men, by their own confession, helpless for terror of it, what power must there be in the substance of one?

But this mass of republicans – vociferous, terrified, and mischievous – is the least part, as it is the vilest, of the great European populace who are lost for want of true kings. It is not these who stand idle, gibbering at a shadow, whom we have to mourn over; – they would have been good for little, even governed; – but those who work and do *not* gibber, – the quiet peasants in the fields of Europe, sad-browed, honest-hearted, full of natural tenderness and courtesy, who have none to help them, and none to teach; who have no kings, except those who rob them while they live, no tutors, except those who teach them – how to die.

I had an impatient remonstrance sent me the other day, by a country clergyman's wife, against that saying in my former letter,[57] 'Dying has been more expensive to you than living.' Did I know, she asked, what a country clergyman's life was, and that he was the poor man's only friend?

Alas, I know it, and too well. What can be said of more deadly and ghastly blame against the clergy of England, or any other country, than that they are the poor man's only friends?

Have they, then, so betrayed their Master's charge and mind, in their preaching to the rich; so smoothed their words, and so sold their authority, – that, after twelve hundred years' entrusting of the gospel to them, there is no man in England (this is their chief plea for themselves forsooth) who will have mercy on the poor, but they; and so they must leave the word of God, and serve tables?[58]

I would not myself have said so much against English clergymen, whether of country or town. Three – and one dead makes four – of my dear friends (and I have not many dear friends) are country clergymen; and I know the ways of every sort of them; my architectural tastes necessarily bringing me into near relations with the sort who like pointed arches and painted glass; and my old religious breeding having given me an unconquerable habit of taking up with any travelling tinker of evangelical principles I may come across; and even of reading, not without awe, the prophetic warnings of any persons belonging to that peculiarly well-informed 'persuasion,' such, for instance, as those of Mr Zion Ward 'concerning the fall of Lucifer, in a letter to a friend, Mr William Dick, of Glasgow, price twopence,' in which I read (as aforesaid, with unfeigned feelings of concern) that 'the slain of the Lord shall be M A N -Y; that is, man, in whom death is, with all the works of carnality, shall be burnt up!'

But I was not thinking either of English clergy, or of any other group of clergy, specially, when I wrote that sentence; but of the entire Clerkly or Learned Company, from the first priest of Egypt to the last ordained Belgravian curate, and of all the talk they have talked, and all the quarrelling they have caused, and all the gold they have had given them, to this day, when still 'they are the poor man's only friends' [. . .]

A year or two ago, a man who had at the time, and has still, important official authority over much of the business of the country, was speaking anxiously to me of the misery increasing in the suburbs and back streets of London, and debating, with the good help of the Oxford Regius Professor of Medicine[59] – who was second in council – what sanitary or moral remedy could be found. The debate languished, however, because of the strong conviction in the minds of all three of us that the misery was inevitable in the suburbs of so vast a city. At last, either the minister or physician, I forget which, expressed the conviction. 'Well,' I answered, 'then you must not have large cities.' 'That,' answered the minister, 'is an unpractical saying – you know we *must* have them, under existing circumstances.'

I made no reply, feeling that it was vain to assure any man actively concerned in modern parliamentary business, that no measures were 'practical' except those which touched the source of the evil opposed. All systems of government – all efforts of benevolence, are vain to repress the natural consequences of radical error. But any man of influence who had the sense and courage to refuse himself and his family one London season – to stay on his estate, and employ the shopkeepers in his own village, instead of those in Bond Street – would be 'practically' dealing with, and conquering, this evil, so far as in him lay; and contributing with his whole might to the thorough and final conquest of it.

Not but that I know how to meet it directly also, if any London landlords choose so to attack it. You are beginning to hear something of what Miss Hill has done in Marylebone, and of the change brought about by her energy and good sense in the centre of one of the worst districts of London.[60] It is difficult enough, I admit, to find a woman of average sense and tenderness enough to be able for such work; but there are, indeed, other such in the world, only three-fourths of them now get lost in pious lecturing, or altar-cloth sewing; and the wisest remaining fourth stay at home as quiet house-wives, not seeing their way to wider action; nevertheless, any London landlord who will content himself with moderate and fixed rent (I get five per cent. from Miss Hill, which is surely enough!), assuring his tenants of secure possession if that is paid, so that they need not fear having their rent raised, if they improve their houses; and who will secure also a quiet bit of ground for their children to play in, instead of the street, – has established all the necessary conditions of success; and I doubt not that Miss Hill herself could find co-workers able to extend the system of management she has originated, and shown to be so effective.

But the best that can be done in this way will be useless ultimately, unless the deep source of the misery be cut off. While Miss Hill, with intense effort and noble power, has partially moralized a couple of acres in Marylebone, at least fifty square miles of lovely country have been Demoralized outside London, by the increasing itch of the upper classes to live where they can get some gossip in their idleness, and show each other their dresses.

That life of theirs must come to an end soon, both here and in Paris, but to what end, it is, I trust, in their own power still to decide. If they resolve to maintain to the last the present system of spending the rent taken from the rural districts in the dissipation of the capitals, they will not always find they can secure a quiet time, as the other day in Dublin, by withdrawing the police,[61] nor that park-railings are the only thing which (police being duly withdrawn) will go down.[62] Those favourite castle battlements of mine, their internal 'police' withdrawn, will go down also; and I should be sorry to see it; – the lords and ladies, houseless at least in shooting season, perhaps sorrier, though they *did* find the grey turrets dismal in winter time. If they would yet have them for autumn, they must have them for winter. Consider, fair lords and ladies, by the time you marry, and choose your dwelling-places, there are for you but forty or fifty winters more in whose dark days you may see the snow fall and wreathe. There will be no snow in Heaven, I presume – still less elsewhere (if lords and ladies ever miss of Heaven).

And that some may, is perhaps conceivable, for there are more than a few things to be managed on an English estate, and to be 'faithful' in those few[63] cannot be interpreted as merely abstracting the rent of them. Nay, even the *Telegraph*'s beau-ideal of the landowner, from a mechanical point of view, may come short, somewhat. 'Cultivating huge farms for himself with abundant machinery; – ' Is that Lord Derby's ideal also, may it be asked? The Scott-reading of my youth haunts me, and I seem still listening to the (perhaps a little too long) speeches of the Black Countess who appears terrifically through the sliding panel in *Peveril of the Peak*, about 'her sainted Derby.'[64] Would Saint Derby's ideal, or his Black Countess's, of due ordinance for their castle and estate of Man, have been a minimum of Man therein, and an abundance of machinery? In fact, only the Trinacrian Legs of Man,[65] transposed into many spokes of wheels – no use for 'stalwart arms' any more – and less than none for inconveniently 'heroic' souls?

'Cultivating huge farms for himself!' I don't even see, after the sincerest efforts to put myself into a mechanical point of view, how it is to be done. For himself? Is he to eat the corn-ricks then? Surely such a beau-ideal is more Utopian than any of mine? Indeed, whether it be praise- or blame-worthy, it is not so easy to cultivate anything wholly for oneself, nor to consume, oneself, the products of cultivation. I have, indeed, before now, hinted to you that perhaps the 'consumer' was not so necessary a person economically, as has been supposed[66]; nevertheless, it is not in his own mere eating and drinking, or even his picture-collecting, that a false lord injures the poor. It is in his bidding and forbidding – or worse still, in ceasing to do either. I have given you another of Giotto's pictures,[67] this month, his imagination of Injustice, which he has seen done in his time, as we in ours; and I am sorry to observe that his Injustice lives in a battlemented castle and in a mountain country, it appears; the gates of it between rocks, and in the midst of a wood; but in Giotto's time, woods were too many, and towns too few. Also, Injustice has indeed very ugly talons to his fingers, like Envy; and an ugly quadruple hook to his lance, and other ominous resemblances to the 'hooked bird,'[68] the falcon, which both knights and ladies too much delighted in. Nevertheless Giotto's main idea about him is, clearly, that he 'sits in the gate'[69] pacifically, with a cloak thrown over his chain-armour (you can just see the links of it appear at his throat), and a plain citizen's cap for a helmet, and his sword sheathed, while all robbery and violence have way in the wild places round him, – he heedless.

Which is, indeed, the depth of Injustice; not the harm you do, but that you permit to be done, – hooking perhaps here and there something to you with your clawed weapon meanwhile. The baronial type exists still, I fear, in such manner, here and there, in spite of improving centuries.

My friends, we have been thinking, perhaps, to-day, more than we ought of our masters' faults, – scarcely enough of our own. If you would have the upper classes do *their* duty, see that you also do yours. See that you can obey good laws, and good lords, or law-wards,[70] if you once get them – that you believe in goodness enough to know what a good law is. A good law is one that holds, whether you recognize and pronounce it or not; a bad law is one that cannot hold, however much you ordain and pronounce it. That is the mighty truth which Carlyle has been telling you for a quarter of a century – once for all he told it you, and the landowners, and all whom it concerns, in the third book of *Past and Present*[71] (1845, buy Chapman and Hall's second edition if you can, it is good print, and read it till you know it by heart), and from that day to this, whatever there is in England of dullest and insolentest may be always known by the natural instinct it has to howl against Carlyle. Of late, matters coming more and more to crisis, the liberty men seeing their way, as they think, more and more broad and bright before them, and still this too legible and steady old signpost saying, That it is *not* the way, lovely as it looks, the outcry against it becomes deafening. Now, I tell you once for all, Carlyle is the only living writer who has spoken the absolute and perpetual truth about yourselves and your business; and exactly in proportion to the inherent weakness of brain in your lying guides, will be their animosity against Carlyle. Your lying guides, observe, I say – not meaning that they lie wilfully – but that their nature is to do nothing else. For in the modern Liberal there is a new and wonderful form of misguidance. Of old, it was bad enough that the blind should lead the blind[72]; still, with dog and stick, or even timid walking with recognized need of dog and stick, if not to be had, such leadership might come to good end enough; but now a worse disorder has come upon you, that the squinting should lead the squinting. Now the nature of bat, or mole, or owl, may be undesirable, at least in the day-time, but worse may be imagined. The modern Liberal politico-economist of the Stuart Mill school is essentially of the type of a flat-fish – one eyeless side of him always in the mud, and one eye, on the side that *has* eyes, down in the corner of his mouth, – not a desirable guide for man or beast [. . .]

Read your Carlyle, then, with all your heart, and with the best of brain you can give; and you will learn from him first, the eternity of good law, and the need of obedience to it: then, concerning your own immediate business, you will learn farther this, that the beginning of all good law, and nearly the end of it, is in these two ordinances, – That every man shall do good work for his bread: and secondly, that every man shall have good bread for his work.[73] But the first of these is the only one you have to think of. If you are resolved that the work shall be good, the bread will be sure; if not, – believe me, there is neither steam plough nor steam mill, go they never so glibly, that will win it from the earth long, either for you, or the Ideal Landed Proprietor.

Faithfully yours,
J. RUSKIN.

NOTES

Like all students and editors of Ruskin, I am deeply indebted to *The Library Edition of the Works of John Ruskin*, edited by E. T. Cook and Alexander Wedderburn (see my Select Bibliography, p. 43). In the following notes, all references to works by Ruskin not included in the present selection are to that edition; volume and page references are cited thus: X, 195. (For the benefit of those readers who may wish to pursue their interest further, I have made such references more often than is strictly necessary; the more casual reader is advised to ignore them.) I have drawn on Cook and Wedderburn's annotations more than it has been possible to acknowledge. When I quote their footnotes verbatim, however, I make concise acknowledgements thus: Cook and Wedderburn, X, 195.

Ruskin was an exceptionally allusive writer. He read widely and was able to quote effortlessly from memory. Many of these notes therefore simply acknowledge his sources. When precise references seemed useful I have given them – e.g. to specific lines in Dante or Shakespeare – but I have not thought it necessary to do this in all cases. There are quotations from the Bible on almost every page of Ruskin. Wherever these occur I give chapter and verse in the customary manner (e.g. Genesis i.3), even when the passage is well-known or when the source struck me as of no special interest. This is because Ruskin's quotations are rarely decorative: understanding frequently gains from consultation of full contexts – and I am not the best judge of what other readers may glean from them.

I have included a good deal of editorial commentary in these notes in order to reduce the introductory material elsewhere. The reader who desires a more general impression of Ruskin's work will find most of them inessential.

THE KING OF THE GOLDEN RIVER

1. p. 57 *without any one's finding it out*: The goldsmith's trade had great significance for Ruskin. This is not surprising, as it brings so many of his interests together: beauty in art and nature, craftsmanship, geology and wealth. In Letter 22 of *Fors Clavigera* (1872) he notes that 'all the great early Italian masters of painting and sculpture, without exception, began by being goldsmiths' apprentices'. Gold is something of a crux in Ruskin's thought. It is valued, rightly, because it is beautiful and durable; it is one of the gifts of nature which man can graciously adapt to his

uses. But when it becomes, as it does for the Black Brothers, a source of greed –
becomes in effect a token of one man's power over another – then it ceases to have a
value that avails for life.

Note, too, that the brothers intend to adulterate their gold. Adulteration was,
for Ruskin, one of the products of capitalism that most clearly condemned it. It
showed that the desire for profit could lead the producer to betray his calling –
that the capitalist was motivated by selfishness, not by any wish to provide for the
community.

2. p. 63   *It was, indeed, a morning . . . peaks of the eternal snow*: One of
the descriptive passages most clearly indebted to Turner, particularly to the later
Alpine paintings and watercolours. Especially characteristic is the contrast between
on the one hand the savagery of the slopes and on the other the peace of the snow
peaks.

3. p. 67   *And the sky where the sun . . . far into the darkness*: Another
passage reminiscent of Turner. Like the description of the sunset which 'passes
judgement' on Hans at the end of Chapter III (p. 65 above), this anticipates Ruskin's
magnificent description of Turner's *Slavers throwing overboard the dead and dying*
(see Introduction, pp. 11–12).

4. p. 70   *And thus the Treasure Valley became a garden . . . regained by love*:
The paradisal valley is an Eden, and the moral of the tale is Christian and redemptive.
It should be noted, however, that Ruskin's paradise is not supernatural. On the
contrary, it is nature herself – a nature in which relationships are just and governed
by love.

THE NATURE OF GOTHIC

1. p. 77   *the division of our subject . . . first chapter of the first volume*: Ruskin's
survey of Venetian architecture, which occupies the second and third volumes of *The
Stones of Venice*, is divided into three periods: Byzantine, Gothic and Renaissance.
These names, however, are no more than convenient labels; Venetian architecture,
as Ruskin is at some pains to insist, is eclectic. Thus, the Byzantine period includes
buildings that are mainly western Romanesque in style, and even those which are
undeniably Byzantine (or eastern Romanesque) show the influence of Islamic
architecture. In the chapter cited here, in fact, Ruskin distinguishes *four* periods, the
second being the transitional phase referred to in what follows. The buildings of this
phase are 'of a character much more distinctively Arabian; the shafts become more
slender, and the arches consistently pointed instead of round . . . This style is almost
exclusively secular.' It is during this period that the distinctively Venetian ogival (or
onion-shaped) arch emerges. The influence of northern Gothic architecture appears
in Venetian churches in the thirteenth century and, before long, unites with the
transitional style to give birth to a variant of Gothic that is uniquely Venetian.

2. p. 80   *but I presume . . . that architecture arose*: Ruskin's presumption is
probably correct. The term seems to have originated in France, where it was used to

describe the architecture of both the Dark and the Middle Ages. It first occurs in English in the seventeenth century.

3. p. 82   *13th and 14th paragraphs . . . first volume of this work*: IX, 291. Ruskin always numbered his paragraphs. When he refers to others of his books, he gives paragraph rather than page references.

4. p. 82   *Greek, Ninevite, and Egyptian*: By Ninevite, Ruskin means Assyrian and possibly Mesopotamian in general. Ruskin never visited Greece or the Middle East, so his knowledge of the schools in question was confined to what he had seen in western European museums. His generalizations about Greek art are often wide of the mark; in later life he came to regret many of them.

5. p. 83   *the mediæval, or especially Christian, system of ornament*: Ruskin always thinks of Romanesque and Gothic architecture as expressive of Christian teaching. Like many other nineteenth-century art historians, he regards Gothic as the uniquely Christian style. His view of the Renaissance style as a reversion to paganism must be seen as a corollary of this assumption (see Introduction, pp. 15–16).

6. p. 85   *the flesh and skin which . . . is to see God*: Cf. Job xix.26.

7. p. 86   *Go, and he goeth . . . Come, and he cometh*: Matthew viii.9.

8. p. 86   *the Irish peasant . . . thrust through the ragged hedge*: 'At the time Ruskin wrote, agrarian crime had been prevalent in Ireland. In 1847 a Coercion Act was passed; in 1848 the "Young Ireland" rebellion broke out, and the Habeas Corpus Act was suspended; in 1850 the Irish Tenant-Right League was formed; in the same year "several landlords were murdered by discontented tenants"' (Cook and Wedderburn, X, 195).

9. p. 87   *that old mountain servant . . . 'Another for Hector!'*: A story told by Sir Walter Scott in his Preface to *The Fair Maid of Perth*: 'In the battle of Inverkeithing, between the Royalists and Oliver Cromwell's troops, a foster-father and seven brave sons are known to have . . . sacrificed themselves for Sir Hector Maclean of Duart – the old man, whenever one of his boys fell, thrusting forward another to fill his place at the right hand of the beloved chief, with the . . . words . . . – "Another for Sir Hector!"'' Scott's novels and poems, their values and preoccupations, exercised an influence on Ruskin throughout his life.

10. p. 87   *the great civilized invention of the division of labour*: Adam Smith's *The Wealth of Nations* begins with these words: 'The greatest improvement in the productive powers of labour, and the greater part of the skill, dexterity, and judgement with which it is anywhere directed, or applied, seem to have been the effects of the division of labour'. With this ironic use of the phrase 'division of labour' Ruskin for the first time signals his opposition to the Political Economists. The reader should note therefore that Ruskin's economic criticism begins with a theory of labour.

11. p. 88   *The men who chop up the rods . . . vibration like hail*: 'Ruskin is no doubt describing what he had seen at the [Venetian] glass works of Murano' (Cook and Wedderburn, X, 197).

12. p. 88 *endeavouring to put down*: 'The abolition of the slave-trade, so far as this country was concerned, was enacted in 1807; the abolition of slavery in British colonies, in 1833. The anti-slavery movement then took a further development, being directed towards treaties with other countries regarding the right of search and other measures for the suppression of the trade; as, for instance, in Brazilian waters (1845). It is to such efforts as these that Ruskin is here alluding' (Cook and Wedderburn, X, 197).

13. p. 90 *I have already defined . . . the hands of childhood*: In *The Stones of Venice I* (IX, 290).

14. p. 90 *I shall endeavour to show elsewhere*: In *Modern Painters III*, which he was to publish in 1856. There Ruskin argues that the characteristic that distinguishes higher from lower art is invention: it is fundamentally *imaginative* (V, 63–4).

15. p. 95 *as I shall hereafter show . . . characteristic of the age*: In *The Stones of Venice III* (XI, 225–6). This paragraph establishes a connection between Ruskin's architectural work and his study of landscape art. The love of nature he found in Gothic architecture is expressed through particulars. The classical purity and symmetry of Renaissance architecture involves the exclusion of such particulars. It was not until the rise of English landscape painting, in Ruskin's view, that a devotion to natural forms returned to art. For Ruskin the discovery of this link seemed to justify his contention that Turner and the best of the English landscapists were fundamentally religious painters, as devotional in their way as the medieval sculptors had been.

16. p. 95 *The grouped shaft*: A shaft is the main part of a column, between the base and the capital. The piers and columns of Gothic churches tend to be made up of groups of shafts clustered together. The main shaft supports the wall directly above it. The more slender shafts attached to it reach above it to support the roof-vaulting on either side.

17. p. 95 *The introduction of tracery . . . window lights*: Each vertical division of a mullioned window (i.e. a window whose parts are divided by stone) is called a 'light'. 'Tracery' is the intersecting ribwork in the 'head' of a window (i.e. the upper part where the pointed arch begins). In early Gothic, tracery was just a decorative way of piercing the stone infilling in the arched head; its purpose was simply to admit more light. As the style developed, however, the decorative aspect became more pronounced. 'Bar tracery', which first appears in England in the thirteenth century, is defined by Nikolaus Pevsner as 'Intersecting ribwork made up of slender shafts, continuing the lines of the mullions of windows up to a decorative mesh in the head of the window' (Glossary to *The Buildings of England*). The vocabulary of forms commonly used in ecclesiastical tracery is reminiscent of natural foliage and is therefore called 'foliation': the main forms are the trefoil (three leaves), quatrefoil (four) and cinquefoil (five). In the second half of 'The Nature of Gothic', which is not reprinted here, Ruskin analyses foliation in some detail. For him it is one of the authenticating signatures of true Gothic, being central to what he now goes on to discuss as the style's 'Naturalism'.

18. p. 96 *Nature, of course ... variation perpetually*: This passage, very characteristic of Ruskin's early writings, is reminiscent of *Modern Painters*. The suggestion that Nature is herself an artist derives from that part of his thought that is rooted in Natural Theology.

19. p. 97 *'they love darkness rather than light'*: John iii.19.

20. p. 98 *the early English*: English Gothic is normally divided into three phases. The first, Early English, is characterized by the introduction of the pointed arch pure and simple, with little or no tracery. It is thus not greatly different from Norman (or English Romanesque) architecture; and it is not always clear whether Ruskin judged it to be true Gothic or not. The second phase, Decorated, begins with the introduction of bar tracery and ribbed vaulting. The last phase, Perpendicular, is distinguished by vertical lines that culminate in very slightly pointed arches – both in the window traceries and in its highly elaborate systems of vaulting. The Perpendicular style, and the still more decorated Flamboyant style, which is found on the continent, Ruskin considered decadent.

Ruskin's emphasis on the decoration of capitals in this passage is an important part of his theory of architectural ornament. Classical architecture is normally divided into three 'orders', each of which can be identified by its capitals: the orders are Doric, Ionic and Corinthian. Ruskin saw Gothic as deriving its character from the Corinthian, the most richly ornamented of the three orders. This is because it goes further than the other two in pursuing the analogy between natural and architectural forms – in this case, the column and the tree. The Corinthian capital is decorated with formalized acanthus leaves. Romanesque and Gothic sculptors developed this convention further, often giving each capital its own particular leaves and adding other decorations, such as fruit, beasts, birds and human heads. Thus, it was through the Corinthian capital, as Ruskin saw it, that the naturalism and variety he so valued came into 'Christian architecture'.

21. p. 98 *Seven Lamps of Architecture*: See VIII, 101.

22. p. 99 *'And behold, it was very good'*: Genesis i.31: God's judgement of his own Creation on the sixth day.

23. p. 99 *triglyph*: A vertically grooved section of a Doric frieze: so, abstract and invariable.

24. p. 99 *them that wake and them that sleep*: See 1 Thessalonians v.10.

25. p. 100 *error and abuse*: At this point Ruskin embarks on several pages of digression, much of it interesting but of more relevance to the argument of *Modern Painters* than to that of the book in hand. He begins by dividing artists into 'three great classes': 'the men of facts' (those who are preoccupied mainly with accurate representation), 'the men of design' (those who are only concerned with abstract values) and 'the men of both'. For some purposes, pure fact and pure design are adequate, but the greatest art must always attend to both. He then analyses the errors of attitude that each of these classes is prone to: which brings him to a second set of classes. This time the categories are moral ones: Purists, who 'perceive, and pursue, the good, and leave the evil'; Naturalists, who 'perceive and pursue the good and evil together'; and Sensualists, who 'perceive and pursue the evil, and leave the good'. At

their best, in Ruskin's view, only the Naturalists are capable of the highest forms of art (as here, in Gothic sculpture). It is important to note, therefore, that when he praises Naturalism he is thinking not only of those who depict the beautiful forms of nature but of those who, praising the good, have the courage to look upon evil. Of this kind of artist, Turner is Ruskin's exemplar (see 'The Two Boyhoods', pp. 151–3).

26. p. 100   *the mosaic of Torcello (Romanesque)*: Torcello is one of the islands on which the Venetian Republic was founded. In 829, however, most of Torcello's inhabitants moved to the present site, the island of Rivus Altus (or Rialto). Torcello has been virtually uninhabited for many centuries. The cathedral there is one of the few Venetian buildings that are western Romanesque (as opposed to Byzantine) in style. Ruskin here refers to the great mosaic of the Last Judgement which covers the west wall of the building, and which he has already discussed in Chapter II of this volume of *The Stones*.

27. p. 101   *St Maclou at Rouen*: A tiny fifteenth-century church which, elaborately decorated, is one of the gems of French Flamboyant architecture. Ruskin praises it in *The Seven Lamps*, but, as the next few paragraphs of the present chapter indicate, he had ambivalent feelings about it because of the decadence of the style.

28. p. 102   *work together for good*: Romans viii.28.

29. p. 103   *Lombardic and Romanesque sculpture*: Strictly speaking, Lombardic architecture is a branch of Romanesque. Presumably Ruskin uses the term Romanesque here to describe architecture that is indigenously Italian, stylistically continuous with Roman architecture. The Lombards were the Germanic invaders who settled in northern Italy and inter-married with the Italian people. The austerely beautiful architecture of their churches was much praised by Ruskin. Among those he admired were S. Michele in Pavia, S. Zeno in Verona and Sant'Ambrogio in Milan.

30. p. 103   *the nature of his material*: Truth to material, though he nowhere uses the phrase, is an important doctrine of Ruskin's. Cf. 'The Work of Iron', pp. 123–4, and my note 14, p. 325, for a fuller exposition.

31. p. 104   *a prophecy of the development . . . recovery of literature*: To the modern reader this sounds like a description of early Renaissance art and how it anticipates the revival of learning in the fifteenth and sixteenth centuries. But Ruskin sees early Renaissance painting and sculpture as the culmination of medieval art.

32. p. 104   *I have before alluded . . . interlacing of branches*: In both *The Seven Lamps* and *The Stones of Venice I* (see VIII, 88, and IX, 226).

33. p. 104   *anchoret*: i.e. anchorite – a hermit.

34. p. 104   *crosslet*: A narrow slit-like window in the shape of a cross.

35. p. 104   *That sentence of Genesis*: i.30.

36. p. 105   *the dove of Noah . . . an olive branch, plucked off*: Genesis viii.9–11.

37. p. 105   *until we have occasion . . . influenced by it*: In Volume III, Chapter III, 'Grotesque Renaissance' (XI, 135 *et seq.*).

38. p. 105   *I have before had occasion*: In *The Stones of Venice I* (IX, 186).

39. p. 107   *the Protestant spirit . . . was expressed in its every line*: An instance of the intellectual contortions Ruskin's devout Evangelicalism led him into at this

stage of his career. There can be little doubt that he was embarrassed by the fact that the buildings he praised were without exception Catholic. With his loss of faith in the 1850s, he came to detest this aspect of his early books. (For a fuller account of this, see note 12, p. 329 below.)

40. p. 108 *'unperplexed question up to Heaven'*: An allusion to Elizabeth Barrett Browning's *Casa Guidi Windows* (1851). The passage in question is a description of Florence,

> where Giotto planted
> His campanile like an unperplexed
> Fine question Heavenward . . .

Ruskin was an enthusiastic admirer of Mrs Browning's poetry.

41. p. 108 *idle in the market*: Matthew xx.3. A reference to the parable of the vineyard, which was to provide the title for *Unto this Last* (see pp. 157–8).

42. p. 109 *We have now, I believe . . . Gothic architecture*: In the second part of the chapter, Ruskin goes on to 'define' the 'outward form' of Gothic architecture. The analysis is outstandingly good but is not included in this selection, being too dependent on its context in *The Stones of Venice* as a whole.

THE WORK OF IRON,
IN NATURE, ART, AND POLICY

1. p. 116 *'breath of life'*: Genesis ii.7.

2. p. 117 *There is only one metal . . . trodden under foot*: Another example of Ruskin's ambivalent attitude to gold. The pavement of gold is in the new Jerusalem (Revelation xxi.21).

3. p. 117 *a globe of black, lifeless, excoriated metal*: There is in this sentence a hint of apocalyptic vision. The suggestion of a world overrun by heavy industry, in which there is no room for organic life, anticipates Ruskin's later work and the despair that permeates it.

4. p. 117 *a kind of soul in me . . . helpful in the circles of vitality*: Ruskin is exceptionally oblique in this part of the lecture. I take it that the phrase 'a kind of soul' is meant to evoke the word 'spirit', the Latin root of which means 'breath' – 'breath of life'. Then, Ruskin always took the word 'holy' to mean 'helpful' (cf. *Unto this Last*, p. 192, and my note 57, p. 337). There is thus buried in this nearly pantheistic account of elemental harmony a reference to the Holy Spirit.

5. p. 118 *'Come unto these yellow sands'*: Ariel's song, which leads the shipwrecked Ferdinand to Miranda; *The Tempest*, I.ii.376.

6. p. 118 *that look of warm self-sufficiency . . . among the green fields*: The alternative to the industrial waste-land. The key-word here is 'self-sufficiency', suggesting both contentment and right economy.

7. p. 118 *how a bit of agate . . . was made, or painted*: Ruskin gives a beautiful

explanation of this in *The Ethics of the Dust*, his slightly arch dialogue on crystallography, written for schoolgirls (XVIII, 332–5).

8. p. 120   *But Nature paints . . . poor and rich together*: Here we see the two poles of Ruskin's career coming together. The divinely ordered Nature of *Modern Painters I* is the source of the ideas of value and justice he was shortly to explore in *Unto this Last*.

9. p. 121   *who had profound respect for purple*: Because it was used to signify imperial power or aristocratic descent. Notice, however, that for Ruskin nobility is a *moral* quality. He insists upon this at the end of the paragraph when he ascribes the purple of porphyry to 'your *humble* oxide of iron'.

The Queen of the Air (1869), Ruskin's study of classical mythology, contains the following passage on purple:

> As far as I can trace the colour perception of the Greeks, I find it all founded primarily on the degree of connection between colour and light; the most important fact to them in the colour of red being its connection with fire and sunshine; so that 'purple' is, in its original sense, 'fire-colour', and the scarlet, or orange, of dawn, more than any other, fire-colour. I was long puzzled by Homer's calling the sea purple; and misled into thinking he meant the colour of cloud shadows on green sea; whereas he really means the gleaming blaze of the waves under wide light. Aristotle's idea (partly true) is that light, subdued by blackness, becomes red; and blackness heated or lighted, also becomes red. Thus, a colour may be called purple because it is light subdued (and so death is called 'purple' or 'shadowy' death); or else it may be called purple as being shade kindled with fire, and thus said of the lighted sea; or even of the sun itself, when it is thought of as a red luminary opposed to the whiteness of the moon: 'purpureos inter soles, et candida lunæ sidera;' or of golden hair: 'pro purpureo pœnam solvens scelerata capillo;' while both ideas are modified by the influence of an earlier form of the word, which has nothing to do with fire at all, but only with mixing or staining; and then, to make the whole group of thoughts inextricably complex, yet rich and subtle in proportion to their intricacy, the various rose and crimson colours of the murex-dye, – the crimson and purple of the poppy, and fruit of the palm – and the association of all these with the hue of blood; – partly direct, partly through a confusion between the word signifying 'slaughter' and 'palm-fruit colour', mingle themselves in, and renew the whole nature of the old word; so that, in later literature, it means a different colour, or emotion of colour, in almost every place where it occurs: and casts around for ever the reflection of all that has been dipped in its dyes.

> (XIX, 379–80)

As can be seen from this passage, it would be hard to over-estimate the significance of colour in Ruskin's work. Beauty in Nature makes manifest the indwelling presence of God. Colour is vital to our sense of visual beauty. In both *The Stones of Venice II* and *Modern Painters III*, Ruskin contends 'that colour is the most *sacred* element of all visible things' and in the latter volume he associates sensitivity to colour with love – 'love, I mean, in its infinite and holy functions'. (See V, 281 and 142–3.)

10. p. 121 *the noblest colour ever seen on this earth*: Ruskin anticipates the theme of the second essay of *Unto this Last*, which is punningly entitled 'The Veins of Wealth': 'it may be discovered that the true veins of wealth are purple – and not in Rock, but in Flesh . . .' (For the idea that blood is purple, see the previous note.)

11. p. 122 *the type which has been thus given . . . has noble antitype*: Ruskin was immersed in medieval typology, i.e. 'the study of symbolic representation' (*O.E.D.*), according to which a 'type' is a symbol, figure or emblem and the 'antitype' that which the type shadows forth. Thus, for example, in medieval Biblical exegesis, the story of Jonah, with his three days in the whale's belly, is a type of the Crucifixion and Resurrection of Christ.

12. p. 122 *On the other side . . . using their fancy or sensibility*: A reference to the new government Schools of Design. (See my Commentary, p. 113.)

13. p. 122 *no art is possible*: In the original text, a footnote refers the reader to an earlier lecture in *The Two Paths*. There Fine Art is defined as 'that in which the hand, the head, and the *heart* of man go together' ('The Unity of Art', XVI, 294).

14. p. 123 *whatever the material . . . qualities of that material*: Another instance of Ruskin's doctrine of truth to material (cf. 'The Nature of Gothic', p. 103). He despised mere *imitation* in art and contrasted it with his highest virtue, *truth*. Thus, in his *Mornings in Florence* (1875–7), for instance, he criticizes the fifteenth-century sculptor Desiderio da Settignano, whose technique was so refined that he could make marble look like real drapery. For Ruskin this was no more than a cheap conjuring trick, the aim of which was empty display. Good sculpture expresses both the nature of the subject (in this case, drapery) and the character of the stone.

15. p. 123 *a window look like an opaque picture*: Ruskin is thinking of the stained glass in Gothic Revival churches. Modern craftsmen in this field tended to apply techniques of pictorial naturalism to what is essentially a two-dimensional medium.

16. p. 124 *Mr Munro*: Alexander Munro (1825–71) was a Gothic Revival sculptor loosely connected with the Pre-Raphaelite Brotherhood, and Ruskin was the Pre-Raphaelites' most notable champion. Munro sculpted a number of statues for the Oxford Museum of Natural History, a building in 'Veronese Gothic' inspired by Ruskin's architectural ideas. The building was designed by Benjamin Woodward, but Ruskin was deeply involved in the planning and was personally responsible for the schemes of decorative sculpture. It was built between 1855 and 1859, the period in which *The Two Paths* was written.

17. p. 125 *pleasances*: A Middle English word meaning enclosed gardens 'laid out with shady walks, trees and shrubs, statuary, and ornamental water' (*O.E.D.*).

18. p. 126 *seneschal*: Another medieval word: a steward.

19. p. 126 *not one of my special subjects of study*: 'But he had studied ironwork with some care . . . The lecture was illustrated with several sketches of foreign ironwork, too rough, however, for engraving . . .' (Cook and Wedderburn, XVI, 392).

20. p. 127 *some good trellis-work enclosing the Scala tombs*: The Scaligeri or lords of la Scala were the rulers of Verona in the thirteenth and fourteenth centuries, the period of Veronese Gothic art. The greatest of them, Can Grande della Scala, is mainly remembered as a patron and protector of Dante during the latter's period of exile. The tombs of the family are near the centre of Verona inside a wrought-iron enclosure and decorated with some magnificent Gothic sculpture, praised by Ruskin in *The Stones of Venice* and elsewhere.

21. p. 127 *Here, for example, are two balconies*: An engraving of these balconies, derived from a daguerreotype of Ruskin's, is the frontispiece to some editions of *The Two Paths*.

22. p. 129 *this everlasting law of life*: Ruskin is thinking of God's commandment to Adam: 'In the sweat of thy face shalt thou eat bread, till thou return unto the ground . . .' (Genesis iii.19). For Ruskin, as for Dante (who influenced him deeply on this subject), the practice of *usury* is in defiance of this commandment. Usury means making money *not out of work* but out of other money – money-lending, in effect. The practice was condemned by the medieval church and also by most of the early Protestants. Dante considers it a form of unnatural vice. With the rise of capitalism, dependent as that system is on lending at interest, the prohibition gradually disappeared. By the time he wrote *Fors Clavigera* in the 1870s, Ruskin had decided that *all* gain by means of interest was vicious.

23. p. 129 *In the dream of Nebuchadnezzar . . . part of clay*: See Daniel ii.33.

24. p. 130 *'He doth ravish the poor . . . your hands in the earth'*: All these quotations are from the Psalms. It is clear from the order in which they are given, which is not consecutive, and from the inaccuracy of quotation here and there, that Ruskin was quoting from memory. Moreover, some verses are quoted from the Authorized Version, others from the Book of Common Prayer. The exact references are to *Psalms* x.9, 8, 2, 3, 7, 8; xiv.4; xxxvii.14; lxxiii.8, 6; lviii.4, 2.

25. p. 130 *but to weigh them . . . anything but that*: Cf. *Unto this Last*, p. 203.

26. p. 131 *Nabal or Dives*: Nabal is the rich farmer in 1 Samuel xxv who refuses hospitality to King David's soldiers, although they have protected his land. Dives (Latin for 'rich') is from Christ's parable of Dives and Lazarus – the rich glutton and the beggar at his gate (Luke xvi.19–31).

27. p. 131 *passing by on the other side, and binding up no wounds*: An allusion to the parable of the Good Samaritan (Luke x.31, 33).

28. p. 131 *the pest-house*: i.e. the plague house.

29. p. 132 *Epaminondas*: Theban commander responsible for the defeat of Sparta in 371 B.C. An example of heroism against the odds, he was renowned for his nobility of character.

30. p. 133 *Whenever we buy such goods . . . somebody's labour*: Cf. *Unto this Last*, pp. 187–8, 202.

31. p. 133 *Front de Bœuf, or Dick Turpin*: The former is the rapacious Norman baron, oppressor of the Saxon underdog, in Scott's *Ivanhoe*; the latter, the legendary highwayman who rode from London to York to establish an alibi.

32. p. 134 *Vanity Fair*: From Bunyan's *Pilgrim's Progress*.

33. p. 134 *strike open the private doors of their chambers*: Ruskin was obsessed with this idea. Compare the following passage from his pamphlet *The Opening of the Crystal Palace* (1854):

> . . . it is one of the strange characters of the human mind, necessary indeed to its peace, but infinitely destructive of its power, that we never thoroughly feel the evils which are not actually set before our eyes. If, suddenly, in the midst of the enjoyments of the palate and lightnesses of heart of a London dinner-party, the walls of the chamber were parted, and through their gap, the nearest human beings who were famishing, and in misery, were borne into the midst of the company – feasting and fancy-free – if, pale with sickness, horrible in destitution, broken by despair, body by body, they were laid upon the soft carpet, one beside the chair of every guest, would only the crumbs of the dainties be cast to them – would only a passing glance, a passing thought be vouchsafed to them? Yet the actual facts, the real relations of each Dives and Lazarus, are not altered by the intervention of the house wall between the table and the sick-bed – by the few feet of ground (how few!) which are indeed all that separate the merriment from the misery.

A similar preoccupation – with *seeing* the misery of the poor – occurs in the last paragraph of *Unto this Last* (p. 228).

In the present lecture, notice the reiteration of the verb to *look*. It is in Ruskin's verbs of seeing and looking that the connection between art critic and social critic is revealed.

34. p. 135 *a Borgia or a Tophana*: 'The cruel lady of Ferrara' is of course the notorious Lucrezia Borgia (1480–1519), daughter of Pope Alexander VI and sister of Cesare Borgia. The Borgias pursued their interests with utter ruthlessness, and many murders were attributed to them. Lucrezia, as Duchess of Ferrara, became an important patron of the arts and learning.

'Tofana, a woman of Naples, who died 1730; immortalised by her invention of an insidious poison, called by her "Manna of St Nicolas of Bari," but more commonly "Aqua Tofana"' (Cook and Wedderburn, VI, 403).

35. p. 135 *'The poison of asps . . . swift to shed blood'*: Romans iii.13, 15.

36. p. 136 *No human being . . . so free as a fish*: Ruskin's contempt for liberty, like his emphasis on the value of sight, begins in his writings on art and continues into his social criticism. Cook and Wedderburn compare this sentence with a passage from *The Seven Lamps of Architecture* where he remarks that 'the majesty of things in the scale of being' is proportional to their obedience (VIII, 250).

37. p. 137 *How wantonly we have wasted . . . science might have prevented*: A reference to the notorious problems of disease among soldiers fighting in the Crimean War.

38. p. 138 *in the present state of political events*: Ruskin is thinking of the Indian Mutiny (1857–8) and possibly also of the recently concluded Crimean War (1854–6).

39. p. 158   *I have personally seen its effects*: A reference to the uprising of 1848.
In that year the Austrians were driven out of Venice. By August 1849, however, they
had returned and crushed the rebellion. Shortly afterwards, in October, Ruskin
began the first of his longer stays in Venice and witnessed many effects of the
recently concluded struggle.

40. p. 138   *Gideon sought it . . . in the days of Gideon'*: Gideon is the Israelite
general who subdued the Midianites because the Lord was with him. In Judges
vi. 21–4, he has a vision of the angel of the Lord: 'And the Lord said unto him, Peace
be unto thee; fear not; thou shalt not die. Then Gideon built an altar there unto the
Lord, and called it Jehovah-shalom: unto this day it is yet in Ophrah of the
Abi-ezrites.' (Ruskin's 'God send peace' is an approximate translation of the Hebrew
'Jehovah-shalom'.) Gideon then goes on to subdue the Midianites, after which 'the
country was in quietness forty years in the days of Gideon' (Judges viii. 28).

41. p. 138   *as Menahem sought it . . . 'his hand might be with him'*: 2 Kings
xv. 19.

42. p. 138   *'Peace, peace,' when there is No peace*: Jeremiah viii. 11 and vi. 14.

43. p. 139   *shall beat their swords . . . war any more*: Isaiah ii. 4.

THE TWO BOYHOODS

1. p. 144   *Giorgione*: The nickname of the Venetian painter, Giorgio da Castelfranco (c. 1477–1510), means literally 'Big George'. Vasari in the *Lives of the
Painters* says of him: 'Because of his physical appearance and his moral and
intellectual stature he later came to be known as Giorgione; and although he was of
humble origin, throughout his life he was nothing if not gentle and courteous'.
Ruskin's 'Brave Castle' translates Castelfranco.

2. p. 144   *the marble city*: i.e. Venice. Castelfranco fell within the Venetian
empire, and it was in Venice that Giorgione pursued his brief career.

3. p. 145   *a respectable barber's shop*: Cook and Wedderburn, writing in 1905,
note that 'The region described by Ruskin has been cleared and rebuilt since he wrote'
(VII, 376). Turner's father was a barber.

4. p. 145   *'Bello ovile dov' io dormii agnello'*: 'The fair sheepfold wherein I used
to sleep, a lamb' – Dante's allusion to Florence, his birthplace, in *Paradiso*, xxv, 5.

5. p. 145   *Enchanted oranges . . . chests of them on the waves*: The paintings
alluded to are *The Garden of the Hesperides* and *The Meuse: Orange Merchantmen
going to pieces on the Bar*. Both are in the Tate Gallery, London.

6. p. 145   *by Thames' shore we will die*: Joseph Mallord William Turner was
born in Covent Garden in 1775 on St George's Day (23 April) and died in Chelsea, in a
house overlooking the Thames, in 1851.

7. p. 146   *about his St Gothard*: Turner's drawing of *The Pass of Faido*. Plate 21
in *Modern Painters IV* is an engraving after this drawing. It illustrates one of
Ruskin's most brilliant passages of detailed critical analysis.

8. p. 147   *poissardes*: fishwives.

9. p. 147 *Which, accordingly . . . to that order of things*: 'The pictures referred to are: (1) "The Battle of Trafalgar, as seen from the mizen starboard shrouds of the *Victory*," exhibited in 1808, and usually called "The Death of Nelson," . . . ; (2) "The Battle of Trafalgar," painted for George IV, and by him presented to Greenwich Hospital in 1829 . . . ; the "*Téméraire*," exhibited in 1839 . . .' (Cook and Wedderburn, VII, 379). The full title of the third painting is *The Fighting* Téméraire, *towed to her last berth*: it is now in the National Gallery, London.

10. p. 148 *devouring widows' houses*: Matthew xxiii.14: 'Woe unto you, scribes and Pharisees, hypocrites! for ye devour widows' houses, and for a defence make long prayer: therefore ye shall receive the greater damnation.'

11. p. 149 *of our Lady of Safety*: i.e. of Santa Maria della Salute, the great seventeenth-century basilica that stands at the entrance to the Grand Canal. It was built in thanksgiving when Venice was delivered from the plague. Literally translated, *salute* means 'health', but Ruskin, who was fond of exploring the roots of words, translates it variously as 'safety', 'salvation' and 'saving' (cf. *Unto this Last*, p. 209). The church was not built until after Giorgione's death.

12. p. 149 *shaping the whisper of death*: In *The Stones of Venice I* Ruskin writes that 'the most curious phenomenon in all Venetian history is the vitality of religion in private life, and its deadness in public policy' (IX, 24); and he goes on to praise 'the magnificent and successful struggle which she maintained against the temporal authority of the Church of Rome' (IX, 27). It is hard not to find this view of Venice eccentric, and there can be little doubt that the young Ruskin, as an ardent Evangelical, was eager to make the Republic's Erastian policy look like incipient Protestantism. That was in 1851. By the time he wrote 'The Two Boyhoods', Ruskin had lost the simple certainties of his youthful faith, and the account he gives here is, though similar, more critical and less sectarian. In *St Mark's Rest* (1877) and the abridged Traveller's Edition of *The Stones* (1879), he abandons this view altogether (cf. 'The Nature of Gothic', pp. 107–8).

13. p. 149 *Liber Studiorum*: A series of Turner's prints which illustrates the different branches of landscape painting as he practised and understood them. The *Liber* was published between 1807 and 1819.

14. p. 150 *I cannot ascertain in what year*: 'It was in 1785, when he was ten years old . . .' (Cook and Wedderburn, VII, 383).

15. p. 151 *deep-scented from the meadow thyme*: Turner's sketch of Kirkstall Abbey in Yorkshire, from which his *Liber Studiorum* print is derived, is now in the British Museum, London. Ruskin dates it as 'about 1795' (XIII, 254), which is probably a few years too early.

16. p. 151 *happy to work upon the walls of it*: Many of the great Venetian painters are known to have frescoed the external façades of palaces on the Grand Canal. This apparent waste of artistic effort – all of them have decayed – seemed to Ruskin the ultimate proof of their devotion both to their art and to the city. Later in *Modern Painters V* he tells of having seen 'the last traces of the greatest works of Giorgione yet glowing like a scarlet cloud, on the Fondaco de' Tedeschi' (VII, 438–9). These last traces have now vanished.

17. p. 151 *by Bolton Brook*: Bolton Abbey, another of the ruined abbeys of West Yorkshire, is on the River Wharfe. Both Turner and Ruskin valued this exceptionally picturesque setting (see 'Traffic', p. 247), and Ruskin is probably thinking here of Turner's early sketch of Bolton, now in the British Museum. Whitby Abbey, also ruined, is on the east coast of Yorkshire; it was another of Turner's early subjects.

18. p. 152 *Fallacy of Hope*: *The Fallacies of Hope* is the title of an epic poem Turner seems to have projected but never completed. Nothing of it survives beyond the fragments quoted by Turner in the catalogue entries for his Royal Academy canvases. The theme of the poem is the decline and fall of empires, particularly those whose power was founded on the sea. The analogy with England is clear. These verse fragments effectively demonstrate that such efforts as the spectacular sunset that reduces the *Téméraire* to ghostliness were intended symbolically. The message is plainly pessimistic. Ruskin was the first critic to notice this, and its effect is to be felt in the opening sentences of *The Stones of Venice*:

> Since first the dominion of men was asserted over the ocean, three thrones, of mark beyond all others, have been set upon its sands: the thrones of Tyre, Venice, and England. Of the First of these great powers only the memory remains; of the Second, the ruin; the Third, which inherits their greatness, if it forget their example, may be led through prouder eminence to less pitied destruction.

All three empires, and the fleets that expressed their power, were recurrent subjects of Turner's. The surviving fragments of his verse have been collected together in *The Sunset Ship: the Poems of J. M. W. Turner*, edited, with an essay, by Jack Lindsay, Lowestoft (Scorpion Press), 1966.

19. p. 152 *weeping of the mother . . . beasts of the field*: Two paintings are referred to here: *The Tenth Plague of Egypt* and *Rizpah, the Daughter of Aiah*. Both are in the Tate Gallery.

20. p. 152 *That old Greek question again*: In 'The Lance of Pallas', an earlier chapter in this Part of *Modern Painters*, Ruskin addresses himself to the tragic awareness of Homer and the Greek dramatists. The central question of Greek literature, as he understands it, is: '. . . beyond . . . mortality, what hope have we?' (VII, 275). Ruskin's attitude to the question may be judged from a sentence earlier in the same chapter: 'all great and beautiful work has come of first gazing without shrinking into the darkness' (VII, 271).

21. p. 152 *Salvator or Dürer*: i.e. Salvator Rosa (1615–73) and Albrecht Dürer (1471–1528). Salvator was a Neapolitan painter of the Baroque period, who was much admired in eighteenth- and early nineteenth-century England as a painter of the Picturesque and Sublime. His use of stark *chiaroscuro* (i.e. sharp contrasts of light and dark) has a lurid quality, especially when the subject is a robber band in savage mountain landscape. Ruskin despised his work as typifying the 'sensuality' and corruption of post-Renaissance art. Dürer, by contrast, he admired greatly, but with reservations, finding in his subject-matter a touch of morbidity. In this section of *Modern Painters*, the two men are made to represent two contrasting ways – both

inferior to Turner's or Tintoretto's – of looking into the darkness. The 'robber's casual pang' and the 'flying skirmish' mentioned later on in this paragraph are meant to typify Salvator and Dürer respectively.

22. p. 153 *'Put ye in the sickle, for the harvest is ripe'*: The quotation is from the book of Joel, when the prophet tells how God will be known in his judgement:

> Prepare war, wake up the mighty men, let all the men of war draw near; let them come up:
>
> Beat your plowshares into swords, and your pruninghooks into spears: let the weak say, I am strong . . .
>
> Put ye in the sickle; for the harvest is ripe: come, get you down; for the press is full, the fats overflow; for their wickedness is great.

> (Joel iii.9, 10 and 13)

The angels in what follows are from a comparable passage in Revelation (xiv.14–20), and the hemlock is from Hosea (x.4). Turner was much preoccupied with apocalyptic subjects in his later work. It seems likely that Ruskin had in mind such paintings as *Skeleton falling off a horse (c.* 1830) and *The Angel standing in the Sun* (1846), both in the Tate Gallery.

UNTO THIS LAST

In the course of these notes, Adam Smith's *The Wealth of Nations*, David Ricardo's *The Principles of Political Economy and Taxation* and John Stuart Mill's *The Principles of Political Economy* are referred to as 'Smith', 'Ricardo' and 'Mill' respectively. I am greatly indebted to P. M. Yarker's edition of *Unto this Last*, London and Glasgow (Collins), 1970, which I refer to as 'Yarker'.

1. p. 161 *to follow out the subjects opened in these papers*: A reference to *Munera Pulveris*, which began appearing in *Fraser's Magazine* in January 1863.

2. p. 161 *given in good Greek . . . Latin by Cicero and Horace*: This insight seems to have impressed Ruskin as he prepared himself for the writing of *Munera Pulveris* – i.e. at more or less the same time as the composition of this Preface (May 1862). Of Greek works, Plato's *Republic* was the major influence on his political thought, but Book V of the philosopher's *Laws*, with its more specifically economic observations, was what he consulted most frequently at this time. Still more important to him than the *Laws* was Xenophon's dialogue the *Economist*, which he was eventually to include in the *Bibliotheca Pastorum* (1876), his library of major texts for the renewal of England (see note 75 on p. 355 below). In his Preface to that edition he writes that the book 'contains a faultless definition of wealth, and explanation of dependence for its efficiency on the merits and faculties of its possessor' (XXI, 27). The Latin works he frequently cites for their bearing on Political Economy are the second of Horace's *Satires* and the *De Officiis* of Cicero.

Ruskin was much criticized for relying so much on ancient authorities – he also makes much use of Shakespeare, Dante and the Bible. It is hard to deny the justice of this criticism; Ruskin never reconciled himself to the fact that modern economies are more complex than ancient ones. Nevertheless, an important strategy of argument was involved. He was concerned with those aspects of commerce (in both senses of the word) which cannot change because they express fundamental truths of human nature. Thus, economic *justice* cannot and should not be understood in relative terms. What is just is always, immutably, just and nothing more or less.

3. p. 161   *The most reputed essay . . . in modern times*: i.e. Mill. Ruskin's many attacks on this book refer to the two-volume edition of 1848.

4. p. 161   '*Every one has a notion . . . nicety of definition*': The sentences Ruskin omits from this quotation are worth considering. Mill writes:

> The enquiries which relate to it are in danger of being confounded with those relating to any other of the great human interests. All know that it is one thing to be rich, another to be enlightened, brave, or humane; that the questions how a nation is made wealthy, and how it is made free, or virtuous, or eminent in literature, in the fine arts, in arms, or in polity, are totally distinct enquiries. Those things, indeed, are all indirectly connected, and react upon one another. A people has sometimes become free, because it had first grown wealthy; or wealthy because it had first become free. The creed and laws of a people act powerfully upon their economical condition; and this again, by its influence on their mental development and social relations, reacts upon their creed and laws. But though the subjects are in very close contact, they are essentially different, and have never been supposed to be otherwise.

It is not difficult to see why the author of *The Stones of Venice* should have baulked at this. To trace the interconnectedness of 'the great human interests' was for Ruskin the whole end of study. Any study so specialized that it failed to take this into account was bound, in Ruskin's eyes, to distort the truth. However, there is some injustice to Mill at this point; Mill does go on to give a definition of wealth – 'all useful or agreeable things which possess exchange value'. In fact, Ruskin directs his argument against precisely this definition.

5. p. 161   *House-law (Oikonomia) . . . Star-law (Astronomia)*: 'House-law' is a literal translation of the Greek word from which 'economy' is derived; 'Star-law' bears the same relation to 'astronomy'. Such etymology-based coinages are a device Ruskin learnt from Carlyle. The idea was to bring out the 'original' meaning of the word and so to direct the reader's mind to the fundamental principle behind it. The disparity between modern usage and the root meaning exposes the disparity between modern practice and the original principle. The plainness of the Anglo-Saxon monosyllables in place of the Greek (or Latin) compels the reader to contemplate the term's moral implications.

6. p. 162   *wealth radiant and wealth reflective*: A development of the analogy between astronomy and economics. One kind of wealth is like the stars (radiant); the other is like the planets (reflective). This anticipates one of the book's central arguments: the distinction Ruskin draws between intrinsic wealth (vitality – that which radiates life) and riches (the system of tokens which represents intrinsic wealth

for the purpose of exchange). Thus, modern Political Economists are like astonomers who study borrowed light without reference to its source.

7. p. 162   *Pope's assertion*: In the *Essay on Man*, IV, 248:

> An honest man's the noblest work of God.

Ruskin's argument is here directed against the hypothesis of 'economic man' (see Introduction, pp. 26–7). Ruskin implies that moral qualities such as honesty, being inherent in all men, make nonsense of the hypothesis.

8. p. 162   *there are yet in the world . . . fear of losing employment*: This is, as the footnote indicates, an attack on Smith. It is also another instance of Ruskin's misrepresentation of his opponents. As Yarker puts it, 'In the passage cited, Smith, who was a Professor of Moral Philosophy, was not excluding other restraints from dishonesty than the fear of unemployment, but was merely saying that the need to please his customer was a more influential check on a tradesman than were the rules of his Corporation . . .' (Yarker, 120).

9. p. 163   *in her first church*: i.e. San Giacomo di Rialto, founded in A.D. 421. The church is in the Rialto market, the original centre of Venice. In his notes to the art collection he established in Oxford, Ruskin wrote: 'The inscription was put upon [the church] by Doge Domenico Selvo when he decorated it within and without, about the year 1090. I discovered the inscription myself [in 1876]' (XXI, 268). The sentence quoted is preceded by the words, 'Be thy true cross, oh Christ, the salvation of this place'. The inscription was to Ruskin a vindication of all he had written about early Venice and economic justice.

10. p. 163   *the Eighteenth paragraph of Sesame and Lilies*: See pp. 262–3.

11. p. 163   *captains*: i.e. industrialists. The expression is taken from Carlyle's *Past and Present*. One chapter is entitled 'Captains of Industry'.

12. p. 163   *in the sequel*: i.e. in *Munera Pulveris*.

13. p. 163   *the worst of the political creed . . . wish him to arrive*: Ruskin was anxious to resist the charge of Socialism.

14. p. 164   *honourable instead of disgraceful to the receiver*: A reference to the feelings of shame and humiliation associated with the corrective workhouse. The New Poor Law of 1834, which introduced these institutions, was inspired by Utilitarian ideas.

15. p. 164   *'a labourer serves . . . deserved well of his country'*: XVI, 113.

16. p. 165   *'de publico est elatus'*: In a letter to his father dated 6 October 1861, Ruskin translates this phrase as 'They carried him forth at public cost'. However, the word *elatus* ('he was carried forth'), is a misreading for *datus* ('given'). The passage quoted in Ruskin's footnote is translated as follows: 'Publius Valerius, universally regarded as the foremost citizen, both in military and in civil qualities, died in the following year . . . ; he was a man of extraordinary reputation, but so poor that money was wanting for his burial, and it was furnished from the treasury of the state. The women of Rome went into mourning for him, as they had for Brutus.'

17. p. 167   *'The social affections . . . the new conditions supposed'*: A caricature of the 'economic man' hypothesis.

18. p. 168   *We made learned experiments . . . to deal with its chloride*: 'Ruskin possibly refers to the experiment by Pierre Louis Dulong, who in 1811 first made nitrogen trichloride by passing chlorine gas through a solution of ammonium chloride in water. Dulong correctly assigned the formula NC_3 to the resulting compound; but the experiment cost him an eye and three fingers' (Yarker, 132).

19. p. 168   *the late strikes of our workmen*: Ruskin seems to have given much thought to the builders' strike of 1859. A letter on the subject dated 4 September 1859 suggests that *Unto this Last* had its origin in that event (XXXVI, 317–19).

20. p. 169   *It is not the master's interest . . . sickly and depressed*: There was much discussion of the regulation of wages throughout the nineteenth century. The classical argument, which begins in Smith, is well summed up by Ricardo: 'The natural price for labour is that price which is necessary to enable the labourers, one with another, to subsist and to perpetuate their race, without either increase or decrease.' Ruskin rejects this 'Iron Law of Wages' (as it was called). In its place he puts the concept of a *just* economic return for labour expended.

21. p. 169   *For no human actions . . . by balances of justice*: This is in effect Ruskin's rejection of Utilitarianism – in particular of the idea that a just society is one that manages to balance off the divergent interests of its members: 'the greatest happiness of the greatest number'. Against this idea he goes on to argue that 'That country is the richest which nourishes the greatest number of *noble* and happy human beings' (my italics).

22. p. 170   *through the community . . . to the servant himself*: The Utilitarians argued, as their heirs still do today, that the employer's self-interest is ultimately of benefit to the employee too: only thus can employment be provided and wages earned. Ruskin attacked this argument again and again.

23. p. 171   *whosoever will save . . . whoso loses it shall find it*: Cf. Matthew xvi.25.

24. p. 171   *Hard Times*: Charles Dickens's most concentrated and systematic attack on Utilitarianism and the Manchester School of Political Economy was published in 1854 and dedicated to Carlyle. Bounderby is Dickens's caricature of the modern industrialist who runs his factory according to the principles Ruskin is here attacking. *Bleak House* and *Master Humphrey's Clock* are also by Dickens.

25. p. 173   *How far it is possible . . . diminishing their number*: On this question the most important theory of the day was Mill's theory of the 'wages-fund'. This was much disputed at the time, and Mill was eventually to reject it himself. He argued that there was, at any one time, a finite amount of capital available for the cost of labour – i.e. for wages. Once this fund had been exhausted, no further money was available for the purpose. It followed that, if wages were fixed at a rate above that of the wages-fund, the result would be unemployment. Unemployment of this kind could only be dealt with by means of state intervention, probably by taxation. Subsidized in this way, the working population would increase, causing more unemployment and spiralling taxation. Moreover, the use of taxation to solve the problem would reduce the efficiency of the workforce by removing competition and the fear of unemployment. Eventually, 'Taxation for the support of the poor would

engross the whole income of the country' (Mill). Ruskin thought the wages-fund theory was nonsense, favouring the more modern view that workers are paid out of anticipated profits – i.e. on credit. He was also very much in favour of income tax as an instrument of social justice (see *Fors Clavigera* p. 303).

26. p. 173   *six-and-eightpence*: Six shillings and eightpence was the fee normally paid for a solicitor's letter.

27. p. 175   *die daily*: 1 Corinthians xv.31.

28. p. 177   *the hero of the Excursion from Autolycus*: The hero of Wordsworth's long poem *The Excursion* is a pedlar of deep human sympathies and philosophic mind. Autolycus, the 'snapper-up of unconsidered trifles' in *The Winter's Tale*, is also a pedlar but, by contrast, a cheat and a thief.

29. p. 178   *paternal authority and responsibility*: Ruskin had advocated 'paternal government' in *The Political Economy of Art*. The whole argument of *Unto this Last* is based on an analogy between nation and family.

30. p. 180   *the laws of mercantile economy . . . those of political economy*: Ruskin's distinction is characteristically semantic and etymological. *Political* economy should be concerned with the wealth of the *polis* (the state or the community). It has nothing to do with 'the science of getting rich', which he calls 'mercantile economy, the economy of "merces" or of "pay"' (p. 181).

31. p. 181   *power over labour*: This agrees with Smith, but Ruskin wishes to take the matter further: to see how that power is used – whether for good or ill.

32. p. 182   *as we shall see presently*: See p. 188.

33. p. 182   *the beneficialness of the inequality*: Ruskin was never an egalitarian, but he opposes the view that inequality necessarily promotes economic health. He considers that an inequality established by just means and directed towards the interest of the community *is* beneficial, but unjust inequalities, though they may seem to favour the individual, are actually harmful to everyone.

34. p. 184   *Suppose two sailors cast away*:

In this analogy Ruskin illustrates two principles: the 'debt-analysis' theory of currency ('All money, properly so called, is an acknowledgment of debt', as he says in the footnote, [p. 185]); and the diminution of the total wealth of the community by 'the establishment of mercantile wealth', or in other words, by greed.

He deals more fully with the debt-analysis theory of currency in *Munera Pulveris*, where he explains that the legal tender of a country is, in the final analysis, an acknowledgement of indebtedness to the holder of it on the part of the State for goods and services rendered, or to be rendered, to the community as a whole. When a workman receives his wages in currency, the notes and coins in his wage-packet are an acknowledgement that society owes him a stipulated quantity of goods and services in return for his week's work. 'Legally authorized or national currency, in its perfect condition, is a form of public acknowledgement of debt,' said Ruskin, 'so regulated and divided that any person presenting a commodity of tried worth in the public market, shall, if he pleases, receive in exchange for it a document giving him claim to the return of its equivalent, (1) in any place, (2) at any time, (3) in any kind' (XVII, 195) . . . It is notable that Mill, who habitually thinks in terms of agencies and commodities rather than people, does not refer to the concept of indebtedness. Characteristically Ruskin makes this concept (with its moral overtones) the essential factor in his analysis.

(Yarker, 143)

35. p. 186 *a political diminution . . . in substantial possessions*: An illustration of the kind of inequality that, 'unjustly established', is *not* beneficial. Good will and charity on the part of the healthy sailor – non-economic factors – would have strengthened the economy of the 'polis'.

36. p. 186 *to superintend the transference . . . from one farm to the other*: Ruskin's second fable describes the evolution of the capitalist entrepreneur. It is not an attack on middle-men *per se*. The point is that this particular entrepreneur considers only what he takes to be his own interest and fails to consider that of the 'polis' as a whole.

37. p. 187 *The whole question . . . one of abstract justice*: The systematic practice of the 'science of getting rich' leads – if the logic of Ruskin's fables is accepted – not to more wealth but less. It is only when the 'moral or pathetic attributes of riches' (which he refers to in the next paragraph) are taken into account that material wealth can increase. So, paradoxically, it is only the adoption of the moral standards Ruskin's opponents call 'sentimental' that can produce the effects Political Economists claim to desire. It is important to remember at this point that Ruskin is thinking of the poverty and degradation to be found in the great cities of the richest nation on earth.

38. p. 187 *pathetic*: i.e. of the emotions.

39. p. 187 *Dura plains*: Daniel iii.1: 'Nebuchadnezzar the king made an image of gold . . . he set it up in the plain of Dura.' This was the idol before which Shadrach, Meshach and Abednego were burnt alive. Political economy is, similarly, a false god to which living men and women are daily sacrificed. (Cf. 'Traffic', p. 249.)

40. p. 187 *the purchase-pieces . . . the citizen and the stranger*: See Matthew xxvii.6–7. The thirty pieces of silver paid to Judas for the betrayal of Christ were used, after his suicide, to buy 'the potter's field, to bury strangers in'. Not only strangers, says Ruskin, but fellow-citizens too. (See my Commentary, p. 158.)

41. p. 188 *to rush riotously upstairs . . . not regularly paid*: An allusion to the strikes mentioned on pp. 168–9. Note the use of a domestic analogy: Ruskin is thinking of 'house-law'.

42. p. 189 *Byzants*: 'Byzants, or bezants, the gold coins struck at Byzantium, were common in England till superseded by the noble, a coin of Edward III' (Cook and Wedderburn, XVII, 55).

43. p. 189 *adamant of Golconda*: Golconda was an ancient Indian fortress, once famous for its diamonds. 'Adamant' originally meant 'diamond'.

44. p. 189 *These are My Jewels*: The words of a great Roman mother introduc-

ing her sons to a richly bejewelled guest. The story is told by the early Roman historian, Valerius Maximus.

45. p. 190   *a Jew merchant*: i.e. King Solomon, seen here in particular as the author of the book of Proverbs. Ruskin's account of Solomon is couched in ironic language intended to imply the utter irrelevance of wise kings and authors of holy scripture to the 'practical' modern businessman who studies Political Economy.

46. p. 190   *the Gold Coast*: Not the African Gold Coast, but Ophir (see 1 Kings ix.26–8), which is thought to have been on the coast of the Yemen.

47. p. 190   *a statue of the old Jew . . . principal public buildings*: Ruskin refers to the so-called 'Judgement Angle' of the Ducal Palace in Venice. The sculpture, which depicts the Judgement of Solomon, had been discussed by Ruskin in *The Stones of Venice* (X, 332, 359, 363).

48. p. 190   *'The getting of treasures . . . them that seek death'*: Proverbs xxi.6.

49. p. 190   *'Treasures of wickedness . . . delivers from death'*: Proverbs x.2.

50. p. 190   *advertisement*: Advertising is barely mentioned in *Unto this Last*. Nevertheless, Ruskin considered it one of the most pernicious features of capitalism and thought it should be banned. In later life he forbade the advertising of his own books.

51. p. 190   *the King's daughter, all-glorious within*: Cf. Psalms xlv.13.

52. p. 191   *'He that oppresseth the poor . . . surely come to want'*: Proverbs xxii.16.

53. p. 191   *'Rob not the poor . . . the soul of those that spoiled them'*: Cf. Proverbs xxii.22, 23.

54. p. 191   *'The rich and the poor . . . God is their light'*: Cf. Proverbs xxii.2 and xxix.13. (The translation is Ruskin's own, from the Latin of the Vulgate.)

55. p. 191   *'sun of justice'*: The Wisdom of Solomon (Apocrypha) v.6: 'the sun of righteousness rose not upon us'. Ruskin goes on to conflate this quotation from one of Solomon's supposed writings with an allusion to Malachi iv.2: 'But unto you that fear my name shall the Sun of righteousness arise with healing in its wings . . .' The substitution of 'justice' for 'righteousness', partially explained in Ruskin's footnote, owes something to the Latin of the Vulgate (*sol justitiae*).

56. p. 191   *'Man, who made me a ruler . . . over you?'*: Luke xii.14.

57. p. 192   *the Helpful One and the Just*: Cf. Acts iii.14: 'the holy one and the just'. Ruskin believed (mistakenly) that 'holy' and 'helpful' were originally synonymous. In his view, the vague piety of 'holy' concealed the true meaning of the word. (Cf. 'The Work of Iron', p. 117, and my note 4, p 323.)

58. p. 192   *'Just, and having salvation'*: Zechariah xi.9.

59. p. 192   *and desired a murderer . . . to be granted to them*: See Mark xv.6–15, where the people of Jerusalem call on Pilate to release Barabbas in preference to Christ.

60. p. 192   *where demand is, supply must follow*: 'The quantity of every commodity . . . naturally regulates itself in every country according to the demand' (Smith).

61. p. 192   *nor only desert, but plague-struck*: 'The subject of inundations,

especially in Italy, was presently to occupy much of Ruskin's thought . . .' (Cook and
Wedderburn, XVII, 61). He wrote a good deal on the subject; see, for example, the
footnote on p. 217.

62. p. 192   'Length of days . . . riches and honour': Proverbs iii.16.

63. p. 193   water of Marah: Exodus xv.23: 'They could not drink the waters of
Marah, for they were bitter.'

64. p. 193   black mail: 'A tribute formerly exacted from small owners in the
border districts of England and Scotland, by freebooting chiefs, in return for
immunity from plunder' (O.E.D.).

65. p. 193   represented by Dante: A reference to Dante, Paradiso, xviii. In this
canto, Dante is shown a vision of the just in heaven. Their spirits fly across the sky,
forming themselves into successive letters that spell out the first verse of the Wisdom
of Solomon. (The Latin words, as Dante quotes them, provide Ruskin with the title of
this third essay: 'Who judge the earth'.) Other spirits then fly down to the final M of
terram and, mingling with the first spirits, transform the letter into the image of an
eagle – for Dante, a symbol of Roman law and justice. All this takes place in the light
of the planet Jupiter, which Dante calls the temperate star. The god Jupiter is the
nearest Roman equivalent of God the Father, so the presence of the planet locates the
source of law and justice in divine love.

66. p. 193   the light of the body, which is the eye: Cf. Matthew vi.22.

67. p. 194   called to be 'saints' . . . 'chosen to be kings': Romans i.7; Revelation
i.6.

68. p. 194   mercy and judgment: Psalms ci.1.

69. p. 194   'makes men . . . that have no ruler over them': Habakkuk i.14.

70. p. 194   equivalent time and labour: Obviously this is a broadly simplified
formula, as Ruskin was aware. It is not possible to calculate exact equivalents, not
least because labour takes many different forms. Ruskin is attempting to give
practical expression to his concept of the just wage and is by implication challenging
the 'Iron Law of Wages'.

71. p. 194   This difference will be analyzed in its place: An indication that
Ruskin had a longer book in mind. He returns to this difference on pp. 215–16 but
does not have room to analyse it fully.

72. p. 195   the law of justice only: Not, that is to say, the 'abstract justice'
referred to on pp. 186–7.

73. p. 195   'interest': 'Not commercial "interest", but the "fruit of labour"'
(Yarker, 151).

74. p. 196   Twenty smiths, or twenty thousand smiths: This tellingly simple
example is Ruskin's response to the 'wages-fund' theory.

75. p. 196   practically: i.e. in practical terms.

76. p. 197   his first definition of labour: To be found in the opening paragraph of
Mill.

77. p. 197 actual quantity: This discussion of positive feelings towards work
may be compared to the account of medieval labour in 'The Nature of Gothic'
(pp. 83–91).

78. p. 198   *It is easier . . . compel him to take for it*: 'Ruskin elaborated this very involved statement in a letter to *The Pall Mall Gazette* in 1867. This letter shows that by "what a man ought to have for his work" Ruskin meant "the quantity of food and air which will enable a man to perform it without actually losing any of his flesh or his nervous energy" (XVII, 473). This view foreshadows the idea of a "living wage", first so called by Sir Andrew Clark in the *Westminster Gazette* on 24 November 1900' (Yarker, 152–3). Of course, Ruskin is also concerned with the worker's other needs, in particular his need to have and support a family.

79. p. 200   *Thirty-five or forty per cent*: 'The calculation refers, it should be noted, not to the share of their wages which they pay in taxation, but to the share of the total taxation which is derived from their wages' (Cook and Wedderburn, XVII, 71).

80. p. 200   *repeal of the corn laws*: Laws restricting the import of corn kept the price of bread artificially high for most of the first half of the nineteenth century. Their repeal in 1846 is generally regarded as a triumph for those who believed in Free Trade, among them the Manchester School liberals.

81. p. 200   *competition is at an end*: Ruskin's footnote is deliberately paradoxical. Free Trade was normally championed by those in favour of economic competition.

82. p. 200   *never perceiving . . . wages would permanently fall*: The 'Iron Law of Wages' (see note 20 on p. 334 and note 70 on p. 338) guaranteed that wages would be controlled by the cost of living.

83. p. 201   *causing a large quantity . . . consumed unproductively*: 'As Ruskin has just pointed out, taxation on the necessities of life is paid by the employer, not the employee, since wages must be high enough to cover the cost of living. He now suggests that the labour needed to cover this extra cost to the employer is "unproductive", since instead of ploughing it back as capital, the employer must pay it to the State' (Yarker, 154).

84. p. 201   *any real over-population in the world*: An allusion to the population theories of T. R. Malthus (see Introduction, p. 20). Ruskin argued that the problem of population had to be seen in a world context. He was thinking in particular of the opportunities for new cultivation that colonization afforded.

85. p. 201   *those magnificent lines of Pope*: *Moral Essays*: Epistles iii, 'To Allen, Lord Bathurst, on the Use of Riches', lines 107–10.

86. p. 201   *I shall examine hereafter*: A reference to the essays Ruskin was not allowed to complete.

87. p. 201   *as will be seen in the sequel*: Another reference to the essays Ruskin did not complete.

88. p. 202   *of one man to all others*: Ruskin's belief in the Platonic ideal of the philosopher king here blends with Carlyle's belief in the hero as leader. (See Introduction, p. 25).

89. p. 202   *'Soldiers of the Ploughshare . . . Soldiers of the Sword'*: Ruskin quotes from *The Political Economy of Art* (XVI, 26).

90. p. 202   *last volume of Modern Painters*: VII, 207. The quotation is not accurate.

91. p. 202   *in my last paper*: A mistake: he says it in the first paper, p. 167.

92. p. 203   *the source of all evil*: See I Timothy vi.10: 'For the love of money is the root of all evil' (Cf. 'Of Kings' Treasuries', p. 274).

93. p. 203   *mammon service*: Cf. Matthew vi.24.

94. p. 203   *'Tai Cristian . . . e l'altro inòpe'*: Dante, *Paradiso*, xix, 109–11. In Cary's translation this reads:

> Christians like these the Aethiop shall condemn,
> When that the two assemblages shall part,
> One rich eternally, the other poor.

These lines are spoken by the 'eagle' referred to earlier (see note 65) – in effect by the souls of the just. The first line of this tercet alludes to Matthew xii.41: 'The men of Nineveh shall rise in judgement with this generation, and condemn it.' The Aethiop, like the 'men of Nineveh', is the righteous pagan who, without the benefit of revelation, is yet able to condemn the wickedness of the damned.

95. p. 204   *so as to be understood by the public*: 'The MS. continues: "Most persons confuse the value of a thing with its price (which is as though they should estimate the healing powers of a medicine by the charge of the apothecary); confuse the wealth (or the possessions which constitute the well-being of an individual) with riches (or the possessions which constitute power over others); and, finally, confuse production, or profit, which is an increase of the possessions of the world, with Acquisition or Gain, which is an increase of the possessions of one person by the diminution of those of another. This last word, production, indeed, which one might . . ."' (Cook and Wedderburn, XVII, 77).

96. p. 204   *Ed. in 2 vols. 8vo, Parker, 1848*: i.e. the first edition. The chapter on capital begins on p. 67 of that edition.

97. p. 205   *in the 'comparative estimate of the moralist'*: The full question reads: 'Political economy has nothing to do with the comparative estimation of different uses in the judgment of a philosopher or of a moralist'. The 'distinction' Mill is concerned with here is that between value in use and value in exchange. The distinction was first defined in Smith.

98. p. 205   *'the stock of permanent means of enjoyment'*: The full quotation reads: 'All labour is, in the language of political economy, unproductive, which ends in immediate enjoyment, without any increase of the accumulated stock of permanent means of enjoyment'. In Mill's definition, labour which leads to an increase in material wealth is productive. That which does not – being consumed as it is bought – is unproductive.

99. p. 205   *Mr Helps' estimate in his essay on War*: See Sir Arthur Helps, *Friends in Council*, New Series (1859). Helps (1813–75) was an essayist, playwright and novelist. He shared Ruskin's views on a variety of ethical and aesthetic questions.

100. p. 206 *'any support to life or strength'*: Mill's definition of 'productive consumption'.

101. p. 206 *'The word "value" . . . value in exchange'*: In Mill's system, 'Value in use . . . is the extreme limit of value in exchange'.

102. p. 206 *of no value to either*: It might be argued that this is merely playing on two different senses of the word 'value' – that in this expression the word is simply synonymous with 'use'. But it is at the heart of Ruskin's argument that the two senses are fundamentally the same. This is why he so often resorts to etymology.

103. p. 207 *Christopher Sly*: See *The Taming of the Shrew*, Induction, scene ii.

104. p. 207 *the opening definitions of four chapters*: Another reference to the essays Ruskin was not allowed to complete.

105. p. 207 *'Utility is not the measure . . . essential to it'*: For Ricardo, see Introduction, p. 20.

106. p. 207 *'Suppose that in the early stages . . . labour realized in each'*: Ruskin deliberately misrepresents Ricardo's argument by cutting the words 'both being the produce of the same quantity of labour' from the first sentence quoted and 'whatever might be the quantity of production' from the second. Ricardo is trying to show that 'the total quantity of labour necessary to manufacture' commodities and 'bring them to the market' affects their exchange value relative to one another. As usual, however, Ruskin's distortion can be justified. He wishes to expose as a fallacy the idea that value is *purely* an economic concept.

107. p. 209 *For ever it avails . . . the Maker of things and of men*: This is Ruskin's theory of 'intrinsic' value. As he says in *Munera Pulveris*, 'All wealth is intrinsic, and is not constituted by the judgment of men' (XVII, 164). Compare his view of what constitutes value in art: 'all great art', he writes in *Modern Painters V*, 'is the expression of man's delight in God's work, not in *his own*' (VII, 263).

108. p. 209 *'I will cause . . . and I will Fill their treasures'*: Proverbs viii.21.

109. p. 209 *Madonna della Salute*: See 'The Two Boyhoods', p. 149, and my note 11, p. 329.

110. p. 10 *George Herbert*, The Church Porch, *Stanza 28*:

> Wealth is the conjurer's devil,
> Whom when he thinks he hath, the devil hath him.
> Gold thou mayst safely touch; but if it stick
> Unto thy hands, it woundeth to the quick.

111. p. 210 *'habet'*: Literally, 'he has it' – meaning 'he is wounded'. In the Roman circus, when a gladiator was struck down, the crowd would shout this word.

112. p. 210 *'quo plurimum posset'*: From the Roman historian, Livy. 'The reference is to the devotion of M. Curtius, who leapt into the chasm which had appeared in the Roman Forum, and which no human power had availed to fill up. The gods required the sacrifice of the best . . .' (Cook and Wedderburn, XVII, 87).

113. p. 211 *'cheereth god and man'*: Judges ix.13.

114. p. 211 *'Dionusos,' hurtful*: 'The actual meaning of the word Dionysus is, however, matter of uncertainty. "Zeus of Nysa" (a supposed place) was the favourite

derivation among the ancients. Of modern guesses, "son of Zeus" seems as good as any . . . Ruskin's derivation is not clear' (Cook and Wedderburn, XVII, 88).

115. p. 211   *'the possession of the valuable by the valiant'*: Ruskin's adaptation of a sentence from Xenophon's *Economist*. In *Munera Pulveris* he translates the sentence more literally thus: 'things are only property to the man who knows how to use them' (XVII, 288).

116. p. 212   *whence that of Pope: Moral Essays*, iii,201–2. Quoting from memory, Ruskin omits the first word, 'Yet'. This is the poem also quoted on p. 201 above.

117. p. 212   *Arist. Plut. 582*: 'Aristophanes, *Plutus* 582. "Zeus is poor indeed!" [Cf. my Commentary on 'Traffic', p. 231.] The lines next quoted are not the immediately preceding ones, but lines 558–9: (*Poverty*) "My people are better than Wealth's; for by him gross and bloated men are presented . . ."' (Yarker, 162).

118. p. 213   *'Catallactics'*: 'The term was first used by Whately in his *Lectures on Political Economy* (1831): "The name I should have preferred as the most descriptive, and on the whole least objectionable, is that of Catallactics, or the 'Science of Exchange'"' (Cook and Wedderburn, XVII, 92).

119. p. 214   *to turn stones into bread*: See Matthew iv.3–4. Ruskin alludes to the temptation of Christ in the wilderness, so the other 'father' is the devil.

120. p. 214   *can but give you a serpent*: See Matthew iv.3–4.

121. p. 214   *'As a nail between the stone joints . . . buying and selling'*: This verse is from Ecclesiasticus (Apocrypha) xxvii.2, and not, as Ruskin seems to have thought, from the Wisdom of Solomon.

122. p. 214   *Zechariah's roll*: Zechariah v.1: 'Then I turned, and lifted up mine eyes, and looked, and behold a flying roll.' The remaining quotations in this paragraph are also from Zechariah v, but Ruskin uses the Greek Old Testament (the Septuagint) instead of the Authorized Version. 'Curved sword' is translated from the Septuagint, as are 'injustice' (where the AV has 'resemblance') and 'Babel' (where the AV has 'Shinar').

123. p. 215   *by the gate of Bethlehem*: See 2 Samuel xxiii.15–17.

124. p. 215   *quantity of labour*: By this expression Ruskin means both actual labour and, according to his debt analysis theory, general labour (i.e. currency).

125. p. 215   *the Poor of the Flock (or 'flock of slaughter')*: Both phrases are quotations from Zechariah xi.7. The quotation that follows, which is from verse 8, provides Ruskin with the second of the epigraphs to *Unto this Last* (see my Commentary, p. 158).

126. p. 216   *for which they reserved another word*: i.e. τίσις. Tisiphone was one of the Furies, whose duty it was to exact retribution for acts of impiety. Ruskin often refers to her, particularly in connection with economic evils.

127. p. 216   *upas-tree*: The 'poison-tree' of legend: said to originate in Java.

128. p. 217   *'he that gathereth not, scattereth'*: Matthew xii.30.

129. p. 217   *the wife is said to be . . . as the olive branch*: Psalms cxxviii.3.

130. p. 217   *the seventh season*: The great classical physician Galen divided the

year into seven seasons. The phrase which follows may be translated: 'not in the seed-time, nor in the planting-time, but in the season of ripeness'.

131. p. 217 *arrows in the hand of the giant*: Cf. Psalms cxxvii.4.

132. p. 218 *Capital*: On the question of capital, Ruskin differs from the orthodox economists only in emphasis, but the emphasis is of some importance. The definition of capital given in this paragraph is not significantly different from Mill's. But Ruskin finds it impossible to consider the root (capital) without also considering the fruit (consumption). This simple metaphor is a potent one, since it draws attention to the continuity of the whole process. The end of wealth – as common sense should tell us – is not more wealth, but consumption. Mill misses this point because he sees capital as part of the process of production, so not in the same department of the subject as consumption. Most modern economists, following John Maynard Keynes, accept Ruskin's view of the matter rather than Mill's. Ruskin's argument reflects the whole basis of his disagreement with Mill: that in dividing objects of study into mutually exclusive departments, he misses the over-arching truth.

133. p. 218 *caput vivum, not caput mortuum*: i.e. living head, not dead one. '"Caput mortuum," the term used by the old chemists to designate the residuum of chemicals when all their volatile matter had escaped' (Cook and Wedderburn, XVII, 98).

134. p. 218 *Prince Rupert's drops*: 'Molten glass, dropped into water, forms pear-shaped globules which, each being a vacuum, explode when fractured. Said to have been introduced by Prince Rupert' (Yarker, 164–5).

135. p. 218 *'splendescere sulco'*: 'Shining in the furrow' (Virgil, *Georgics*, i,46).

136. p. 218 *Ixion*: 'Ruskin here moralises the legend of Ixion, who had promised his father-in-law, Deioneus, a valuable present, but had not given it. Deioneus in consequence stole the horses of Ixion, who thereupon – "the first among the heroes to shed blood of kindred craftily" (Pindar, *Pyth.* ii.32) – invited his father-in-law to a banquet, and threw him into a secret pit, filled with fire. Ixion was unable to obtain expiation from gods or men, till at last Zeus received him in pity and purified him. Pindar, in the same ode, tells the story of Ixion's infatuation, and of his eternal punishment on the wheel. "Ixion," says the poet, "writhing on his winged wheel, proclaims this message unto men, To him who does thee service make fair recompense." From this passage, and from later lines in the same ode – where the poet teaches the worthlessness of riches if not joined with the happy gift of wisdom – Ruskin seems to have taken a clue for his own interpretation of the story' (Cook and Wedderburn, XVII, 99).

137. p. 218 *clouds are without water*: Cf. Jude 12.

138. p. 219 *Demas' silver mine*: In *Pilgrim's Progress*: 'a little Hill called Lucre, and in that Hill a *Silver-Mine*, which some of them that had formerly gone that way, because of the rarity of it, had turned aside to see; but going too near the brink of the pit, the ground being deceitful under them, broke, and they were slain . . . A little way off the road, over against the *Silver-Mine*, stood Demas (gentleman-like) to call to Passengers to come and see.'

139. p. 219   *embracing a cloud (or phantasm)*: When Zeus discovered that Ixion planned to seduce his consort, Hera, he shaped a cloud into her image. So when Ixion tried to embrace her, he clasped nothing. Zeus then punished him by binding him on to a wheel of fire for all eternity.

140. p. 219   *'Ephraim feedeth . . . after the east wind'*: Hosea xii.1.

141. p. 219   *'l'aer a se raccolse'*: Dante, *Inferno*, xvii,105: in Cary's translation, 'Gathering the air up with retractile claws'. Geryon is the winged monster on whose back Dante and Virgil descend from the Seventh to the Eighth Circle of Hell. He represents Fraud.

142. p. 219   *So also in the vision . . . before quoted*: from Zechariah v.3 ff. See p. 214.

143. p. 219   *the Plutus of Dante*: In *Inferno*, vii, 1–15. Plutus, the god of Riches, is discovered by Dante and Virgil at the brink of the Fourth Circle. He is furious at their intrusion and shouts at them incoherently. When Virgil rebukes him, he falls to the ground.

144. p. 219   *the Ezekiel vision is true . . . the wheels go by them*: See Ezekiel i.15 ff.

145. p. 220   *demand for commodities is not demand for labour*: Another reference to Mill's theory of the wages-fund (see note 25). This is the theory that wages are not paid from what is earned by current production but out of a pre-existing fund of capital set aside for that purpose. According to this theory, the nature of the product could not affect the wages paid towards its manufacture, nor could its success or failure on the market. If it sold well and made a profit, however, part of the profit could be set aside for its continued production; this would have the effect of diverting larger and larger amounts of the wages-fund away from other products in favour of the successful one. To Ruskin this argument is both illogical and hypocritical. In his judgement, workers are paid out of current production, their wages being, in effect, a form of credit. Thus the argument is an excuse to deny work-people their just rewards.

146. p. 220   *He distinguishes between labourers . . . the purchase of velvet is not*: Mill's example has been generally judged obscure. Behind it is the distinction (outlined in note 98) between immediate and permanent means of enjoyment, unproductive and productive labour. The velvet presumably stands for luxury goods which are immediately enjoyed; the pleasure gardens are a permanent means of enjoyment. According to the classical theory, saving is consumption forgone. The consumption of luxuries, in Mill's view, depressed the economy: diverting capital away from further production, it exhausted the wages-fund and thus caused unemployment. The laying-out of pleasure grounds, by contrast, created employment. In Ruskin's view, however, wages were paid not out of a pre-existing fund but in advance. Therefore, when the consumer chose to buy anything, he in effect provided employment for the workers who made it. Thus consumption involved moral responsibility: the consumer had the power to decide whether workers were to spend their days in unhealthy textile mills or in the open air. Hence Ruskin's distinction between good and bad consumption.

147. p. 221 *Mr Mill's great hardware theory*: See pp. 204–5 above.

148. p. 221 *capitalists' wealth*: Ruskin later observed that in this context he should have said 'cash', not 'wealth'.

149. p. 221 *purchasing of each other . . . annually*: i.e. the amount France and Britain spent on armaments.

150. p. 221 *reap what you have sown*: Cf. Galatians vi.7.

151. p. 222 *two months ago*: i.e. in the second essay, pp. 189 above.

152. p. 222 *pursue them elsewhere*: When publication of the essays was curtailed, Ruskin was allowed to increase the length of the last one. His practical recommendations had to be deferred.

153. p. 222 *the greatest number of noble and happy human beings*: Ruskin is playing on the favourite tags of his opponents. The Utilitarians, for instance, aimed at 'the greatest happiness of the greatest number': Ruskin's introduction of *nobility* is therefore significant. The Political Economists argued that that country was richest whose people owned the largest number of material things; Ruskin's redefinition of wealth therefore colours his use of the word 'richest'. And the emphasis on 'number' – and quantification in general – prepares us for his attack on the Malthusian argument in the next paragraph but one.

154. p. 222 *the Economy of Heaven*: A reference to the revolt of Lucifer and the rebel angels. Cook and Wedderburn (XVII, 105) cite 2 Peter ii.3–4: 'And through covetousness shall they with feigned words make merchandise of you: whose judgement now of a long time lingereth not . . . For if God spared not the angels that sinned, but cast them down to hell . . .'

155. p. 222 *But is the nobleness consistent with the number*: Mill and the other political economists endorsed the Malthusian theory of a natural balance between population level and the means of subsistence. If the poor did not observe this balance they would starve, and their starvation would be their own responsibility. Ruskin does not wholly disagree with the theory, but he objects to the moral assumptions implicit in its expression. He argues that the burden of responsibility lies with the rich for their failure to provide education for the poor. The reference to animal population in what follows may owe something to the comparison of men and rabbits that occurs in Mill: 'the conduct of human creatures is more or less influenced by foresight of consequences, and by impulses superior to mere animal instincts'. Ruskin also insisted – rightly – that the world was by no means overcrowded.

156. p. 223 *'Nay,' says the economist . . . 'people down to the same point of misery'*: Ruskin is probably thinking of Mill's remarks on the repeal of the Corn Laws. Mill considers the possibility of workmen's wages rising as a result of it: 'If they content themselves with enjoying the greater comfort while it lasts, but do not learn to require it, they will people down to their old scale of living.'

157. p. 223 *Suppose it were your own son*: The hypothesis is an appropriate one, as Ruskin habitually takes the family as a model for the just state. In the just state, as in the family, the strong take responsibility for the weak.

158. p. 223 *they cannot receive education*: 'Education is not compatible

with extreme poverty. It is impossible effectually to teach an indigent population' (Mill).

159. p. 223 *the Sabbath . . . but to save*: See Luke xiii.11–16.

160. p. 223 *It is continually the fault or the folly of the poor that they are poor*: In Mill's view, '. . . the working classes . . . obey a common propensity, in laying the blame of their misfortunes . . . on any shoulders but their own'. Mill's view of the matter is plainly influenced by Malthus.

161. p. 223 *The life is more than the meat*: Matthew vi.25.

162. p. 224 *Ye sheep without shepherd*: See both Numbers xxvii.17 and Matthew ix.36.

163. p. 224 *'natural rate . . . maintain the labourer'*: Cook and Wedderburn (XVII, 108) cite two passages from the chapter 'On Wages' in Ricardo: 'The natural price of labour is that price which is necessary to enable the labourers, one with another, to subsist and to perpetuate their race, without either increase or diminution.' Ricardo adds: 'The power of the labourer to support himself, and the family which may be necessary to keep up the number of labourers, does not depend on the quantity of money which he may receive for wages, but on the quantity of food, necessaries, and conveniences become essential to him from habit, which that money will purchase.'

164. p. 225 *the meditative, muscular, and oracular labourers*: i.e. lawyers, soldiers and clergymen. Presumably Ruskin means us to recall his argument concerning these professions in 'The Roots of Honour'.

165. p. 225 *That chapter and the preceding one*: i.e. Mill, Book IV, Ch. vii, 'On the Probable Futurity of the Labouring Classes', and Ch. vi, 'Of the Stationary State'.

166. p. 225 *the apple of Sodom and the grape of Gomorrah*: See Genesis xix. God destroyed the 'cities of the plain' because their citizens were given over to unnatural vice. Dante, a considerable influence on Ruskin, puts usurers and sodomites in the same circle of Hell. Both are guilty of 'violence against nature'.

167. p. 226 *'rejoices' in the habitable parts of the earth*: See Proverbs viii.31.

168. p. 226 *The desire of the heart is also the light of the eyes*: Cf. Proverbs xv.30.

169. p. 226 *man doth not live . . . unknowable work of God*: Cf. Deuteronomy viii.3; Matthew iv.4.

170. p. 226 *'remain content . . . which Providence has placed them'*: This 'quotation' is based on a maxim from the Church catechism: '. . . do my duty in that state of life unto which it shall please God to call me' (Book of Common Prayer).

171. p. 227 *'justice and peace have kissed each other'*: Psalms lxxxv.10. Ruskin again substitutes 'justice' for the Authorized Version's 'righteousness'.

172. p. 227 *'sown in peace of them that make peace'*: James iii.18.

173. p. 227 *as is shown in the language of all nations*: Another rather fanciful piece of etymology. Various Greek, Latin, French and English words connected with buying and selling are derived by Ruskin from words meaning 'come' and 'become'.

174. p. 227   *having a raven-like mind . . . look for rest for their feet*: Cf. Genesis viii.7–8, the story of Noah and the ark.

175. p. 227   *'hath builded her house . . . her seven pillars'*: Proverbs ix.1.

176. p. 227   *her paths are peace*: Proverbs iii.17.

177. p. 228   'ὅσον ἐν ασφοδέλῳ μέγ ὄνειαϱ': Hesiod, *Works and Days*, 41: 'how great blessing lies in mallow and asphodel', that is, in simple things which even the poor enjoy.

178. p. 228   *the light of the body*: Matthew vi.22.

179. p. 228   *where the Wicked cease . . . the Weary are at rest*: See Job iii.17.

TRAFFIC

1. p. 233   *All good architecture . . . life and character*: This, one of Ruskin's most enduring convictions, provides the theme of two of his most influential books, *The Seven Lamps of Architecture* (1849) and *The Stones of Venice*.

2. p. 234   *good taste is essentially a moral quality*: Another enduring theme, which occurs as early as the first volume of *Modern Painters*: 'He who has followed up [the] natural laws of aversion and desire . . . so as to derive pleasure always from that which God originally intended should give him pleasure, and who derives the greatest possible sum of pleasure from any given object, is a man of taste . . .' (III, 109–10). See Introduction, p. 9.

3. p. 234   *to hunger and thirst after justice*: Matthew v.6 – except that the Authorized Version gives 'righteousness' instead of 'justice'. See *Unto this Last*, p. 191, where Ruskin explains this emendation in a footnote.

4. p. 235   *it is the taste of the devils*: No aspect of Ruskin's art criticism is more difficult for the modern reader to accept than his belief that there are good and bad *subjects* for painting. When he criticizes Dutch genre painters such as Teniers in more detail, he argues that a corrupt attitude to the subject is clear from the *treatment*. Nevertheless, it is important to place this opinion within the larger context of Ruskin's theory of art. 'The art of man', he says in *The Laws of Fésole*, 'is the expression of his rational and disciplined delight in the forms and laws of the creation of which he forms a part' (XV, 351). The objection to Teniers' art is that it delights in the degradation of nature – specifically, of human nature. The rest of this paragraph is based on that assumption.

5. p. 235   *On the necessity . . . taste among all classes*: A book by Sir John Gardner Wilkinson, a distinguished Egyptologist.

6. p. 235   *Newgate Calendar*: Subtitled the *Malefactors' Bloody Register*, this was a popular chronicle of notorious crimes, first published in 1774. It was revived in the 1820s when Ruskin was a boy.

7. p. 236   *'They carved at the meal . . . through the helmet barr'd'*: Sir Walter Scott, *The Lay of the Last Minstrel*. The 'two great peoples' are Britain and France. Ruskin was greatly troubled by the arms race the two countries engaged in

throughout the 1860s and 70s, particularly because he was something of a Francophile.

8. p. 237   *Armstrongs*: The popular name for the large-bore ordnance designed by W. G. Armstrong (1810–1900) and used in the Crimean War.

9. p. 237   *and for the black eagles . . . if I mistake not*: Both Prussia and Austria had black eagles on their flags. Ruskin is referring to the Schleswig-Holstein question and the British government's unwillingness to go to the assistance of Denmark in that conflict.

10. p. 237   *I have done it elsewhere before now*: Notably in *The Stones of Venice*.

11. p. 238   *'This is the house of God and this is the gate of heaven'*: Genesis xxviii.17. The story Ruskin goes on to retell is that of Jacob and the ladder (Genesis xxviii.10–22). It is characteristic of the author of *Modern Painters* to insist, in spite of his own passion for church architecture, that nature herself is the sacred place.

12. p. 238   *lightning when it shines from the east to the west*: See Matthew xxiv.27.

13. p. 239   *'Thou, when thou prayest . . . in secret'*: Matthew vi.5–6.

14. p. 239   *Lares . . . Lar*: The Romans called their tutelary or household gods *Lares*. (*Lar* is the singular.)

15. p. 239   *do you mean to build as Christians or as infidels*: It was a fallacy of Victorian art history – one much promoted by Ruskin and by the architect and Gothic Revival apologist, A. W. N. Pugin – that Gothic architecture was a uniquely Christian style. The corollary was that Renaissance architecture, based as it is on Roman architecture, was fundamentally a pagan style. Ruskin was aware that early Christian architecture in the West was also Roman in style, and that Roman was one of the many styles that contributed to Gothic. His sense of the symbolic resonances of Gothic in church architecture seems to have blinded him to the implications of these facts. (See Introduction, pp. 15–16, and 'The Nature of Gothic', pp. 83–91.)

16. p. 239   *I have had also to show that good architecture is not ecclesiastical*: In *The Stones of Venice II* Ruskin had argued that 'it is the test of a noble style that it shall be applicable to both' the dwelling house and the church (X, 123).

17. p. 241   *the Greeks essentially worshipped . . . was, to the Greeks – Foolishness*: Ruskin draws directly on St Paul, 1 Corinthians i.22–3: 'For the Jews require a sign, and the Greeks seek after wisdom: But we preach Christ crucified, unto the Jews a stumbling-block, and unto the Greeks foolishness.'

18. p. 241   *the word, of which we keep . . . Jupiter the revealer*: Ruskin's etymology is generally accepted. Both *Zeus* and *Jupiter* are cognate with the Sanskrit *Dyaus-pitar*, as are the Latin *deus*, the French *dieu* and probably the English *day* and *dew*. (Dyaus-pitar was the Vedic god of the sky.) Ruskin probably learned this from Max Müller, *Lectures on the Science of Language* (see note 10, p. 350).

19. p. 241   *crowned with the olive spray*: Hence the title of the book from which this lecture is taken. Ruskin was much preoccupied with Athene's significance. In *The Queen of the Air* (1869), he substantially develops this account of the symbols associated with her.

20. p. 242 *It is, of all architecture . . . when built by the noble*: i.e. Gothic. It is worth noting that in this, the period of his 'unconversion', Ruskin not only has reservations about institutional Christianity but also about the architecture that in his view most perfectly embodied it.

21. p. 242 *'Oppositions of science, falsely so called'*: 1 Timothy vi.20. This is a reference to the philosophical disputes that mark the last phase of classical Greek civilization.

22. p. 242 *Tetzel's trading*: Johann Tetzel was the papal agent whose sale of indulgences in Germany in 1517 caused Luther to nail his ninety-five theses to the door of the church in Wittenberg. Thus Tetzel is normally regarded as the immediate cause of the Reformation and the break-up of medieval Christendom.

23. p. 243 *And the Master of Christians . . . selling of doves, not impious*: In Matthew xxi.12–13, Jesus enters the temple in Jerusalem and overthrows 'the tables of the money-changers, and the seats of them that sold doves'.

24. p. 243 *supplying people with food, or clothes*: A constant theme of Ruskin's. See *Unto this Last*, pp. 178–9.

25. p. 244 *Britannia of the Market*: What follows is a grotesque parody of the allegorical painting and sculpture that Ruskin celebrates elsewhere in his writings on Gothic art and architecture.

26. p. 245 *the study of spending*: See *Unto this Last*, pp. 217–22.

27. p. 245 *make Ossa like a wart*: Hamlet, V.i.305. Ossa is a high mountain in Thessaly. When the giants wanted to overthrow Zeus, they tried to climb up to heaven by piling Mount Ossa on top of Mount Pelion. So to 'pile Ossa on Pelion' is to add difficulty to difficulty without getting any nearer one's goal.

28. p. 245 *Plutus*: The god of wealth.

29. p. 246 *Pallas*: i.e. Pallas Athene.

30. p. 246 *I asked you what it was, when I was last here*: In the lecture 'Modern Manufacture and Design', delivered at Bradford in 1859, and published in *The Two Paths* (1859).

31. p. 246 *'they should take who have the power, and they should keep who can'*: Wordsworth, 'Rob Roy's Grave'.

32. p. 247 *to be in Jerusalem as stones*: 1 Kings x.27.

33. p. 247 *'men may come . . . go on for ever*: From Tennyson's 'The Brook':

> For men may come and men may go,
> But I go on for ever.

34. p. 248 *the Sons of God . . . daughters of men*: See Genesis vi.2.

35. p. 248 *'their spot was not the spot of his children'*: Deuteronomy xxxii.5.

36. p. 248 *that indeed*: The long quotation which follows is Ruskin's own translation of a passage from the *Critias*.

37. p. 248 *of gold and of possessions*: 'Here Ruskin, probably by accident, omits a few words: "neither were they intoxicated by luxury, nor did wealth deprive them

of their self-control; but they were sober, and saw clearly that . . .'" (Cook and Wedderburn, XVIII, 457).

38. p. 248 *faded and became extinct*: A mistranslation. Cook and Wedderburn give 'was beginning to fade away' (XVIII, 457).

39. p. 249 *The rest is silence*: Hamlet's dying words: *Hamlet*, V.ii.372.

40. p. 249 *this golden image . . . the plain of Dura*: See Daniel iii.1. See also *Unto this Last*, p. 187, and my note 39, p. 336.

41. p. 249 *following those trodden ways . . . which are peace*: Proverbs iii.17: 'Her [i.e. Wisdom's] ways are ways of pleasantness, and all her paths are peace.' A verse Ruskin was fond of quoting – e.g. in *Unto this Last*, p. 227.

42. p. 249 *temples not made with hands*: See Acts vii.48.

OF KINGS' TREASURIES

1. p. 255 *some connection . . . for different classes of youth*: Ruskin took a practical interest in education for most of his life. At the time of this lecture he was patron of a progressive school for girls at Winnington Hall, Cheshire, whose principal, Margaret Bell, had been influenced by his ideas. He was also a governor of Christ's Hospital and an Examiner in the Oxford Examinations of Middle Class Schools.

2. p. 256 *the last infirmity of noble minds*: Milton, *Lycidas*, 71, the poem which Ruskin analyses later on in this lecture.

3. p. 260 *my life was as the vapour*: Cf. James iv.14.

4. p. 261 *in parables*: See Luke viii.10: 'but to others in parables; that seeing they might not see, and hearing they might not understand.' For Ruskin's use of parables, see Introduction, pp. 22–3.

5. p. 262 *the peerage of words*: As will be clear from other writings in this collection, Ruskin was fascinated by the roots of words. The quest for the 'original' meaning of a word is part of his conservatism, for changes in meaning inevitably involve the loss of a purer denotation. (See, for example, *Unto this Last*, p. 161, and my note 5, p. 332.)

6. p. 263 *a false Latin quantity*: The duration of a syllable in Latin verse is determined by its length and not, as it is in English, by stress. A syllable pronounced with the wrong length is said to be 'a false quantity'.

7. p. 263 *'ground-lion'*: A literal translation of the Greek word 'chameleon'.

8. p. 264 *the Word of God . . . choked*: See Matthew xiii.4, 7.

9. p. 264 *'He that believeth not shall be damned'*: Mark xvi.16. 'In all the three passages referred to the Greek is κατακρίνω. In the Authorised Version it is translated "damn" in the first case, "condemn" in the others; in the Revised Version "condemn" has been substituted in the former' (Cook and Wedderburn, XVIII, 68).

10. p. 265 *Max Müller's lectures*: *Lectures on the Science of Language* (1861 and 1864). Müller was a German-born philologist who became a British subject and

Professor of Comparative Philology at Oxford. He was responsible for making the pioneer discoveries of German philology more widely known in England. Ruskin admired his work and drew on it for his etymological analyses.

11. p. 266 *For Milton reads . . . quite honestly*: The quotation is from Matthew xvi.19, where Christ chooses St Peter as the 'rock' on which the Church shall be built. In other words, from a Roman Catholic point of view, the saint is appointed the first pope. Milton as a Puritan would not have agreed with this interpretation.

12. p. 267 *Bill and Nancy, knocking each other's teeth out*: Bill Sykes the burglar and his girl, Nancy, from Dickens's *Oliver Twist*.

13. p. 268 *but it was St Paul's*: See Acts xx.28, where St Paul, addressing the elders of Ephesus, says: 'Take heed therefore unto yourselves, and to all the flock, over the which the Holy Ghost hath made you overseers, to feed the church of God, which he hath purchased with his own blood'.

14. p. 268 *'The wind bloweth . . . born of the Spirit'*: John iii.8. In the original Greek, the same word is used for both 'wind' and 'spirit'. (Cf. 'The Work of Iron', p. 117, and see my note 4, p. 323.)

15. p. 268 *'puffing up'*: See 1 Corinthians xiii.4: 'charity vaunteth not itself, is not puffed up . . .'

16. p. 269 *clouds, these, without water*: See Jude 12; and cf. *Unto this Last*, p. 218.

17. p. 269 *Milton and Dante in their interpretation of this power*: See Dante, *Purgatorio*, ix, 117 et seq.

18. p. 269 *'have taken away . . . not in themselves'*: See Luke xi.52.

19. p. 269 *'He that watereth, shall be watered also himself'*: Proverbs xi.25.

20. p. 269 *'Take him . . . and cast him out'*: See Matthew xxii.13. The 'rock-apostle' is St Peter again.

21. p. 270 *'to mix the music . . . with heavenly doubts'*: See R. W. Emerson, 'To Rhea':

> He mixes music with her thoughts,
> And saddens her with heavenly doubts.

22. p. 271 *the scene with the bishops . . . the character of Cranmer'*: 'That is, hypocrisy and mock humility (*Richard III*, iii.7) against [Cranmer's] honesty and true humility (*Henry VIII*, v.1–2)' (Cook and Wedderburn, XVIII, 77).

23. p. 271 *the description of St Francis . . . lo perfido assassin*: See Dante, *Paradiso*, xi and xii, where the founders of the two mendicant orders (the Franciscans and the Dominicans) are described as 'two Princes' ordained by Providence on behalf of the Church to be our 'guides'. St Francis and St Dominic – contemporaries, and both admired by Dante, as by Ruskin – here represent the good priest. By contrast, the Italian quotations refer to bad priests encountered by Dante in Hell (*Inferno*, xxiii, 124–6, and xix, 49–50). The first of them is Caiaphas, the Jewish high priest responsible for the arrest of Jesus: 'Then I saw Virgil wonder over him that was distended on the cross so ignominiously in the eternal exile'. The other is Pope

Nicholas II, who is being punished for buying and selling ecclesiastical preferment – the sin of simony. Dante stands beside him 'like the friar who is confessing a treacherous assassin'.

24. p. 271   *the Ecclesiastical Courts*: Ruskin is alluding to the controversy surrounding the publication in 1860 of *Essays and Reviews*, a collection of polemical essays on important religious issues of the day. The authors were 'advanced', broad church clergymen with whom Ruskin sympathized. In 1864, two of the contributors were charged with heresy in the ecclesiastical Court of Arches and found guilty. They were later acquitted on appeal.

25. p. 271   *'Break up . . . sow not among thorns'*: Jeremiah iv.3.

26. p. 271   *outcries against sensation lately*: Another contemporary controversy: the question whether sensational novels caused harm. The Archbishop of York had recently spoken on the subject.

27. p. 272   *'the angels desire to look into'*: 1 Peter i.12.

28. p. 273   *see noble nations . . . without an effort or a tear*: A reference to the Polish insurrection, savagely put down by the Russians in the year of this lecture, 1864. Ruskin considered the British government's inaction to be partly responsible for the carnage.

29. p. 273   *'injustice' or 'unrighteousness' of sensation*: Ruskin habitually treated 'just' and 'righteous' as synonyms. He justifies the practice in a footnote to *Unto this Last*, p. 191.

30. p. 273   *A great nation . . . having done a single murder*: A reference to a murder which had received much attention in the newspapers.

31. p. 273   *and for a couple of years . . . in the wrong*: A reference to the American Civil War. The supply of cotton to the Lancashire mills had been affected by a blockade of the Confederate ports.

32. p. 273   *and large landed estates . . . at the cannon's mouth*: A reference to the Opium Wars of 1840 and 1856, which were caused by Chinese opposition to the opium trade.

33. p. 273   *and then debate . . . the lives of its murderers*: Ruskin refers to a resolution passed by the House of Commons. The Queen was to appoint a Royal Commission to look into the future of the death penalty. Ruskin was in favour of capital punishment.

34. p. 273   *'perplexed i' the extreme'*: Othello, V.ii.348.

35. p. 274   *it is sending a Minister . . . lambs in spring*: The reference is to the appointment of a new ambassador to Russia shortly after the atrocities referred to on p. 273.

36. p. 274   *the root of all evil*: 1 Timothy vi.10 (cf. *Unto this Last*, p. 203).

37. p. 274   *'When I come again, thou shalt give me fourpence'*: An ironic reference to the parable of the Good Samaritan. When the Samaritan leaves the injured man at the inn, he gives the innkeeper twopence. 'Take care of him,' he says; 'and whatsoever thou spendest more, when I come again, I will repay thee' (Luke x.35).

38. p. 274   *with scorpion whips*: See 1 Kings xii.11, 14.

39. p. 275   *multipliable barley-loaves*: A reference to the feeding of the five thousand (John vi.9).

40. p. 275   *we have surrendered . . . to pay for ships*: 'Ruskin refers to the extinction of public zeal in this country for Arctic discovery which followed the expedition under Sir Edward Belcher in 1852–1854' (Cook and Wedderburn, XVIII, 86).

41. p. 276   *a portion for foxes*: Psalms lxiii.10.

42. p. 276   *a whole kingdom . . . announced by that fossil*: The fossil in question was that of Archaeopteryx, the first fossil bird, which was discovered in 1861. It is now in the Natural History Museum in South Kensington.

43. p. 277   *'What d'ye lack?'*: A common street-cry.

44. p. 277   *in Venice . . . the palaces containing them*: When Ruskin was living in Venice between 1848 and 1851, the city had only recently been recaptured by the Austrians. In consequence, there was much evidence of military control.

45. p. 278   *'towers of the vineyards'*: See Isaiah v.2.

46. p. 278   *I will print the paragraph in red*: In most editions of *Sesame and Lilies*, it is printed in red.

47. p. 279   *a certain passage which some of us may remember*: The passage in question is Matthew vii.9: 'What man is there of you, whom if his son ask bread, will give him a stone?' The ironic tone is characteristic of Ruskin at this time. His readers live, he implies, in a Christian country, yet are so indifferent to Christ's commandments that they not only fail to keep them but cannot even recall the turns of phrase they were expressed in. (Cf. the description of Solomon as an obscure 'Jew merchant' in *Unto this Last*, pp. 190–1.)

48. p. 280   *'Ere the fresh lawns . . . eyelids of the Morn'*: Another quotation from *Lycidas*, 25–6. But Milton writes of 'high lawns', not fresh ones: evidence, perhaps, that Ruskin was quoting from memory.

49. p. 280   *But the poor like to die . . . reconciled to the conditions*: For Ruskin's views on pensions and the workhouse, see *Unto this Last*, p. 164.

50. p. 281   *Satanellas, – Roberts, – Fausts*: Three popular operas of the nineteenth century, all of which are concerned with the diabolical: Balfe's *Satanella*, Meyerbeer's *Robert le Diable* and Gounod's *Faust*.

51. p. 281   *carburetted hydrogen ghost*: 'Ruskin plays on the word, with reference to "Pepper's Ghost" – an illusion caused by reflection from a mirror by the aid of some strong illuminating agent, such as carburetted hydrogen gas – which was attracting the public at the Polytechnic in 1864' (Cook and Wedderburn, XVIII, 96).

52. p. 281   *Lazarus at the doorstep*: Luke xvi.20, the parable of Dives and Lazarus.

53. p. 281   *or ever shall be*: Ruskin's target in this paragraph is the ritualistic Anglo-Catholicism of the Oxford Movement. The Movement combined Anglican services with Catholic ritual and was very attentive to the forms of worship. Ruskin's anger here has much to do with his awareness of the fact that many of the

architectural paraphernalia he mocks at had been inspired by *The Seven Lamps of Architecture* and *The Stones of Venice*.

54. p. 282   *as the idolatrous Jews . . . dig to detect*: See Ezekiel viii.7–12. Particularly relevant to Ruskin's point here, though he does not quote them, are the words 'Son of man, hast thou seen what the ancients of the house of Israel do in the dark, every man in the chambers of his imagery?'

55. p. 282   *Chalmers*: Thomas Chalmers (1780–1847), Scottish theologian; active in the foundation of the Scottish Free Church.

56. p. 282   *the last of our great painters*: i.e. Turner. The watercolour of Kirkby Lonsdale was one of Ruskin's favourites. In *Modern Painters IV*, he uses it to illustrate Turner's 'acute sense of the contrast between the careless interests and idle pleasures of daily life, and the state of those whose time for labour, or knowledge, or delight, is passed for ever' (VI, 381).

57. p. 283   *'Art thou also . . . one of us'*: Isaiah xiv.10 (The quotation is not quite accurate.)

58. p. 283   *that old Scythian custom, when the head of a house died*: This custom is described by the Greek historian Herodotus.

59. p. 283   *the ice of Caina*: The outermost ring of the Ninth and last Circle of Hell (Dante, *Inferno*, xxxii). The last circle consists entirely of ice. It is named after Cain, the first murderer, and is occupied by those who, like Cain, have murdered their own kindred.

60. p. 284   *whose spirit is entering into Living peace*: Ruskin's own adaptation of Romans viii.6.

61. p. 284   *'Visible governments . . . the burdens of more'*: From *Munera Pulveris* (XVII, 245).

62. p. 284   *'people-eating'*: Iliad, i, 231.

63. p. 284   *The true kings . . . hate ruling*: A reference to Plato's *Republic* (i, 347).

64. p. 284   *'gran rifiuto'*: Dante, *Inferno*, iii, 60: 'the great refusal'. Dante's famous condemnation of the pope who resigned his office, typifying all rulers who through weakness fail to exercise their authority and so bring ruin on their subjects.

65. p. 284   *Trent cuts you a cantel out here*: See *1 Henry IV*, III.i.101. When the kingdom is divided up between the different lords, Hotspur complains that his share is too small because the course of the River Trent reduces it by a 'cantel'. (A cantel is a part cut out.)

66. p. 284   *say to this man . . . 'Come,' and he cometh*: Matthew viii.9. These are the words of the centurion who asks Christ to heal his servant. He is describing his own authority. A constant theme of Ruskin's is that it is the duty of all governors to govern. Hence his contempt for *laissez-faire* liberals who believe there should be as little government as possible.

67. p. 285   *'do and teach'*: Matthew v.19.

68. p. 285   *only the power of the moth and the rust*: This sentence and the rest of the paragraph depend heavily on Matthew vi.19–21:

Lay not up for yourselves treasures upon earth, where moth and rust doth corrupt, and where thieves break through and steal:

But lay up for yourselves treasures in heaven, where neither moth nor rust doth corrupt, and where thieves do not break through nor steal:

For where your treasure is, there will your heart be also.

69. p. 285 *a Fourth kind of treasure . . . valued with pure gold*: See Job xxviii.12–19. The 'Fourth kind of treasure' is wisdom: hence the mention of Athene, Goddess of Wisdom, in the next sentence. Ruskin now returns from questions of practical government to the theme of books – the Kings' Treasuries of his title. Once again the version of government is Platonic: Ruskin's kings are philosopher-kings.

70. p. 285 *potable gold*: 'The term used in alchemy for gold dissolved in nitro-hydrochloric acid, supposed to contain the elixir of life' (Cook and Wedderburn, XVIII, 102).

71. p. 285 *Angels of Conduct, Toil, and Thought*: 'For Athena, "the Spirit of Wisdom in Conduct"; Vulcan, "the Spirit of Wisdom in Adaptation, or of serviceable labour"; and Apollo, "the Spirit of Light and a mountain Spirit, because the sun seems first to rise and set upon the hills,' see [Ruskin's] *Cestus of Aglaia* [XIX, 64–5]' (Cook and Wedderburn, XVIII, 102).

72. p. 285 *the path which no fowl . . . eye has not seen*: Job xxviii.7, the same chapter as that referred to in note 69 above.

73. p. 285 *the one that will stand . . . all work of mine*: i.e. *Unto this Last*. The 'single sentence' is the footnote on p. 221.

74. p. 286 *It will be long, yet, before that comes to pass*: 'The first Act, authorising municipalities to provide Free Libraries out of the rates, was passed in 1850, but progress under it had been very slow. In 1860 there were only 23 such libraries in England and Wales, and in 1870 only 35' (Cook and Wedderburn, XVIII, 104).

75. p. 286 *a royal series of books in them*: Through his Guild of St George, Ruskin was to initiate such a series himself. He called it the *Bibliotheca Pastorum*, 'The Shepherds' Library', and the first volume, *The Economist of Xenophon*, was published in 1876. (For Xenophon, see note 2 on p. 331.)

FORS CLAVIGERA

1. p. 294 *since the fighting in Paris*: The defeat of France in the Franco-Prussian War in January 1871, the month in which Ruskin began *Fors Clavigera*, was followed by the revolt of the Paris Commune. The authority set up by the Commune was predominantly Socialist and Republican in complexion. From 18 March to 21 May, Paris was besieged by troops under orders from the legitimate Versailles government of Louis-Adolphe Thiers. Ruskin's sympathies went out to the poor of Paris, but he was also greatly alarmed by reports in the press of churches and other monuments being pillaged and despoiled by the Communards. Letter 6 of *Fors* ends with a

Postscript, dated 25 May, which quotes a Reuter telegram to the effect that the Louvre was then on fire. The damage turned out to be relatively insignificant.

2. p. 294 *I am myself a Communist of the old school*: In earlier writings Ruskin had gone to some lengths to reassure the public that his ideas entailed neither Socialism nor Communism. In *Fors*, however, he adopts a number of political self-descriptions to ironical effect. Thus in Letter 1 he calls himself 'a violent Illiberal' and in Letter 10 'a violent Tory of the old school' (pp. 306–7). His aim is partly to question mindless partisanship and partly to shock the reader out of complacency. What the sequel indicates, of course, is that Ruskin was neither a Communist nor a Tory of anything that might be called a *new* school.

3. p. 295 *I have spent many days . . . our English school myself*: An allusion to his teaching for the Working Men's College.

4. p. 295 *'To do good work, whether we live or die'*: The first article of what Ruskin was to call the St George's vow, set down in Letter 2. The other articles were:

> (2.) To help other people at [their work], when you can, and seek to avenge no injury.
>
> (3.) To be sure you can obey good laws before you seek to alter bad ones.

5. p. 295 *in my 'arrogant' way*: In Letter 6, Ruskin had defended himself against the charge of arrogance. This was an objection to his absolutism and the autocratic tone of *Fors*. He replied that, in *Fors*, he never expressed opinions – only things he *knew* to be true!

6. p. 295 *and told us, three thousand years ago*: Ruskin is thinking of ancient Greek society as represented in myth. A key figure in *Fors* is the hero Theseus, who, as ruler of Athens, shared his meals with his people.

7. p. 295 *which Garibaldi came to fight for*: In Letter 1, Ruskin had written:

> The moment a Republic was proclaimed in France, Garibaldi came to fight for it as a 'Holy Republic'. But Garibaldi could not know, – no mortal creature could know, – whether it was going to be a Holy or Profane Republic. You cannot evoke any form of government by beat of drum. The proclamation of a government implies the considerate acceptance of a code of laws, and the appointment of means for their execution, neither of which things can be done in an instant.

The hero of Italian unification, Garibaldi had been disappointed by the failure of the Republican movement in his native country. The newly united Italy was a kingdom.

8. p. 295 *do common or simple work for his dinner*: See 2 Thessalonians iii.10: 'if any would not work, neither should he eat'.

9. p. 295 *the Chelsea farmer . . . in last number*: Sir Thomas More – lawyer, humanist, man of letters, Lord Chancellor of England, martyr and saint – is referred to obliquely at the end of Letter 6. He was born in 1478 – not in 1480, as Ruskin goes on to say – and was executed for high treason in 1535. His treason was his refusal to assent to the Act of Supremacy, which made Henry VIII supreme head of the Church of England.

10. p. 295 *the 'Place of Wellbeing,' or Utopia*: Ruskin is mistaken: 'Utopia' is

taken from a Greek word meaning nowhere. When he objects in the next sentence to 'that stupid way' of using the word, he is presumably thinking of those who use 'utopian' to mean 'impossible' or 'impractical'.

More's great Latin work *Utopia* is partly a satire and partly a work of political speculation. It describes the polity of an imagined country in which goods are held in common, men and women share the same national system of education, and religious difference is tolerated. The book was published in 1516. The quoted passages which follow are from Book II and slightly condensed; the translation is Ruskin's own.

11. p. 296   *I spare you, for once . . . general sense, to me, too*: 'The magistrates are, says More, called "in the old language of the Utopians," "Syphograuntes," and this is the word here rendered "government" by Ruskin. The word may have been intended for nothing more than unintelligible jargon' (Cook and Wedderburn, XXVII, 118).

12. p. 297   *if we may be gathered up . . . called unclean too*: A reference to St Peter's vision (Acts x.9–16), in which he is taught not to despise the Gentiles as unclean.

13. p. 298   *on the outsides of houses, where the people can see them*: Cf. 'The Two Boyhoods', p. 151, and my note 16, p. 329.

14. p. 298   *Hôtel-de-Ville*: town hall.

15. p. 298   *the fountains . . . with precious marbles, and the like*: Like those which Ruskin admired at Siena (by Jacopo della Quercia) and Perugia (by Giovanni Pisano). They are discussed in *Val d'Arno* (1874), his Oxford lectures on Tuscan sculpture.

16. p. 298   *instead of a common poverty . . . to receive his dole of, annually*: The existence of a National Debt in a rich nation seemed to Ruskin a profound condemnation of an economy based on interest. In *Fors*, Letter 1, he advocates 'a National Store instead of a National Debt', a proposal earlier made in *Munera Pulveris* (XVII, 164 *et seq.*). He had argued there that – wealth being intrinsic – a nation's currency should be based on the store of preservable goods (food and clothing) that, through labour, it is able to accumulate.

17. p. 299   *Privatus illis . . . Commune magnum*: 'With [our ancestors] private estates were small and the common wealth great' (Horace, *Odes*, II.xv.13–14).

18. p. 299   *When the French cried . . . and not of the Re in it*: The Latin word *respublica*, from which 'republic' is derived, is literally translated as 'the public (*publica*) thing (*res*)'.

19. p. 299   *a Common-Illth*: For this coinage of Ruskin's, see *Unto this Last*, p. 211.

20. p. 299   *that is to say, full crimson . . . phoenix or flamingo colour*: '"Blue blood" and "true blue" being originally Spanish phrases, the old families of Spain who trace their pedigree beyond the time of the Moorish Conquest claiming that they have *venas ceruleas*, whereas the blood in the veins of the common people is black' (Cook and Wedderburn, XXVII, 122). Note how this piece of verbal play enables Ruskin to figure both as a red in the present letter and as a true-blue Tory in Letter

10. For the meaning of purple and the colour of blood, see also 'The Work of Iron', p. 121, and my notes 9 and 10 on pp. 324–5.

21. p. 299   *so that Dante . . . so fire-colour she was, all through*: 'Our queen' is the lady who gives her name to this letter of *Fors*: Charity. The three theological virtues (Faith, Hope and Charity), together with the four cardinal virtues, take part in a divine pageant which Dante witnesses in the Earthly Paradise. Charity is described, in the words Ruskin quotes in his footnote, as 'so red that hardly would she be noted in the fire' (*Purgatorio*, xxix, 122–3).

22. p. 300   *Tyrian-red*: The ancient city of Tyre was famous for a crimson dye manufactured there. It was made from molluscs.

23. p. 300   *not to the hills, but to their graves*: 'Speech . . . on the Army Regulation Bill on June 19 . . . Colonel North was objecting to the inclusion in the drafts for India of soldiers under the age of twenty-one' (Cook and Wedderburn, XXVII, 124).

24. p. 301   *petroleuse*: An incendiary who set buildings on fire with paraffin. (The word is a coinage of 1871.)

25. p. 301   *canaille*: rabble.

26. p. 301   *it is like manna . . . worms in the morning*: See Exodus xvi.20.

27. p. 301   *even to Cœur-de-Lion's tar-and-feather extreme*: *Fors* is recurrently concerned with the careers of various heroes of medieval chivalry. The extreme authoritarian streak in Ruskin finds much to admire in the laws of Richard I, some of which he quotes in Letter 3. About to embark on the Third Crusade, Richard decreed that any of his troops found guilty of theft should be tarred and feathered and put ashore on the first land sighted. Ruskin particularly valued Richard's laws for a more admirable principle: they classed misrepresentation and deception as forms of theft.

28. p. 301   *worse in kings and rich people than in poor*: Cf. Letter 10, pp. 307–8.

29. p. 301   *So that we can understand . . . and licked king's blood*: The allusion is to the story of Naboth's vineyard in 1 Kings xxi. Ahab, King of Samaria, covets the vineyard of a man named Naboth who lives near his palace. When Naboth refuses to give it him, the King's wife Jezebel arranges for him to be falsely accused of blasphemy. He is condemned to death by stoning and Ahab takes possession of the vineyard. Then God sends the prophet Elijah to denounce Ahab and Jezebel with the words: 'Thus saith the Lord, Hast thou killed, and also taken possession? . . . In the place where dogs licked the blood of Naboth shall dogs lick thy blood, even thine' (xxi.19). In 1 Kings xxii, Ahab is killed and dogs lick his blood. In 2 Kings ix, Jezebel is thrown from a window and dogs eat her flesh.

Ruskin goes on to compare this story with the Franco-Prussian War, fought over the vine-growing provinces of Alsace and Lorraine. The last sentence of this paragraph alludes to a famous passage from Shakespeare (*Macbeth*, II.ii.61–4) that Ruskin frequently quotes.

30. p. 302   *the prosperity of their neighbours . . . their own also*: Cf. Ruskin's fables of the two and three sailors in *Unto this Last*, pp. 185–6.

31. p. 302   *'Invidia' . . . 'Charitas'*: 'Invidia' (Envy) is one of the Seven Deadly Sins. There are also in medieval typology seven virtues, subdivided (as in the passage

quoted from Dante and discussed in note 21 above) into three theological virtues and four cardinal. The greatest of the virtues is 'Charitas' (Charity) – see 1 Corinthians xiii.13. In the Arena Chapel in Padua there is a set of monochrome frescoes by Giotto depicting the virtues and vices. Each letter of *Fors* had a frontispiece, five of which were autotype reproductions of these frescoes. Thus, 'Invidia' was used for Letter 6 and 'Charitas' for Letter 7. Letter 10, as will be seen, had 'Iniustitia' (Injustice).

32. p. 302 *And the guilty Thieves of Europe ... are the Capitalists*: Cf. Ruskin's footnote on p. 221 of *Unto this Last*.

33. p. 302 *that Meteorological question ... from above downwards*: A reference back to Letter 4:

> The *Spectator* ... says that 'the country is once more getting rich, and the money is filtering downwards to the actual workers.' But whence, then, did we filter it down to us, the actual idlers? This is really a question very appropriate for April. For such golden rain raineth *not* every day, but in a showery and capricious manner, out of heaven, upon us; mostly, as far as I can judge, rather pouring down than filtering upon idle persons, and running in thinner driblets, but I hope purer for the filtering process, to the actual workers.

34. p. 302 *'Shall there be dew upon the fleece only'*: See Judges vi.37.

35. p. 303 *Do you see in* The Times *... why he dares not*: On the abdication of Napoleon III's government, the new National Assembly had elected Thiers its chief executive. In August 1871, he became the first president of the Third Republic. A redoubtable liberal, Thiers had declared that he would never be responsible for introducing income tax in France. The *Times* correspondent had suggested that French objections to the necessary inquisition involved were such that false returns would inevitably have been made. Ruskin was greatly in favour of income tax.

36. p. 303 *it makes publicly known ... how he gets it*: Cf. *The Crown of Wild Olive*: 'let every man who wishes well to his country, render it yearly an account of his income, and of the main heads of his expenditure; or, if he is ashamed to do so, let him no more impute to the poor their poverty as a crime, nor set them to break stones in order to frighten them from committing it' (XVIII, 505). Ruskin's belief in financial openness led him, as his ideas for the Guild of St George developed, to lay open his own accounts in the pages of *Fors* – mainly by way of example, but also to demonstrate that he could practise what he preached.

37. p. 303 *Look back at them*: See note 4 above.

38. p. 304 *the 'Charity' of Giotto*: See note 31 above. It is always important for Ruskin that Giotto (1266?–1337) and Dante (1265–1321) were contemporaries, and that Dante recognized Giotto's exceptional greatness.

39. p. 304 *we will have our cauldrons ... with baboon's blood*: Cf. *Macbeth*, IV.i, the famous cauldron scene. Hecate was the Greek goddess regarded as the protectress of witches. Ruskin violently objected to the Darwinian theory and frequently caricatured the descent of man from the apes in this way. As is so often the case with his response to modern science, the hysteria seems to have been provoked by only too clear an understanding of the theory.

40. p. 304 '*Pay me that thou owest*': Matthew xviii.28. The 'great religious and reformed nation' was Prussia. The debt in question was the indemnity of 5,000 million francs demanded by Prussia at the outset of the peace negotiations.

41. p. 305 *whose Dominion is . . . from generation to generation*: Slightly misquoted from Daniel iv.3.

42. p. 306 *a speech of Lord Derby's*: Derby, a former Foreign Secretary, was a prominent member of the Conservative opposition. (At the time of writing, Gladstone and the Liberals were in power.)

43. p. 306 *your Liberal paper*: The *Telegraph* supported the Gladstone government.

44. p. 306 *the* Pall Mall Gazette: A paper founded by Ruskin's publisher, George Smith, in 1865. It had begun as an independent paper with a serious concern for public affairs and the arts. Ruskin had contributed letters to some of the early numbers. By 1871, however, it had begun to favour the Conservatives.

45. p. 306 *I will tell you plainly*: At this point begin nine paragraphs of personal history which were to become, with slight modifications, the opening paragraphs of Ruskin's autobiography, *Praeterita* (1885–9).

46. p. 307 *a violent Tory of the old school*: See note 2 above.

47. p. 307 *the affectation to write like Hooker . . . having long tried*: Richard Hooker (1554?–1600), theologian and political theorist, wrote *Of the Laws of Ecclesiastical Polity*. The book is noted for the gorgeousness of its prose style. The young Ruskin fell under Hooker's influence, and the prose of *Modern Painters II* was strongly affected by him. In later life, Ruskin disapproved of the self-consciously fine writing in his early books.

George Herbert (1593–1633), the metaphysical poet and author of the prose work 'A Priest to the Temple', was, like Hooker, a country clergyman. Ruskin was a passionate admirer of Herbert's verse and frequently quoted it from memory in his writings.

Both Herbert and Hooker are commonly thought of as founders and pillars of the Anglican cultural tradition.

48. p. 307 *Tydides or Idomeneus*: Greek warrior kings in Homer's *Iliad*. Tydides is the patronymic of Diomedes, King of Aetolia. Idomeneus was King of Crete.

49. p. 308 *Redgauntlet*: The hero of Scott's novel of the same name, a courageous young knight who undergoes many adventures in eighteenth-century Scotland. Scott's life and works are among the recurrent minor themes of *Fors*.

50. p. 308 *'an entirely honest merchant'*: John James Ruskin had died in 1864. The epitaph his son wrote for him is worth quoting in full: 'He was an entirely honest merchant, and his memory is, to all who keep it, dear and helpful. His son, whom he loved to the uttermost and taught to speak truth, says this of him.'

51. p. 309 *and I used to read the* Abbot *. . . the island of Loch Leven*: Ruskin refers to characters and places in the two novels named, both of which are by Scott. *The Abbot*, which deals with the period when Mary, Queen of Scots, was a prisoner in Lochleven Castle, is the sequel to *The Monastery*.

52. p. 309 *the FitzJames . . . no Knight of Snowdoun*: The persons mentioned all figure in Scott's heroic poems *The Lady of the Lake* and *Marmion*, both of which deal with Scotland in the sixteenth century.

53. p. 309 *I always wore . . . on the 29th of May*: i.e. on the anniversary of the Restoration in 1660. The oak-apple, or acorn, recalls the preservation of Charles II after the Battle of Worcester in 1651. Pursued by parliamentary troops, he took refuge in an oak-tree in the grounds of Boscobel House.

54. p. 309 *against the Emperor before his fall*: Napoleon III fell from power as a result of the French defeat in 1871. Ruskin had been – somewhat surprisingly – a keen admirer of his, but, as the following paragraph indicates, his ardour cooled as the Emperor went ahead with the reconstruction and modernization of Paris.

55. p. 310 *with L. N.'s*: i.e. with the Emperor's initials (Louis Napoleon).

56. p. 310 *déjeûner à la fourchette*: Dinner with forks.

57. p. 311 *in my former letter*: i.e. Letter 4 (XXVII, 77). The tutors who teach the peasants 'how to die' are, of course, the clergy.

58. p. 311 *leave the word of God, and serve tables*: Acts vi.2.

59. p. 311 *the Oxford Regius Professor of Medicine*: Ruskin's lifelong friend, Henry Acland.

60. p. 312 *what Miss Hill has done . . . the worst districts of London*: The reference is to Octavia Hill, the social reformer. Ruskin met her when in her late teens she studied drawing under him. In 1864 she and Ruskin embarked on a project to improve housing conditions for the poor in London. They began with six dwellings in Marylebone, which Ruskin had inherited from his father. The experiment met with some success; as W. G. Collingwood puts it, 'They showed what a wise and kind landlord could do by caring for tenants, by giving them inhabitable dwellings, recreation ground, and fixity of tenure, and requiring in return a reasonable and moderate rent' (*The Life and Work of John Ruskin*).

61. p. 313 *as the other day in Dublin, by withdrawing the police*: 'On August 6, 1871, an Amnesty meeting held in Phoenix Park was dispersed by the police, and many injuries were inflicted. The affair was the subject of debate in Parliament (August 17), and shortly afterwards the Government gave way on the point and allowed meetings to be held in the Park' (Cook and Wedderburn, XXVII, 176).

62. p. 313 *nor that park-railings . . . will go down*: In 1866, radicals demonstrating in favour of Parliamentary Reform pulled down the railings in Hyde Park. Matthew Arnold makes much of the incident in *Culture and Anarchy*.

63. p. 313 *'faithful' in those few*: See Matthew xxv.23.

64. p. 313 *'her Sainted Derby'*: Another Scott reference – to *Peveril of the Peak*.

65. p. 313 *the Trinacrian Legs of Man*: The three legs joined together which are the emblem of the Isle of Man. The Earls of Derby were feudal lords of the island. Trinacria was the Latin name for Sicily and means 'with three promontories'. Heraldry is another of the minor themes of *Fors*.

66. p. 313 *I have, indeed, before now . . . as has been supposed*: See Letter 7, p. 302 above.

67. p. 313   *another of Giotto's pictures*: See note 31 above.

68. p. 314   *'hooked bird'*: From the Greek epithet γαμψῶνυε.

69. p. 314   *'sits in the gate'*: Psalms lxix.12.

70. p. 314   *good lords, or law-wards*: One of Ruskin's favourite etymologies – one, however, which appears to be mistaken. 'Lord' almost certainly means 'loaf-keeper'.

71. p. 314   *Past and Present*: One of Carlyle's most powerful works of social criticism, which exerted an incalculable influence over such medievalizing writers as Tennyson, Morris and Ruskin. In it, Carlyle contrasts the England of the 'hungry Forties' – the era of severe poverty, unemployment, industrial development, Chartist agitation and *laissez-faire* government – with the administration of Bury St Edmunds Abbey in the twelfth century. Abbot Sampson is the most sympathetic of Carlyle's heroes, a man whose severity is tempered with justice and compassion. As such, he must be seen as a key model for Ruskin's ideal of the paternal king or governor. Published in 1843, *Past and Present* was among the first of several important Victorian books which criticized the age of industrial progress by contrasting it with idealized medieval societies. Ruskin's *The Stones of Venice* is therefore indebted to it.

Carlyle was also an important influence on *Fors*, frequently cited and immoderately praised. The style of his *Latter-Day Pamphlets* – colloquial, improvisatory, prophetic statements on current events – clearly helped Ruskin to achieve the more various and subtle manner of his Letters.

72. p. 315   *that the blind should lead the blind*: Matthew xv.14.

73. p. 315   *That every man shall do . . . good bread for his work*: As so often in Ruskin, the Biblical text behind this is God's command to Adam: 'In the sweat of thy face shalt thou eat bread' (Genesis iii.19).

In every corner of the world, on every subject under the sun, Penguin represents quality and variety – the very best in publishing today.

For complete information about books available from Penguin – including Pelicans, Puffins, Peregrines and Penguin Classics – and how to order them, write to us at the appropriate address below. Please note that for copyright reasons the selection of books varies from country to country.

In the United Kingdom: Please write to *Dept E.P., Penguin Books Ltd, Harmondsworth, Middlesex, UB7 0DA*

If you have any difficulty in obtaining a title, please send your order with the correct money, plus ten per cent for postage and packaging, to *PO Box No 11, West Drayton, Middlesex*

In the United States: Please write to *Dept BA, Penguin, 299 Murray Hill Parkway, East Rutherford, New Jersey 07073*

In Canada: Please write to *Penguin Books Canada Ltd, 2801 John Street, Markham, Ontario L3R 1B4*

In Australia: Please write to the *Marketing Department, Penguin Books Australia Ltd, P.O. Box 257, Ringwood, Victoria 3134*

In New Zealand: Please write to the *Marketing Department, Penguin Books (NZ) Ltd, Private Bag, Takapuna, Auckland 9*

In India: Please write to *Penguin Overseas Ltd, 706 Eros Apartments, 56 Nehru Place, New Delhi, 110019*

In Holland: Please write to *Penguin Books Nederland B.V., Postbus 195, NL–1380AD Weesp, Netherlands*

In Germany: Please write to *Penguin Books Ltd, Friedrichstrasse 10–12, D–6000 Frankfurt Main 1, Federal Republic of Germany*

In Spain: Please write to *Longman Penguin España, Calle San Nicolas 15, E–28013 Madrid, Spain*

In France: Please write to *Penguin Books Ltd, 39 Rue de Montmorency, F-75003, Paris, France*

In Japan: Please write to *Longman Penguin Japan Co Ltd, Yamaguchi Building, 2–12–9 Kanda Jimbocho, Chiyoda-Ku, Tokyo 101, Japan*

PENGUIN CLASSICS

Arnold Bennett	**The Old Wives' Tale**
Joseph Conrad	**Heart of Darkness**
	Nostromo
	The Secret Agent
	The Shadow-Line
	Twixt Land and Sea
	Under Western Eyes
E. M. Forster	**Howard's End**
	The Longest Journey
	A Passage to India
	A Room With a View
	Where Angels Fear to Tread
Henry James	**The Aspern Papers** and **The Turn of the Screw**
	The Bostonians
	Daisy Miller
	The Europeans
	The Golden Bowl
	Portrait of a Lady
	Roderick Hudson
	Washington Square
	What Maisie Knew
	The Wings of the Dove
Rudyard Kipling	**The Day's Work**
	The Light That Failed
	Wee Willie Winkie
D. H. Lawrence	**The Plumed Serpent**
	The Rainbow
	Selected Short Stories
	Sons and Lovers
	The White Peacock
	Women in Love

FOR THE BEST IN PAPERBACKS, LOOK FOR THE 🐧

PENGUIN CLASSICS

Richard Jefferies	**Landscape with Figures**
Thomas Macaulay	**The History of England**
Henry Mayhew	Selections from **London Labour** and **The London Poor**
John Stuart Mill	**On Liberty**
William Morris	**News from Nowhere** and **Selected Writings and Designs**
Walter Pater	**Marius the Epicurean**
John Ruskin	**'Unto This Last' and Other Writings**
Sir Walter Scott	**Ivanhoe**
Robert Louis Stevenson	**Dr Jekyll and Mr Hyde**
William Makepeace Thackeray	**The History of Henry Esmond**
	Vanity Fair
Anthony Trollope	**Barchester Towers**
	Framley Parsonage
	Phineas Finn
	The Warden
Mrs Humphrey Ward	**Helbeck of Bannisdale**
Mary Wollstonecraft	**Vindication of the Rights of Woman**
Dorothy and William Wordsworth	**Home at Grasmere**